American Prophecy

American Prophecy

Race and Redemption
in American Political Culture

George Shulman

University of Minnesota Press I Minneapolis I London

Portions of chapter 5 previously appeared as "American Political Culture, Prophetic Narration, and Toni Morrison's *Beloved*," *Political Theory* 24, no. 2 (1996): 295–314, and as "Narrating Clinton's Impeachment: Race, the Rights, and Allegories of the Sixties," in *Public Affairs: Politics in the Age of Sex Scandals,* ed. Paul Apostolidis and Juliet A. Williams (Durham, N.C.: Duke University Press, 2004).

"Ode to Failure," by Allen Ginsberg, from *Collected Poems, 1947–1980,* by Allen Ginsberg (New York: HarperCollins Publishers, 1984), 737. Copyright 1984 by Allen Ginsberg. Reprinted by permission of HarperCollins Publishers.

Published by the University of Minnesota Press
111 Third Avenue South, Suite 290
Minneapolis, MN 55401-2520
http://www.upress.umn.edu

Library of Congress Cataloging-in-Publication Data

Shulman, George M.
    American prophecy : race and redemption in American political culture / George Shulman.
        p.   cm.
    Includes bibliographical references and index.
    ISBN 978-0-8166-3074-5 (hc : alk. paper) — ISBN 978-0-8166-3075-2 (pb : alk. paper)
        1. Political culture—United States.   2. Prophecy.   3. United States—Race relations.   4. Prophecy in literature.   5. Bible. O.T.—Prophecies.   I. Title.
    JA75.7.S55 2008
    306.2089'00973—dc22

                                                                    2008017607

Printed in the United States of America on acid-free paper

The University of Minnesota is an equal-opportunity educator and employer.

15 14 13 12 11 10 09 08   10 9 8 7 6 5 4 3 2 1

Ode to Failure

Many prophets have failed, their voices silent
ghost-shouts in basements nobody heard their dusty laughter in family attics
nor glanced at them on park benches weeping with relief under empty sky
Walt Whitman viva'd local losers—courage to Fat Ladies in the Freak Show!
    nervous prisoners whose mustached lips dripped sweat on chow
    lines—
Mayakkovsky cried, Then die! my verse, die like the workers' rank & file
    fusilladed in Petersburg!
Prospero burned his power books & plummeted his magic wand to the
    bottom of dragon seas
Alexander the Great failed to find more worlds to conquer!
O Failure I chant your terrifying name, accept me your 54 year old Prophet
epicking Eternal Flop! I join your Pantheon of mortal bards, & hasten this
    ode with high blood pressure
rushing to the top of my skull as if I wouldn't last another minute, like the
    Dying Gaul! to
You, Lord of blind Monet, deaf Beethoven, armless Venus de Milo, headless
    Winged Victory!
I failed to sleep with every bearded rosy-cheeked boy I jacked off over
My tirades destroyed no Intellectual Unions of KGB & CIA in turtlenecks
    & underpants, their woolen suits and tweeds
I never dissolved Plutonium or dismantled the nuclear Bomb before my skull
    lost hair
I have not yet stopped the Armies of entire Mankind in their march toward
    World War III
I never got to Heaven, Nirvana, X, Whatchamacallit, I never left Earth,
I never learned to die.

                                            —Allen Ginsberg

Contents

Preface

THIS BOOK is animated by a central paradox: Though prophetic language is a passionate frame of reference that sets the horizon of American politics, the Hebrew prophets are not typically included in the canon of political thought, and neither their language nor their heirs figure in currently prevailing forms of political theory. By exploring how great critical voices have revised prophecy to reshape ideas of American nationhood and democratic politics, especially in regard to race, I assess prophecy's danger and value as a language in and for politics.

My premise is that prophetic language is axiomatic in American life. Almost 30 percent of Republican voters declare themselves "born-again" Christian evangelicals, but Rev. Jerry Falwell and Rev. Pat Robertson were not speaking only to this constituency when they declared that 9/11 was God's just punishment of his chosen people for tolerating abortion and homosexuality. According to polls, roughly 60 percent of American adults expect Jesus to return, and they say the book of Revelation is a prophecy of apocalypse they take literally and believe is being fulfilled now. But when President George W. Bush described his war on terror in moral terms of good and evil and in millennial terms of redeeming the Middle East from captivity, his language echoed even more widely.[1]

For the idea of a chosen people and "redeemer nation," called to redeem all humanity from despotism and immorality, resonates even among avowedly secular citizens. Such redemptive language entwines democracy and a special American nationhood: Only forty years ago, Martin Luther King Jr. invoked redemptive language to cast racial apartheid as a national failure to honor a democratic promise; now, evangelical Republicans narrate a "jeremiad" depicting the nation's decline from its sacred and virtuous origins. Both draw on a deep symbolic structure and prevailing narrative form to name the circumstances, confront the vicissitudes, address the meaning, and authorize the reconstitution of collective life.

Stories of special origins, corruption, and renewal; ideas of sin and individual responsibility; standards of moral judgment; symmetries of crime and punishment; tropes of suffering; pleas for forgiveness; promises of rebirth; poetics of redemption—this language is not marginal to American politics, nor is it a possession of the "Republican Right." Those canonized as *the* Hebrew prophets forged this language, which first shaped the entire Bible and now inhabits American culture, gripping even those who would escape it. It concerns not only nationhood but morality, not only religion but the personal meaning of freedom, not only codes of conduct but intimately lived senses of personhood. An originally biblical language is now a vernacular for ordinary as well as political life, providing the stories and the narrative frameworks by which people—singly and collectively—give purpose to life. Falwell's claim about God's punishment is intelligible to those who reject it, because it bespeaks an unthought symbolic order and a daily idiom of which "religion" is only the surface.

These claims are not novel to scholarship in American studies, which shows the cultural vigor and political importance of biblical religiosity and the "jeremiad" as a "prophetic" story. By redefining the founding principles and purposes of a special "American" identity, many scholars argue, elites and social movements authorize contrasting claims and action. Tropes of corruption and redemption have been used repeatedly to justify domination and exclusion—in the name of defending a chosen people against subversion linked to female desire, independent women, demonized others, nonreproductive sexuality, and urban life. Currently, indeed, prophetic language authorizes imperial power, racial domination, and patriarchal codes. Yet compelling voices in American politics also use prophetic speech to defend democratic projects claiming to redeem "America" as a symbol of possibility. To project the communitarian face of liberal individualism, or to contest this liberal nationalism and enlarge the democratic imagination, differently situated critics take up and rework prophetic language.[2]

Prophecy in America is thus a biblical genre, a vernacular idiom, and a political language, gripping and yet capacious, available for opposing uses. I turn to prophecy, therefore, not to find a philosophic answer to the question of political theology but to engage a rhetoric crucial to American life, not to document its importance but to assess its political bearing. Sociologist Robert Bellah once depicted a salutary political dialectic within a dominant "civic religion" between biblical language and

constitutional liberalism, but, especially since 1980, the language has
been captured by or ceded to "Christian" or "New Right" constituencies
in the Republican Party. During what Michael Rogin terms a "counter-
subversive" moment, whose twinned aspects are "culture war" and "war
on terror," I pursue political questions in rhetorical form: Should small-*d*
democrats reclaim and revise this language, so deeply tied to domination and to struggle against it? If a language has such power to harm,
can that power be used differently? If it frames what politics means for
Americans at axiomatic levels, must we rework it because we are mute
without it? Or must we work through it to move beyond it?[3]

When I began this book, it seemed obvious that prophecy is *inherently*
a problematic genre for democratic politics. We may recall that Hebrew
prophets criticize social injustice and idolatry of wealth and ritual, but
also that they speak in the name of a God whose higher authority is
beyond question. In liberal theory's terms, they recognize neither "negative liberty" nor inalienable rights as they declare what God requires.
Hebrew prophecy is remembered for questioning pervasive practices
long deemed legitimate, but in Aristotelian terms, it does not credit a
valid contest among compelling truths and worthy goods; no prophet
argues that freedom depends on this plurality and its public mediation
by citizens engaging in speech and action. After all, they militantly defend monotheism against what we now call multiculturalism! Their God
makes profound demands for justice, but also for a unitary community
purged of "other gods." God's messengers presume there is one right
way to view and live in the world; other ways are not worthy adversaries
but false prophecy dooming the nation. They courageously speak truth
to power, but they seem to demand assent, not invite conversation.

Reading back from Falwell to biblical forebears, appeals to divine authority seem inescapably dogmatic, and community under God seems
to impose excessive cultural unity. By figuring Hebrews as the children
or the spouse of God, prophecy casts adult agency as willful rebellion or
self-destructive adultery; a rhetoric of fidelity or corruption thus seems
to moralize social practices and demonize cultural difference on behalf of an impossible purity. Whereas a story of decline from origins
seems to idealize the past and reify first principles, a messianic story of
redemption seems to escape history, devalue politics, and justify—even
generate—violence. Even if we grant that prophetic language raises
fundamental political questions—about authority, the constitution of

community, the meaning of suffering—biblical answers seem to justify closure rather than openness, unity rather than plurality, nostalgia rather than experiment.

Justifications of racial domination and culture war in American history *are* enabled by the monotheist cultural politics that frames biblical prophecy. Claims to divine authority and absolute moral truth and narratives of corruption and redemption *do* engender self-righteousness and violence, which close spaces for political contest. Redemptive language *still* weds moral dichotomy to violent purification of practices, people, and impulses deemed an unacceptable stain on human life. Given Christian Right evangelism and the long shadow of 9/11, it seems credible to count prophecy as a language to avoid. Against those who serve higher authority and unequivocally defend the one right way to live, figures like Machiavelli, Friedrich Nietzsche, Hannah Arendt, and—not least—Groucho Marx seem a needed countertradition.

This argument captures the dangerous impact of the hegemonic form of prophecy in American history, but it is too simple. I develop a more complex view through engagement with the figures I analyze in this book: Frederick Douglass and Henry Thoreau in the nineteenth century, and Martin Luther King Jr., James Baldwin, and Toni Morrison in the twentieth. Why do I write more generously about them than about the Hebrew prophets? Less because these figures are so different—though the differences matter greatly—and more because of what they oppose: white supremacy, not the worship of gods other than Yahweh. Whereas biblical attacks on idolatry seem to discredit a pluralism I value, opposition to white supremacy in the name of equality is deeply appealing. But critics of slavery and of white supremacy link injustice to idolatry, which they interpret less as a mistaken idea (of God or race) and more as reified categories tied to domination and enabling its disavowal. Like the Hebrew prophets, they depict not a plurality among valid ways of life but a regime of power whose constitutive practices make the freedom (and identity) of some depend on the servitude of others.

Their prophetic critique of slavery and white supremacy compels a rethinking of our assumptions about dogmatism and plurality, about judgment of injustice and openness to difference, about the conditions of fundamental as opposed to incremental change. Their prophetic rhetoric also seems an extraordinarily resonant form of political speech. Partly, critics use prophecy to address enfranchised citizens: about the disavowals that imprison them in captivity and despair and the acknowledgments—of racial domination and of the democratic principles—that might free them. Partly, critics of white supremacy use prophecy to invert the sacred iconography of American exceptionalism: Casting the Promised Land as Egyptian bondage or Babylonian captivity, they forge a subaltern political community between nation and empire. From prophecy they draw modes of address and registers of voice by which they try to reconstitute an exclusionary regime and redeem the catastrophic history of a subjugated people.

To face race in America is to be compelled toward prophecy. For American liberalism is constituted by disavowing its deep connection to racial domination, and cognate forms of "democratic theory"—from rational choice to discourse ethics—echo this willful innocence. By avoiding race, liberalism defaults on a democratic project and offers a conception of politics that is impoverished by fear of what it takes race (as blackness) to signify: passion, irrationality, embodiment, impurity. At worst, liberal norms of pluralism, tolerance, or deliberation are the smiley face of white supremacy. At best, they prove inadequate to the task of naming, let alone confronting, it. Critics of white supremacy repeatedly turn to prophecy, therefore, to pose questions unvoiced in—and dimensions of experience silenced by—the liberal ordinary. In principle, these critics could use other genres of political speech besides prophecy, but they are gripped by it, and they see no other powerful *vernacular* to provoke acknowledgment of domination and its disavowal, to depict accountability, to affirm democratic commitments, and to redefine collective purpose. They do not cede this language to adversaries, but rework it.

Because white supremacy compels critics toward prophecy as a *political* language addressing domination and collective action, and because they would animate a *democratic* politics by avowedly prophetic speech, I have come to discern political values and democratic resources in a voice I had only feared, to see a tension rather than a polarity between prophecy and politics. By focusing on race, therefore, this book works out that tension and dramatizes prophecy's ambivalent meaning, to rethink how we theorists conceive what is political.[4]

I still find Jeremiah in Jerry Falwell, so to speak, but now also in Frederick Douglass, Henry Thoreau, and Martin Luther King Jr., who inflect theism very differently, as well as in James Baldwin and Toni Morrison, who revise prophecy in nontheist ways to bring an erotic poetics to national politics and to reimagine diasporic community. How do these figures echo Jeremiah? They insist faith is a condition of worldly free-dom. They announce realities we must acknowledge if we are to flour-ish. Depicting the freedom of some premised on the subordination of others, they make unequivocal judgments of constitutive injustice and of we citizens who disclaim it. They depict a culture beset not by an ignorance to be remedied with more information but by a systemic derangement about what (and who) we count as real. They depict not a plurality of faiths but a disavowal of reality. To address audiences in-vested in denial, they take up a complex rhetorical task and political of-fice: By acts of witness and narration, they try to shift how people judge the past and its meaning, to provoke acknowledgment not only of what is forgotten or disavowed but also of the meaning of principles they have practiced in viciously exclusionary ways. Only such "repentance" frees people imprisoned by willful innocence of their history while sig-naling their capacity to practice their principles differently. Baldwin thus makes whites the protagonists in a tragedy of crime and misrecognition, characters whose captivity, haunting, and contingent redemption he narrates to initiate democracy in America.

We theorists may interpret "abolitionist" voices as dogmatic, yet equality stands fast for us as a commitment, and we are unequivocal about the evil of white supremacy and its unfortunate centrality in Ameri-can history. We worry about the dangers of redemptive rhetoric, but we too want whites to acknowledge and overcome—why not say repent of and redeem?—a history of racial domination. We value pluralization of perspectives, but we recognize that not every version of history enables a fruitful relationship to the past. We even may credit that a story making white supremacy central to our history is a condition of democratic pos-sibility, period. Because prophecy depicts such fateful judgments and choices about practices and stories, it is a needed—albeit dangerous—political practice.

Because the danger is great, it is tempting to split good and bad forms of prophecy, as if to exorcise Jerry Falwell but save Frederick Douglass, as if defining "true" prophecy could separate valuable and dangerous uses, to assure democratic outcomes. But the voice of judgment—adversarial and aggressive—that I reject in one seems appealing and justified in the other. Indeed, what attracts my figures to prophecy and gives their language compelling political resonance are the very registers of voice that political theorists may spurn under the sign of dogmatism, moral-ism, or fundamentalism. To take prophecy whole is to discover how its political value is inseparable from what we find dangerous about it: the exercise of authority in claims about willful blindness and judgment of injustice, in uncompromising and aggressive calls to conflict over fateful and costly choices, in intense avowals of solidarity, in urgent demands for accountability on behalf of reimagined community, and in poetic promises of redemption—not to mention intensities and cadences of speech that raise the temperature in the body politic.

A profound ambiguity thus marks the political meaning of prophecy: Registers of speech we find disturbing or potentially antidemocratic can perform truly democratizing and politicizing work. In form and content such speech and claims are essential, but essentially risky, in a democratic politics. We thus trace how critics use prophecy to make visible crucial dimensions of politics, and how their speech can go awry; seeing how risk is tightly wound with value, we face claim making about practices and choices as a needful political act, and a terrifyingly contingent one, because we cannot guarantee a good outcome. But fear of doing evil deprives us of the capacity to do good.

Whereas many theorists respond to neoliberal and post-9/11 politics by reaffirming constitutional liberalism, investing in deliberative democracy, or imagining an ethos of pluralization or cosmopolitanism, I have concluded that we lose too much if we simply abjure prophetic language. The political challenge is to fashion political counterprophecy, democratic forms of prophetic speech. Rather than dismissing a prophetic voice as inherently flawed or seeking an alternative to it, I use critics of white supremacy to analyze not only that voice's danger but its powerful appeal, capacity for reworking, and political value. Partly I explore how these critics work both with and against inherited prophetic idioms. Partly I explore how they fashion counterprophecies to confront the limits of liberalism by making democratic claims in political ways. Partly I explore how they try to politicize the redemptive rhetoric bequeathed by biblical prophecy as they struggle to imagine and foster a possibility for new possibilities.

My approach has obvious limitations. I set aside other idioms in the American ordinary to focus on those I identify here. Some may say I read liberal political thought ungenerously. But liberalism already has many defenders and elaborators, most of whom (not all!) repeat what I find here: a sustained complicity with white supremacy that cannot be overcome solely by liberalism's methods—rights claims, juridical redress, public policy, legislative politics. These need to be animated—and also unsettled—by prophetic practices that unrelentingly expose the hierarchies held in place, not undone, by the liberal ordinary.

Focusing on the figures in this book, however, also means simplifying the complexity of the American racial system in which a black–white binary intersects with a category of "ethnicity" and so with the subject formation of native peoples, Mexican natives, and Chinese laborers in the nineteenth century; Europeans in the twentieth century; and immigrants from Asia, India, and Hispanic cultures since 1965. I focus on the black–white binary not to depict this complex reality but to invoke the political meaning of "race." For in American political rhetoric, "race" is not just a powerful biologistic fiction; it denotes a history organized by slavery and the specific historic experience of African Americans. In the democratic imaginary, then, "race" is also a trope connoting the reality of power and inequality, of embodiment and difference, in contrast to prevailing idioms of formal equality, individualism, ethnic mobility, or multiculturalism. In turn, my figures address white supremacy mostly as a black–white dynamic, but they thereby raise issues—of idolatry and finitude, domination and disavowal, embodiment and agency, accountability and collective purpose—at the heart of democratic life.

Indeed, to address the crisis, and sense of crisis, in American life now, visionary storytelling by those who bear witness seems ever more essential: To name the constitutive exclusions, amnesia, and anxious dream of sovereignty that make imperial power and repressive action seem credible answers to wounded national identity. The office of those who bear witness is not only critical or disenchanting, though, for by passionate language that seizes audiences, prophetic testimony can make dead bones live. Prophecy can elevate people's "expectations and requirements," Thoreau says, by animating values they imagine as static, dramatizing commitments they reify by forgetting, and energizing democratic solidarities they invoke in name only. In these and other ways, prophetic visions, questions, claims, demands, and energy—provoking, recalcitrant, haunting, passionate, and poetic—may be especially needful now.

The example of these critics, at least, suggests how we ourselves might wrestle with the legacy of this language in the world and within ourselves. To explore how Douglass and Thoreau and Baldwin, King, and Morrison take up—in some regards reworking and in other regards resisting—this language, is to create what Alasdair MacIntyre calls an "argumentative retelling" of prophecy.[5] Situated in relation to prophetic idioms, their political concerns, theoretical insights, and rhetorical strategies speak powerfully to each other and to us. For as each figure retells American history to confront racial domination, together they form a conversation about the deepest issues in American life, about the political and rhetorical difficulties in addressing them, and so about the value and danger of prophecy as a language in and for politics. To invoke the ambivalent conclusion of Morrison's novel *Beloved*, "this is not a story to pass on"—we must not pass by or ignore this story, but nor can we simply bequeath it to others unchanged.[6]

Acknowledgments

A PROJECT this long in the making incurs many debts and warrants many acknowledgments.

To begin with, this book would not have been possible without the support of my colleagues at the Gallatin School of Individualized Study. Lisa Goldfarb and Stacy Pies taught me to hear and read poetry, which helped me read everything else. Dean Frances White and Acting Dean Ali Mirsepassi gave me leave time and every other kind of encouragement. When I received a fellowship from the National Endowment for the Humanities, they helped make it a full year and then funded the fabulous work of a student assistant, Jillian MacClearie. Dean Susanne Wofford helped fund the index. My faculty colleagues were supportive of my efforts to link teaching and writing. As its name suggests, our school was an incubator of interdisciplinary study, and it was enormously fruitful to my scholarship to translate ideas, not into lectures but into discussion-based seminars organized around close reading of texts. My ideas about prophecy, race, and politics, but also about authority and rhetoric, took shape through undergraduate teaching, and I thank years of students for their intellectual creativity and political energy.

Several friends and colleagues saved this book because they took it seriously when I lost faith: Barbara Dudley, Peter Euben, Lisa Goldfarb, Harvey Goldman, George Kateb, Melissa Orlie. Early on, Hanna Pitkin and Jack Schaar helped me get past a stuck place, and Michael Rogin affirmed and so enabled a new direction before he died. At that point, Stephen White at the University of Virginia, Linda Zerilli at Northwestern University, and Peter Euben at Duke arranged for talks that helped me clarify and solidify that new direction. So did a conference on identification set up by Ernesto Laclau at Essex, which created a terrific conversation with Victoria Hattam, Joe Lowndes, Anne Norton, and Linda Zerilli. I was able to sharpen my work on Morrison through talks at Columbia University, City University of New York, and University of Oregon, and I am grateful to Ross Posnock, Jennifer Gaboury, and Joseph Lowndes for arranging them. More recently, Cora Kaplan and Bill Schwartz at University of London invited me to a conference on James Baldwin that enriched my work and broadened my world of interlocutors.

The book would also have been inconceivable without my participation in several different intellectual conversations.

One was a reading group on political theory and political identification. By reading and discussion, Kevin Bruyneel, Edmund Fong, Victoria Hattam, Joseph Lowndes, Priscilla Yamin, and I worked through poststructural critiques of identity to rethink the formation of political subjectivity.

A second is a reading group that Ross Posnock and I convened to bridge American literature and political theory by focusing on race. Its members included Aliyah Abdur-Rahman, Alyson Cole, Tanya Friedel, Jennifer Gaboury, Robert Gunn, Victoria Hattam, Tom Jacobs, Megan Obourn, Cyrus Patel, Shireen Patel, Lindsay Reckson, Dan Skinner. Our abiding concern was embodiment: How are raced and gendered categories inscribed and yet resisted in literary art, national narratives, and lived experience?

There is a third cluster of colleagues, mostly but not entirely in the field of political theory, whose work has deeply affected mine and with whom I have been in conversation—sometimes only internally, sometimes privately, and sometimes publicly—about political theory, modernity, and democratic politics. Among these I specifically want to acknowledge Talal Asad, Lawrie Balfour, Jane Bennet, Wendy Brown, Rom Coles, Mary Dietz, Tom Dumm, Anne Norton, and especially George Kateb and William Connolly, whose political-theory classes inspired me as an undergraduate so many years ago and whose texts have remained essential to my thinking. Over many years, the work and conversation of these folks has consistently enriched me by enlarging my theoretical vocabulary, challenging my assumptions, and modeling an exemplary generosity.

Speaking more directly about the book, several colleagues read specific chapters: Jane Bennet, Lawrie Balfour, Alyson Cole, Rom Coles, Lisa Goldfarb, Victoria Hattam, George Kateb, Hanna Pitkin, Eric Santner, John Schaar, Linda Zerilli. Other colleagues read most or all of the chapters and sometimes several versions: Peter Euben, Harvey Goldman, Bonnie Honig, Melissa Orlie, Mark Reinhardt. Without their emotional encouragement and intellectual feedback, this book would not have been finished, or would have been much worse than it is.

Three other acknowledgments remain to be made:

First, I am indebted in every way to Michael Rogin, who bridged political theory, American literature, and the study of American politics and who revealed the centrality of race to each. I wish every sentence of this book could live up to his political outrage and intellectual creativity—not to mention his fabulous sense of humor, especially about the darkest things.

Second, in the land of the living I have been sustained by several people who are both friends and intellectual interlocutors: Peter Euben, Harvey Goldman, Vicky Hattam, Bonnie Honig, Melissa Orlie, and Linda Zerilli, who have profoundly shaped my view of politics and of theory while generating many a good laugh over the vicissitudes of life and career.

Last but by no means least there is my family, whose love, humor, and abiding insistence on pleasure in life sustains me every day. To them, Mimi, my wife, and Taylor, my son, I dedicate this book.

1. Introducing Jeremiah's Legacy

Placing Prophecy in American Politics and Political Theory

Precisely when its dubiousness as a pragmatic record is recognized, the narrative reveals its function in creating a people in politics and history.
—Eric Voegelin, *Order and History*, vol. 1, *Israel and Revelation*

Where discourse lives an authentic life . . . the word is not a material thing but rather the eternally mobile . . . medium of dialogic interaction. . . . The life of the word is contained in its transfer from one mouth to another, from one conflict to another, from one generation to another generation. . . . When a member of a speaking collective comes upon a word, it is not . . . free from the aspirations and evaluations of others, uninhabited by other voices. . . . The word enters his context from another context, permeated with the interpretations of others. His own thought finds the word already inhabited.
—Mikhail Bakhtin, *Problems of Dostoevsky's Poetics*

THIS IS an introductory chapter that sets the frame for my substantive readings of Thoreau, King, Baldwin, and Morrison. It briefly describes my method of interpreting prophecy as a social practice and rhetorical form open to revision. Then it introduces the instantiations of "prophecy" that guide subsequent chapters. First is the Hebrew voice of prophecy, to identify key markers of biblical prophecy as a genre. Second is prophecy as an American idiom, to identify the capaciousness and political contingency of the ways biblical prophecy is translated and used. Third is "prophecy" as an object in American studies, to identify the central scholarly debate about its political and cultural role. Last is prophecy introduced into the conversation of political theory, to identify the theoretical questions my readings pursue.

Characterizing Prophecy

We should begin by noting that "prophecy" is not easily defined, and it is surely not defined once and for all by the canonical books of the Bible.

It is a social practice of many cultures, in forms that modern commentary links to shamanism, ecstatic vision, charismatic authority, founder myths, and social criticism. It thus names the public role of those who address a community by mediating its relationship to the larger realities conditioning its existence and choices. As a social practice, prophecy is open to revision and intense conflict, for people argue about the definition of the role and about whose words to recognize as having authority. Simon and Garfunkel's lyrics "the words of the prophets are written on subway walls and tenement halls" signal how such mediating voices surround us still, as we count some and ignore others—at our peril.

But in this book, "prophecy" connotes the genre canonized in the prophetic books of the Hebrew Bible, and the ways their speech and example is taken up by Jesus and Paul, reworked by Martin Luther and John Calvin in the Protestant Reformation, by Puritans in the English Revolution and first American founding, and by slaves, nationalists, and reformers in the United States. Prophecy (and deep assumptions about it) are also reshaped as John Milton and William Blake—then Samuel Coleridge, Ralph Waldo Emerson, and Walt Whitman—transform prophetic ideas to fashion a political and secular conception of "the poet." Once Blake claims that prophets are poets who invent the gods later reified by priests into rigid truths, other figures in the romantic movement can affirm that human beings, by poesis, compose visions of God or optics on reality. Once Percy Bysshe Shelley depicts how imaginative vision makes the poet an "unacknowledged legislator," Emerson can make poetic genius a capacity democracy emancipates in citizens. Protestant religiosity and its romantic alter ego, in tandem and tension, inflect biblical prophecy in ways that become central to the imagination of democracy and of American nationhood.[1]

Allen Ginsberg and Martin Luther King Jr. speak "prophetically," then, not because they predict the future or engage in social criticism but because they bespeak and inflect these Protestant and romantic registers of voice. From Milton to Blake, from the jeremiads of Douglass and Thoreau, or from Abraham Lincoln's meditation on the inexorable workings of a just God, to Ginsberg's ecstatic poetry, to King's worldly practice of redemption, to the richly ambiguous texts of Baldwin and Morrison, or to the punitive literalism of the Christian New Right, prophecy is both replenished and remade.

Scriptural literalism and theocratic rule are powerful now; in them we see anxiety over difference, hatred of women, fear of sexuality, aversion to democratic plurality. But ministers and mullahs rule by emptying language of its ambiguity, while using its capacity to excite and incite. We are rightly disturbed by their literalism and terrified by the passion it mobilizes. But we acquiesce in that power if we accept the view that language, especially so-called religious language, is simple in meaning, or if we reduce prophetic poetry to a didactic message. My contrary practice is to recover prophecy not as scripture with fixed meaning but as living poetry open to infusions of new meaning. My avowedly secular goal is to show the richness of language where it now seems least present, to affirm the passion of language even when it is dangerous, and so to sustain a sense of democratic possibility when it seems most besieged.

If we assume, in that case, that prophecy "is" a genre of speech and form of action that people at once live, problematize, and revise—to address the demands of their day—then our interpretive challenge is to honor the richness and political contingency of this remaking while crediting the weight of its dominating practice. Even if we focus on heretical Protestant and romantic inflections of prophecy, though, the first task is to identify the elements that moderns draw from biblical prophecy. We must seek, not an account of what biblical prophecy really is, but the modes of address, registers of voice, primal stories, and constitutive metaphors that modern figures "hear" in it.[2]

Hearing Hebrew Prophecy

Most commentators and translators recognize Hebrew prophecy as an *office:* Prophets are "called"—often responding only reluctantly—to a public responsibility. The Hebrew word *navi,* whose root means "to bubble forth," "to utter" or proclaim, "to call" (not only "be called by"!) God, is later translated as *pro-phetes* in Greek, "fore-speaker and interpreter." At first, *navi* are the ecstatics who lead peasant militias into battle against nearby empires, to create a confederation of tribes that call themselves Hebrew. *Navi* voice their war God's unconditional blessing of a relatively egalitarian way of life. The *navi* Samuel thus opposes kingship, which he links to the worship of gods other than Yahweh, but once the tribes overrule him, subsequent *navi* speak for the royal house, supporting state building and centralized priest-mediated worship under David and Solomon.

After Solomon dies in 922 BC and Israel splits into two kingdoms, most *navi* support the regimes, but figures later canonized as *the* prophets sustain Samuel's opposition. Amos and Hosea appear around 750 BC, preaching to the northern kingdom before it is destroyed by Assyria; in the southern kingdom, Micah and Isaiah warn of a similar fate. In 587 Babylon does invade, destroying the Jerusalem temple, taking a captive people into exile. Jeremiah endures this disaster and addresses its meaning; other prophets emerge during the Babylonian exile. Over several hundred years, until the exile, those we might call "house prophets" repeat the ideology that God unconditionally supports the monarchical regime, while those we now deem canonical declare that a just God judges the conduct of kings, priests, and people. Claiming to speak God's words, they accuse each other of false prophecy.[3]

Orthodox redaction reads this era teleologically as if true prophecy is obvious, but Max Weber grasps the uncertainty: "Prophecy and counterprophecy confronted each other in the street. Both equally claimed ecstatic legitimation and cursed one another. Where is Yahweh's truth? everybody had to ask." Facing imminent invasion by Assyria or Babylon, Hebrews question the justice of a God who seems to have reneged on the promise of unconditional support, and the power of a God who seems unable to protect them. As the "dramatic narrative" ordering the monarchical world regime loses credibility, they face what Alasdair MacIntyre calls an "epistemological crisis." Adversaries hurl "curses and invective," says Weber, because they disagree, not about the application of self-evident principles, but about how even to depict their God, situation, choices. Then, and now, people must distinguish true and false prophets as they debate what prophecy is.[4]

Such uncertainty leads to the colloquial belief that prophecy means making predictions, whose truth retroactively verifies a speaker's authority. But few prophets, and no poets, accept this view. As Martin Buber argues, to be a prophet "means to set the audience, to whom the words are addressed, before the choice and decision. . . . The future is not already fixed in this present hour; it is dependent on the real decision . . . in which man takes part in this hour." A "true prophet does not announce an immutable decree," but "speaks into the power of the decision lying in the moment" in a way "dependent on question and alternative" and "call and response." This view of Hebrew prophecy as a political office posing fateful collective decisions to an audience is specified by biblical texts.[5]

First, prophets are *messengers* who *announce* truths their audience is invested in denying. Addressing not an error in understanding but a partly willful blindness, they announce realities we must acknowledge if we are to flourish. Amos denies monarchical ideology by making the unprecedented announcement that a just God makes blessings conditional on conduct, and indeed, may destroy the Hebrews because they value ritual over justice. But when Nietzsche denies a teleology wiring divine providence into the nature of things, he also uses the prophetic persona to *announce* "the death of God."

Second, the office means *bearing witness,* though not in a legal sense, as prophets *testify to what they see and stand against it.* "The Lord hath a controversy with his people and he will plead with Israel," Micah says, bearing God's point of view to provoke self-reflection. His God thus asks, "What have I done unto thee? Wherein have I wearied thee? Testify against me" (Mic. 6:1–3).[6] The office is interrogatory and dialogic, seeking relation in the call-and-response of speech. But testimony also bears judgment: Prophets stand with people whose exclusion makes the whole partial. As bearing witness makes present what has been made absent—the poor and God—biblical prophets testify *against* injustice and idolatry. Jesus thus identifies God with "the least of us"; Frederick Douglass "stands with God and the slave" to bear witness against slavery and the idol of race in a republic.

Third, prophecy is the office of *watchmen* who *forewarn:* They name danger to forestall it. Amos warns of the danger in conduct that dispossesses others: "Ye have built houses of hewn stone, but ye shall not dwell in them; ye have planted pleasant vineyards, but ye shall not drink wine of them" (5:11). But disaster occurs because Hebrews do not "amend their ways" to prevent it. Foreseeing the danger in conduct, prophets seek what they call a "turn"—from a life oriented by disavowal. The Hebrew "turn" is translated as "repentance"; those who "hearken" to the warning "turn" to the realities they now disavow, and they reconstitute community. Still, the relentless consequences of prior choices may overwhelm that possibility. James Baldwin warns of "the fire next time" not because he believes that God punishes the wicked but to provoke a turn before it is too late.

Fourth, therefore, prophecy is the office of *singers* who ask and answer the question, What is the meaning of our suffering? They help people endure catastrophe and exile by *poetry* that endows a painful history with meaning. From Jeremiah's lamentations to the sorrow songs and spirituals of slaves and their heirs, the office of prophecy is to voice traumatic loss and hopes of redemption. Invocation of loss and projection of possibility, risking the nostalgic and the messianic, are two sides of songs addressing decision and action in a present: Why are we here? What is to be done? How do we go on?

In each mode of address, the office of prophecy is a public vocation mediating between a community and powerful realities it does not understand or control. In each regard, prophets make claims about the circumstances and difficulties—and fateful decisions—*of the whole;* indeed, in this way they reconstitute the very "we" they seem to invoke as a given. In each regard, they seek to *redeem* the community they address and whose fate they commit to sharing. Prophecy is thus a performance to incite audiences to self-reflection and action. Not only a rhetorical act, prophecy is an embodied form of symbolic action: Hosea marries a prostitute to symbolize God's sense of betrayal by people who "love" other gods; Isaiah walks around Jerusalem wearing a heavy yoke to signify the danger in allying with another state. Students who sit in at segregated lunch counters assume the office of those who bear bodily witness to their testimony in speech.

In cultures bearing biblical traces, though, "prophecy" also names a literary and political *genre* with characteristic—though not fixed— narrative forms and tropes, cadences of speech, tones of voice, and registers of feeling, which speakers and actors draw on to address fundamental political questions. The genre entails three narrative forms: theodicy, jeremiad, and lamentation.

When Amos "announces" that a just God has declared war on the Hebrews because of their conduct, he invents what we now call a *theodicy*. For when he declares that imminent invasion is mandated by a just God—he asks, "Shall there be an evil in a city and the Lord hath not done it?" (3:7)—he makes events into signs of a just God's blessings and punishments. This "theodicy of misfortune" makes the universe "ethically rational," Weber says, investing agency and suffering with a moral meaning authored by God.[7] If we interpret events as God's just judgment, we will amend our ways to seek pardon. Linking agency, punishment, and forgiveness, prophets make the unprecedented and problematic invention of a collective subject responsible for its acts because it can act otherwise.

Amos explains God's grievances with the Hebrews' conduct: "I brought [thee] up from the land of Egypt," his God declares, but the

Hebrews "have despised the law of the Lord and have not kept his commandment" (2:4). Accordingly, he says, "Hear this word that the Lord has spoken against you, O children of Israel, against the whole family which I brought up from the land of Egypt, saying, you only have I known of all the families of the earth; therefore I will punish you" (3:1–2). The Hebrews have brought on this disaster because, despite warnings, they disobeyed their God. By this unrelenting yet reassuring logic, theodicy makes meaningful the otherwise senseless destruction of the northern kingdom and its people and initiates both the collective ethos that Weber calls "joint liability" and what Nietzsche calls "the bad conscience." But what does "obeying" God mean?[8]

Most Hebrew prophets denounce injustice and idolatry. They testify that the wealth of a few is gained by oppressing others, as if they are not members of the same community, as if they do not even count as real. The rich and powerful "store up violence and robbery in their palaces" by "turning aside" the poor "from their right," Amos declares (3:10; 5:12). Rulers "abhor judgment and pervert all equity"; they "build up Zion with blood and Jerusalem with iniquity" according to Micah (3:9–10), who laments a general condition: "There is none upright among men; they all lie in wait for blood; they hunt every man his brother with a net" (7:2). Yet "they lean on the Lord and say, 'Is not the Lord among us?'" (3:11) because they perform rituals they believe God has mandated.

Prophets thus testify against idolatry, which is worshiping other gods than Yahweh, and worshiping Yahweh in the wrong way—by ritual rather than justice. "I hate, I despise your feast days," says Amos's God. For, God asks the Israelites, "have ye offered me sacrifices and offerings in the wilderness forty years?" (5:21, 25). God is not "pleased with thousands of rams" says Micah; rather, "he hath showed thee, O man, what is good, and what doth the Lord require of thee, but to do justly, to love mercy, and to walk humbly with thy God?" (6:7–8). Not a Platonic form to perceive or a law to obey, justice is a practice acknowledging interdependence and limitations; in Amos, justice is a "mighty stream" buoying our action and nourishing our life.

Idolatry, therefore, is not a philosophical mistake: The worship of other gods sustains imperial states and social inequality; ritualized worship of Yahweh empowers a priestly elite but ignores social relations and daily conduct. A people ruled by God, in contrast, seeks relations of relative social equality or nonrule among themselves and assumes "joint liability" for the whole, from whose fate no one—rich or poor—is exempt.

To oppose idolatry is to resist states, "religion," or law as worldly authorities endowed with inappropriate meaning; in contrast to the reification Weber associates with "the massive ritualism of the priests," prophecy enjoins what he calls "the ethical righteousness of deeds."[9]

Accordingly, obeying God means not submission but action, not ritualized worship but "doing justly," not following a law but counting the reality of those Morrison later calls "the dis-remembered and unaccounted for."[10] Like Socrates, prophets thus ask, What do you value? Is what you value worth valuing? Is what you call justice really just? To whom is justice due? Like him, too, they answer by exemplary action, not doctrine. But their mode of speech is not by the better argument but by the testimony and narrative of one who bears witness. Reflection is framed not by seeking to define "justice" as such but by asking, Are you upholding your covenant (with your God and each other) to live in a certain way? Prophets make no "moral" claim to a rule or law for all people at all times but instead tell a story of infidelity to a founding covenant that once redeemed *this* people from Egypt.

Here we see the second crucial narrative form in prophecy: By a *jeremiad* prophets narrate conduct as a decline from origins, to address a community about its constitutive commitments and current difficulties, to make its future contingent on a "decision" about its conduct. Through profoundly resonant tropes of captivity and founding, of covenant and corruption, of repentance and covenant renewal, prophets identify the fateful choices that form, endanger, and redeem their community.[11]

Their story of a covenanted relationship begins with redemption from Egypt. Isaiah says of his God: "In all their affliction he was afflicted . . . in his love and in his pity he redeemed them; and he bare them" (63:9). Hear the pathos and anger: "I have nourished and brought up children and they have rebelled against me" (1:2). As Baldwin says, though, every accusation contains a plea: to "hearken" to God's voice and "amend" our ways, but also to restore community. Indeed, Hosea dramatizes the meaning of covenanted bonds by depicting the Hebrews not as rebellious children but as God's adulterous "wife of whoredoms" (1:2), who has taken other "lovers." The dangerous legacy of prophecy appears not only in theodicy's moral(istic) logic, but here, in this patriarchal jeremiad of covenant and infidelity. It yields a salutary idea of covenant renewal and a cultural politics of purification that links idolatry to female desire in ways that both pathologize agency and police actual women.

Promising to "allure her and bring her into the wilderness and speak comfortably unto her" and hoping that "she will sing . . . as in the days of her youth" when she "came up out of Egypt," Hosea's God seeks remarriage by reciprocal acts of human atoning and divine forgiving (2:14–15). "We will say no more to the work of our hands, ye are our gods" (Hosea 14:3), and God will say "to them which were not my people, thou art my people, and they shall say thou art our God" (Hosea 2:23). (Morrison uses these lines, quoted by Paul in the Epistle to the *Romans,* as the epigraph to *Beloved.*) If Hebrews "turn" toward each other and God to renew covenants, they "shall abide many days without a king, without a prince, without a sacrifice and without an image" (Hosea 3:4). Amos imagines community redeemed from dispossession: "They shall build the waste cities and inhabit them . . . plant vineyards and drink the wine thereof . . . make gardens and eat the fruit of them" (9:14). For Micah, "They shall sit every man under his vine and fig tree, and none shall make them afraid." Indeed, "all people will walk every one in the name of his god, and we will walk in the name of the Lord our God for ever and ever" (4:4, 5).

Whereas Aristotle severs politics from the household to defend plurality, Hebrew prophets use marriage as a metaphor to imagine community as a chosen and libidinal bond in which people commit to each other, to a God demanding justice, and to covenant as a central practice. Jeremiads make infidelity a key political trope, to put a premium on commitment, not plurality. The danger to democracy in demands for unity is obvious, but the democratic resources in a trope of fidelity can be seen in thinkers from Machiavelli and Arendt to Douglass and King.

For critics who seek participation or oppose slavery can draw on prophecy to depict democratic community constituted by *covenant* as a social practice and by specific promises. Partly, we hear a political claim in conditional terms: To live without kings and exploitation, we *must* resist idolatrous investments in worldly authority, and we *must* sustain contrary practices of covenant and equality. Partly, critics pose political choice in terms of fidelity to equality as a commitment or to covenant as a founding practice. Machiavelli's citizens resist "corruption" by "returning" to their origins, not only to "first principles" but to "themselves," to the needs that brought them together, and to their capacity for action. Douglass and King thus oppose white supremacy by jeremiads in which covenant renewal reenacts 1776 to recover what Arendt calls "the lost treasure" of the revolutionary tradition.[12]

The "turn" we translate as "repentance" thus is a *redemptive* political practice. Redemption means "deliverance from"—from kings, priests and idols, exploitation and imperial rule, corruption or self-betrayal. And it means "recovering" what has been lost—rights and autonomy, land and material blessings, capacities for cooperative action, closeness to God. Hosea adds to redemption's meaning: A "whore" is redeemed or *made worthy* if she atones for her crimes, makes good the injuries she has caused, repairs the breach with her husband, heals her self-inflicted wounds, and draws value from her suffering. Redemption means not only covenant renewal as a return to origins, but the purification of a stain on a human being. Lamenting that "the faithful city [has] become a harlot" (1:21), Isaiah's God pleads, "Wash you, make you clean." This means "put away the evil of your doings from before mine eyes; cease to do evil, learn to do well" (1:16–17). But as he implores—"come now, and let us reason together, . . . though your sins be as scarlet, they shall be as white as snow" (1:18)—he also imagines redemption as a "spirit of burning" that humbles "every one that is proud and lofty" (4:4, 2:12).

Here we see the dimensions—profound, politically fruitful, and disastrous—of the redemptive vision that prophets articulate cumulatively. The literal and the figurative are joined by a poetry relating worldly and internal dimensions of life: Desire and imagination within are ruled by a "pride" that, in worldly practices, in groups and states, holds people captive. For King no less than Isaiah, overcoming pride in and as worldly hierarchy and purifying pride internally are two sides of a deliverance both personal and political, enjoyed by bodily selves in a land made fruitful. Isaiah thus feels called to "preach good tidings unto the meek . . . to bind up the broken-hearted, to proclaim liberty to the captives and the opening of the prison to them that are bound" (61:1).[13]

When is struggle with "pride" a salutary practice of wrestling with the power and partiality that are part of life? When does "deliverance" mean the complete and completed abolition of a pride seen only as a stain on life? How does redemption come to mean escaping, rather than turning to and confronting, history? In the name of delivering us from injustice, does redemptive language seek an impossible purity, fostering violence though it promises peace? Such questions address even covenant renewal, if it is invested with a promise of communitarian fullness without remainder. But once the Hebrews are exiled, prophecy surely changes tone.[14]

By a third narrative form, a *lamentation* that depicts the suffering of exile, prophets dramatize loss, and they imagine another kind of redemption to sustain a people in the face of traumatic dispossession. "The Lord shall set his hand a second time to recover the remnant of his people . . . from the four corners of the earth" (Isa. 11:11–12). Crushing the empires by which he once punished them, God makes "a highway for the remnant of his people, as it was to Israel in the day he came up out of Egypt" (Isa. 11:16). For Jeremiah, a "remnant" redeemed from exile will make a "new covenant" that "circumcises the heart":

> I will make a new covenant with the House of Israel and the House of Judah: not according to the covenant that I made with their fathers in the day I took them by the hand to bring them out of the land of Egypt; which covenant they broke, though I was a husband unto them. . . . But this shall be the covenant. . . . I will put my law in their inward parts and write it in their hearts. . . . And they shall teach no more every man his neighbor and brother, saying, Know the Lord, for they shall all know me, from the least of them unto the greatest of them. (Jer. 31:31–34)

Breaking the vicious cycle of crime and punishment, Jeremiah imagines a new beginning: Divine forgiveness breaks repetition, and divine love, by initiating a change of heart, renews the capacity to begin. To depict a present defined not by a past that haunts it or by a future that redeems it, he imagines a new Exodus, as if to inaugurate what Harold Rosenberg calls "the tradition of the new."[15] In Isaiah's parallel vision, the Hebrews become God's suffering servant, by whom humanity is redeemed:

> The mountain of the Lord's house shall be established in the top of the mountains . . . and all nations shall flow unto it. And many people shall go up to the mountain of the Lord . . . and he will teach us of his ways and we will walk in his paths. For out of Zion shall go forth the law, and the word of the Lord from Jerusalem. And he shall judge among nations and rebuke many people; and they shall beat their swords into plowshares and their spears into pruning hooks; nation shall not lift up sword against nation, neither shall they learn war anymore. (Isa. 2:2–4)[16]

Prophets would "redeem" the suffering of war and exile because, as Arendt says, "we can no more master the past than we can undo it. But we can reconcile ourselves to it. The form for this is the lament, which arises out of all recollection." Still, exile-as-loss is named but then overcome as lamentations promise a recovered plenitude that escapes worldly and historical limits. This-worldly practices of covenant renewal give way to God's grace, which alone redeems a remnant not only from exile but from the carnal particularity that Philip Roth calls "human stain." People are thus redeemed from worldly authority and political conflict: As each wholeheartedly embodies God, so community embodies justice without remainder. These visions of redemption prefigure Jesus's glad tidings, which depict a body unified by practices of covenanted commitment and loving forgiveness and which imagine this reborn community bearing a universal good.[17]

How are prophecy and redemption taken up by political theory? To speak too simply, Leo Strauss sees the origins of prophecy in Moses as founder and in *law* to ground standards of judgment and contain political power. Emphasizing God's changing *word*, Eric Voegelin invokes Paul and Augustine to depict "prophetism as the struggle against the law" and against any territorial political community. He recovers the antinomian voice of critique obscured by Strauss, but by severing prophecy from worldly community. If Strauss's "Jerusalem" signifies irretrievable faith in absolute standards, and if for Voegelin it signifies continuing faith in a living word, each recovers it to warn against lodging redemption in modern rationalism.[18]

Their splitting of biblical prophecy, and their engagement with redemption, is paralleled by more recent secularizers. To speak too simply again, Norman O. Brown uses Baruch Spinoza to depict a historical sequence in which prophetic revelation is announced as law, internalized by later prophets as conscience, translated by Jesus into love, and cast by philosophers as the natural light of reason in each and all. By interpreting universal community as "love's body," Brown rejects Strauss's reduction of prophecy to law and rejects Voegelin's split of spirit and word from flesh and history, to fashion a "Dionysian Christianity" that secularizes redemption. But his de-territorialized philosophy abstracts speech from actual cultures and replaces politics with ethics.[19]

Inversely, Michael Walzer secularizes prophecy as "social criticism" authorized not by law, revelation, or reason but by the "core values" of a particular community. He turns prophecy from theist absolutes to "internal criticism" of tradition, but he reifies its validating authority. Against Christian and secular universalisms, he defends attachment to community, but he elides its exclusionary entailments. To draw from prophets a model of consensual and social-democratic practice, he must deny their marginality, sanitize their antinomian wildness, and disown their messianic narratives. Likewise, his this-worldly, prosaic, and meliorist view of "redemption" avoids the twinned legacies of racial domination and biblical language in American politics.[20]

To turn to American politics is to recover in its wholeness a biblical prophecy whose every aspect entwines resources and risks, but also to discover how prophecy is an office and genre remade by critics who draw on its resources—and reenact or resist its dangers. In this sense Weber calls Hebrew prophets "world-political demagogues" because these "speakers in public" use vulgar and incendiary language to address the fate of the whole. Their heirs do not recover a law or revelation but are gripped by performances of vision and judgment that they transfigure to fashion their own dramatic personae and voices. In rhetorically artful and emotionally urgent ways—as messengers, witnesses, watchmen, and singers—these heirs speak to elicit affect, provoke self-reflection, and incite action. In counterpoint, liberal theory since Thomas Hobbes sees prophecy as "comprehensive doctrine," dangerously coercive, or as possession by an "enthusiasm" that threatens rational self-control and public order. Let us turn, then, to the prevailing voice of prophecy in the United States, to hear how it is used for opposed political projects.[21]

American Prophecy as a Semantic Field

On September 13, 2001, Rev. Jerry Falwell called the destruction of the World Trade Center in New York City a divine punishment of American immorality. "God continues to lift the curtain and allow the enemies of America to give us probably what we deserve." He explains why:

[When we] throw God out of the public square . . . and destroy 40 million little innocent babies, we make God mad. . . . The pagans, the abortionists, the feminists, the gays and lesbians who are actively trying to make that an alternate lifestyle, the ACLU, People for the American Way—all of them who have tried to secularize America—I point the finger in their face and say, "you helped this happen."

For Falwell, representative government is underwritten by "Christian ideals" and "traditional moral standards" that entail patriarchal codes and compulsory heterosexuality. Bearing witness against the corruption of this cultural frame, he warns, "America is in imminent peril. We are rotting from within." Still, "has America crossed the line of no return?" He quotes 2 Chronicles 7:14: "If my people, which are called by my name, humble themselves and pray, and seek my face, and turn from their wicked ways, then will I . . . forgive their sin, and will heal their land." But, he continues, "scriptures remind us that . . . Israel, the apple of God's eye, was destroyed . . . because the people failed to repent" of their "idolatry."[22]

Falwell speaks in "prophetic" terms, we might say, because he attributes our fate to our (choices about our) conduct as judged by a just God and because he situates claims about conduct in a story about a specific (chosen) people, its founding covenant, corruption, and contingent fate. By a *theodicy* of divine justice, and a *jeremiad* about founding promises betrayed, a "prophetic" voice posits the practices we must renounce (and those we must sustain) if we are to flourish. He thereby casts innovation since the 1960s as a violation of God's absolute commands and as the corruption of a constitutive national legacy. Judged by his example, prophecy seems antithetical to a democratic politics.

On the one hand, theodicy seems to replace politics by divinely commanded moral law and democratic debate by theocratic rule in the name of scriptural authority. Absolute claims about the "end"—the purpose and conclusion—of history, as if we could know it, and absolute claims about moral law deny not only the contingency in life but the plurality and interpretive ambiguity that generate disagreement and require consensus building. By reducing political judgment to moral absolutes and complex social change to moral melodrama—a willfully self-destructive refusal to obey divine commands—theodicy seems to seek redemption *from* politics. In Nietzsche's terms, theodicy creates a "true world" by which to devalue and escape the actual one.

On the other hand, a jeremiad seems inherently nostalgic if it calls us to literal recovery of an idealized origin, and it seems inherently punitive toward people and practices made to signify "corruption." In both ways jeremiads give corruption a gendered and racialized meaning, authorizing "culture war" to save an imminently endangered people. What must be purified from the political body? Hebrew prophets say social injustice and idolatry, but by ignoring social injustice, Falwell foregrounds the troubling cultural politics of a story in which plurality is depicted as infidelity. If redemption means "more perfect union," must prophecy purify the difference in which politics lives?

So it seems, from Falwell's example. He demonizes adversaries: He depicts not a struggle within each person over good and evil, but a struggle between the innocent and the guilty over conduct determining the fate of the nation. But there are other alternatives. In his second inaugural speech, Lincoln holds North and South jointly responsible for the "offense" of slavery and for the horrific bloodshed of the Civil War. By construing slavery as a national issue, he also makes the carnage meaningful as a just God's punishment of a guilty people. Indeed, justice requires that violence continue until the blood shed by the sword fully redeems the blood shed by the lash. Imagine this speech as an answer to Falwell on 9/11! But *how* Lincoln argues is as important as *what* he claims.

He quotes a prophetic judgment: "Woe unto the world because of offenses! For it must needs be that offenses come; but woe unto that man by whom the offense cometh!" But: "If we shall suppose" that God "gives to both North and South this terrible war, as the woe due to those by whom the offense came, shall we discern therein any departure from those divine attributes which believers in a Living God always ascribe to Him?" By saying "if we shall suppose" slavery to be an offense and war a punishment, he makes a prophetic story an interpretative choice. He makes it credible from the perspective of a faith that he does not declare as his own and that he enables others to refuse. Amos or Falwell simply proclaim God's just punishment; Lincoln names their faith a supposition. Still, it helps him depict human actors lacking sovereignty, it helps him imagine how the suffering of war could redeem the crime of slavery, and it tells him why "we the living" must redeem this history by a "new birth of freedom."[23]

When Lincoln narrates a theodicy to relate human action to divine providence, he enters the semantic field of prophecy. If his humility toward (suppositions about) God's purposes marks his distance from prophecy, he still insists on the joint liability of the whole nation for the offense of slavery, narrates the devastating consequences of conduct, and seeks the meaning (even justice) in suffering as a condition of possibility. Yet by refusing to presume his own innocence or to demonize his adversary and by enabling critical distance from his own perspective, he inflects theodicy differently than does Falwell, and he opens a space of dialogue. As he registers the horror of slavery and war and names our need to endow them with meaning, he also suggests a way to credit both our wish for redemption and the poesis needed to satisfy it. Does he tap into the visionary quality of prophecy but open its claims to debate?

While Lincoln's "if we shall suppose" contrasts with Falwell's theodicy, Frederick Douglass's speech "The Meaning of July Fourth for the Negro" fruitfully contrasts with Falwell's jeremiad. This 1852 speech, delivered to a rally of abolitionists, is the most powerful and artful jeremiad in American history. Douglass begins by creating rhetorical and political distance: He notes that even the abolitionists compare the celebration of "*your* national independence" and "*your* political freedom" to the "Passover" ritual of "the emancipated people of God," but, he says, "the distance between this platform and the slave plantation from which I escaped is considerable." He stands with slaves: "Are the great principles of political freedom . . . embodied in that Declaration of Independence, extended to us?" The "rich inheritance . . . bequeathed by your fathers is shared by *you,* not by *me.* The sunlight that brought light and healing to you has brought stripes and death to me. This Fourth of July is *yours,* not *mine. You* may rejoice, *I* must mourn."[24]

Still, he depicts national origins in rebellion, covenant, and the principle of equality. He defends "*your* fathers" because of "the principles they contended for," because "they loved their country better than their own private interests," and because they chose "revolution to peaceful submission and bondage." Calling the Declaration of Independence "the ring-bolt to the chain of your nation's destiny," he declares, "The principles contained in that instrument are saving principles. Stand by those principles, be true to them on all occasions, in all places, against all foes, and at whatever cost."

By celebrating 1776, not 1787, to make revolution a heroic paternal legacy, he casts self-declared sons of founders as a pathetic post-heroic generation, lacking the courage and ideals of fathers who had attacked inherited authority. These sons would have been Tories in 1776, though they "eulogize the wisdom and virtues of their fathers." Likewise, "it was fashionable for the children of Jacob to boast 'we have Abraham as our father' when they had long lost Abraham's faith . . . [and] repudiated the deeds which made his name great." Indeed, "Need I tell you that the Jews are not the only people who built the tombs of the prophets and garnished the sepulchers of the righteous?"

Creating distance between fathers and sons, between those sons and the slaves with whom he overtly stands, and between founding principles and present conduct, Douglass takes up prophecy. He positions himself at the margins of society with those it enslaves or excludes, even as he names himself a fellow citizen. "My subject, fellow-citizens, is American slavery. I shall see this day . . . from the slave's point of view. Standing there, identified with the American bondman, making his wrongs mine, I do not hesitate to declare, with all my soul, that the character and con-

duct of this nation never looked blacker to me than on this 4th of July."
Standing "with the slave" also means "standing with God . . . [and] in
the name of humanity which is outraged, in the name of liberty which
is fettered, in the name of the Constitution and the Bible which are dis-
regarded and trampled upon," to "question and denounce . . . everything
that serves to perpetuate slavery—the great sin and shame of America!"
Using a jeremiad to *announce* that American freedom depends on slavery and to *bear witness* against this injustice and its disavowal by whites, he
also *warns* of the danger they bring on themselves: "Fellow-citizens . . .
Be warned! A horrible reptile is coiled up in our nation's bosom; the ven-
omous creature is nursing at the tender breast of your youthful republic;
for the love of God" destroy "the hideous monster."

Douglass stands with those Jacques Rancière calls "the part that has
no part," and by putting the slave's injury into speech, Douglass announces what Rancière calls the "wrong" that constitutes the whole as
partial, but through principles the enfranchised can recognize. He thus
enacts what Rancière calls "dis-agreement," reaching across difference
to reconstitute the regime.[25] Partly, Douglass denounces the exclusion
at the origins of political community and the amnesia that sustains its
identity; by remembering what it forgets, he denies its identity with itself, and exposes the abyss between how people see themselves and the
actuality of their history and conduct. Partly, he invokes the professed
God or crucial commitments of the people he addresses: Not speaking
as a rebel rejecting the core ideals of the Republic but using their authority to justify his own, he casts himself as truly faithful to the legacy they
desecrate, and at once affirms the principles they profess and models a
democratic way to practice them.

Does he, nostalgically, seek a literal return to origins? "My business,
if I have any here today," he says, "is with the present." For he embodies
in carnal bodies (or "blackens") the ideals whites profess abstractly, to
"return" to first principles not as an authority whose meaning is fixed by
the past but as commitments he infuses with new meaning. He "returns"
not to a dead past but to revolution as an event, to provoke the reconstitution of community Lincoln calls rebirth. But while he reworks a jeremiad, he also doubts the capacity of white "fellow-citizens" to recognize
him and heed his warning.[26]

He thus casts blacks as Hebrews exiled in Babylon. To call them to
"join . . . in joyous anthems" is "to copy the example of a nation whose

crimes, towering up to heaven, were thrown down by the breath of the Almighty, burying that nation in irrevocable ruin." As he quotes the psalmist's "plaintive lament" for a "woe-smitten people":

By the rivers of Babylon, there we sat down. Yea! We wept when we remembered Zion. There, they that carried us away captive required of us a song; they who wasted us required of us mirth, saying, Sing us one of the songs of Zion. How can we sing the Lord's song in a strange land? If I forget thee, O Jerusalem, let my right hand forget her cunning. If I do not remember thee, let my tongue cleave to the roof of my mouth. (Ps. 137:1)

He will not sing a July Fourth anthem to entertain the class subjugating his people. They want a minstrel performance to relieve their bad conscience and to gain voyeuristic pleasure from the pathos and art of their slaves. By refusing, he models a voice of black prophecy not addressed to whites, or addressed to them only indirectly. His real audience is their captives, strangers in a strange land.

Recasting the white republic as a doomed empire, Douglass redefines its despised captives as exiled Hebrews still chosen by God to play a special role in history: Though marked as merely particular, exclusion invests them in a desire for liberty and so in a universality that whites betray. If the millennial promise in prophetic lamentation seemed to escape history, Douglass here puts it to worldly political purposes. By lamentation he names a defining rupture and imagines community built not on a founding covenant but on memories of uprooting, hope of redemption, and self-affirming organizing. Here he models how black critics in America rework a diasporic narrative: By a redemptive project of narrating trauma, they form community as a nonterritorial "nation" in a space between empire and exile. If we begin not with scripture promising divine rescue but with prophecy before scripture, we can imagine not only how prophets feel called by God, but also how they *summon* God on behalf of their people, conjuring powers hidden in their situation and in themselves.[27]

To compare Douglass to Falwell is to see that prophecy is a genre open to reworking, not only based on the social position and political purposes of the speakers but also on the startling ways they remake the meaning of biblical stories and tropes. Still, such differences in *what* they say presume a parallel in *how* they speak, especially by contrast to Lincoln. Both Douglass and Falwell claim minority positions, standing on the margins to criticize a dominant regime, even as each invokes the authority of a biblical and liberal consensus. Indeed, both invoke an orthodoxy whose axioms they do not question, whether theism or equality. Both depict a national problem—a sin and a shame—in which all are complicit. Both seek polarized political subjects: Good sons must redeem the "sin and shame" of the nation because bad sons have betrayed its defining origins. Both bear witness by using what Kimberly K. Smith calls "dominion of voice" to address the affective dimensions of politics. Each manifests the power of a speech act in tension with canons of reasonable or civil argument.[28]

Douglass imagines a critic telling him, "Would [you and your fellow abolitionists] argue more and denounce less, would you persuade more and rebuke less, your cause would be much more likely to succeed," to which Douglass responds, "Where all is plain, there is nothing to be argued." "Would you have me prove that the slave is a man?" Douglas denies that an "argument" could persuade whites to *count* him as human when they refuse to, despite all the evidence: "Would you have me argue that man is entitled to liberty? . . . You have already declared it. Must I argue the wrongfulness of slavery? Is that a question for republicans?" In the end, every man "beneath the canopy of heaven . . . know[s] that slavery is wrong for *him*." Surely Douglass is arguing even as he denies the value of argument, giving reasons to oppose slavery even as he denies the efficacy of reasons. His point, though, is that the political and rhetorical challenge is not to *justify* an argument more effectively or less offensively, but to confront what Stanley Cavell calls a refusal of "acknowledgment."[29]

The problem is not an ignorance to be remedied by knowledge or argument, but a perception of what and who we count as real; not just a gap between our professed ideals and actual conduct, but a motivated blindness (Baldwin says "innocence") about the other, about our conduct, and so about who we think we are. What kind of speech is needful? "At a time like this" says Douglass, "scorching irony, not convincing argument is needed. . . . For it is not light that is needed, but fire; it is not the gentle shower, but thunder. We need the storm, the whirlwind, and the earthquake. The feeling of the nation must be quickened; the conscience of the nation must be roused." Speech must compel people to see that "there is no nation on earth guilty of practices more shocking and bloody than the people of the United States. . . . for revolting barbarity and shameless hypocrisy, America reigns without a rival."[30]

Douglass, whose charged exclusion constitutes American freedom in American slavery, would "scorch" rather than seduce whites, as if thunder and fire, not light, could provoke the self-recognition that biblical prophets call repentance. Indeed, if the central issue is that we refuse to count others as real, or if we are invested in denying conditions—say, slavery, world hunger, or global warming—we need to count as real, he must find a form of speech that names such refusals and works through such denials, and he must do so as a precondition of a dialogue that cannot otherwise happen. Audiences may feel defensive, not because a speaker is artless but because they are being called to account for their conduct. Does such declamation end conversation, or does its intensity provoke responses we cannot predict? Such speech enacts strong judgment, but does it remain an invitation to community?

In a situation characterized by blindness rather than pragmatism, or as Ahab saw, by forms of pluralism and reason within a larger madness, critics must use poetry and metaphor to reach the affective dimensions of life and to recast what we count, at visceral levels, as real and valuable. That is why so many critics of white supremacy turn to prophecy. What is at once disturbing and needful in prophecy, therefore, appears in the declamatory voice stating realities we deny but need to acknowledge, in the adamant judgment about how to interpret our professed commitments, and in the imperative voice demanding fateful decisions about constitutive practices—registers of voice shared by adversaries like Falwell and Douglass. At issue, then, is the deeper political bearing of an office and genre whose common use enables divergent projects. We turn next, therefore, to how scholars of American studies assess prophecy, and then from their debate about hegemony to conversations in political theory.

Prophecy as an Object of American Studies

Puritans carrying the Reformation from Europe and people of African descent undergoing uprooting and enslavement forged constitutively "American" religious and political idioms from biblical texts. Whereas Louis Hartz and Perry Miller depict an ascendant liberalism burying Puritanism and prophecy, therefore, I follow a "second generation" of post–New Left thinkers and historians who, confronting white supremacy and the Vietnam War and refracting the civil rights and student movements, reconceive how Puritanism and prophetic language relate to the formation of liberalism and nationalism, race and empire, social movements and democratic projects. Here I contrast two scholars—

Robert Bellah and Sacvan Bercovitch—to depict the central debate in American studies about prophecy, that is, about the commonality of and difference between Falwell and Douglass and the broader idioms they call upon.[31]

In 1968, Bellah repeats Tocqueville: Liberalism requires the supplement of a "civil religion," for "a good society" cannot emerge from "the actions of citizens motivated by self-interest alone." By joining "the biblical" and "the republican," he modernizes Tocqueville's claim that the American Republic hinges on relating "the spirit of liberty and the spirit of religion." He thus initiates a "communitarian" critique of a "liberalism" defined as rights-based individualism and interest-group politics in a constitutional framework. Anchoring American nationhood not in John Locke only but also in Puritan faith and republican virtue, his jeremiad, *The Broken Covenant,* denounces the way civil religion has become "an empty and broken shell."[32]

Partly, Puritanism generates worldly asceticism and an acquisitive individualism. Partly, biblical language justifies racial domination in the name of defending morality. Partly, revivalism has taken politically reactionary forms. Partly, as Michael Rogin argues, "the peculiarly American form of liberal nationalism" has joined "Protestant Christianity with westward expansion," to separate old and new worlds, but also to separate a chosen (white and civilized) people from racialized others who signify license and servility.[33] Bellah himself quotes Herman Melville's famous performance of this nationalism:

Escaped from the house of bondage, Israel of old did not follow after the ways of the Egyptians. . . . And we Americans are the peculiar, chosen people—the Israel of our time; we bear the ark of the liberties of the world. Seventy years ago we escaped from thrall; and, besides our first birthright—embracing one continent of earth—God has given to us for a future inheritance, the broad domains of the political pagans, that shall yet come and lie down under the shade of our ark, without bloody hands being lifted.[34]

As Rogin argues, this messianic project, of extending freedom to "political pagans," takes jeremiadic form: "Since the Puritan founding, American history has proceeded by consciousness of decline from the faith of the founders and efforts at heroic renewal. Made in the name of the fathers to revitalize the sons, these efforts regenerate a world grown dead in sin."[35]

But Bellah does not abandon "civil religion." He takes the prophet's role in a jeremiad against a world grown dead in sin. The problem is not prophecy as such, he insists, but who uses it for what ends: For Bellah, William Lloyd Garrison and Eugene V. Debs signify the potential in standing with outcasts to attack elites, seeking collective accountability for problematic practices, and undertaking democratic renewal. He quotes Garrison mocking the idea that the fate of the world depends on America: "As if God had suspended the fate of all nations . . . upon the result of a wild and cruel 'experiment' by a land-stealing, blood-thirsty, man-slaying and slave-trading people in one corner of the globe!" Still, Bellah affirms the value of speaking in national terms: "Whatever we might wish, the national community exercises control over our fate and in part over the fate of the world." Moreover "no one changes a great nation without appealing to its soul [and] stimulating national idealism." He invokes Debs to fault students for not tying their politics to "any genuinely American pattern of values," the "better instincts of American patriotism," or "the deeper moral instincts of Americans." This "failure guarantees isolation and ineffectiveness," while a corporate regime "undermines essential American values and constitutional order."[36]

To summarize Bellah's *political* logic: "Culture is the key to revolution; religion is the key to culture." Liberalism is embedded in a civil religion, and by jeremiads critics announce its bad conscience about self-interest, technical reason, and capitalism while articulating commonality and purpose. The risk in politics is not faith or comprehensive doctrine, for freedom requires myth or "imaginative vision" to frame it. Nor is theism a threat to democratic plurality, for "biblical religion" enables both citizen empowerment and "democratic self-restraint." The danger is that critics cede the republican and biblical language that gives their dissent consensual ground.[37]

Twenty years of New Right hegemony might persuade Bellah to agree with Sheldon Wolin: "Civil religion is the incorporation of religious practice into the system of governance and control."[38] Millennial militancy, providential presumption, punitive sanctimony, and state power make "biblical religion" not an endangered resource but a toxic, all-too-alive legacy. Still, many scholars echo Bellah, invoking what I call a "left Puritan" tradition to seek "native ground" for democratic projects in a "hellfire nation," a never-secular America. Cornel West and Eric Dyson echo the "prophetic" voice of African American jeremiads. Historians like Christopher Lasch, Sean Wilentz, David Chapelle, Michael Kazin, or James Marrone, theorists like Michael Sandel or Eldon Eisenach, and activists like Jim Wallis distinguish an individualistic and procedural liberalism from a republicanism or populism tied to "biblical religion." To resist intensifying neoliberalism and to overcome marginality, these figures (and many others) seek in extant moral and religious traditions consensual resources for a "progressive" politics.[39]

One great scholarly enemy of this "left Puritanism" is Sacvan Bercovitch. Bellah's heirs contrast King and Falwell, as if to separate true and false prophecy in politics, but the prophetic language binding them, Bercovitch argues, is an ideology that in fact sustains liberal nationalism. For Bellah's heirs, prophecy draws from a consensual civil religion to contest liberalism and chasten nationalism, but Bercovitch depicts a hegemony entwining prophetic language and liberal politics. People must *relinquish* prophecy if they are to address the limits of liberalism and loosen the grip of nationalism on democratic possibility.

In America, Bercovitch argues, faith in self-determination and commitments to rights, individualism, and popular sovereignty are secured by *Puritan* views of moral self-control and providential history. But liberal hegemony in the United States is sustained because differently situated groups continue to argue about inequality, identity, and difficulty through the genre of the jeremiad, which he calls a "prescribed ritual form" that "directs an imperiled people of God toward the fulfillment of their destiny."[40] Like biblical prophets, American critics "teach a special people to comply with the terms of its covenant" by "waking [their] countrymen up to the fact that they are desecrating their own beliefs." But the American jeremiad makes criticism a "rite of assent" to "American" identity: "The very exposure of social flaws" is "a ritual of socialization." The jeremiad enables but "contains" social criticism because it reauthorizes the (liberal) origins it invokes. Because "America" begins in a universalist promise, though, jeremiads also justify progressive change: "Endless secular improvement" will overcome every obstacle to redeem a founding promise of freedom for all. To be "American" means to turn against the past and embrace the new and yet to affirm liberal axioms and a national frame. Narrowed "symbolically and substantively to the meaning of America," criticism is "at once endless and self-enclosed," and politics is reduced to revivals redeeming a national promise. Conflict means not "moral and social alternatives" to liberal nationalism but competing calls for the "cultural revitalization" of its authentic but jeopardized values.[41]

A Canadian immigrant claiming to stand outside the symbolic order that invests America with redemptive meaning, Bercovitch depicts a "poly-ethnic, multi-racial, openly materialistic, self-consciously individualistic people, knit together in the bonds of myth, voluntarily, with a force of belief unsurpassed by any other modern society." Astonished, he depicts a "secular modern nation living in a dream" that collapses the sacred and the secular, and to disclose this "collective fantasy," he imagines the United States "recognized for what it is, not a beacon to mankind as Winthrop proclaimed . . . not the political Messiah as the young Melville hymned . . . not even a covenanted people robbed by un-American predators of their sacred trust," but "one more profane nation in the wilderness of this world." What would it mean if "America" were "severed once and for all from the United States?" The question is jolting. That it is rarely posed indicates the hegemony whose grip he would help us slip.[42]

What do we learn from Bercovitch? Rather than split the biblical and republican from the liberal, he shows how a liberal capitalist regime is sustained by a "prophetic civic identity." Denying separate "strands" of discourse, he makes the "liberal-communitarian" debate moot. Moving from consensus to hegemony to show cultural idioms as forms of power, he depicts dissent "contained" because the "form" of criticism renews both liberal axioms and a national frame. The "refusal to abandon the national covenant," indeed, marks critics as "American." For "the dream that inspired them to defy the false Americanism of their time" also "compelled them to speak their defiance as keepers of the dream." He thus distinguishes, not Falwell and Douglass, but Debs and Emma Goldman, or King and Malcolm X, to expose the hegemonic gravity defining how critics "must" speak to be legitimate. Contingent yet intractable, the "must" signals the strategic and internal pressures driving critics to redeem the society they condemn.[43]

Bellah, fearing marginality, seeks in prophecy a consensual ground for dissent; Bercovitch, fearing incorporation, affirms a critical marginality by refusing its hegemony. He rightly identifies the dominant way prophecy has been practiced, but the problem in his view of hegemony is disclosed by focusing on race. For, partly, the nation is produced by violent domination in ways he does not credit. And, partly, liberal nationalist hegemony is fractured and contested in ways he obscures because he elides race. For as black voices, and those of white critics who identify with them, use prophecy to resist white supremacy, they develop a critical view of the liberal faith, jeremiadic form, and national frame that rule American politics. Demonstrating contingency in what prophecy can mean, they make visible aspects of politics occluded by liberalism, to advance an agonal rather than a communitarian or consensual politics. While Bercovitch splits an incorporated inside (and repetition of the same) from a radical outside, critics of white supremacy use prophecy to forge a politics that mediates part and whole to reconstitute community.

Engagement with Bellah and Bercovitch thus reveals the issues we inflect in Thoreau, King, Baldwin, and Morrison. One is how they rework inherited discursive forms against the grain, not only the jeremiad but also other aspects of prophecy, even prophecy as a theistic practice. A second relates prophecy to liberal hegemony and democratic politics, for these figures use prophetic speech to expose and cross the line between the liberal and the democratic. A third concerns whether stories that redeem a *democratic* promise must also replenish a *national* frame for politics. If we refuse a national fantasy of inclusion, which justifies exclusion and devalues politics, we also should resist the fantasy of escaping the nation, which still is *the* organizing center of political life. From Thoreau to Morrison, these critics invoke *and trouble* national political identity by dramatizing what is costly, fantastical, and fateful in it.

We conclude this chapter and enter the theory conversation about prophecy and politics, however, by reopening Bercovitch's rejection of redemptive rhetoric: For he sees it sustaining national fantasy and displacing politics, while many contemporary political theorists also argue that theist and secular forms of redemption devalue political life. We move from American studies to political theory, from Americanizing a Marxian critique of hegemony to democratizing a Nietzschean critique of redemption, by reading redemptive language as a symptom not of hegemony but of resentment at "fundamental pre-requisites of life." We put to political theory the question that Bellah and Bercovitch pose in national terms: Must we rework or relinquish redemptive language to democratize politics? A focus on race will inflect every response in unexpected and illuminating ways.[44]

From Prophecy in America to Prophecy in Political Theory

Prophecy is mostly absented from current conversations in political theory, and for two reasons. One is linked to Nietzsche and Arendt: The legacy of "Jerusalem"—theist absolutes and redemptive rhetoric— seems inherently antipolitical. A second reason is that political theorists tend to orient themselves by canonical engagements with modernity in European rather than American terms, through the Holocaust rather than white supremacy, and so in genres other than prophecy, whose political revision in America remains theoretically unexplored. Prophecy goes missing if or when we theorists split politics and redemption, Europe and America, modernity and race. But focusing on modernity and race in America reveals prophetic practice remaking the relation of redemption and politics. Indeed, biblical idioms and transfigured American instantiations offer a distinctive approach to central issues in political thought. Let us unpack these claims.

Surely, ideas of redemption derive from prophecy, and the language of *deliverance from* seems to generate inherently antipolitical conceptions of authority, community, and history. First, biblical prophecy bequeaths the idea of fidelity to true authority or to the one right way to live, an idea that seems to redeem people from existential responsibility for choices and moral ambiguity about them, as well as from plurality and the judgments it entails. Second, biblical prophecy bequeaths the idea that fidelity to authority creates communitarian fullness, an idea that seems to redeem people from partiality, conflict, and injustice. Third, biblical prophecy bequeaths a dream of closing the gap between art and life, for by depicting the "end" of history and of suffering, prophetic narrative ends, or redeems us from, the problem of their meanings. The absent Aristotelian space in Marx signals a similar logic: By linking truth to authority, authority to communitarian fullness, and political identity to a teleological narrative endowing suffering with meaning, Marxism also displaces politics in the name of redemption.

I identify with and have learned from a cohort of theorists who criticize the redemptive logics in biblical or theistic forms, in Marxist teleology, in nationalism and other forms of identity politics, in communitarianism, in "moralism" as a resentful political disposition—and in theories of deliberation promising to "redeem validity claims." On behalf of "agonistic" democratic practices, rather than a liberal politics of negative liberty, this post-theist, post-Marxist, postidentity theorizing—so indebted to Michel Foucault and Jacques Derrida—values contingency and action, receptivity to difference, and resignification of signs in a view of politics as a struggle to defer closure.[45]

Increasingly since 9/11, however, theorists are crediting the inescapability of faith and the necessity of commitment, affirming more than processual accounts of community, and recognizing both the political necessity of coming to terms with the past and the necessarily narrative ways we do so. Theorists now presume "the ubiquity of faith," as William Connolly aptly puts it, and seek resources in Carl Schmitt on "political theology," Walter Benjamin or Jacques Derrida on messianism, Emmanuel Levinas on transcendence and ethics, and Giorgio Agamben on witnessing. They explore "states of exception" as being analogous to miracles and seek forms of authority analogous to the apostolic. Conceptions of community, once cast only in terms of "contingent foundations," now entail moments not only of disidentification but of affirmation. As community bears the grip of "wounded attachment," so theorists explore the meaning of trauma, the relation between mourning and melancholy, and the ethics of vulnerability. Invoking the idea of a witness, theorists seek "fearless speech" or "testimony" in which the idea of truth reappears.[46]

Faith, theology, ethics, trauma, and speech—constitutively prophetic issues—are featured increasingly in the work of political theorists in the United States. We seek in Continental philosophers a vocabulary post-Marxist, postidentity, and now postsecular. Obviously, European thinkers differ greatly among themselves in the ways they work through the Judeo-Christian legacies shaping late-modern political life. But our encounter has not been an occasion to take *prophecy* seriously in its biblical forms, let alone in its American figurations. Our work seems cut off from the place where we Americans live and from the prophetic voices haunting it.

It is strange, really: Theorists read Agamben or Arendt on a genocide that Americans did not cause or experience directly, but not Douglass, W. E. B. Du Bois, Baldwin, or Morrison, who draw on prophetic idioms to address the racial holocaust that Americans caused and experienced directly, whose legacy still grips the life of each and all. We address the meaning of (late) modernity by way of European philosophy and meditations on the messianic, but not on local ground in nearby idioms. Is our cosmopolitanism a kind of evasion? We profess to value "local knowledge," but do we? Surely, theorists must take sustenance wherever they find it, but still, why there and not also here, why in languages of political theology or ethics but not also of prophecy?[47]

If I echo Emerson by complaining that theorists living in America ignore their native ground, I mean to endorse not cultural chauvinism or American exceptionalism but efforts like Stanley Cavell's to put Anglo-American and Continental voices in conversation to overcome this split.

Whereas Cavell uses American romanticism as a bridge, however, I use prophecy. But also, the common ground he discloses is "the ordinary," while the ground I disclose is a history of racial violence, which at once defines the American ordinary and rejoins America to imperial Europe. Whereas he turns philosophy to the ordinary as a therapy for skepticism, therefore, I follow the examples of Douglass and Baldwin, who draw on prophecy to confront another (but related) kind of disavowal. Cavell laments that Emerson and Thoreau are unread by philosophers; I wonder why Baldwin or Morrison are not read *as*—let alone by—political theorists.[48]

Partly, I have argued so far, the reputation of prophecy is linked to redemption as an antipolitical trope: Because we reify prophecy as a practice, we seek alternatives to, not reworkings of, it. But also, these American figures are not counted as philosophical or political. Is it still necessary to argue that literary texts do profound theoretical or philosophical work? Is our range of references still constrained by the racial history behind the canon? As Baldwin and Morrison indeed argue, the legacy of modernity is divided because it is founded not only in the Enlightenment, but by slavery, which haunts American politics, cultural practices, and theoretical productions. Moreover, enlightenment remains entangled in faith, and secularism in religion, as the subjection and resistance of African Americans attests. A torn legacy entwining slavery, freedom, and religion, this modernity is reworked by the American figures I call prophetic. To hear them is to confront a modernity neither white nor secular, to reimagine the meaning and making of "countermodernity."

Prophecy as Political Theory

By the criteria of a biblical literalism anchored in theism, Thoreau and King may not, and Baldwin and Morrison do not, count as prophetic. But prophecy is a genre open to reworking, and each revitalizes it as a form of political theory and practice, not as a theology dangerous to politics. In turn, they enable us to rethink three issues central to the European canon, to a democratic imaginary, and to postsecular politics: first, how we conceive the meaning of authority and practice of judgment; second, how we conceive the meaning of political identification and community; third, how we conceive the power and meaning of the past. To rethink these issues, which inhere in prophecy as an office and a genre, is to recast the political meaning of redemption.

First, as the office of messengers and witnesses, prophecy raises the issue of *authority* with unrivaled profundity and intensity. Prophetic voices ask not whether we are ruled by authority, but which authority rules in and through us. From Jeremiah to Blake, Thoreau, and Baldwin, prophecy asks, What gods do you already serve? What is your animating faith? Do you serve Mammon, the god of success, or the authority of the state, which Nietzsche calls a "cold idol"? We can avoid or defer the question of authority—of which faith we presume, of what commitments we orient by—but we always answer it. Accordingly, they neither belittle as infantile the effort to answer this question, nor treat any answer as only dangerous, for freedom and flourishing depend on it. Rather, they declare, Here is my table of values, what is yours? And thus they expose our "idolatry" of gods and institutions we already endow with authority and impel us toward choices about our commitments. But if they thereby rupture a consensus, do they answer the question of authority in ways that enable politics?

If authority is the capacity of an institution, idea, or person to elicit our assent, as John Schaar argues, the image of announcing messengers suggests despotic authority: As an absolute authority entitled to unalloyed obedience, God's law of laws or word is a command to obey. Politics seems at once framed and radically displaced by divinely centered notions of law or truth: Prophets question what we assent (or give authority) to, but they close down the space of contest if they invoke extrapolitical authority dictating our fate or announcing one right way against a plurality of alternatives. If monotheism means absolute sovereignty issuing law as command and fate as decree, then prophetic authority is exercised on behalf of orthodoxy and subjection, though it promises redemption. Likewise, in ways that Bellah seeks and Bercovitch fears, prophecy "contains" politics if, in Durkheimian senses, it invokes authority on behalf of stable moral order or cultural coherence.[49]

But we follow Blake, for whom prophets are poets and gods their poetic inventions, later reified by priests as law and "religion." In words so powerful as to become what Wallace Stevens calls "supreme fictions" that subsequent generations live by, they remake the deep axioms by which people orient self-reflection and agency. In this sense, prophets raise the question of authority in terms of the framework, or passionate frame of reference, people live by. Isaiah invokes God and Douglass invokes equality not as truths to prove or as justifications of action but as commitments without which a form of life is unimaginable and impossible. We inherit them, but they lose authority, unless we make them our own, make them anew. In this existential sense, prophets can return to origins not to fix authority conceived as a noun but to renew it as a verb: God or justice are not substances to define rightly as grounds of justification but commitments to risk and remake in action. Exercising authority not by justifying but by enacting a principle or idea, they live by love rather than duty, surrender rather than subjection, faith rather than certainty. Against the image of a superego god and its minions, they exercise authority in democratic—because exemplary—ways.[50]

For Douglass, Thoreau, and Baldwin, messengers also announce the unsaid and witnesses testify to what has been unspeakable. When Amos announces a God of justice and Nietzsche the death of God, they speak in "prophetic" ways to declare truths we avoid at great cost to ourselves and others. Prophecy is the office that announces the reality of what (and who) we had not counted as real, that "remembers" what we forget or refuse to see: a just God or a universe beyond good and evil, the relentless haunting of actors by a past never past, the misrecognition or "vanity" on which identity depends, the servitude enabling our freedom, the others whose reality we deny. Such claims are imperative and conditional, stating what we must acknowledge in order to flourish. Their unequivocal, compelling character is entailed not by theism or moral absolutism, but by grasping the meaning of acknowledgment and its refusal. Such claims seek not subjection to orthodoxy but a "turn" toward what has been disavowed. Again, prophecy links authority not to truth as theology, law as command, or faith as consensus but to bearing witness and warning. By saying what they see and standing against it and by warning to forestall danger, prophets also declare, indeed demonstrate, that we can act otherwise. In these modes of speech, they exercise authority on behalf of freedom by exposing choice and inciting action.

To follow Buber, prophecy is the office that calls people to fateful "decision" about what and who they count as real, and about which commitments they practice, and how. Still, the Schmittian aura of "decision" highlights the dangers in this prophetic practice of authority. Declaring, "Here I stand, I can do no other," prophetic figures do not move if we are offended, and would fail their office if they did move, because they depict not a valid pluralism of views and practices but amnesia, disavowal, and complicity in evil. Jeremiah and Baldwin know their perspectives (on idolatry say, or race) are contestable, but we who contest them cling to "innocence," as Baldwin puts it, by denying the meaning of our conduct and history. Weber calls these critics "titans of the holy curse" because they offer, not opinions whose comparable validity we must grant to achieve civility, but fateful judgments on which our lives depend.[51] Impatient with procedure and compromise, they depict decisive choices between constitutive practices. Fidelity to a "jealous God" (Exod. 20:5)—or equality as a first principle—means fostering some practices and overcoming others.

Many political theorists see this voice of authority and kind of claim making as a great danger, never needful. For the point of politics is to resist closure: Fidelity to openness itself seems the best way to resist the exclusion or injustice entailed by authorizing any framework or optic. We do not authorize a comprehensive doctrine, but we value multiple goods, privatize those goods to de-politicize conflict, or defend pluralization to defuse it. To counter "scorching irony," we practice Kenneth Burke's "humble irony," which fosters kinship between adversaries. Because dogmatism demonizes those who live by different faiths, we invoke faith's contingency or contestabiity to engender a "critical responsiveness" of one to another.[52]

But in abolitionist prophecy, fidelity to democratic norms means withdrawing legitimacy from pervasive practices we must not pluralize or privatize: White supremacy is not a worthy practice whose forgoing is a loss to lament, or a valid faith to reconcile with others, but a social practice empowering some by subjugating others. Slavery, apartheid, and institutional racism do signal a "white" identity produced by denying dependence on the difference it posits, but they also signal a democratically authorized structure of domination cutting across every subject position and dimension of life. By prophetic speech, therefore, critics provoke profound conflict about first principles and how to practice them. Still, Baldwin hears a plea in every accusation, and for Cavell, every claim spoken to another is an invitation to community.

Like Douglass, Thoreau and Baldwin thus would reconstitute a regime, and since they must question the authority of majority rule and pluralist ideals, it is no surprise they are cast as invasive moral fanatics opposed to democratic traditions. But if forbearance allows complicity in domination, the appearance (even the reality!) of moralism is not the great danger. Their passionate commitment and aggressive claim making are not (only) symptoms of orthodoxy but conditions of vibrant political life, which entails profound judgments about opposed practices and conflict between constituencies invested in them. American prophecy thus suggests that our aversion to authority may lead us to devalue crucial, albeit disturbing, registers of voice and essential, albeit dangerous, dimensions of politics.

The office of prophecy also raises a second basic political issue, about the meaning of *political identification*, because prophets address the issue of authority in regard to a specific community, a "we" whose decision and reconstitution they incite. As with authority, so with community: Prophets ask not whether we identify with others, but with whom and on what basis. As with authority, we can defer the question, but we always answer it in our speech and action. As the office of prophecy judges those answers, so their answers enter debates about *community* that cross between American studies and political theory.

Theorists who reject the assumptions of liberal political thought about sovereign subjects, individualism, and rational deliberation have turned toward culture or language as the ground of politics. But then they take two different paths. Bellah, Walzer, and Sandel offer a "thick" view of community, centered by fidelity to a "comprehensive doctrine" or by the orienting authority of "core values." Their critics worry that such visions of "community" seem to promise political unity, justice without remainder, and communal plenitude—by constituting members who internalize communal authority and the terms of consensus.[53]

Insofar as this is a "prophetic" vision of community, it signals the dangers that postidentity theorists see in identity substantialized as a noun, a state of being: Sameness effaces a differentiated "I," and by demonizing differences projected outward, identity closes off a space of plurality within. In biblical prophecy and in Falwell's proclamations, this danger appears in casting people as an adulterous wife needing to be redeemed by renewed fidelity to God: Such tropes pathologize plurality as idolatry and justify repressive unity as fidelity to true identity. Less dramatically, Walzer and Bellah enact the power they elide in "consensus," as they construe marginality not as a sign of difference to welcome but as a flaw to overcome.[54]

"Postidentity" theory points to real dangers in prophecy and political identification, but consider another reading. For Thoreau and Baldwin speak not of belonging and core values but of domination in a regime constituted by exclusion. They teach *estrangement* from collective identity by criticizing the "vanity" of any identity claiming, as if to escape contingency and transience, a ground in the nature of things. Like biblical prophets, they also model profound tensions between identification with and critical distance from the people they engage. In the cauldron of this doubleness they forge an individuality whose "pathos of solitude" and inwardness confound what communitarians say "belonging" means. But unlike the adherents of postidentity theory, these prophetic critics imagine politics less as plurality and more as adversarial conflict over practices that empower some by harming others. Isaiah and Douglass expose the idolatry that reifies a "we," but they do so to forge alternate solidarities and reconstitute a regime.

They presume that identification is not only dangerous but also a positive good. How so? Partly, if we *presume* difference or noncoincidence in politics, association must be *created*. Politics appears not only in acts of disidentification with inherited or ascribed identities, but in the *achievement* of (alternate) identification. Partly, politics arises not only from plurality but from domination's creation of bosses and workers, masters and slaves, a regime of the normal and a queer nation. *Power* requires forging a "we," creating a *space together,* not only between us, with some and against others. Contesting domination means struggling over contrasting ways of answering the questions, With whom do you identify? And on what basis? The work of politics, and prophecy, is to rework or shift how we answer these questions.

Fundamentally, prophets rework political identification to create a collective subject for whose fate members are liable and from whose fate none are exempt. Hannah Arendt thus says,

The reason for my responsibility must be my membership in a group which no voluntary act of mine can dissolve. . . . This kind of responsibility is always political, whether it appears in the older form, when a whole community takes on itself to be responsible for whatever one of its members has done, or when a community is being held responsible for what has been done in its name.

Quoting Jeremiah to Germany, Arendt argues that "we are always responsible" politically "for the sins of the fathers," but not "guilty of their misdeeds either legally or morally." This "vicarious responsibility" is "the price we pay for the fact that we live our lives not by ourselves but among our fellow-men." Correspondingly, critics of white supremacy use prophecy to testify to the "collective responsibility" of a nation for its conduct, but they also project a counternational black subject as its interlocutor, adversary, redeemer—(un)armed prophet. In Rancière's terms, they forge a "part that has no part" into a political subject, to reconstitute the whole that disavows it.[55]

Political identification is necessary, then, both to enable political power and to instantiate political responsibility. From Isaiah to Baldwin, therefore, prophets do not reify identity as an object but mediate (rather than pluralize) parts and wholes. They also challenge contemporary theories in their answers to the question, Identify (with whom) *on what basis?* Arendt echoes prophecy by founding political community on covenants, which create a theater of appearance for action, a constitutional frame for contest, and a collective subject liable for its actions. But in ways that confound models of voluntary contract, as well as ironic distancing by postidentity theory, prophecy from Hosea to King, Baldwin, and Morrison also depicts community as a *bond of love.* Identifications bear "love and murder," Baldwin says;[56] invested with desire, disappointment, and anger, they are open to reworking but subject to repudiation, as the example of Paul (not Jesus) or Richard Wright (not Baldwin) signals. By emphasizing only the value of belonging or only the danger in identification, theorists may avoid this pathos of ambivalence in attachment. But by enacting it, prophets can fold powerful adversarial arguments, about idolatry or white supremacy, into a vision of community as always partial, at risk of failure—and open to reconstitution.[57]

By mediating parts and whole, prophecy offers an alternative both to unity and to pluralism, while engaging attachments by ambivalence rather than affirmation or distancing. Prophets voice ambivalence not only because attachment is ambivalent, but because they depict people not only standing together but standing for—and identifying with—a principle beyond themselves and a promise to orient by it, whether that principle is a God of justice or an ideal of equality. Though a particular attachment, political community also must aspire to universality, for what are we if we do not live for or by something larger than ourselves? A generative ambivalence—and danger—lives in this tension between attachment to concrete others in the actuality of their needs and limits, and to ideals bearing their aspiration to universality.

The greater danger in prophecy may not be exclusive, narrow, or intense attachment but the universalist or redemptive promise lodged in it. For then we argue ferociously to define the ideal we are chosen to bear, or the principle without which we do not deserve to exist, while we devalue—and envy—the nonelect, who lack the transfiguring purpose that redeems "mere" existence. In such terms prophetic critics refuse the meaning of whiteness and the nationalism of a chosen American people, yet still magnify the meaning of black agency and aspirations for freedom. With Bercovitch, we theorists see magnification only as dangerous, but prophecy suggests how it is needful.

Prophetic practices of identification show that not only dogmatists have adversaries, and that not every identification (with some, against others) is demonizing. We could avoid idealization and demonization by crediting that *any* identification is knotted, imperfect, costly. Prophecy thus enters the conversation of theory by modeling mediators whose identification is torn between a god and a people and between the enfranchised and the disavowed; who therefore testify to a profound doubleness toward both national and racial bonds; who cast those bonds as constitutive fatalities and as chosen allegiances to rework; and who wrestle with magnifying or deflating them. Prophets thus suggest generative ambivalence toward identification: As Victoria Hattam puts it, they claim and forge identification, yet signal its partial, imperfect, invented, and contingent—say political—character.[58]

The third issue that prophecy brings to political theory follows from the second because a political identification is not only an erotic and chosen bond mediated by a first principle, but a historical relationship that poses the question, How do we imagine the constitutive power of *the past*, and how do we *come to terms with it* as a condition of our agency? For Bellah, an American culture invested in liberal autonomy must be returned to its Puritan origins to confront both the haunting power of its violent history and the reality of evil. For Bercovitch, even that jeremiad is a ritual imprisoning people in the liberal and Puritan origins it replenishes. For Michael Rogin, racial violence and its disavowal are an origin repeated not only by amnesiac whites but even by the reformers trying to overcome it. In contrast to these stories, post-Nietzschean political theory often casts agency in terms—of natality, states of exception, and miracle—that rupture history, as if to suspend its causal or constitutive power. How, then, does prophecy engage the relationship of origins and agency? It has spoken in two modalities: Each can displace political life in the name of an impossible redemption, but each can address the "power of decision lying in the moment."

In its jeremiadic modality, prophecy risks idealization of the past, moralizing a "corrupt" present as a decline from pure origins to which people could return. Whereas Weber narrates the inevitable routinization of charisma, prophets narrate infidelity to principle; whereas Foucault depicts unavoidable imbrication in discourse, prophets denounce a culpable corruption; whereas Bercovitch depicts jeremiads anthropologically as rituals of consensus, prophets judge a guilty people. Prophets can moralize historical process by linking agency and culpability, but their jeremiads can refuse reification in political ways. Douglass, Thoreau, and King make founding violence an origin haunting the present, but they still narrate jeremiads. They "return" to equality as a first principle and to revolution itself, not to repeat the past but to refound a republic in struggle against slavery. They transform how we judge the meaning of our history to change who "we" are. For them, the past is a resource whose promise we can still redeem. They may be mistaken: They do not know in advance whether their faith lives in us and can still bear fruit. By narrating a "return" to origins, do they create a trap, or a legacy from which to spring?

In its second modality, the past is not a resource but a problem. Prophets still narrate a story of origins, but now as a disastrous trauma, a catastrophic uprooting we must "redeem" or make meaningful as a condition of our agency. We define ourselves not by a "legacy of freedom" but by an exile and captivity that is haunting and imprisoning because it is horrific and because it has been denied. This exilic modality includes a messianic poetry that promises an escape not only from trauma in history but from history as trauma. Still, Douglass and King use promises of redemption and resurrection (or rebirth) for world building in Babylon, while Baldwin and Morrison dramatize the need to come to terms with traumatic origins from which none can escape. Their narrative art compels us to ask, Is the political task to enable a "mourning" by which the dead can bury their dead, or to avow and live within, not leave behind, constitutive losses?

On the one hand, then, prophetic voices call into being the "we" whose past they narrate in terms of an American republic and subaltern counterpublics. To both audiences, on the other hand, prophets "redeem" a past no one can change or escape, to foster a fruitful relationship to it. Not any story will do, they insist: Our stories *must* make idolatry/race central to our regime, or put traumatic uprooting at the origin of our community, if we are to discern the true conditions of our agency and make a future different from the one the past seemed to dictate. Our capacities to act and create depend on which stories we tell and which we pass on. Here again, the office of prophecy discloses a "power of decision" in our hands.

To say that freedom and fruitfulness are possible only on certain terms is to speak a language of redemption. As Jeremiah, Thoreau, King, Baldwin, and Morrison also ask, What could release us from a history of repetition?—so prophecy twins freedom and redemption in ways only

Nietzsche rivals. Like him, they do not ask whether we seek redemption, but how: They do not defuse our longing for redemption, which would deprive politics of energy, but assess the projects in which we lodge it and commit to those that yield the blessing of more life. That is why these figures are not only "American" critics recasting prophecy to oppose white supremacy, but political thinkers reworking redemptive language to foster political life. What can we learn from them?

2. Thoreau, the Reluctant Prophet
Moral Witness and Poetic Vision in Politics

What is called politics is comparatively something so superficial and inhuman, that, practically, I have never fairly recognized that it concerned me at all.
—Henry Thoreau, "Life without Principle"

The word prophecy . . . is much misused . . . narrowed to prediction merely. That is not the main sense of the Hebrew word. . . . The great matter [in prophecy] is to reveal and outpour the God-like suggestions pressing for birth in the soul.
—Walt Whitman, *Specimen Days*

Individual poets, whatever their imperfections may be, are driven all their lives by that inner companion of the conscience which is, after all, the genius of poetry in their hearts and minds. I speak of a companion of conscience because to every faithful poet the faithful poem is an act of conscience.
—Wallace Stevens, *Opus Posthumous*

WHY FOCUS first on the ways that Henry Thoreau takes up and revises prophecy? A story can introduce the reasons. The week after John Brown raided Harpers Ferry in October 1859, Thoreau personally organized three public events so he could defend Brown and his raid. Public opinion in the North already cast Brown as a "monomaniac" and murderer, but Thoreau linked him to Puritans and Revolutionary fathers who, unlike enfranchised northern whites, would not sacrifice the principle of equality to expedience. Because the Dred Scott case effectively nationalized slavery, Thoreau argued, Brown's self-sacrificing violence was needed not only to free slaves but to redeem northern whites from self-betrayal and save their republic from self-destruction. Thoreau's impassioned, incendiary speech initiated a decisive shift in northern public opinion, a shift that really registered in the South and encouraged southern support for secession. In a year the Civil War began.

Brown enacts one version of prophecy in action: Declaring that he serves a just God and lamenting that the sin of slavery cannot be redeemed any longer without violence, he gives life to biblical idioms that still enable both antiracist politics and the moralized violence Edmund Wilson calls "patriotic gore." Even today, Brown is a Rorschach test of American racial politics: Thoreau's defense of him is affirmed almost without exception in African American commentary, but otherwise Brown is typically condemned for moral fanaticism and political terrorism. Joining American slavery and freedom, Brown compels us—as he did Thoreau—to relate prophecy, redemption, and politics. How should we understand this knot and Brown's embodiment of it? Why was the author of *Walden*—famous for huckleberry parties, naturalist observation, and antipolitics—inspired to defend him? To answer such questions we need to grasp Thoreau's deep sense of kinship with Brown and assess the political meaning of his defense of Brown and his violence. That means retracing Thoreau's struggle with prophecy in politics.[1]

The argument of this chapter, indeed, is that Thoreau *struggled with* and *revised* prophecy in ways represented in—and risked by—his defense of Brown. At the center of Thoreau's life and work is a tension between the Protestant idiom and jeremiadic narrative of his civil disobedience and antislavery lectures, and *Walden*'s "romantic" idiom and narrative of rebirth in nature. Those who define conscience as moralism, and those who define romanticism as withdrawal to personal cultivation, criticize him for seeking antipolitical forms of purity. Indeed, Sacvan Bercovitch says that Thoreau's Protestant and romantic idioms together show the hegemony of American liberal culture in its individualistic premises and redemptive rhetorics. Though in tension, we might conclude, these idioms enable his abiding antipolitics, which binds him to the regime he rejects while depriving him of any way to transform it.

I dispute these claims, first by asking why and with what effect Thoreau crafts a prophetic voice in his antislavery lectures, and second by asking why and with what effect he draws on romantic idioms to place the poet in the office of prophet and thereby to revise prophecy as a genre and practice. He does reject "what is called politics," as he himself puts it, for what is *called* politics can ignore crucial aspects of importance. I therefore find unexpected affinities—not only evident tensions—between Thoreau's prophecy and political life. By inhabiting the office of (moral) witness and by creating a poetry of wilderness regeneration, I will argue, he engages a political world he always distrusted and maligned, always wished he could escape, and always dreamed of transforming.

On the one hand, Thoreau is one of the few American thinkers to have connected white supremacy to the problem of mass society: While the mobile freedom of some is premised on the subordination of others, that fluidity generates conformity rather than independence among the enfranchised. Denouncing "slavery in Massachusetts," he *twins* these two forms of servitude, which still mock celebrations of an American freedom. When he says "it is hard to have a southern overseer, it is worse to have a northern one; but worst of all is when you are the slave-driver of yourself"—we need not take the bait in his provocative ranking to see "slavery" as a master trope in his texts (*Walden*, 4).[2]

Everything he wrote is haunted by imperial expansion and the destruction of native peoples, by chattel slavery and northern complicity, by new forms of labor, false fates, and subjection to them. Indeed, he is the great antebellum analyst of worldly asceticism, which divides the self and entombs it in a world of dead things. Bearing witness to the captivity his neighbors impose on others and the death-in-life they impose on themselves, he connects politics to culture, but he neither invokes a moral and religious consensus in Bellah's sense nor recapitulates liberal nationalism as Bercovitch argues.

On the other hand, therefore, everything he wrote conceives freedom not as a given but as an achievement. *Cultivation* is his other master trope: His concern, even in his famous 1849 essay, is not to *justify* civil disobedience but to *cultivate* a people capable of it. He sees that only "freer and less desponding spirits" can stand with "the fugitive slave, the Mexican . . . and the Indian," to resist an unjust state. His essay locates that identification on "the freer and more honorable ground" ("Disobedience," 9) of a jail, while in *Walden* a trope of wilderness represents a project of cultivation that joins citizenship to resistance rather than docility.

To analyze empire, slavery, and servitude and to cultivate resistance to them, however, Thoreau speaks in prophetic forms and terms, which he draws from biblical and Protestant sources but also inflects by what we now call romanticism and its exalted idea of poetry. The crux of my argument concerns Thoreau's *translation* of prophecy as he moves between Protestant and romantic, theistic and poetic, moral and aesthetic registers of language. In his jeremiads, he speaks as a witness and watchman announcing collective liability and demanding a decision about the servitude that enables American freedom. But *Walden* adopts a *poetic* persona: The epigraph to *Walden* announces, "I do not propose to write an ode to dejection, but to brag as lustily as chanticleer in the morning, standing on his roost, if only to wake my neighbors up." He announces a "dawn" meant to arouse "neighbors" not to injustice but to their imprisonment by despair, self-loathing, and resentment. How does he relate and use these two personas and registers of voice, and how do they each, separately and together, bear on politics?

Thoreau's practice of prophecy and his relationship to politics reflect his indebtedness to, and struggle against, a Protestant tradition that Søren Kierkergaard calls "a religion for adult men," which runs from Luther and Calvin to Garrison, Douglass, Debs, and King. Radical Protestantism produced a language of authority and covenant, moral autonomy and personal conscience, bearing witness, calling, and redemption that was and still is a crucial aspect of the American vernacular. Thoreau's slavery lectures surely draw on this tradition and idiom: Linking "manliness" to moral witness and conscience to embodied action, he models how citizens can resist a liberal constitutionalism authorizing slavery and war.[3]

Walden, however, shows how this religious and moral language generates worldly asceticism, racism, an inner slave driver, and reformers who displace private woe into resentful action toward redeeming others. Thoreau struggles with this legacy in himself and his neighbors by an "experiment" in nature that draws on a nontheist and secular idea of poetry. As if to address the dangers and poison in (his own) conscientious militancy, to supplement—both trouble and revise—that abolitionist voice, he fashions another, avowedly affirmative register of prophecy.

Partly, he casts life in aesthetic and libidinal, not only moral, terms to juxtapose "the wild" and "the good," to embrace the multivocal "obscurity" of "extra-vagant" language, to grasp how imagination "instills and drenches" meaning into a universe that "obediently answers our conceptions" (*Walden,* 176, 270–71, 79). Partly, he dramatizes how a capacity to be alone is a key condition of a democratic community that does not insist on unity. But partly, his personal narrative is a parable of refounding community, by redoing a wilderness experiment he depicts as a violent, self-destructive failure. In *Walden* he does not reject the office or genre of prophecy but reworks its historic practice by a poesis rich in possibility.

As any space for speech and dialogue closes down after Dred Scott, however, he increasingly despairs about the political value of his poetic myth making. By defending Brown, Thoreau articulates the political crisis behind his despair, as well as an alternative to it. He bears witness to the deep kinship he feels for someone empowered by the same fundamentalist flame whose burning heat he had drawn on in his own abolitionist politics, though he had transfigured this flame by his poetic visions of rebirth in nature. Working through these two registers of voice, we can grasp what is both understandable and distressing in Thoreau's defense of Brown's righteous violence and assess how his own life is at once completed and betrayed by it.[4]

My substantive chapters begin with Thoreau, then, because in tension and tandem his Protestant and romantic registers of prophetic voice address the central issues raised by prophecy as an office and genre: the problem of authority, the practice of judgment, the living of faith; the remaking of political identification and the reconstitution of community; and the meaning of coming to terms with the past and its power. Importantly, Thoreau not only writes in voices of prophecy: His life follows the arc of prophecy as a genre, albeit not by design, as he moves between cultivation in the wilderness and moments of speech in public to summon "the power of decision lying in the present." After all, in biblical prophecy from Hosea to Jesus, "wilderness" is a liminal space and passage, always related to a settled community and (political) engagement with it. But things could have gone differently. Thoreau might have cultivated his powers but not been called to speak, or he might have been called to speak for Brown but been unprepared. Imagine, then, his acute sense of contingency as a fate as he steps into the place not only of a Douglass or Brown but of prophecy as a political vocation.[5]

Political Captivity and "Resistance"

A brief chronology helps initiate our analysis. In 1845, when he was twenty-eight, Thoreau went to Walden Pond—"by accident on July 4th" he later writes—about a mile from his home in Concord. During the summer of 1846, when he went to jail briefly for withholding taxes to protest the Mexican War, he also wrote his first draft of *Walden*, which appeared six drafts and eight years later. He left his hut in September 1847. In January 1848 he gave the first version of his "resistance to government" lecture, soon renamed "Civil Disobedience." If he declared a kind of independence by going to the pond, his lecture renewed that declaration by using the jail as a critical perspective: "Under a government which imprisons any unjustly, the true place for a just man is also a prison," the "more free and honorable ground" on which "the state places those who are not *with* her but *against* her" ("Disobedience," 9).

By 1854, the Kansas–Nebraska Act had repealed the Missouri Compromise by opening territories to slavery or not on the basis of "popular sovereignty," that is, based on the votes of the local populace. It ignited violent conflict and generated the Republican Party, whose platform Lincoln articulated: The Constitution allowed slavery in southern states and the pursuit of fugitive slaves, but no slavery in the territories. That summer of 1854, shortly before *Walden* appeared in print, Thoreau rejected this platform as he stoked an uproar over the Fugitive Slave Act and the increasing nationalization of slavery.[6]

Anthony Burns had escaped from slavery in Virginia and lived in Boston's community of free blacks, but he was captured, and after a week-long trial, Massachusetts allowed his deportation. As state and federal troops escorted Burns to the ship returning him to slavery, fifty thousand people lined Boston streets to protest. This event profoundly shifted New England public opinion: "We went to bed old-fashioned, conservative, Compromise Union Whigs," one observer noted, "and waked up stark mad Abolitionists."[7] A non- or antiabolitionist majority now found slavery a threat to its freedoms, not just a "somewhat foreign form of servitude," to quote *Walden* (4). Thoreau, for years involved in the underground railroad, which ran through his family home, joined Garrison, Wendell Phillips, and Sojourner Truth at a July 4 rally protesting Burns's deportation.

Garrison read the Fugitive Slave Act, set a copy on fire, and received a thunderous response when he declared, "Let the crowd say Amen." After burning Burns's deportation documents, he read proslavery passages in the U.S. Constitution, quoted Isaiah to denounce it as a "covenant with death and agreement with hell," and promised, "So perish all compromises with tyranny." Thoreau's lecture at this rally, "Slavery in Massachusetts," put the state on trial by depicting enfranchised whites as enslaved. Their concern is, typically, displaced: "The house is on fire, and not the prairie," for "there is not one slave in Nebraska; there are perhaps a million slaves in Massachusetts." The real issue is "her own slaveholding and servility." He ridicules July Fourth: "The joke could be no broader if the inmates of prisons were . . . to hire the jailors to do the firing and ringing for them, while they enjoyed it through the grating. This is what I thought about my neighbors" ("Slavery," 22).

"Civil Disobedience" in 1848 and "Slavery in Massachusetts" in 1854

frame the political context of *Walden* and reveal the Protestant or abolitionist register of prophecy with which that text struggles. Each lecture is
organized by prophetic questions and manifests the prophetic presumption that his peers live in denial and need to be aroused and warned. His
core claim is that "they who have been bred in the school of politics fail
now and always to face the facts" ("Slavery," 19). What "facts" does he
announce to move people from disavowal to acknowledgment?

First, the United States is an ex-colonial but slaveholding and imperial republic. That is because, second, enfranchised northern men support war and chattel slavery, both of which are national, not sectional,
issues. "Practically speaking, the opponents of reform in Massachusetts
are not a hundred thousand politicians in the south, but a hundred
thousand merchants and farmers here. . . . I quarrel not with far-off
foes, but with those who, near at home, cooperate with and do the bid-
ding of those far away, and without whom the latter would be harmless."
He believes that state power must be authorized by the consent of the
governed and majority rule, but he also sees that slavery and war are authorized democratically and constitutionally. Indeed, third, democratic
norms work to sustain gross injustice, for those "*in opinion* opposed to
war and slavery" are led by "undue respect" for the authority of majorities and law to become the "most *conscientious* supporters" of the regime
and "the most serious obstacles to reform" of the very evils they condemn ("Disobedience," 4, 5). He thus bears witness to another essential
fact: "Whatever the human law may be, neither an individual nor a nation can ever commit the least injustice against the obscurest individual
without having to pay a penalty for it" ("Slavery," 22). What is the penalty
to which he bears witness??

Thoreau invokes a prophetic idea of joint liability not only because
there must be accountability but because those who allow slavery impose
on themselves another kind of servitude.

The mass of men serve the state . . . not as men mainly but as machines, with
their bodies. They are a standing army and the militia, jailors, constables . . . etc.
In most cases there is no free exercise whatever of the judgment or of the moral
sense, but they put themselves on a level with wood and earth and stones. . . .
Yet such as these are commonly esteemed good citizens. . . . Most legislators,
politicians, lawyers, ministers and office-holders serve the state chiefly with their
heads; and, as they rarely make any moral distinctions, they are as likely to serve
the Devil, without *intending* it, as God. A very few, as heroes, patriots, martyrs,
reformers in the great sense, and *men*, serve the state with their consciences also,
and so necessarily resist it for the most part; and they are commonly treated by it
as enemies. ("Disobedience," 3)

Here is the prophetic question: The "good citizens" always serve authority, but which, and how? What is "commonly esteemed" good citizenship is a *conscientious* reification by which people subordinate the "free
exercise of the judgment" and become thoughtless bodies "on a level
with wood and earth and stone." Idolatry names their undue respect for
the authority of law and majorities, compared to exercising authority
directly by their own "moral sense" and political deliberation as citizens.

About fundamental issues, people should not "judge according to
precedent" but should "establish a precedent for the future." Granted,
"it is to some extent fatal to the courts when the people are compelled to
go behind them . . . but think of leaving to any court in the land to decide
whether more than three millions of people, in this case a sixth part of
the nation, have a right to be freemen or not!" Thoreau seeks a political,
not a legal, decision: "I would much rather trust to the sentiments of the
people. In their votes you would get something of some value, at least,
however small." He seeks dialogue and decision in public meetings as
"a true Congress," but majority rule still displaces responsibility: "If the
majority vote the Devil to be God, the minority will . . . obey the successful candidate—trusting that some time . . . they may reinstate God"
("Slavery," 23, 24, 27).

To resist the subjection he attributes to "undue respect" for the authority of legal precedent and majority rule, Thoreau invokes the authority his culture claims to lodge in conscience, in equality as a principle,
and in the idea of active consent. He would unsettle—though he does
not reject—liberal constitutionalism and resist the broader filio-piety it
bespeaks. For those "standing so completely within the institution" of
the Constitution do not ask "what it behooves a man to do here in America today with regard to slavery"; rather, they accept it as "part of the
original compact." Figures like Daniel Webster cannot say the compact
"is itself the evil" because he is "not a leader but a follower. His leaders
are the men of '87" ("Disobedience," 16–17). While Lincoln famously
sought a "political religion" to "reverence" the Constitution, Thoreau
sees constitutional reverence as voluntary entombment: "Society is not
animated, or instinct enough with life. . . . All men are partially buried
in the grave of custom, and of some we see only the crown of the head
above ground. Better are the physically dead, for they more lively rot."[8]

Thoreau draws on the genre of prophecy, and assumes the office, to
announce the captivity that citizens impose on others and to bear witness to its penalty, a political entombment they impose on themselves.

He names a servitude he attributes to idolatry as undue respect, but he also bears witness to a capacity for choice and action that might animate deadened men and an entombed social body. He models how citizenship, infused with the "moral" and "manly," resurrects the dead. This rebirth goes behind the compact and founders of '87, to Revolutionary fathers and transcendental Puritans cast as rebels.

How then does he "stand outside" and speak "with authority" about the institutions, compacts, customs, and conventions that good sons are "buried" within? Partly, he invokes the perspective of outcasts on those who "esteem themselves children of Washington and Franklin." Partly, he invokes embodied consent, which makes rather than follows precedent, to de-reify institutions by revealing coauthorship "behind" them. But since people consent to slavery and war, he also invokes the idea of *rightful* power by depicting a "moral sense" both transcendental and internal:

The question is not whether you, or your grandfather seventy years ago, did not enter into an agreement to serve the Devil, and that service is not accordingly now due, but whether you will not now, for once and at last, serve God—in spite of your own past recreancy or that of your ancestors—by obeying that eternal and only just CONSTITUTION which He, and not any Jefferson or Adams, has written in your being. ("Slavery," 27)

Against the Faustian pact that premises the freedom of some on the servitude of others, he invokes a divinely inscribed constitution that he never theorizes because he is not trying to justify civil disobedience. A *capacity* to judge and an *idea* of right, available to all because it is "written in" human beings by God, *enable* people to resist the constitution written by subjection to worldly authority:

Among human beings, the judge whose words seal the fate of a man furthest into eternity is not he who merely pronounces the verdict of the law, but he, whomever he may be, who from love of truth, and unprejudiced by any custom or enactment of men, utters a true opinion or *sentence* concerning him. He it is that *sentences* him. Whoever can discern truth . . . finds himself constituted judge of the judge. ("Slavery," 24)

Accordingly, even when he faces "the brute force" of an implacable majority, he says:

But just in proportion as I regard this as not wholly a brute force, but partly a *human* force, and consider that I have relations to those millions as . . . *men*, and not mere brute and inanimate things, I see that appeal is possible, first and instantaneously from them to the Maker of them, and secondly, from them to themselves. ("Disobedience," 15)

Appealing to a constitutional capacity for judgment to resist a constitution written by convention, he exposes the reification that makes relations among humans seem like relations among (brute and inanimate) things. In turn, to join "the moral sense" to action is to exemplify "action from principle":

> The perception and performance of right changes things and relations; it is essentially revolutionary and does not consist wholly with anything which was. It not only divides states and churches, it divides families; aye, it divides the individual, separating the diabolical and the divine.

Just as Jesus brings not peace but a sword, so "all change for the better, like birth and death . . . convulse the body." Thus does "the perception and performance of right" signify the rebirth of adults and revolution in their social body ("Disobedience," 7).

Asserting "the citizen" must never "for a moment or in the least degree resign his conscience to the legislator," Thoreau infuses the "moral sense" of "the man" into the activities of citizens acting in concert. Condemning the displacement of responsibility that splits spirit from body, he calls on his neighbors to "cast your whole vote, not a strip of paper merely, but your whole influence," saying, "let your life be a counter-friction to stop the machine." His own "action from principle" is meant to recall and inspire "corporations of conscientious men." Such association is instrumentally effective: "A minority is powerless while it conforms to the majority," but "irresistible when it clogs [the machine] by its whole weight" ("Disobedience," 8, 9). But by what action?

Given "the present posture of affairs," the indispensable mode of engaging the issue of slavery is to confront any who have "voluntarily chosen to be an agent of the government," and who thereby allow themselves to be divided into an officeholder and a human being. "How shall he ever know what he is and does as an officer of the government, or as a man, until he is obliged to consider whether he shall treat his neighbor . . . as a neighbor and well-disposed man or as a maniac and disturber of the peace?" Minorities withholding consent, to provoke dialogue and self-reflection, comprise his "definition of a peaceable revolution, if any such is possible" ("Disobedience," 8–9). Likewise, against what is "commonly esteemed" good citizenship, Thoreau insists, "We should be men first, and Americans at a later and more convenient hour"; deflating a nation claiming providential sanction, he weds "America" to the devil rather than God and severs it from its utopian promise. But by bearing witness to "action from principle," which joins natality and egalitarian ideals, he relocates that utopian promise with those who stand against rather than with the state. In these very terms, however, he appeals to his audience as bearers of a specific history in which theist faith, personal conscience, and political consent are avowedly linked to liberty. By returning to these origins they can recover the judgment and action severed by constitutional piety, regenerate their own authority, and create rather than repeat precedent. He thus demonstrates what his peers forget: both an endowment that constitutes them as creatures of judgment and action, and the historical origin of their political community in capacities to withhold consent and initiate the unprecedented.[9]

How shall we assess the politics entailed by the prophetic terms and form of this argument? His language is pervasive: Like Lincoln and Douglass, he tells a jeremiad about a crisis in a house divided. In Machiavellian terms, he narrates a (re)turn to equality as a first principle he creatively reinterprets, but also to "origins" in "action from principle" as a generative capacity to (re)constitute power. But Thoreau is an "unarmed prophet" who also orients politics by appeals to the moral sense or divinely inscribed constitution of his audience. The danger is not *that* he speaks a "moral" language to condemn slavery, for no self-evident political action follows from the claim that slavery is "wrong" or unjust. At issue is *how* he conceives and practices his notion of "the right."[10]

Clearly, he feels authorized because he imagines a prepolitical "moral sense" and conscience "inside" the self, which empowers the self against worldly authority. Neither a social voice internalized nor a citadel ruling a conquered city, as Nietzsche and Sigmund Freud argue, conscience is a permissive authority enabling and entitling an "I"; as Blake claims, "The voice of honest indignation is the voice of God."[11] But Thoreau splits the subject: The divine/manly is wholly distinct from the brute/diabolical. In his masculinized individualism, "moral sense" names a pure *inside* threatened by contamination from culture, the "outside," and a *higher* authority threatened by "lower" passions associated with material interest, compromise—politics. To serve any other authority is to become a brute or slave; to honor it redeems the human from its debasement. Depicting a "mass" of men because each is emasculated, he projects (maternal) abjection to dramatize moral autonomy as separation, (re)birth of manliness.

Slaves who accept being ruled by man rather than God, Frederick Douglass likewise argues, commit a sin; they must see their submission as a sin, even if they cannot overcome it. Though masters call defiance a sin, Douglass calls his fight with his master, Edward Covey, a "resurrection from the tomb of slavery to the heaven of freedom" because "however long I might remain a slave in form, the day had passed when I could be a slave in fact." But he insists on the worldly reality of violent domination: Slaves are "taunted with a want of the love of freedom, by the very men who stand upon us and say, submit or be crushed." He sees the abyss between slavery as a trope and a fact, even as he uses one to contest the other. But Thoreau presents an idealized persona whose moral integrity, pure and heroic, signals an unconditioned capacity to defy any worldly condition.[12]

By this persona of potency and plenitude, Thoreau struggles to overcome his own sense of weakness, write himself into being, and address the docility of his peers, but by abstracting conscience and action from the actualities always conditioning them. Never able to inhabit fully his impossible ideal, he casts "what is political" as a wholly ignoble contamination. So he fumes, "We are not a religious people but we are a nation of politicians" ("Slavery," 24). Separating pure principle from contaminating involvement with others, he insists, "the only obligation which I have a right to assume, is to do at any time what I think right" ("Disobedience," 2).

Hannah Arendt thus claims, "Thoreau argued his case not on the ground of a *citizen's* moral relation to law, but on the ground of individual conscience, and conscience's moral obligation." Seeking purity by fidelity to moral principle, his language of "conscience is unpolitical. It is not primarily interested in the world where the wrong is committed or in the consequences that the wrong will have for [its] future course." In contrast, Lincoln frames politics by the same moral claim about slavery, but he also argues that citizens must recognize other authorities—of the Constitution (which permits slavery in the South) and of majority rule (which reflects pervasive racism)—as well as recalcitrant historical circumstance and the worldly plurality of opinions and interests. *Political* responsibility means mediating such conflicting claims to *build* a consensus that sustains community.[13]

If prophecy means orienting action only by conscience or by what is "right," it seems inimical to political responsibility. It displaces a "political" sensitivity to context and unintended consequences. It avoids the Machiavellian lesson that a principle holds good only if advanced by groups exercising power on its behalf—which puts every actor at moral risk. It avoids the fact that *political* judgment must be forged by counting as real and engaging a plurality of others. Absolute standards, and self-righteous certainty about them, thus seem to sanction either "disunion" from evil or its violent purification, but not a politically mediated and morally ambiguous engagement with it. Addressed repeatedly not only to Thoreau but to abolitionism, these arguments link prophecy to a dogmatic, invasive, purifying, and polarizing approach to politics that seems antithetical to democratic norms and practices. But consider another reading.[14]

Thoreau's Abolitionist Prophecy as Politics

Start with Thoreau's claim to "speak practically and as a citizen" ("Disobedience," 2).[15] Simply put, he believes he exercises political judgment by attending to context, weighing the "cost" of prevailing practices and of inaction about them, addressing the idioms and concerns of a specific (abolitionist) audience, and modeling forms of "minority action." He knows that critics of abolitionism tend to minimize the injustice and political danger of slavery—as its critics even today tend to presume that slavery would have died by itself. Because of his sense of the grip of slavery, indeed, he is unsure if moral suasion (or "peaceable revolution") can work. But he is rethinking the forms of judgment and action available to an abolitionist minority.

Partly, he uses prophecy to make slavery and its consequences the paramount issue for the Republic as a whole and for every enfranchised member. Partly, then, he uses prophecy to demonstrate the "office" of citizen: He models capacities for judgment, dialogue, and action he would cultivate in his neighbors. He thus weighs the costs of injustice to identify when action is necessary. "If the injustice is part of the necessary friction of the machine of government, let it go, let it go. . . . If the injustice has a spring, or pulley . . . exclusively for itself, then perhaps you may consider whether the remedy will not be worse than the evil." But,

when friction comes to have its machine and oppression and robbery are organized, I say, let us not have such a machine any longer. In other words, when a sixth of the population of a nation that has undertaken to be the refuge of liberty are slaves, and a whole country is unjustly overrun and conquered by a foreign army and subject to military law, I think that it is not too soon for honest men to rebel and revolutionize. What makes this duty the more urgent is the fact that the country so overrun is not our own, but ours is the invading army. ("Disobedience," 8)

At issue is not harmony with his conscience but injustice against others so great that "this people must cease to hold slaves and make war on Mexico, though it cost them their existence as a people" ("Disobedience," 4). Arendt, horrified at this assertion, approves of Lincoln's claim that his only goal is saving the Union, with or without slavery, but Thoreau weighs the cost of union to others and the cost of inaction to its members. To those (like Lincoln) who fear that a politics oriented by what is "right" will ignite violence, he responds that the violence is already ongoing against others; in fear of risking violence among the enfranchised one enshrines the order founded by this violence. For we can rectify *this* injustice only by risking mortal (national) existence: The "cost" of freedom *is* profound conflict because people disagree about the rightness of practices constitutive of their society.

Thoreau thus speaks as a citizen, but not in consensual terms. He is trying to destroy a consensus by making the North antislavery, that is, by changing its political judgment about the meaning—the rightness and cost—of slavery. What Eileen Kraditor says in defense of Garrison applies to Thoreau:

The point is not that Garrison created an atmosphere of moral absolutism but that the choice which the nation faced was objectively between absolutely antagonistic moral systems. Garrison's real choice was not between democratic and undemocratic, or fanatical and reasonable agitation; it was between anti-slavery agitation and silence.[16]

A "prophetic" project is "abolitionist" in the sense that it would shift (or "polarize") political judgment of a prevailing practice, say idolatry or slavery, precisely to provoke a crisis. Still, how should antislavery abolitionists weigh the forms of action available to them? "Unjust laws exist: shall we be content to obey them, or shall we endeavor to amend them, and obey them until we have succeeded, or shall we transgress them at once?" Granted, "men generally, under such a government as this, think they ought to wait until they have persuaded the majority to alter them. They think that, if they should resist the remedy would be worse than the evil" ("Disobedience," 7). In most cases Thoreau *agrees* with "men generally": One should use electoral politics or constitutional procedure. But in regards to slavery he depicts a state of exception and calls for a decision. Still, what action is "right," in the sense of appropriate?

We are not in a revolutionary situation, he argues: A vast majority of citizens support slavery, and a majority of the minority who oppose slavery (though not white supremacy) are "conscientious" supporters of the regime. Their constitutional reverence is crucial: He must show

how they bear conflicting loyalties (to law and to "the right" disclosed by conscience) that cannot be reconciled but must be ranked; only a different ranking disrupts their conscientious passivity. By demonstrating his own ranking, he politicizes the issue of authority at the center of prophecy and displays how judgment enacted even by a minority makes a worldly difference. As a minority of a minority, he declares: "Those who call themselves Abolitionists should . . . not wait til they constitute a majority . . . before they suffer the right to prevail through them. I think that it is enough if they have God on their side." Aware that men "are as likely to serve the Devil, without intending it, as God" and that "obstinacy" is as much a danger as "undue regard for the opinions of men," he endorses "the perception and performance of right" by "corporations with a conscience" ("Disobedience," 8, 15).

As Arendt sees in Tocqueville but not in Thoreau, "association" transforms conscience into a public opinion whose power depends on numbers. She even credits that anti–Vietnam War protestors argue "on moral grounds, but so long as there is freedom of association and with it the hope that resistance in the form of refusal to participate will bring about a change in policy," their action "is essentially political" because "the center of consideration is not the self" but the "conduct" and "fate of the nation." But protestors quoted Thoreau, not Tocqueville, because Thoreau showed how a minority can clog the machine "by its whole weight" by action that also shifts a consensus about what Arendt calls "the fate of a nation and its conduct." Deflating electoral politics, Thoreau relocates speech and action in civil society and everyday life, to confront neighbors with "facts" they need to acknowledge rather than disavow. He does not call "action from principle" political, but says it opposes injustice, weighs the cost of loyalty to contrasting authorities, and takes (as well as demands) responsibility for the consequence of "private" as well as "public" actions; by provoking neighbors to self-reflection and speech, it seeks solidarity to create power and provoke dialogue.[17]

In Puritan terms, Thoreau refuses, not endorses, the separation of grace and works: Rooting the "moral sense" in bodies in social space and historical time, he demands personal responsibility, whose absence makes covenant the tomb of the spirit, not its worldly testament. Relevant here is Jonathan Schell's account of the Polish Solidarity movement: "Its simple but radical principle" is "to start doing things you think should be done and start being what you think society should become." If you wish to produce results today, "what area of life is . . . more . . . within your grasp than your own action?" A corollary principle is that, since "the journey and the destination are the same," action must not "be degraded by brutality, deception or any other disfigurement." This "solidarity," in its immediacy and its assumption that means are ends in the making, shows "corporations with a conscience" creating power where none had been. (Contra Schell, though, both Douglass and Thoreau doubt that moral suasion or deliberation can suffice to eliminate an institution as entrenched as slavery.)[18]

Call this a sixties reading of Thoreau, whose joining of moral authenticity, personal autonomy, and embodied action made him an exemplar at a time when imperial war and racial apartheid also compelled critics and citizens to relocate action outside and beneath "what is called politics." Henry Abelove thus reads Thoreau as initiating "queer" politics, not because he loves men, though he does, but because he affirms an eccentric life beyond bourgeois domesticity and because, rather than seek rights or recognition from the state, he uses symbolic action to create nondomestic and highly visible sites of outrage and excitement. In the shadow of Weber, who cast constitutionalism and popular sovereignty as ideologies that authorize violent and bureaucratic regimes, we should not so hastily dismiss Thoreau's effort to embody antinomian critique in beloved community.[19]

Conflict about the sixties still may fuel arguments about Thoreau: Is the problem the regime he faces, or his unrealistic expectations, his moralistic anger at neighbors who must fail him, and so his self-imposed marginality? Rather than invent and impose expectations, however, he affirms expectations that people already profess as public truths. Rather than make neighbors feel abject or guilty, he politicizes a despair they already voice in private. Perhaps he is right to be enraged about slavery and complicity in it, and rather than show inappropriate anger at a world that fails him, he binds justifiable anger to faith in human capacities for judgment and action otherwise. His voice is strident, and because he holds others to account for their conduct, they do feel defensive: They accuse him of lacking the authority to judge them, or they unmask what seems like his claim to a superior moral position. But his judgments are those of a peer and witness, not a father. He does not invent the facts he laments, the standards he invokes, or the cross they constitute; he does intensify the contradiction his neighbors live, but to show its penalty and how to resist it.

He establishes rhetorical distance, but he speaks a daily idiom and uses an ordinary encounter with a tax collector to symbolize dialogue about personal and political responsibility. Peter Euben's view of Socrates is apt here: "By chastising fellow citizens for not living up to their own ideals, while subjecting those ideals to critique and reinterpretation," he would "reestablish the conditions of political deliberation and moral discourse." But Thoreau puts Socratic practice in prophetic form; as one whose office is to bear witness—against injustice and to the generative power of action from principle—he practices prophecy as a form of democratic authority.[20] For his authority with others rests not on the divine origin of his moral claim, nor on a claim to special knowledge, but on avowing his positioned or particular experience, honoring the meaning of his words in his action, using idioms resonant to others, and inviting their response. His political authority, then, finally rests with those he addresses, who may not recognize their situation, language, or capacities in his testimony and may rebuff it. He suffers the pathos of any prophetic witness: Here he stands, he can do no other, but he also must endure the freedom (and hostility!) of his audience. They can refuse his claims and deny any community with him, but he has no right *not* to judge them:

If I could convince myself that I have any right to be satisfied with men as they are and to treat them accordingly, and not according, in some respects, to my requirements and expectations of what they and I ought to be, then . . . I should endeavor to be satisfied with things as they are and say it is the will of God. ("Disobedience," 15)

Thoreau turns to prophecy, therefore, to perform the "expectations and requirements" to which he holds himself and others accountable: He does not justify but rather seeks to cultivate such standards in those he addresses, whose despondency has precluded creative action. By what Douglass calls scorching irony, Thoreau testifies to "facts" that his peers deny at great cost to others and to themselves. By exemplary action, he also affirms both commitment making and their own professed commitments, while testifying to the necessity of a decision about how to practice them. In contrast to the angry, relentless judgment he links to prophecy in an unjust world, however, *Walden* announces "irrepressible satisfaction with the gift of life." How and why, then, and why does he revise prophecy?[21]

Recasting Prophecy as Poetry

Thoreau revises prophecy in ways signaled by romanticism: He turns from a God outside nature to a divinized nature, and he imagines "the poet" in the office of the prophet. By turning to nature and poetry, what

problems would he solve? Partly, I argue, he would address worldly asceticism, including the prevailing character of "moral reform" and the
Protestant orthodoxy of (his own) abolitionism. Partly, he crafts a poetic persona to remedy the resentment in prophecy and its notion of
redemption. Naming the unvoiced despair that drives his peers toward
resignation or moralism, and seeking to sustain his own faith in possibility, sorely tested by horrific injustice and his sense of complicity in
it, Thoreau thus makes a prophecy that emphasizes newness, initiative,
and poesis. Partly, his story about his own self-cultivation, whereby he
earns the right to the words we are reading and achieves the faith in
possibility that he announces, is also a political parable of refounding
political community by confronting and redoing its violent history in a
"wilderness."

By my reading, then, he does not flee society and history but criticizes the frontier romance of an exceptional nation that can escape time
into space. Though the wilderness trope creates rhetorical distance,
he is not transcending his culture but dramatizing and testing the key
terms and myths of its self-understanding. This very engagement makes
his revised prophecy powerfully resonant, yet his poetry of rebirth and
myth making are vulnerable to unmasking. To explore how, we proceed
in stages, from his account of the problem to his crafting of a poetic
prophecy in response.

Recasting the Prophetic Problem

Walden is not a jeremiad of first principles violated; rather, it depicts
a death-in-life created by idolatrous labor. It addresses captivity, not in
citizenship as subjection but in alienated "labor," the "slave driver" that
compels it, and the despair sustaining both. "I would fain say something," the book begins, "not so much concerning the Chinese and
Sandwich Islanders as you who read these pages, who are *said* to live in
New England; something about your condition, *especially* your *outward*
condition or circumstance in the world, in this town, what it is, whether
it is necessary that it be as bad as it is, whether it cannot be improved as
well as not" (*Walden*, 1, my emphasis).

He thus begins with a prophetic interrogatory framed by the trope of
death-in-life. Using slavery as a trope, he moves between the horrific violence of chattel slavery and the self-imposed forms of servitude prophets
call idolatry. Because abolitionists attack slave labor as "foreign" compared to "free labor," he feels compelled to say, "I sometimes wonder

that we can be so frivolous, I can almost say, as to attend to the gross but somewhat foreign form of servitude called Negro Slavery, there are so many keen and subtle masters that enslave both North and South." In "Economy," *Walden*'s famous first chapter, he therefore links subjection to alienated labor and property, but also to being "the slave-driver of yourself." He roots servitude in the "public opinion" that equates worth and material success and in the "private opinion" that Nietzsche calls the bad conscience, whose unending labor mortifies the flesh to redeem it (*Walden*, 4, 5).

Enfranchised men imprison themselves by their very pursuit of autonomy and self-respect in acquisitive terms, which binds them to markets, the accumulation of property, the esteem of others, and the slave-driver within. Echoing Karl Marx and Nietzsche, Thoreau turns from the formally political in his account of freedom twinned with servitude. "America is said to be the arena on which the battle of freedom is to be fought; but surely it cannot be freedom in a merely political sense that is meant. Even if we grant that the American has freed himself from a political tyrant, he is still the slave of an economic and moral tyrant. . . . Is it a freedom to be slaves or a freedom to be free of which we boast? We are a nation of politicians concerned only about the outmost defenses of freedom."[22]

"What is *called* politics" avoids these economic and moral questions, which he casts in terms of "outward conditions" and "labor," as well as in terms of their "inward" aspect. For "everywhere, in shops, offices, and fields, the inhabitants appeared to me to be doing penance in a thousand remarkable ways." The *Oxford English Dictionary* defines penance as a "religious discipline voluntarily undertaken in token of repentance, and by way of satisfaction, for sin"; we "undergo some penalty" by "acts of self-mortification" to express "penitence." Since Thoreau also defines a sacrament as a "visible and outward sign of an inward and spiritual grace," he argues that social practices relate inner spirit and worldly action (*Walden*, 2, 56). To call our practices penance means they are "works" that bespeak guilt rather than faith, as we seek redemption by self-mortification.

Despite incessant activity, we are *said* to live because we devalue both the beauty of a world we instrumentalize and our worth, which we "spend" our lives to prove. We "labor" to redeem but in fact entomb ourselves. Assuming that "the cost of a thing is the amount of what I will call life which is required to be exchanged for it, immediately or in the long run," Thoreau weighs the "sacrifice" of "life" for "the advantages of civilization." Using a pervasive Franklin-esque idiom of "keeping accounts," he satirizes the deranged logic of a culture that idolizes wealth and accounting but leaves people impoverished in the senses that count most, unable to account for—or voice—their own discontent.

He links the hunger for property to an idolatry that despoils and devalues the world:

> I respect not his labors . . . who would carry the landscape, who would carry his God to market . . . who goes to market *for* his God as it is . . . whose fields bear no crops, whose meadows no flowers, whose trees no fruits, but dollars; who loves not the beauty of his fruits, whose fruits are not ripe for him til they are turned to dollars. Give me the poverty that enjoys true wealth. (*Walden*, 64)

The self is also instrumentalized: "It is very evident what mean and sneaking lives many of you live . . . trying to get into business and . . . out of debt . . . lying, flattering, voting, contracting yourselves into a nutshell of civility, or dilating into an atmosphere of thin and vaporous generosity," to "persuade your neighbor" to buy your services. Thoreau often says "you" in this distancing way, but as often includes himself, for he adds: But "public opinion is a weak tyrant compared with our own private opinion," of which any of us becomes "the slave and prisoner." Indeed, "what a man thinks of himself" "determines or rather indicates his fate. Self-emancipation in the West Indian provinces of the fancy and imagination—what Wilberforce is there to bring that about?" (*Walden*, 4–5).

Thoreau witnesses "incessant anxiety," and by asking what it "is about and how much it is necessary that we be troubled" (*Walden*, 7–8), he reveals another sense of labor:

> Men labor under a mistake. . . . By a seeming fate, commonly called necessity, they are employed, as it says in an old book, laying up treasures which moth and rust will corrupt. . . . When we consider what, to use the words of the catechism, is the chief end of man, and what are the true necessaries and means of life, it appears as if men had deliberately chosen the common mode of living because they preferred it to any other. Yet they honestly think there is no choice left. (*Walden*, 3–5)

As a result, "we are not where we are, but in a false position. . . . we suppose a case and put ourselves in it, and hence are in two cases at the same time, and it is doubly difficult to get out." We profess, he goes on, to live by consent or choice, and we claim to have chosen this way of life deliberately—on purpose, with care—yet we think there is no other choice, as if our social practices are necessary, our life fated. Because we suppose a fate, "what is called resignation is confirmed desperation," a "stereotyped but unconscious despair," which precludes testing, to confirm or revise, the case we suppose. Despair is the "inward condition" of which our practices are the external sign, which makes them a diabolical sacrament. We "lead lives of quiet desperation" because this despair is unsaid, unavowed (*Walden*, 273, 5).

Thoreau links fantasy (supposing a case) to despair (supposing no choice is left), and both to "fate," which is "being determined to run on a track." But "man's capacities have never been measured; nor are we to judge of what he can do by any precedent," because "so little has been tried," and because "there are as many ways [to live] as there can be drawn radii from one center." Possibility is untried rather than exhausted, but we are invested in our mistake. "How vigilant we are! Determined not to live by faith if we can avoid it," we "reverence our life" as it is and deny "the possibility of change" (*Walden*, 7–8).

As Cavell says, "The choice is not between belief and unbelief but between faith and idolatry."[23] Thoreau thus speaks in a prophetic mode of address "if only to wake my neighbors up" to the labors by which they hold themselves captive, the choices they could make but do not even see, and the despair that seems safer than change. We hear the urgent intensity in his insistence that we face, every moment, a choice—a "decision"—between sleep or awakening, fate and faith, death-in-life or rebirth-into-life. In a prophetic idiom, he raises *political* questions about the *necessity* of social practices, the *possibility* of living otherwise, and the despair imposing a fate we suppose.

He therefore agrees that "countless reforms are called for"; he too is "sick," not of an "incurable disease" but "of tradition, conformity, and infidelity." But he distances himself from "reformers." Partly, they merely "hack at the branches of evil" rather than "striking at the root," because they do not address the "mode of life" that produces the "misery which they strive in vain to relieve" (*Walden*, 63). In this way he opposes the "sentimental" reform that new elites undertake in schools, prisons, asylums, and family regimes. But partly, Thoreau raises Emerson's and Nietzsche's question about motivation: He seems to make reform—or politics—*only* a displacement of private woe; by redeeming others, reformers would redeem themselves from a disease they can only see as evil or lack in others. For "if anything ail a man, so that he does not perform his functions, especially if his digestion is poor . . . if he has failed in all his undertakings hitherto, if he has committed some heinous sin and partially repents, what does he do? He sets about reforming the world" (*Walden*, 63).

At bottom, resentment animates their moralism: "To [their] eyes the globe itself is a great green apple," and they worry "that the children of men will nibble before it is ripe." Fearful of wayward desire in people they treat as heathens or children, reformers seek social control or normalization. Such projects reek of bad faith: "There is no odor so bad as that which arises from goodness tainted. It is human, it is divine carrion. If I knew for a certainty that a man was coming to my house with the conscious design of doing me good, I should run for my life" (*Walden*, 63, 60).[24]

To inspire our participation in genuine change, a reformer "must not rely solely on logic and argument . . . but see that he represents one pretty perfect institution himself, the center and circumference of all others, an erect man." In this pre-Freudian and self-exposing idiom, an "erect" man exemplifies what he says. But what spirit should embodied words impart?

He should impart his courage and not his despair; his health and ease, not his disease; and take care that this does not spread by contagion. It is rare that we are able to impart wealth to our fellows, and not surround them with our own cast off griefs as an atmosphere, and name it sympathy. . . . Even the prophets and redeemers have consoled the fears rather than satisfied the free demands and hopes of man! We know nowhere recorded a simple and irrepressible satisfaction with the gift of life. (*Walden*, 64)[25]

If "prophets and redeemers" surround us with their own "cast off griefs," they console fears rather than inspire free demands and hopes, imparting despair, not satisfaction with the gift of life. If "moral reform" is a symptom of the larger problem of worldly asceticism, what sort of reform (of reform) can get to those roots? How can reformers, or "prophets and redeemers," motivated by dissatisfaction to bear a critique, still impart satisfaction with the gift of life?

The Persona of Prophet as Poet

Given his view of those who are "said to live" and of self-declared reformers among them, Thoreau carefully specifies his audience:

I do not mean to prescribe rules to strong and valiant natures, who will mind their own affairs whether in heaven or hell . . . ; nor to those who find their encouragement and inspiration precisely in the present condition of things, and cherish it with the fondness and enthusiasm of lovers—and to some extent I reckon myself in this number; I do not speak to those who are well-employed, in whatever circumstances, and they know whether they are well-employed or not; but mainly to the mass of men who are discontented, and idly complaining of the hardness of their lot or of the times, when they might improve them. (*Walden*, 12)

He does not claim to address everyone, but only those who resentfully suffer their lives, a "mass of men" he calls "the poor" in a spiritual sense. He includes himself among those who find their inspiration in the present "to some extent," both to separate himself from those who simply celebrate as progress the "mode of living" he criticizes, and to insist that his criticism is not animated by resentment. What distinguishes the idly complaining and the well-employed is not an ignorance to be remedied but "a want of enterprise and faith." Declaring himself "convinced by both faith and experience that to maintain one's self on earth is not a hardship but a pastime," he creates a carefully crafted persona to awaken people to their despair and to "turn" them toward a faith in possibility (*Walden*, 58, 174, 58).

In this spirit we can hear his epigraph to *Walden*: "I do not propose to write an ode to dejection, but to brag as lustily as chanticleer in the morning . . . if only to wake my neighbors up." He crafts his prophetic persona as a cockerel:

The note of this once wild Indian pheasant is certainly the most remarkable of any bird's, and if they could be naturalized without being domesticated, it would soon become the most famous sound in the woods, surpassing the clangor of the goose and the hooting of the owl. . . . It would put the nations on the alert. Who would not . . . rise earlier and earlier every successive day of his life, till he became unspeakably healthy, wealthy, and wise? This foreign bird's note is celebrated by the poets of all countries along with the notes of their native songsters. All climates agree with brave Chanticleer. He is more indigenous even than the natives. His health is ever good, his lungs are sound, his spirits never flag. (*Walden*, 104)

What does this passage suggest about Thoreau's revised prophecy?

As an affirmative voice linked to poetry, Chanticleer is unlike the owl, the proverbial voice of philosophy, whose wisdom is melancholy, because belated and retrospective, and whose sound ("oh-o-o-o—that I had never been born") bespeaks the despairing lament of Silenus. "I rejoice that there are owls. Let them do the idiotic and maniacal hooting for men" to announce "a vast and undeveloped nature," including "the stark twilight and unsatisfied thoughts which all have" (102–3). But owls do not "brag," and though Thoreau criticizes social entombment, he does not mean to write an ode to dejection.

His critique must impart a spirit that *imitates* Chanticleer, who acclaims "expectation of the dawn":

He is blessed over all mortals who loses no moment of the passing life in remembering the past. Unless our philosophy hears the cock crow . . . it is belated. . . . There is something suggested by [the crowing] that is a newer testament—the gospel according to this moment, a *brag* for all the world, healthiness as a spring burst forth. The merit of this bird's strain is its freedom from all plaintiveness. . . . When I hear a cockerel crow . . . I think to myself, there is one of us well at any rate, and with a sudden gush return to my senses.[26]

Chanticleer announces "a newer testament," a song no longer plaintive because it is not haunted by the past but, like spring and dawn, brags of (faith in) beginnings, renewal, possibility.

Turning to context for a moment will help unpack what Thoreau is doing. His turn to nature bespeaks and carries on a larger shift in Anglo-European culture, from Protestant theism to romanticism. Thoreau enacts this struggle to shift authority from a transcendent, inaccessible deity predestining abject yet striving human beings, to a God immanent in nature and incarnated in human beings. Blake initiates the shift by saying, "God becomes as we are that we may be as he is," so that poetic imagination *is* God incarnated in us. We are not Lockean subjects who passively perceive "external" objects; rather, we envision and love what we behold. Thus can Emerson claim, "The religions of the world are the ejaculations of a few imaginative men." It is but a step to the lusty bragging of Chanticleer, who announces a "living earth" and the poetic imagination to conceive and affirm it.[27]

As romanticism lodges authority in nature, the distinctive human quality becomes poesis, our capacity to make order and meaning through language. Yet a central ambiguity shapes the exalted role of poets. Partly, Alfred Kazin says, "the romantic belief is that poetry would *rescue* religion by *replacing* it."[28] That is, romanticism can "replace" religion by casting redemption as attunement not with God but with an inherent moral order in nature. What George Kateb says of Emerson may be true of Thoreau: "He wants the world to have a reason for its existence, and he wants that reason to be a moral one." Then the redemptive dream of prophetic theodicy becomes the "meaning" poets "reveal" in nature: Their calling is to redeem life by announcing that—and showing how—fragments of experience cohere as a morally purposeful whole. Poetry then "answers" Silenus by appearing to close the gap between words and the world, to end the problem of meaning. But as Emerson also says, poets know we reify our tropes and in our idolatry forget that "language is vehicular and transitive," meant to "flow" not "freeze." Then poets must act as "liberating gods" to free us from "fossilized language" and "mind-forged manacles."[29]

Our first question to Thoreau, then, is, What kind of work does poetry and the persona of Chanticleer do for you? What kind of meaning do you make (and what kind of redemption do you perform) by acclaiming dawn? The broad answer is that poetry works as an antidote to worldly asceticism and to abolitionist prophecy by turning us toward *finitude,* our existence in time, in mortal bodies, and in language. Chanticleer announces not the possibility of "redemption from" these conditions of human life, but the possibility that a human meaning can be wrested from them.

By awakening us to dawn, Chanticleer most of all declares the inexorable passage of *time.* He "answers" the question of meaning not by disclosing an "unchanging ground" outside of time that we can know and orient by, but rather by acknowledging the passage of time, which includes dawn. A symbol of always-available possibility, dawn means that (human) nature includes capacities to awaken and begin anew, and if we are awake to them, we affirm contingency and deny that life takes a necessary course. "The morning, which is the most memorable season of the day, is the awakening hour." Since "morning is when I am awake and there is dawn in me," and since "to be awake is to be alive," so "moral reform is the effort to throw off sleep" (*Walden,* 72–73). Accordingly, he says, "My next experiment was the present," that is, to become "present to" the moment as a groundless ground. Like biblical prophets, then, he makes us wretched and elicits a sense of loss, for we are not in our senses and awake to the present but dead to our life, which is so quickly passing away. Like the prophets, he provokes grief to elicit *mourning,* and so decision. "Our moulting season, like that of the fowls, must be a crisis in our lives. The loon retires to solitary ponds to spend it. Thus also the snake casts its slough, and the caterpillar its wormy coat, by an internal industry and expansion." Shedding an old skin is partly the "internal industry" of mourning; this labor requires that we acknowledge our despair, see it as a choice, and affirm the very possibility of other possibilities as well as our capacity to pursue them.

Chanticleer as poet thus displaces Christian theism while inflecting biblical prophecy. Thoreau announces not a providential design driving our actions, but contingency and decision, which he signifies as a "turning," not to God but to the recurring availability of dawn to the wakeful. Announcing not God's command as moral law but seasons recurring, he imagines change not as the repentance that separates the divine and diabolical, but as grief at loss, which may open us to the inner necessities symbolized by molting an old skin. Announcing not judgment of sin, or even mercy beyond good and evil, but satisfaction with life as a gift that requires no redemption, Chanticleer sustains a prophetic focus on faith but resists the relentlessly moral, deterministic ways it has been conceived.

By rooting faith in sentient bodies capable of throwing off sleep, Chanticleer also awakens people to a *separateness* they disavow. Since it is only by acknowledging this separateness that others can be(come) real to us, however, Chanticleer awakens us from utter loneliness (because no reality is outside) to *reality* as an outside comprised of others and nature. On *Walden*'s first page, Thoreau thus says he requires "of every writer, first or last, a simple and sincere account of his own life, and not merely what he has heard of other men's lives; some such account as he would send to his kindred from a distant land; for if he has lived sincerely, it must have been in a distant land to me." Throughout *Walden*, he calls us "strangers," "indwellers," and "sojourners," to emphasize the pathos of distance that "prophets and redeemers" must accept if they are to avoid bad faith, and that citizens must accept if they are not to insist on unity.[30]

Partly, then, Chanticleer also awakens us to finitude by showing us that we live *in* language, which mediates our relationship to nature and each other. We must "spend our lives in conceiving them," for as we "instill and drench" reality with meaning, the universe "answers our conceptions." Poesis is necessary and generative, for we make the world and ourselves as we make meaning, and Thoreau awakens us to its plural, multivocal, and ambiguous character. "Obscurity," he therefore declares, is "inseparable from the very nature" of his poetic vocation, which must keep texts and life open to interpretation. "It is a ridiculous demand which England and America make, that you shall speak so that they can understand you. . . . As if Nature could support only one order of understandings." Rather, he fears "chiefly lest my expression may not be *extra-vagant* enough . . . to be adequate to the truth of which I have been convinced." He imagines "words addressed to our condition exactly, which, if we could really hear and understand, would be more salutary than the morning or spring to our lives, and possibly put a new aspect on the face of things for us." But he must present "the volatile truth of words" in ways that "continually betray the inadequacy of the residual statement" (*Walden*, 79, 271, 88).[31]

How Thoreau speaks is crucial to *what* he says: He must voice the despair we need to acknowledge, but without confirming it, and he must announce vitality in ways that deter readers from entombing it. He trumpets "satisfaction with the gift of life" precisely by "bragging lustily" about it: He imagines our own capacity to imagine, desire, and affirm being *aroused* as we witness him strut his stuff. By this "lusty" and "bragging" persona, he inflects biblical prophecy in each mode of address. "It is not by compromise, it is not by a timid and feeble repentance, that a man will save his soul and *live*, at last." Indeed, since "the greater part of what my neighbors call good I believe in my soul to be bad . . . if I repent of anything it is very likely to be my good behavior." Using biblical (both prophetic and Christian) idioms, he presents the persona of one who *repents* of bourgeois propriety, and of the rancor and despair that have been inseparable from prophetic judgment of life's injustice. "If I seem to boast more than is becoming, my excuse is that I brag (like chanticleer) for humanity rather than for myself; and my shortcomings and inconsistencies do not affect the truth of my statement. . . . I am resolved that I will not through humility become the devil's attorney" (*Walden*, 40).[32]

Let us here identify further how he uses poetry to inflect prophecy. Clearly, he sees prophecy as a public office requiring self-division "if only" to perform the role of witness and messenger, "to wake my neighbors up." Like his biblical forebears, he deploys appearances in a rhetorical project with a political purpose: to demonstrate the "faith" on which freedom depends. Like them, he creates a persona—and risks charges of hypocrisy—to appear exemplary; by maintaining rhetorical distance from his audience, as if he had overcome the disease he diagnoses in them, he models how they might name and move beyond it. He, too, claims he earned his words and sense of authority in a wilderness experience, but he calls it an experiment and he shows the seams between his art and life. A literary achievement and political performance, his persona disturbs the (idea of) authenticity it seems to affirm.

In answer to our first question about poetry, then, he does not answer the question of life's meaning, though he uses dawn to say that natality inheres in (human) nature. He uses poetry and nature to go behind Calvinist theodicy and recover the contingency and faith in possibility we found in biblical prophecy. But unlike biblical prophecy, therefore, he emphasizes poesis and shifts from judging joint liability to affirming human potential. We feel the intensity in his wish to overcome relentless judgment of fault and failure, even as we also still feel it when he asks, Are you awake? How do you spend—waste—your life? But the change in his *criterion* of judgment—from injustice to flourishing—poses the second key question to put to *Walden:* In turning to poetry and nature, does Thoreau abandon the political dimensions in (even his own abolitionist) prophecy?

Thoreau's texts surely suggest so. After wondering in "Civil Disobedience" whether, from the "highest" perspective, politics may not be "worth looking at or thinking of at all," he adds, "They who know of no purer sources of truth, who have traced up its stream no higher . . . wisely stand by the Bible and the Constitution and drink at it there with reverence and humility," but some "continue their pilgrimage toward its fountainhead" (17). Is this not an aspiration to get beyond politics? Exemplifying a transforming experience in nature, Thoreau's story of cultivation can seem both cut off from and antithetical to politics. It emphasizes affirmation of life rather than judgment of injustice. Despite the radical-sounding social critique in *Walden*'s first chapter, critics argue, his cultivation of private infinitude elevates but still replenishes self-making mythology. He seems to inflate autonomy, personalize difficulty, refuse the claim of social bonds, and disavow the power of history. By linking independence from culture to wilderness regeneration, critics also argue, he in fact replenishes the "poetry" of frontier violence. The terms of his nonconformity confirm a cultural consensus he only appears to question. His romantic language of rebirth, at once individualistic and nationalist, echoes in Ronald Reagan's announcement of "morning in America!" No wonder Bellah invokes Puritanism to chasten this voice, but Bercovitch rightly sees this move as closing a circle we must open.[33]

As Stanley Cavell famously argues, however, the prophetic poet addresses a specific political community, and his narrative of a personal experiment is a parable of refounding it. His Thoreau does not seek a ground beyond culture in nature but depicts ordinary language as our groundless ground. Romanticism moves from God to nature, but his Thoreau invests in language a quasi-transcendental authority: We do not invent the meanings of our words but are accountable to and for them. We do not need to "know" an unchanging ground beyond language, but we need to "front" our life in and by it. By invoking the authority of language and returning us to it, his Thoreau casts prophecy and redemption in nontranscendental terms. Cavell's Thoreau is a prophet, then, because he bears not God's word but ours: "The power he claims for his words is that they are not his." He thus "claims to know what everyone knows" but has disavowed. His prophetic vocation is to "return" us to the ordinary meaning of our words, to enable us to recover our voices and thereby refound our lives singly and together. To show the conditions of life we must acknowledge if we are to *live,* he "must assume the condition of language as such . . . until the nation is capable of serious speech again." This "literary redemption of language" also "requires a redemption of the lives we live" by it. Accordingly, he withholds his "consent both from society so-called and from . . . conspiracies of despairing silence which prevent that society from becoming his, or anyone's. The refusal is not in fact though it is in depiction a withdrawal; it is a confrontation, a return, a constant turning on his neighbors."[34]

Like his biblical forebears, Thoreau voices the unsaid, in this case, the "quiet desperation" haunting a culture celebrating self-making, but he does not mean to write an ode to dejection, because acknowledgment is the condition of acting otherwise. Addressing already-formed adults who require, not bonds of familiarity by which to grow up, but estrangement and self-reflection, he narrates a textual experiment that models judgment of the practices they have inherited and the ideas they have taken inside. By a *performance* of withdrawal, and in the textual space it creates, he thaws frozen assumptions—about property and labor, identity and conscience, faith and consent—that make the world seem fated. If severed from this prophetic "turning" on neighbors, his story of cultivation does seem like mere withdrawal. But in literary form and personal terms he provokes a critical political dialogue foreclosed in the world beyond the text. Critics of his antipolitics misread—read literally—a parable of political education in prophetic form.

Building on but in contrast to Cavell, however, I would foreground the fact that Thoreau "returns" people to the ordinary not (only) as the fact of language and living in it but also as the central *myths* of his culture and as racial violence. His Chanticleer announces dawn not anywhere but to a nation whose self-declared errand into a wilderness promises independence from Old World despotism but yields slavery, genocide, and, among the enfranchised, voluntary subjection. How can he not compose an ode to dejection? To what possibilities in *this* place and history could his neighbors awaken? By relating the meaning of wilderness in national and prophetic idioms, he recasts a myth of wilderness regeneration in politicizing, albeit problematic, ways.

Prophecy, Wilderness, and Experiment

Thoreau aspires to rival Homer, "a poet who . . . nailed words to their primitive senses . . . transplanted them to his page with earth adhering to their roots. . . . You will perceive that I demand something which . . . no culture, in short, can give. Mythology comes nearer to it than anything." Poetry, like Blakean prophecy, does not announce God's design but harvests words as if for the first time, the earth of life still clinging to their roots. Not as doctrine but as myth, poetry supersedes (because it precedes) what is called religion. "Poetry" names his aspiration to make what Norman Mailer calls a "myth sufficiently true to offer a life adequately large."[35]

  If we attend to Thoreau's testimony as narrative, he declares independence by moving to a "wilderness" space, but there he reinhabits history and redoes it, partly by retelling national myths about it. He critically reenacts the nation-building myth of an "experiment" in democracy undertaken by people declaring independence of Old World forms. His experiment occurs not privately but as a public demonstration of a proposition, visible to all and subject to failure. Like biblical prophets and Puritans, therefore, Thoreau depicts people who believe they bear a special project but who have betrayed it by the way they have practiced it. Puritanism is crucial to this problem because white heirs sustain not its example of faith in possibility but the instrumental rationality it bequeaths. For Thoreau, Puritanism survives only as what the poet William Carlos Williams later calls a "spiritually withering plague" that anxiously separates soul from body, property from nature, citizen from corporeal being, white from red and black. In response, Thoreau enacts what Williams calls a "descent to the ground of desire" in the body, place, and history. Redoing (and retelling) such a wilderness experiment will bear fruit. But how?[36]

  Partly, Thoreau redoes a history in which "declaring independence" and withholding consent are crucial tropes, first principles, and democratic practices to model and revive. By claiming to begin "by accident" on July 4, he denies providential authorization of the nation and makes political identity into an "accident" whose meaning depends on our poe-

sis, and so a project, enacted in time, subject to risk, change, and failure. Partly, therefore, he begins in wilderness: As in biblical prophecy,
"wilderness" denotes a liminal space between old and new, a space of
contingent possibility, a space of transformation and so of commitment
or covenant, a space of cultivating or preparing for action, and in each
sense a place of loss, anticipation, and terror. Just as Puritans sought
a "wilderness condition" of crisis and choice, to relinquish Egypt and
seek a promised land, so Thoreau invokes wilderness as an experiment
in testing limits and possibility. To "front the essential facts of life" he
experiments in building a house and hoeing beans: If one experiments
in housing rather than entombing the spirit, and the other experiments
in cultivating virtues, each relates the artful and the wild, and both are
metaphors to reimagine citizenship. He takes up, as an "experiment,"
the two tropes—of "house" and "vineyard"—by which biblical prophecy
imagines community.[37]

Accordingly, the "founding" episode in Thoreau's wilderness experiment is not declaring independence but building a house: Every Hebrew prophet addresses the "the house of Jacob" because house (like
family) is a trope for community, but house (unlike family) connotes
world building to "house" passing generations. "Independence" is a
negative space, but freedom means building a house and fashioning
new inhabitants for it. But the danger in building is clear: Echoing prophetic critiques of settlement and temple as a return to Egypt, Thoreau
sees that "most of the stone a nation hammers goes toward its tomb only.
It buries itself alive." The "sentimental reformer," who begins "at the
cornice not the foundation," redecorates a tomb (*Walden*, 37). Can we
build otherwise?

Better to see a dwelling "gradually grow from within outward, out
of the necessities and character of the *indweller* who is the only builder."
Who is that? How is that to build?

Drive a nail home and clinch it so faithfully that you can wake up in the night
and think of your work with satisfaction,—a work at which you would not be
ashamed to invoke the Muse. So will help you God, and so only. Every nail
driven should be as another rivet in the machine of the universe, you carrying
on the work. (*Walden*, 275)[38]

What then is the political meaning of "indwelling?" Partly, as Cavell
translates Thoreau: "Education for citizenship is education in isolation."
Arendt affirms this truth: "Solitude" is "thought to be the habitus of the
philosopher only" and "suspected by the polis of being anti-political,"

but it "is on the contrary the necessary condition for [its] good functioning, a better guarantee than rules of behavior enforced by laws and fear of punishment." Why? "Only he who knows how to live with himself is fit to live with others," she answers. Self-reflection enables political judgment of worldly authority, and citizens who live with(in) themselves do not demand unity. "I would not have any one adopt *my* mode of living on any account," Thoreau says, for, he says, he desires "that there be as many different persons in the world as possible," each pursuing "*his own* way, and not his father's or his mother's or his neighbor's instead." Yet "to act collectively is according to the spirit of our institutions" because we must build a *house* that both reflects and fosters this plurality (*Walden*, 58, 90).[39]

The other founding act and political metaphor in Thoreau's experiment is growing food, the labor of cultivation to "make the earth say beans instead of grass." By hoeing beans he asks, How do we produce our necessities? What do we cultivate in ourselves and others by our labors? Biblical prophets depict a vineyard planted by God to cultivate people who flourish because they are just, and Thoreau asks, "What shall a state like Virginia say for itself at the last day" if "slaves and tobacco have been its staple productions? What ground is there for patriotism in such a State?" But Jeremiah's God laments that a noble vine became a "degenerate plant," as if willfully ruining itself, while for Thoreau human beings are both cultivators and cultivated, and the experiment easily goes awry. If our "chief want" is "high and earnest purpose" rather than "potatoes," however, our "staple production is not slaves or operatives, but men—those rare fruits called heroes, saints, poets, philosophers, and redeemers"—who address the question of their purpose rather than unthinkingly serving another's purpose.[40]

Thoreau himself labors to grow beans, but they are also a writer's metaphor. He cultivates "tropes," he says, "to serve a parable-maker one day," and *Walden* is the parable he makes: His engagement with nature is a labor to "elevate life by conscious endeavor." To clear ground, to *make* the earth say beans by weeding, is to display poesis and its redemptive power. Partly, redemption *is* the literal agriculture of clearing nature; to reclaim anything *for us* is to redeem it by making it worthwhile. Partly, such worldly labor should cultivate virtue, which requires willful "weeding" to assert distinctions of value and engender some goods rather than others. Cultivation is political because such distinctions are subject to contest and failure. Indeed, he despairs that his seeds and tropes will yield no harvest of virtues: "Alas! I said this to myself; but now another summer is gone, and another, and another, and I am obliged to say to you, Reader, that the seeds which I planted, if indeed they *were* the seeds of those virtues . . . did not come up" (*Walden,* 135).[41]

Having asked prophetic questions about the fruits of our labor, he echoes Jeremiah's lament: "The harvest is past, the summer is ended, and we are not saved" (Jer. 8:20). But Thoreau does not mean to write an ode to dejection, and he needs to affirm the possibility of future harvest. He therefore reworks Jeremiah's claim that a remnant will be redeemed by a merciful God, and by a new covenant that enables them to build and plant differently than before. Rather than invoke a God invested in possibility, Thoreau anchors possibility in nature and its cycles; indeed, he poeticizes the meaning of "spring" to affirm the ways that human beings *naturally* engage in transformation and form giving. In contrast to the futural dimensions of biblical prophecy, which projects renewal in linear time, he affirms human poesis by depicting the recurring, violent, and creative transformation of a muddy hillside in spring. Does this myth making simply evade a political crisis around slavery, or does it in some ways enable engagement with it?

Myth and Politics

Awed by flowing mud and emerging foliage, he says, "I am affected as if I stood in the laboratory of the Artist who made the world and me." Witnessing "the creation of cosmos out of chaos," he declares, "no wonder that the earth expresses itself outwards in leaves, it so labors with the idea inwardly." As "the lumpish grub in the earth" becomes an "airy" butterfly, "the very globe continually transcends and translates itself, and becomes winged in its orbit." Inwardly driving all forms, including human institutions, are "somewhat excrementitious" energies, which "suggests that nature has some bowels, and there again is mother of humanity" (*Walden,* 255, 262, 256, 257). Struck that man "is but a mass of thawing clay," he announces, "There is nothing inorganic":

The earth is not a fragment of dead history, stratum upon stratum like the leaves of a book, to be studied by geologists and antiquarians chiefly, but living poetry like the leaves of a tree, which precede flowers and fruit—not a fossil earth, but a living earth. . . . You may melt your metals and cast them into the most beautiful molds you can; they will never excite me like the forms which this molten earth flows out into. And not only it, but the institutions upon it are plastic like clay in the hands of the potter. (*Walden,* 258)

The God of Isaiah or Jeremiah is a potter entitled to smash his creations, a creator who stands outside and struggles with the recalcitrant
agency of his creations. In Thoreau's spring, a mother-earth engenders
"forms" from within. Institutions and cultures should be such forms,
produced from inside out by our "labors," but instead are tombs, frozen
in time. If we create this "winter," we must undergo "a crisis in our lives"
he calls a thawing spring: Such a crisis impelled him to the experiments
in fashioning the faith he now bears. Nature teaches just this overcoming: Spring signals the capacity of nature, and of humans as "part and
parcel of nature," for renewal, or redemption.

Ambiguously situated between "renewal" of life and "rebirth" into
new life, spring symbolizes generative human capacity in a universe that
fosters and receives it. Accordingly, Thoreau also links spring to mutual
forgiveness of the sins that tie us to the past and to rancor. On a "spring
morning . . . even the vilest sinner may return" to community with us,
because we sense in each other "even a savor of holiness groping for
expression, blindly and ineffectually perhaps, like a new-born instinct."
By this jubilee we suspend moral categories and annul the power of the
past, which have ruled the present; by relinquishing judgment and despair, we foster a second innocence. If worldly asceticism constitutes a
self that is contemptible unless redeemed and is redeemed only by self-
denying labor as penance, then redemption from redemption means
overcoming this very moralism. Accordingly, he also affirms violence
and death: "Nature is so rife with life that myriads can be . . . sacrificed
and suffered to prey on one another. . . . The impression made on a wise
man is of universal innocence" (*Walden*, 262–63, 265). Spring shows
that there is no waste; no aspect of life is without value.[42]

Correspondingly, spring symbolizes the "larval" character of social
life. In *Walden*'s last image, Thoreau repeats the story of "a strong and
beautiful bug which came out of the dry leaf of an old table . . . which
had stood in a farmer's kitchen for 60 years." "Who does not feel his faith
in resurrection and immortality strengthened by hearing of this? Who
knows what beautiful and winged life, whose egg has been buried for
ages under many concentric layers of woodenness in the dead dry life of
society," may emerge from its "well-seasoned tomb" to "enjoy its perfect
summer life at last!" No mere lapse of time can make this morning dawn.
"Only that day dawns to which we are awake." But always, "There is more
day to dawn. The sun is but a morning star" (278).

By using poetic imagination and a myth of wilderness, Thoreau fashions a countercultural ethos to resist worldly asceticism and models an experiment in founding a community whose "staple production" is indwellers and citizens. To resist entombment and foster creativity, he also believes, citizens need a myth sufficiently true to offer a life adequately large, and he aspires to create it. But his faith—that possibility is written into (human) nature—is vulnerable to charges of false prophecy.

Herman Melville could be referring to Thoreau when he says, "Say what some poets will, Nature is not so much her own ever-sweet interpreter as the mere supplier of that cunning alphabet, where by selecting and combining as he pleases, each man reads his own lesson." Melville also refuses any vision of universal innocence because human evil bespeaks *depravity* in nature: "All deified nature absolutely paints like the harlot, whose allurements cover nothing but the charnel-house within." That is why Captain Ahab's effort to get at the truth of reality, by striking through the visible appearances he calls a "pasteboard mask," results in apocalyptic self-destruction. Apocalypse, or unveiling, reveals not Christ's coming or earth's beneficent bowels but horror, and our only defense against it is the fragile artifice we call culture. We must affirm the realm of appearances, Melville's story implies, for the (romantic) effort to disclose a truth beneath it will destroy the world.[43]

Like Captain Ahab, Thoreau seeks the "truth" of reality, but to heal Ahabian resentment and restore trust in appearances. In depiction he turns toward nature, but as Cavell rightly sees, Thoreau turns us from skepticism (despair, metaphysics, or "the case we suppose") to the ordinary, to ourselves and our words. He lodges redemption in that turn, in experiences of wildness and spring, and in experiments with building and cultivating. To risk such experiments and surrender to such experiences, however, does require a faith in redemption—say, in the possibility of change or natality—that Melville warns against and refuses.[44]

In *Walden,* Thoreau stands at an avowed remove from both slavery and abolitionist antislavery, but to create a broader form of self-reflection about forms of subjection other than chattel slavery and about the possibility of confronting them. Against Melville, he thinks his myth is "sufficiently true" because in it, worldly asceticism, racial domination, and political captivity—but also capacities for action and overcoming—become "facts" we deny at great cost. He hopes his myth offers "a life adequately large" because an experiment in "fronting" these facts opens people's purposes and practices to question, because such experiments change participants and the world in ways not knowable in advance, because such changes put assumptions and attachments at risk, and because such risks ennoble their bearers.

Still, if the facts of slavery and northern complicity call forth this mythic recasting of prophecy, it cannot redeem him or his neighbors. Chanticleer announces the dawn, but Thoreau awakens every day to the slavery and violence he and his neighbors authorize or allow. His vision of always-available renewal, indeed, only intensifies his rage. A month before *Walden* appears, he delivers "Slavery in Massachusetts" to condemn the Fugitive Slave Act at the July 4, 1854, rally protesting Burns's deportation. No enraptured portrait of "somewhat excrementitious" nature, his speech judges a people who dwell "wholly within hell" ("Slavery," 29).

Before the state "deliberately" sent an innocent man to slavery, "I dwelt in the illusion that my life passed somewhere only between heaven and hell," but now he thinks otherwise: "Suppose you had a small library [to] contemplate scientific and literary pursuits, and discover that [it] is located in hell. . . . do not these things suddenly lose their value in your eyes?" Because "life itself" is "worth less, all things with it, which minister to it, are worth less," which means "I found that hollow which even I had relied upon for solid." He can no more celebrate the redemptive meaning of art in hell than his peers can celebrate liberty while in jail. Nature and art—even projects to cultivate "freer and less desponding spirits" to stand against the state—cannot free him from or console him for the nationalization of a slave regime. "I am surprised to see men going about their business as if nothing had happened." Don't they know that "all beneficent harvests fail as you approach the empire of hell"? Subject to a devaluation no person can escape or enterprise redeem, he rejects the pastoral flight attributed to him: "I walk toward one of our ponds, but what signifies the beauty of nature . . . in a country where both rulers and ruled are without principle?" Politics is inescapable: "It is not an era of repose. We have used up all our inherited freedom." To "save our lives, we must fight for them" ("Slavery," 29–30).

Still, he ends his speech by meditating on a water lily: "It is the emblem of purity . . . as if to show us what purity and sweetness reside in and can be extracted from the slime and muck of the earth. . . . What confirmation of our hopes is in the fragrance of this flower! I shall not so soon despair of the world for it, notwithstanding slavery, and the cowardice and want of principle of Northern men." But he cannot decide how to relate the flower and the slime. He says the lily is "extracted" from the slime, but also "the sweet and pure and innocent are wholly sundered from the obscene and baleful." He struggles with his metaphor:

The foul slime stands for the sloth and vice of man . . . the fragrant flower that springs from it, for the purity and courage which are immortal. Slavery and servility have produced no sweet-scented flower annually, to charm the senses of men, for they have no real life: they are merely a decaying and death, offensive to all healthy nostrils. We do not complain that they *live* but that they do not *get buried*. Let the living bury them; even they are good for manure. ("Slavery," 30)

When the "bowels" of the earth are a "somewhat excrementitious" womb of all living forms, he joins what he "wholly" sunders here. For he cannot fold slavery into a story of rebirth as he folds death and excrement into his story of spring. Slavery and servility cannot be redeemed, for they produce no valuable fruit; they yield the blessing of more life only if and as we bury them.

Five years later, though, John Brown exemplifies the virtuous action that, by burying servility, enables Thoreau to appreciate the sweetness of the lily. Brown's example leads him to assure his audience—contrary to his worry in *Walden*—that "in the moral world, when good seed is planted, good fruit is inevitable, and does not depend on your watering and cultivating; when you plant, or bury, a hero in this field, a crop of heroes is sure to spring up. This is a seed of such force and vitality that it does not ask our leave to germinate" ("Plea," 36).

John Brown, Redemption, and Violence

Brown's raid on Harpers Ferry in October 1859 was not just a "violent act" but a "cultural event," says David Reynolds in the best recent account of Brown's life and the meaning of his raid. Reynolds shows how northern public opinion was universally hostile to Brown at first. No abolitionists defended him at first; it was the New England transcendentalists' speech making that "rescued him from infamy and possible oblivion." Indeed, their words transformed northern public opinion, which southern "fire-eaters" cited as justification for secession. Though the Republican Party responded to this polarization by nominating the moderate Lincoln over the more radical William Seward, northern support for Brown encouraged Southerners to secede. By recasting the meaning of the raid, the transcendentalists played a crucial political role in beginning the Civil War. And Thoreau was "the earliest and boldest" in his defense of Brown; at first only he "took the risk of publicly defending the 'insane' Brown and his 'deluded' followers."[45]

According to Reynolds, Thoreau himself organized a lecture in defense of Brown, rebuffing the local Republican Party committee and local abolitionist society, which asked him not to. Thoreau also asked friends to arrange venues in Worcester and in Boston, where he spoke in the first week of November. According to Thoreau scholar Bob Pepperman Taylor, Thoreau "was asked to stand in for Frederick Douglass, who had fled the country under suspicion that he was implicated in the attack on Harpers Ferry." Whether Thoreau volunteered or was nominated, he experienced a call and answered it. In its review, Garrison's newspaper the *Boston Liberator* was sarcastic: "This exciting theme seems to have awakened the 'hermit of Concord' from his usual state of philosophical indifference." But Thoreau's speech was reprinted in newspapers and reached a large audience. "Just as important," Reynolds argues, "it roused to Brown's defense" the "intellectual leaders" around Thoreau, "notably Emerson, who had huge cultural clout." Indeed, Thoreau initiated the arguments and images that Emerson and others reworked to considerable cultural and political effect, making John Brown central to the iconography and music of the Civil War period and beyond.[46]

How are we to understand the meaning of Thoreau's defense—or idealization—of Brown? That depends partly on how we view the political circumstances at this moment. The space of political debate is closing down by 1859, especially after the 1857 Dred Scott decision. The limited Republican Party platform profoundly disappoints most abolitionists, but virtually none accepts Brown's key political claim, that slavery can be ended only by violence. As he said from the gallows: "I John Brown am now certain that the crimes of this guilty land will never be purged away but with blood. I had as I now think vainly flattered myself that without *very* much bloodshed it might be done."[47] Abolitionists attacked Brown because they endorsed, not Lincoln's compromise, but a continuing project of moral suasion. But behind Brown's denial that moral suasion could eliminate slavery, Lawrie Balfour argues, was his "understanding of the gap in perception about the moral and political implications of the institution." She adds, "Brown realized that the complex of interests, prejudices, and fear that preserved slavery was not susceptible to dissolution through reasoned debate." In effect, abolitionist critics demonized his violence to prop up a "pious hope that slavery could have been eliminated without bloodshed." Debates over Brown even today signal such assumptions about the efficacy of speech and persuasion in politics.[48]

Thoreau's defense reflects his arguably correct view—also the view of Frederick Douglass—that the only choice for antislavery whites was between acquiescing to a "slave power" bent on nationalization and resisting it with force. But Thoreau goes beyond arguing the necessity of violence to celebrating Brown's nobility and self-sacrifice. In important ways, Thoreau is deeply attracted not only to Brown's political clear-sightedness but to his example of devotion to a cause, of wholeheartedly enacting egalitarian ideals at risk to his mortal life. Thoreau shares Brown's abolitionist orthodoxy and his conviction that unless faith was embodied in action, life was lived in bad faith. Thoreau may have been moved by Brown, then, partly by a sense of shame that his life was about words rather than action. In crucial ways, then, Brown appears as Thoreau's own idealized persona, and by rescuing Brown from infamy he vindicates himself.

Yet I think he also enacts a disturbing reversal, as if he sacrifices crucial parts of himself to that defense. Unlike in "Civil Disobedience," his 1848 lament that the state crucifies "heroes and redeemers" it should value, he *seeks* Brown's martyrdom. Depicting a Christ whose immortality depends on chosen death, not on "irrepressible satisfaction at the gift of life," Thoreau's prophetic voice celebrates not joy but sublime sacrifice to and for a cause. *Walden* ends with an image of rebirth, but his John Brown lectures produce redemption by crucifixion. Does he sunder the tensions—between the good and the wild, the right and the artful, speech and action—that characterize his revision of prophecy? Yet we also must say that Thoreau's "wilderness experience" has prepared him to respond to Brown's deed, and his literary art enables him to immortalize it. Even still, to complete the circle, Brown's critics say Thoreau immortalizes holy terrorism.

In one dimension, the meaning of Brown is highly contested and intensely charged in ways that reflect the meaning of race in American history and life. For as Russell Banks writes, Brown "stands more exactly than any other white American on the line that divides our historical imagination. To almost all Americans who regard themselves as white, John Brown was a madman, a fanatic (in spite of his good intentions, some add). To Americans who do not view themselves as white, he was and will always be a hero of the first order." This "clash between historical narratives" marks "the presence of origin myths at war," which bespeak conflicting social positioning and histories and which inflect every response to slavery—and its continuing legacy. There is no innocent reading of John Brown.[49]

In turn, one tradition of political commentary demonizes Brown as a "type," an "armed prophet," a fanatic ideologue armed with self-righteousness and literal weapons he feels authorized to use. He chooses violence *rather than* dialogue *because* he claims divine sanction. Claiming that God "is no respecter of persons" and expects us to oppose slavery, Brown not only announces God's judgment of slavery but enacts its punishment as God's instrument. Because transcendental authority and moral absolutes *inherently* entail self-righteous dogmatism, which in turn *necessarily* generates violence in the name of redemption, "prophecy" is said to foreclose a democratic politics.[50]

Emerson reports Brown saying, "Better that a whole generation of men, women and children should pass away by a violent death, than that a word of [the Bible and the Declaration of Independence] should be violated in this country." In his Cooper Union speech, Lincoln responds that the wrong of slavery does not "excuse violence, bloodshed, and treason. It could avail [Brown] nothing that he might think himself right." Weighing consequences more than intentions and valuing constitutional forms to resolve conflict peacefully, Lincoln lives between ideals and conduct—the space of politics, many say—whereas Brown sees the political as a form of corruption and wars with complex, morally impure—because inherited and mediated—social practices. At issue is his literal violence, but also a heroic (and so patriarchal) model of politics, which inflates individual personality and great deeds and devalues quotidian forms of courage.[51]

But there is another tradition of interpretation, which Thoreau initiated. At first only he defended Brown publicly, but his language is ramified by Douglass and Wendell Phillips, echoed by Emerson, then reworked by Eugene V. Debs and W. E. B. Du Bois fifty years later and by James Baldwin fifty years after that. They credit, first, that equality for him was not a theoretical stance but a daily practice: He departed from most abolitionists in believing as fervently in full racial equality as in antislavery, and he lived a racially integrated life in ways that remain exceptional.[52] Second, he recognized—Reynolds says prophetically—that violence would be necessary to overcome slavery. Third, Brown is cast as a hero because he risks his own life in the service of high ideals and a noble cause—to free blacks from slavery, to free whites from complicity in gross injustice, and so to free a whole nation from its founding crime. Hearing these voices may help us discern what is generative, and not only troubling, in Thoreau's inaugural arguments.[53]

By 1859, Douglass had revised abolitionism to sanction both the party politics and the violence that Garrison had rejected. Douglass no longer condemned the Constitution. "Slavery lives in this country not because of any paper constitution, but in the moral blindness of the American people, who persuade themselves that they are safe, though the rights of others be struck down." Rejecting Garrisonian disunion, he entered party politics to confront this blindness and build political support for using federal power against slavery. Since "slave-holders ruled the American government for the last fifty years" and "made the Constitution bend to the purposes of slavery," the solution is "to let the North now make that instrument bend to the cause of freedom and justice." To that end, "the ballot is needed and if this will not be heeded, then the bullet."[54] "Anti-slavery men should vote" for antislavery candidates and laws, but "when a slave is to be snatched from a kidnapper, physical force is needed, and he who gives it proves himself a more useful anti-slavery man than he who . . . contents himself by talking of a 'sword of the spirit.'" Asserting a slave's right to violently resist tyranny, Douglass had no *moral* qualms about Brown's act. Indeed, he credits Brown with persuading him that war was needed to end slavery. Still, Douglass refused Brown's invitation to join the raid because he believed it would fail: Slaves would see Brown "as a man of words trying to be a man of deeds, and they would not follow him."[55]

Yet afterward, Douglass argues that the raid, "though apparently unavailing," is profoundly effective:

He has attacked slavery with weapons precisely adopted to bring it to the death. Moral considerations have long since been exhausted on the slaveholders. It is in vain to reason with them. . . . Slavery is a system of brute force. . . . It must be met with its own weapons . . . and his blow has sent dread and terror throughout the entire ranks of the piratical army of slavery. His daring deed may cost him his life, but . . . the blow he has struck . . . will prove to be worth its mighty cost.[56]

Douglass uses the image of Samson to depict this blow: "He has laid his hands upon the pillars of this great national temple of cruelty and blood, and when he falls, that temple will speedily crumble to its final doom, burying its denizens in the ruins." As Samson had betrayed his God with Delilah but redeemed himself by this last act of self-sacrifice, so Brown is an exemplary white citizen. He redeems his own complicity in sin by redeeming his nation from its worship of false gods in the temple of slavery, though many will be buried in its ruins.[57]

As if to clarify Douglass's metaphor, James Baldwin later asserts that Brown's goal was "not to liberate black slaves but to liberate a whole *country* from a disastrous way of life. And as horrible as it may sound," Baldwin therefore adds, his raid "was an act of love"—by living the Golden Rule in relation to those in bondage and as "a soul-saving gift to *white* America." Because he bears witness against injustice and its penalty on whites, testifies that the future of the Republic depends on overcoming white supremacy, and stakes his own life on this redemption, says Baldwin, he is "a great American prophet."[58]

Brown's defenders weave his meaning from strategic argument and a poetry of *sublime* sacrifice, as devotion to a just cause, righteous violence, and self-sacrifice are joined to compose a story of political redemption. Though the symbolism of Moses and Christ is pervasive in a biblical culture, Thoreau's use of these tropes does literally prefigure the "patriotic gore" that soon authorizes and then seeks to redeem the violence of the Civil War. In turn, Eugene Debs worries that "history may be searched in vain for an example of noble heroism and sublime self-sacrifice equal to that of old John Brown," for "who shall be the John Brown of Wage-Slavery?" Despite overt national division over John Brown's body, then, we can see why Bercovitch finds in every defense of Brown—beginning with Thoreau's claim that he is "the most American of us all"—a "ritual of consensus" that sustains a "mythos of revolution" as an *American* promise.[59]

Turn now to how Thoreau's speeches announce and invest these themes with meanings specific to his sense of his own prophetic vocation and of its crisis. At issue is Thoreau's view not only of the necessity of violence but of its meaning. On the one hand, he depicts Brown's violent self-sacrifice as a "sublime spectacle" that promises to *awaken* the North, and he depicts violence against slavery as a redemptive form of self-sacrifice for a higher democratic cause ("Plea," 44). On the other hand, Thoreau, like Lincoln at Gettysburg, credits the power of language to conceive and immortalize the spectacle of action that humbles it. In both regards Thoreau at once completes and endangers his poetic revision of prophecy.[60]

His speech is instantly stunning because it reverses his usual flow of attention: Comparing Brown to a "meteor . . . flashing through the darkness in which we live," he declares, "I know of nothing so miraculous in our history." Though "I commonly attend more to nature than to man," he notes, "I was so absorbed in him as to be surprised whenever I detected the routine of the natural world surviving still or met persons going about their affairs indifferent" ("Last Days," 145). The raid and imminent hanging are a "sublime spectacle" that disrupts the ordinary and gives access to transcendence. A darkened, prosaic world is illuminated suddenly by a *human deed* working like *dawn,* each a "transcendental" intrusion that reveals the death-in-life of those "said to live" as "Christians" and "free men"; the raid and the hanging are redemptive because each reveals the capacity of men to act otherwise. But no dawn occurs unless we are awake: Just as those lacking virtue cannot smell the lily, so the North cannot perceive, even denies, the meaning of Brown's raid. Alone in his receptivity, Thoreau feels called to awaken people to the miraculous event.

Brown's raid was universally condemned in the North on grounds of principle and practice. Horace Greeley voiced what was common opinion as well as Republican Party opinion: On the one hand, freeing slaves could be effected best by "quiet diffusion of the sentiments of humanity" without "an outbreak of violence"; on the other hand, Brown was a "monomaniac" and, as the Pottawatomie massacres show, a bloodthirsty murderer.[61] To reverse public opinion Thoreau determines to redeem Brown—by casting him as a redeemer. That means stating "the facts" that those bred in politics disavow:

The slave-ship is on her way, crowded with its dying victims. . . . A small crew of slave holders, countenanced by a large body of passengers, is smothering four millions under the hatches and yet the politician asserts that the only proper way by which deliverance is to be obtained is by "the quiet diffusion of the sentiments of humanity without any outbreak . . . ." What is that I hear cast overboard? The bodies of the dead that have found deliverance. That is the way we are "diffusing" humanity, and its sentiments with it. ("Plea," 39)

Depicting the American Republic as a slave ship, he exposes the centrality of violence to an unjust regime. The "United States" is a "tyrant holding fettered four million slaves" while meanwhile preserving "the so-called peace of our community by deeds of petty violence every day. Look at the policeman's billy and handcuffs! Look at the jail! Look at the gallows! . . . We are hoping only to live safely on the outskirts of this provisional army. So we defend ourselves and our hen-roosts, and maintain slavery" ("Plea," 45).

Against this tyranny, an alternate "society" has emerged to "save all

the fugitive slaves that run to us, and protect our colored fellow-citizens."
He evokes a parallel polis: "The only free road, the Underground Railroad, is owned and managed" by "Vigilant Committees" that have "tun-
neled under the whole breadth of the land." But why do his abolitionist
allies repudiate Brown? Speaking of them, Thoreau says, "We aspire to
be something more than stupid and timid chattels, pretending to read
history and our Bibles, but desecrating every house and every day we
breathe." His gross conflation of northern docility and black enslavement seems fueled by shame at his own passivity. For "our foe" is not a
master treating us as chattel, nor is it the Slave Power as a worldly adversary, but a "universal woodenness . . . [and] want of vitality in man," on
which he blames "bigotry, persecution, and slavery of all kinds." What
causes these? "The curse is the worship of idols, which at last changes
the worshiper into a stone image of himself" ("Plea," 44, 35, 37). Race
and property are the great idols, and the "penalty" of idolatry is dead-
ness, which explains why Brown is seen only as a madman. But reversing
the accusations reveals an idealization whose penalty we also need to
consider.

Brown is called insane, a "monomaniac," because he "thought he
was appointed to do this work, as if it were impossible that a man could
be divinely appointed in these days to do any work whatsoever—as if
vows and religion were out of date . . . as if the agent to abolish slavery could only be appointed by the president or some political party."
Thoreau locates Brown in a lineage of New England antinomians, who
authorize themselves by claiming commission from God. Because he
"set up no graven image between himself and his God" he can rebel
against the idolatry of worldly authority. His "resistance to tyranny here
below" is called "high treason," but he is right that his act bespeaks "the
power that makes and forever recreates man" ("Plea," 46, 37, 43). Brown
thus joins "a class of whom we hear a great deal" but never see:

The Puritans. It would be in vain to kill him. He died lately in the time of
Cromwell, but he reappeared here. Why should he not? Some of the Puritan
stock *are said* to have come over and settled in New England. They were a class
that did something else than celebrate their forefather's day. . . . They were
neither Democrats nor Republicans, but men of simple habits, straightforward,
prayerful, not thinking much of rulers who did not fear God, not making many
compromises, nor seeking after available candidates. ("Plea," 32–33)

Brown also belongs with the heroes of 1776, though he "was firmer and
higher principled" because "they could bravely face their country's foes,

but he had the courage to face his country herself when she was in the wrong." He is "the most American of us all" because no one else "ever stood up so persistently and effectively for the dignity of human nature, knowing himself for a man, and the equal of any and all governments" ("Plea," 32, 40).

What defines this lineage? *Devotion to a cause.* Brown was "a transcendentalist above all, a man of ideas and principles—that was what distinguished him. Not yielding to a whim or transient impulse, but carrying out the purpose of a life." Comparing the "cause this man devoted himself to, and how religiously," to the cause his critics serve, "I see they are as far apart as heaven and earth are asunder." Brown, because of his passionate vocation, "did not value his bodily life in comparison with ideal things." Just as action from principle "divides the diabolical from the divine," so Brown "shows himself superior to nature"—including his own mortal life—because "he has a spark of divinity in him." By witnessing his devotion, "we are lifted out of the trivialness and dust of politics into the realm of truth and manhood" ("Plea," 33, 46, 40).

Thoreau imagines an (armed) prophet enacting the Protestant (and masculinized) idea of vocation as devotion to a cause. Prophecy is neither prediction nor poetic vision but Weber's "ethical righteousness of deeds." Brown is an "embodiment of principle, who actually carried out the golden rule" by opposing slavery. But doesn't violence deny that rule? Because slavery violates God's moral law, "a man has a perfect right to interfere by force with the slaveholder . . . to rescue the slave." Thoreau grants that "they who are continually shocked by slavery have some right to be shocked by the violent death of slave-holders," but whatever method "quickest succeeds to liberate the slaves" is best. Most of "my countrymen think that the only righteous use that can be made of Sharpe's rifles . . . is to fight duels with them when we are insulted by other nations, or to hunt Indians, or shoot fugitive slaves," but "I think for once the Sharpe's rifles . . . were employed in a righteous cause." The question therefore "is not about the weapon, but the spirit in which you use it" ("Plea," 45).

Thoreau recasts Brown's monomania as devotion to a cause, and he makes the "rightness" of violence politically contingent rather than morally absolute. He also addresses the second charge: "Many condemn these men because they were so few" and because they "failed" to free any slaves or the nation from slavery, while getting themselves killed. Of course Thoreau never devalues a minority view: "When were the good and the brave ever not a minority?" And he recasts what we count as success: a life lived by fidelity to its "polestar" and "religiously," by passionate commitment ("Plea," 44). Thoreau believes he is validating *his own* ideal of life by defending Brown, but he wants to say that it is *effective* in the world. How is apparent failure transcendent triumph? Brown's sublime example can *regenerate* northern citizens.

Partly, Thoreau repeats Brown's speech, as if to channel Brown's firm persuasion: I was sent not by man but by "my own prompting and that of my maker," for "I think you [slaveholders] are guilty of a great wrong against God and humanity, and it would be perfectly right to interfere with you so far as to free those you willfully and wickedly hold in bondage." To oppose slavery "is in my opinion the greatest service a man can render God," and "I am here not to gratify any personal animosity, revenge, or vindictive spirit" but because of my "sympathy with the oppressed, that are as good as you and as precious in the sight of God." Calling Brown's words "true as the voice of nature," Thoreau chastises his audience: "You don't know your testament when you see it." Their lack of recognition signals the death-in-life he laments. But, Thoreau continues, "in teaching us how to die," Brown has "taught us how to live." Indeed, Thoreau declares in a self-revealing way, "How many a man who was lately contemplating suicide has now something to live for!" ("Plea," 48, 46).

Thoreau casts Brown as *Christ,* therefore, because he would regenerate those dead to life and because these living dead allow his death. He is "sent to be the redeemer of those in captivity," but "the only use to which you can put him is to hang him at the end of a rope. You who pretend to care for Christ crucified, consider what you are about to do to him who offered himself to be the savior of four millions of men." But Thoreau is *invested* in this death before it happens, as if self-sacrificing martyrdom is a crucial part of Brown's regenerative gift. In his lecture before Brown is executed, Thoreau realizes, "I anticipate a little, that he is still . . . alive in the hands of his foes, but . . . I have all along found myself thinking and speaking of him as physically dead" ("Plea," 47, 40). Brown himself concluded that his act required martyrdom for its completion, to validate his cause and provoke a national crisis. But Thoreau is not speaking so strategically; mortal self-sacrifice in the service of a higher cause can serve (our) life by vitalizing it. Violence is *necessary* to end slavery, but he casts Brown as Christ to depict *self-sacrifice* as regenerative.

"Some eighteen hundred years ago Christ was crucified; this morning, perchance, Captain Brown was hung. These are the two ends of a chain which is not without its links. He is not Old Brown any longer; he is an angel of light." As he becomes "pure spirit himself," he "is more alive than he ever was" because "he has earned immortality." Indeed, "I see now it was necessary that the bravest and humanest man in all the country should be hung," for only this secures the immortality that can bring deadened men back to life. Brown thereby can become an abolitionist icon in the struggle against slavery. Thoreau's final words validate Bercovitch's concern: "I foresee the time when the painter will paint that scene . . . and, with the Landing of the Pilgrims and the Declaration of Independence, it will be the ornament of some future national gallery, when at least the present form of slavery shall be no more" ("Plea," 48).

But Brown's death may serve Thoreau for reasons Thoreau does not state or own: Thoreau sees his idealized image in Brown; to canonize Brown is to establish the criteria that warrant his own claim to immortality. Committed to each man following his polestar, or the fugitive's North Star, Thoreau wants to be known as an exemplar of the capacity for freedom his neighbors disown but could redeem. Not irresponsible or selfish because he serves a higher cause, not a monomaniac but a man who lives by faith, not a failure even though a minority of one, he legitimizes his own testament by vindicating Brown. His own moment has arrived, to redeem himself and not only his neighbors by redeeming Brown.[62]

But the intensity of Thoreau's *idea* of Brown, its idealizing abstraction from the messy actuality of motivation and character, signals the fantasy and shame in an identification that requires sacrificing parts of himself. Surely, his investment in sacrifice is a way to atone for his own aggression, even as he justifies it. Surely, he also struggles with his ambivalence about the efficacy of language and meaning of art by praising Brown for being *artless*. After all, manly integrity means (violent) action, not speech. But Thoreau also praises Brown's eloquence after his capture: He "could afford to lose his Sharpe's rifles" because he "retained his faculty of speech, a Sharpe's rifle of infinitely surer and longer range" ("Plea," 41). He replaced metaphoric bullets with real ones, but he "won his greatest and most memorable victories" by "taking up the sword of the spirit" ("Last Days," 152). His immortality will rest not on his violent act as such but on his (and Thoreau's) words about it. What kind of speech, then, does Thoreau affirm?[63]

Thoreau does not attack those who "demand that you speak so they can understand you." He does not seek "obscurity," or defend "the volatile truth of words" from reduction to their "residual statement." He devoted eight years to revising his *Walden* manuscript, but he now asserts,

"The art of composition is as simple as the discharge of a bullet from a rifle" because "the one great rule of composition" is *"speak the truth,"* which "demands earnestness and manhood, chiefly." He now praises a simplicity of speech that is enabled by character but ruined by learning ("Last Days," 150–51). "Not in the least a rhetorician," Brown did not attend "Harvard," but "went to the great university of the West" to "pursue the study of liberty," not "grammar" ("Plea," 32). Does Thoreau's defense of artless manhood and "plain speech" betray the meaning of his own life? At least, does he devalue the literary—ironic and playful—ways he complicated the moral voice of prophetic witness?

Surely, he misrecognizes Brown, a consummate artist who scripted his life as an antislavery activist and his death as a martyr. A devout, self-righteous, and demanding Calvinist, Brown was repeatedly accused of commercial fraud in a series of failed business endeavors. Says biographer Stephen Oates, "He did have very high standards but was unable to live up to them," until he found his vocation in Kansas. Then "he began to act as if he really had the characteristics" he valued, and soon "the fantasy [of himself] became in a sense the reality, except that the outward qualities of strength—heroic endurance, inspiring leadership, and relentless purpose—concealed inner qualities of weakness—flawed judgment, homicidal impulse, and simple incompetence." But Brown artfully used his Puritan persona to seduce New England transcendentalists from whom he sought financial support. They "saw him as by nature and instinct, a man of action, utterly devoid of artistry and rhetoric," Oates claims, and "never sensed at all that he was, in some ways, more of an artist and a man of words than any of them."[64]

Brown's effort to make life follow art succeeds because Northerners are drawn into his story of redemptive sacrifice, partly because he does wholeheartedly assume the part of a redeemer willing to die to redeem slaves from captivity and whites from their sins, and partly because Thoreau immortalizes that mythic connection. Brown has found a narrative and a vocation by which to transform a self once demeaned by worldly failure into a figure of triumph, but he would have failed again if his performance had not inspired Thoreau.

Thoreau is completely captivated by Brown's performance of artless simplicity in speech and unwavering fidelity in conduct. Thoreau sees no gaps between the words and acts of this heroic self: Wholly invested in words that are fully embodied in action, Brown seems to embody the persona of faith and commitment Thoreau invented through his art but believes he has failed to inhabit. His Brown closes the gap between appearance and "shortcomings"—self-doubt and fear—that he had transfigured in and by his art. Chanticleer depicts an aspiration, but Brown's example suggests that art is necessary only because of weakness and that both can be overcome by sublime commitment. Sacrificing the mortal Brown to sustain an immortal image of manhood and liberty, Thoreau gains solace that his own persona can survive his mortifying weakness and political failure. But to identify with Brown, he kills off that weakness, and devalues the art that transfigures it.

If a democratic political space requires that people credit their mutual weakness and their capacity to artfully transfigure it into power together, Thoreau's persona and language must be problematic. By acknowledging that human beings are constituted in time, which discloses loss, and that possibility is constituted in language, which discloses the gap between art and life; in interdependence, which discloses mutual need; and in plurality, which discloses distance and difference, his *Walden* embeds masculinized political agency in a prophecy that makes finitude the condition of possibility and artful speech the medium of politics. But under the pressure of the slavery crisis, idioms of manhood and liberty authorize not art and action-from-principle but violence and self-sacrifice. Art and politics seem sacrificed to the heroic manhood by which he once enabled them.

We need to credit that this desperate redemption does not flee but registers a desperate political situation in which dialogue is impossible and violence necessary. Thoreau's prose idealizes Brown but never loses sight of the political and racial reality Brown names. Still, we should resist the ways Thoreau tried to redeem this violence: He positions Brown with slaves and against the state, so Brown's godly example authorizes insurrection, but as Brown's holy war against a slave regime becomes a state's holy war against slavery, Thoreau's defense of Brown becomes the language of state power—and of one state's power against others. The meaning and impact—the danger—of prophecy really changes if it moves from margin to center. The Lincoln who condemns Brown is soon called Abraham by self-declared Isaacs, and he endorses self-sacrifice to redeem the crime of slavery and give the union a new birth of freedom. Thoreau's prophetic legacy thus appears not only in critics who use moral witness to stand against the state and with those it dominates, but also in self-declared sons who endorse violence and redemptive self-sacrifice to regenerate their freedom in the father's house.

Walden then reminds us of the value of using "poetry" to inflect the office and genre of prophecy.

These idioms of prophecy are drawn on and transformed one hundred years later during the second Reconstruction: Chapters 3 and 4 trace how Martin Luther King Jr. and James Baldwin inflect the Protestant and romantic registers that Thoreau reworked in tandem and tension. Assuming the office of moral witness and taking on the Protestant idiom of devotion to a cause and redemptive sacrifice, King authorizes black struggle against white supremacy. Baldwin, raised in the biblical language of the black church, works the idiom of prophet as poet to fashion an existentialized and queer prophecy that decisively breaks the bond linking purity and redemption.

Interlude

From Henry Thoreau to Martin Luther King Jr. and James Baldwin:
Race and Prophecy

*It can happen that a man will rise above prejudice of religion, country,
race . . . but it is not possible for a whole people to rise, as it were, above itself.*
—Tocqueville, *Democracy in America*

*If America undergoes great revolutions, they will be brought about by the
presence of the black race. . . . they will owe their origin not to the equality
but the inequality of conditions.*
—Tocqueville, *Democracy in America*

*When life has done its worst, they will be enabled to rise above themselves and
triumph over life.*
—James Baldwin, "Stranger in the Village"

MARTIN LUTHER KING JR. and James Baldwin came to
prominence during what many scholars now call the second Reconstruction, from the late 1940s through the late 1960s, and each figure
has been domesticated since this project of democratization was abandoned. King now is a national icon, cast as a figure who embodied—
who lived and died for—the American Dream; he is contained by an
American exceptionalist story of a nation whose progressive telos is to
fulfill its founding principles. Baldwin, too, has been made into a critic
who stands up for the universalism latent in a national consensus, to
redeem a specifically American promise. Richard Rorty thus celebrates
him for—and reduces him to—the goal of "achieving America." King
and Baldwin now appear as models of Michael Walzer's "internal critics,"
who protest practices they construe as violations of core values, so that
they "begin in revulsion but end in affirmation," as he puts it. Their criticisms, it is widely claimed, embrace what Gunnar Myrdal, at the outset
of this second Reconstruction, called "the American Creed." King and
Baldwin are then incorporated within Bercovitch's "ritual of consensus,"

89

as commentators solicit our (belated) recognition of their belonging to "our" community.[1]

Readings that sanitize King and Baldwin to preserve political (and national) innocence also domesticate the meaning of prophecy. For if, as Hebrew prophets were the first to argue, nations (or groups) are formed by forgetting, by closing the gap between who they are and who they say they are, then the office of prophecy is to expose that gap. Prophets thus reveal a divided personal and political subject, a subject whose disavowal of division is both generative and crippling. To testify to division as disavowal, to use acknowledgment of disavowal to reconstitute personal identity and political community, to bear witness in word and deed both to reconstitution *as* a possibility and to a redemption (finalized by some, not others) that is lodged in it—this is the prophetic practice that King and Baldwin take up and revise. By it, they trouble the false comfort—false prophecy?—in stories of an exceptional nation and its progress.

As we trace where their thinking goes, we will see both figures criticize liberal political thought, for two reasons: because it understates how racial categories are instantiated and replenished by market forces, state institutions, cultural expression, and political rhetoric; and because it overstates the capacity of the nation-state to achieve a universality that overcomes racialization. Each moves beyond a liberal politics as he exposes the inequality that law cannot reach and as he testifies that rational deliberation cannot dissolve white supremacy. Both critics thus show how antiblack racism is crucial to creating "American" citizen-subjects and forging a national subject. But both still appeal to the universalizing rhetoric of American nationhood, to enlist it on behalf of black struggle, while both also imagine a collective black agency that reaches beyond the national form. In the trajectories of their prophecy, both use and trouble but then despair of national allegiance as a resource to advance the promise of freedom for all. As they struggle to name the agents and model the practices that are the predicates of redemption, they make it a question impossible to avoid.[2]

Chapters 3 and 4 recapture the truth that canonization obscures—that the prophetic practices of King and Baldwin live in creative (and increasingly profound) tension with liberal political norms and redemptive American nationalism. But King and Baldwin do not practice prophecy in the same way, and those chapters also identify and assess that difference. It appears in the different ways they inflect the prophetic idioms they inherit and take up, and in the different ways they negotiate with a dominant culture. In both regards, they are related to Thoreau's literary and political example in illuminating ways.

Begin with registers of voice and their inflection. One path from Thoreau to King appears in theist faith, moral witness, corporations with a conscience, and civil disobedience, the register of prophecy by which militant Protestantism elevates or intensifies the democratic elements in a Puritan and liberal culture. King thus passionately identifies with Thoreau's nonviolent opposition to white supremacy and imperial war and with his persona of righteous autonomy and moral courage, a persona that follows a "different drummer" rather than "the drum major's instinct."[3] In ways not sufficiently noted, therefore, King also joins critiques of racial domination and conformity in mass society on behalf of a community that encourages the moral agency of every member. But King emerges from and draws on the semantic field created by the black church and its distinctive appropriation of biblical and Protestant idioms. He does not turn to poetry or the poet to supplement abolitionist orthodoxy; rather, he invokes a biblical vision of redemptive love and beloved community that deflates Thoreau's individualism. Still, both invest redemption in "action from principle," which promises personal and political rebirth by separating the divine and the diabolical.

Whereas King remains within the theistic horizon that is one register in American prophecy and the wider culture, another path runs from Thoreau, a ridiculed "bachelor of nature," to Baldwin, who calls himself a "sexually dubious freak" and whose sexual marginality exposes the repressive bond between the black church and American national identity. Thoreau is not an exemplar for Baldwin, but both stand in profound tension with the religiosity and proprieties that King upholds, and both use literary art to fashion a nontheist prophecy as an antidote to Christian tropes of sin and redemption.[4]

But because Baldwin's translation of theist prophecy draws from a blues aesthetic, Henry James, and existentialism—rather than romanticism—he does not write symbolic order into nature, require spirit to redeem brute matter, or sustain the fiction of an integral subject. Because Thoreau remains invested in the idea of rebirth, he inflects prophecy by a trope of dawn that bears new beginnings, whereas Baldwin inflects prophecy by a tragic sense of human finitude to emphasize the necessity of "accepting" the power of the past, as well as the incompletion, wayward desire, and carnal particularity that mark the human condition.

Thoreau secularizes prophecy by announcing the ever-available possibility of rebirth from (the category of) sin, but Baldwin secularizes it by denouncing the "innocence" of those disavowing the meaning of their conduct, finitude, and history.

If Thoreau never escapes the logic of splitting spirit from flesh and past from present, Baldwin bears witness to the staggering penalty of just this project, to seek "acceptance" of realities we deny but can never escape. Accordingly, the idiom of rebirth bonds the prophetic voices of King and Thoreau, who pursue in theistic and romantic registers the idea of new beginnings rupturing historical repetition, while Baldwin recasts redemption as a practice Nietzsche calls *"amor fati"* (love of one's fate) and Cavell, acknowledgment. Baldwin originates prophecy not in God's word or in nature's signs but in a carnal and historical being struggling to name and "accept" what he calls "the price of the ticket."[5]

But it is important to emphasize the differences not only between theist and secularizing registers of voice but also between the ways that prophetic speakers depict and position themselves toward "American" culture. Thoreau, King, and Baldwin locate themselves in relation to "the house of the fathers," a Puritan, acquisitive, and constitutional regime each anchors in racial domination and empire. But race really affects how each reworks tropes of heir and outcast to link citizenship to resistance.

Disidentifying with those who call themselves Isaacs, Thoreau identifies with fugitive slaves and savages, but he *can* shift identification by associating with a racialized wildness, because he is privileged in the racial and gendered system. In contrast, King and Baldwin are fixed in social place by this racial imaginary. Their political engagement is the other side of an ascribed identity each makes a form of belonging and condition of action, even as each also negotiates the symbolic code that precludes legitimate black agency. Using prophetic speech to address a white republic about its disowned history and unjust conduct, they also address blacks about a suffering they not only witness but undergo in common. The richness of American prophecy thus appears as minoritized voices mediate two audiences or nations about distinct experiences and entwined fates.[6]

Then the differences between King and Baldwin gain added significance. For like Douglass, King refuses the role of outcast scripted for African Americans; he refuses to identify *as* an Ishmael though he stands *with* those cast out. He speaks as a true heir of the founding fathers, to redeem the principles they and their legally recognized sons betray. He conscientiously performs the cultural *rites* that warrant political *rights* to demonstrate to whites and model for blacks the comportment and values proving entitlement to normative manhood and citizenship. Inescapably and intentionally, he also "blackens" signifiers of citizenship to defeat the racial imaginary that makes black agency mean license rather than liberty. Disciplining black subjectivity to secure that distinction, he seeks to form a community that acts to "redeem the soul of America."[7]

In contrast, Baldwin refuses the regime of the normal that binds heterosexuality to manhood and citizenship. He does not, like Douglass or King, narrate a jeremiad radicalized by rooting American freedom in slavery. Rather, he asks whether a society that has never been democratic can "accept" this truth of its history and thereby begin to make a future on different terms. Likewise, he argues that whites must accept the fatality of an entwined history with blacks if they are to draw out its miscegenated blessings. While King's jeremiad seeks repentance to produce a national rebirth that culminates in whites and blacks eating at a common table, Baldwin makes their acceptance of their "wedding," both carnal and figurative, the condition of freedom. Rather than evoking an ideal America to return to or a "true" America to realize, he calls for "accepting" the actual one. It is he, not Emerson, who represents what it means to democratize Nietzsche's effort to secularize prophecy and redemption.

Baldwin and King inflect prophecy differently by profoundly different narratives, but each addresses whites to reconstitute a regime beyond white supremacy, and each believes that exclusion invests blacks in the worldly defense of freedom. For each, black particularity can bear a universal good by opening democratic possibilities once foreclosed by disavowal. Not only does King perform the persona of the prophet politically, therefore, but he also creates an image of black agency as a collective prophet calling the American nation to account. Invoking Mohandas Gandhi and Thoreau, he calls blacks to refute Machiavelli's dictum that "unarmed prophets" must fail, but he thereby imposes on them the prophetic burden of representing the universal in mortal form.

In contrast, Baldwin translates the office of prophecy into the public calling of the artist, which he construes as a lover's responsibility to "disclose the beloved to himself." While Thoreau rejects "philanthropy" and Baldwin rejects "the protest novel"—that is, sentimental or melo-dramatic forms of reform—each seeks a "poetry," a form of speech or testimony embodied visibly in action, to "awaken" people who are "said to live." Linking black collective agency to cultural production, Baldwin imagines art and politics creating a "disagreeable mirror" to shatter the self-protective "innocence" of those who imprison themselves in the idolatry of identity. Still, he too imagines blacks forming a collective protagonist that frees itself by redeeming whites.[8]

What then is at stake as we move from Thoreau to King and Bald-win? First, we see them rework the key "prophetic" questions: about the truths and commitments we endow with authority, about whom we iden-tify with and on what basis, about which and whose stories we tell and how we pass them on. And in each regard these questions compel us toward fateful decisions on which our flourishing and freedom—our redemption—depends. Second, we see them inflect these questions dif-ferently by narrating history and conceiving redemption differently. But third, despite obvious differences, both fashion a language of "love," though one defines it as agape to avoid the particularizing danger of eros, and the other insists on that very tension. For both, love names an energy, a relationship to others, and an arduous engagement across dif-ference. For both, "love" is a redemptive practice, and so of both we ask: What is the *political* bearing of the way you take up and revise prophecy as this practice of redemption?

For Arendt, love in Christian and erotic forms is antipolitical because it collapses the space-between in which action and plurality live, but King and Baldwin argue otherwise. "Love" names an energy of solidarity that has enabled black people to survive in America, but it also names an engagement with adversaries who cannot simply be defined as enemies. Love names a transforming energy and a practice of mediating part and whole by speech and action. In both regards, its political bearing is il-luminated by Jacques Rancière in *Disagreement:* What they call love is the "dis-agreement" that reconstitutes a regime. Because every whole is constituted by exclusion, politics in the fullest sense occurs as "the part that has no part" transforms itself into a political subject by putting its experience of injury into public speech about "wrong," and as it ad-dresses the enfranchised, to refound the whole they have constituted partially. What King and Baldwin call love is then a political practice, not movement beyond it.[9]

As black critics take a prophetic role speaking both to an exclusionary white republic and to an African American community itself divided, the mediating role of prophecy as an office and the complexity of the "we" these prophets invoke are glaringly obvious. By a rhetoric of love, therefore, King and Baldwin seek at once to forge, mediate, and redeem communities they address as parts and wholes. It is politically significant, then, that King defines love in moral and spiritual terms by a theism that invests him in nonviolence and drives him toward self-sacrifice on its behalf: Does he enact a logic of moral purity, or stake his life to keep disagreement within the bounds of speech? Baldwin, who sees the knotted ambivalence by which love is connected to disappointment and violence, troubles King's moral categories and teleology of redemptive sacrifice to deny we can ever resolve a stable whole. By imagining engagement with the darkness within and between us, does he secularize prophecy and redemption for politics? But he would be the first to ask: What is the price of this ticket?

3. Martin Luther King Jr.'s Theistic Prophecy
Love, Sacrifice, and Democratic Politics

If you stick a knife nine inches into my back and pull it out three inches, that's not progress. Even if you pull it all the way out, that's not progress. Progress is healing the wound; America hasn't even begun to acknowledge the knife.

—Malcolm X

If a prophet is one who interprets in clear and intelligible language the will of God, Martin Luther King Jr. fits that designation. If a prophet is one who does not seek popular causes to espouse, but rather the causes he thinks are right, Martin Luther qualified on that score.

—Benjamin Mays, Eulogy for Martin Luther King Jr.

LIKE HENRY THOREAU, Martin Luther King Jr. assumes the office of prophecy and uses the genre as a language in and for politics. As we have seen, Thoreau developed two registers of prophetic voice, one abolitionist and the other romantic, in tandem as well as in tension with each other and with politics. We told a story that revealed unexpected affinities between these registers of prophecy and his political engagement with white supremacy, but it also suggested that while his use of wilderness as a trope was politically fruitful, his turn toward nature could not sustain this engagement. Indeed, the great problem in his use of prophecy was the idea of rebirth common to both his registers of voice, because it entails a logic of splitting for the sake of the new and pure. If the broad question we bring to King is how he takes up the biblical idiom he inherits and inflects toward politics, the specific legacy of our story about Thoreau is to assess how King imagines politics through redemption as rebirth.

King does not seek an antidote to theism in nature, nor does he revise abolitionist orthodoxy by a poetic calling. Rather, he voices a biblical idiom that has been transformed by what Raymond Williams calls the "structure of feeling" created by the black church tradition,[1] which forged a profound and fertile synergy of exodus and resurrection to represent, endure, and overcome white supremacy. Moreover, King is gifted at translating this theistic prophecy into other—constitutional, liberal, and democratic—terms. He adds another dimension of meaning to our sense that prophets mediate not only the divine and the human and part and whole, but also "religion" and secular politics. We imagine prophets as uncompromising purists, an image perhaps validated by Thoreau's persona and acts of solitary witness and cultivation, but King's calling as a prophet means *negotiating tensions*—between theist faith and postwar liberalism, between his speech to black and to white (or national) audiences, and between the effort to transform blacks into a redemptive protagonist and the effort to transform liberal society. In each regard, he at once enacts and *translates* prophecy.

These negotiations reveal that King is, to the civil rights movement, like a wave to the ocean: His capacity to speak and lead depends entirely on his connection to a larger movement. He depends not only on historic black church idioms of redemption, but also on "congregation" as action in concert to transform the noun of ascribed status and racialized essence into an activity, a movement whose potentiality cannot be known in advance. In relation to racialized subordination, King is cast as a Moses redeeming people from captivity and as a Jesus redeeming sin by way of love, the sword of spirit. Joining these two figures we might call the first and the last of the Hebrew prophets, he tests Machiavelli's claim that unarmed prophets must fail, but like a Machiavellian prince he artfully mediates the relationship of the civil rights movement to whites and state institutions, changing his speech with his audiences despite consistent themes. For the differential positions of blacks and whites entail different perspectives: Black political struggle requires a perspective (on power, patience, suffering) unlike that by which he speaks to the privileges that whites presume and to the struggle they must undergo if they would be free.

But we should not assume a simple identification between King and *the* black community compared to strategic negotiation with a monolithic white society. Hebrew prophets do not enact a simple identity with the oppressed; they criticize those they stand with and endure a kind of distance or estrangement even where they seem most at home. Likewise, King engages in a profound struggle over the character of the black church, and thus over a wider black political subjectivity, and in this way over the character of American society as a whole. He is a contested figure in agonal relations to each of his audiences, for as Richard Lischer says, "He never quit trying to shape a 'congregation' of people that would be capable of redeeming the moral and political character of the nation."[2]

To tell a story of his initial success, his radicalization, and his final marginalization is to see his prophetic faith as political and politicizing precisely to the degree that he could sustain these tensions, but it is also to see how, as he risks his faith in action and exposes his redemptive dream to failure, he enters a crisis that drives him toward self-sacrifice and death.

Prophetic Faith and Political Freedom

Not surprisingly, scholars disagree about how King relates his prophetic vocation to politics. But let us begin with the centrality of prophetic language in the civil rights movement before we see how King relates it to constitutional liberalism and American nationalism. In *A Stone of Hope*, David Chappell says, "It may be misleading to view the civil rights movement as a social and political event that had religious overtones. The words of many participants suggest that it was for them primarily a religious event, whose social and political aspects were, in their minds, secondary or incidental." Emphasizing the extent to which participants forged a movement in "prophetic, ecstatic, biblical tones," he calls it an instance "in the great historical tradition of religious revivals."[3]

This claim does not devalue politics. On the contrary, the civil rights movement resisted the other-worldly orientation of the prevailing Christian practice of the black church. Activists believed they could "make religion a greater presence in peoples' day-to-day lives," Chappell says, "only by turning religion's means to political ends." Linking religion to political action seemed "the only way to make religion credible in a world plagued by political injustice," though King's critics argued, conversely, that religion is saved from corruption only by distance from politics. In Chappell's account, religion enables politics, and politics saves—or redeems—religion by making it fruitful. But it is a "prophetic" orientation that "explains" the movement, which he claims could not have occurred or succeeded otherwise. Why? He attributes two different but related gifts to what he calls a prophetic tradition. Each gift offers what is lacking in liberalism, but thereby serves liberal ends.[4]

For Chappell, "liberalism" avows an Enlightenment faith in reason and education to overcome "prejudice," ignorance, and superstition.

In his view, liberalism also avows faith in progress because the "empire of reason" extends human cooperation by procedures and deliberation that produce consensual agreement. What he calls liberalism thus drives the New Deal faith that technocratic reason enables elites to overcome prejudice, resolve social conflict, and design institutions that ensure justice. Liberalism joins faith in rational planning to a narrative of American exceptionalism that depicts the progressive overcoming of social practices—like legal apartheid—that violate an "American creed" rooted in the Enlightenment.

For Chapell (and others), Gunnar Myrdal's *American Dilemma* exemplifies this liberal perspective.[5] On the one hand, it depicts a national "creed" that joins an Enlightenment faith linking reason to norms of dialogue and tolerance and a constitutional faith linking equal rights and representative government to the rule of law. On the other hand, it depicts white supremacy not as a social practice of material domination entailing categories of "race" but as a prejudice of one race against another. Enacted in the discriminatory conduct of individuals and enshrined in legalized segregation, prejudice is said to violate core elements of a creed whites otherwise accept. Because whites are unaware that their prejudice violates their creed, this argument goes, once they see that gap, their conduct will change because their commitment to the creed is profound while their prejudice is anomalous. Still, Myrdal also argues, blacks must overcome the pathologies imposed by generations of domination, to seek and *warrant* assimilation. He thus imagines what Chapell calls a "virtually painless" exit from the nation's racial history, for if racism is only attitude, it is susceptible to (re)education.[6]

Diverse critics in the black community argued that Myrdal had profoundly misunderstood how race works. Most importantly, they claimed, racism is the ideological face of a caste system: Slavery was created to exploit labor, and racism was created to justify that exploitation, to square it with egalitarian norms by impugning the "nature" of the enslaved. After the legal end of slavery, material practices of domination have been sustained by state-sanctioned terrorism and by discourses that still identify intractable defects in the subordinated. (In postwar social science, ghettos signify black pathology rather than racial domination.)[7]

The problem, Myrdal's critics argue, is not white attitudes or prejudice, nor is it ignorance of the gap between a universalist creed and "discrimination" in conduct. The problem is organized domination and the investment of those who call themselves white in their unequal power, superior identity, and material benefits. If prejudice is not a form of ignorance but is motivated by resistance to recognizing how practices of domination violate democratic ideals, and if denial of black humanity is not a cognitive error but a refusal to acknowledge what whites do "know," then education cannot end white supremacy. But what is a credible political response to domination and denial of it?

Chappell argues that a "prophetic" tradition runs from the biblical prophets through Augustine and Luther to the Social Gospel movement, Reinhold Niebuhr, the black church, and King. It bequeaths a profound "realism" about human nature and political possibility, he argues, compared to the "idealism" of rationalist and liberal modes of thought. For it depicts the way prospects for justice are set partly by powerful groups invested in domination and partly by abiding human dispositions toward fear and shortsightedness, vain idolatry of identity, and denial of the reality of others.[8]

For King, "liberalism . . . leaned toward a false idealism" because it "overlooked the fact that reason is darkened" by "our tragic inclination for sin." Indeed, "reason, devoid of the purifying power of faith, can never free itself from distortions and rationalizations" because "reason by itself is little more than an instrument to justify" what we resolve on in our partiality and pride. Standing with those "who are opposed to humanism in the world," he rejects "all forms of humanistic perfectionism." Since power and sinfulness make injustice endemic to institutions, which distribute resources in grossly unequal ways and call it justice, progress toward justice is not automatic. Echoing Hebrew prophecy, he condemns "the irrational notion" that "something in the very flow of time will inevitably cure all ills."[9]

But why act at all if domination inheres in human life? The other gift of prophecy, paradoxically, is hope—not a "liberal optimism" buoyed by faith in progress, Chappell claims, but hope sustained by faith in providence. King thus would supplant "faith in man" by "prophetic faith in God." For Chappell, "It is hard to imagine masses of people lining up for years of excruciating risk . . . without some transcendent or millennial faith to sustain them." Their "hope for improvement in this world could not be sustained without signs that God was on their side," he claims, but each victory becomes a sign, and every adversity a test calling forth renewed faith. As Clayborne Carson argues, King voices faith in "the living reality of a personal God" as a comforting personal presence *and* as a spiritual force intervening in history on the side of righteousness.[10]

God is "on our side" because this is a God of *righteousness,* "no respecter of persons" as John Brown reminds his jailors, and slavery or legalized apartheid deny our dignity and freedom as human beings equal to any others in God's eyes. Faith in *this* God underwrites two crucial ideas: that equality is an absolute moral law, and that we who uphold it are doing God's work and will be divinely supported. "We *will* overcome" *because* our demands echo the central commitment of the God ruling the universe: "The arc of the moral universe is long, but it bends toward justice."[11]

In an early sermon, King declares, "God has planted in the fiber of the universe certain eternal laws which forever confront every man. They are absolute and not relative. There is an eternal and absolute distinction between right and wrong." Thus does "all reality hinge on moral foundations" in a universe governed by "moral laws" and not only "physical laws":

I'm here to say to you . . . that some things are right and some things are wrong. (Yes!) Eternally so, absolutely so. It's *wrong* to hate (Yes, that's right) It always has been wrong and it always will be wrong (Amen!) It's wrong in America, it's wrong in Germany, it's wrong in Russia . . . in China! It was wrong in two thousand B.C. and it's wrong in 1954 A.D. It always has been wrong (that's right!) and it always will be wrong. . . . Some things in this universe are absolute. The God of the universe has made it so.[12]

But this moral law requires actors: "The thing we need in the world today is a group of men and women who will stand up for right and be opposed to wrong, wherever it is." No wonder that King, "fascinated by ideas of refusing to cooperate with an evil system," recalls being "deeply moved" by Thoreau's essay on civil disobedience, which convinced him "that noncooperation with evil is as much a moral obligation as is cooperation with good." In either mode, as King took Thoreau and Gandhi to show, actors must embody their ends in their means, and not do "wrong" in the name of "right." Good and evil are absolute, but the distinction of "diabolical and divine," as Thoreau says, bisects all humans, and each must struggle internally to do right in worldly ways. Each must "love"—seek the good in and of—adversaries: Faith in providence entails a moral dogmatism that, paradoxically or not, precludes violence and demands dialogue with adversaries.[13]

Chappell identifies the twin gifts of realism and hope with Reinhold Niebuhr, whose work greatly influenced King. Insisting on the inescapable reality of power, Niebuhr criticizes the overvaluation of conscience and reason by moralists: Injustice "can be checked only by competing associations of interest and these can be effective only if coercive methods are added to moral and rational persuasion." But such "coercive methods will always run the peril of introducing new forms of injustice." So Niebuhr must ask, "If power is needed to destroy power, how is this new power to be made ethical?" "What is to prevent the instrument of today's redemption from becoming the chain of tomorrow's enslavement?"[14]

Making politics the site "where conscience and power" or "the ethical and coercive" meet, Niebuhr relates Gandhi's nonviolent but coercive form of power to American racial domination. Questioning whether any "disinherited group, such as the Negroes" ever wins justice by *negotiating* with a dominant group, he says, "It is hopeless for the Negro to expect complete emancipation . . . merely by trusting in the moral sense of the white race." Indeed, "the white race in America will not admit the Negro to equal rights if it is not forced to do so." But it is also "hopeless to attempt emancipation through violent rebellion." The only viable politics is "non-violent resistance," and "there is no problem of political life to which religious imagination can make a larger contribution."[15]

Niebuhr imagines that blacks could demonstrate nonviolent "noncooperation" by refusing to pay taxes to a racist state and by using boycotts to refuse exploitive economic exchanges with whites. At the same time, "non-violence expresses moral good will" by "distinguishing between the evils of a social system" and "the individuals involved in it," while it also "protects against the resentment which violent conflict always creates" and "proves this freedom from resentment to the contending party . . . by enduring more suffering than it causes":

The discovery of common elements of frailty in the foe, and . . . the appreciation of all life as possessing transcendent worth, create attitudes which transcend social conflict and mitigate its cruelties. . . . these attitudes of repentance, which recognize that the evil in the foe is also in the self, and these impulses of love, which claim kinship with all men in spite of social conflict, are the peculiar gifts of religion to the human spirit.

Such attitudes require "a sublime madness" that "disregards immediate appearances" to emphasize "ultimate unities." This sublime madness is what Chappell calls prophecy and finds in the civil rights movement.[16]

But Chappell tends to *reduce* King to Niebuhr by ignoring the redemptive dimension in King's theology and practice. For Niebuhr is finally *anti*redemptive in what he claims politics can do, and he increasingly emphasizes that politics can avoid atrocity only by relinquishing aspirations to transform social life. Spiritual development is individual; after all, his most famous book is *Moral Man and Immoral Society.* "Too ready to consign the social order to the hell of power politics," Lischer says, he embraces cold war liberalism. But King never accepts Niebuhr's sense of the limits that "sin" sets on collective possibility. Niebuhr's "Christian realism" disowns what King "would die trying to accomplish," says Lischer, "the injection of Christian love into the social and political process."[17]

While Niebuhr imagines black nonviolence changing the outer conduct of whites, King would transform or redeem them in the process. Arguing that whites "need" and seek (albeit unconsciously) black forgiveness to be released from guilt over domination and that forgiveness also enables blacks to overcome the legacy of their oppression, King makes "beloved community" the goal of political struggle. Crossing difference is a strategic necessity for a minority, but it is also a Christian precept and democratic commitment. Let us turn, then, to King's theology of redemptive love and its embodiment in political practice.

From Preaching to Prophecy

Begin with King's sense of his calling as preacher and prophet. His sermons do not so much teach "the word of God" as *perform* it; his sermons are (meant to be, and to be effective must be) God's word *enacted.* In King we can hear the "preaching" of prophecy as spoken-word poetry performed to an audience; the words arising *in* the speaker take on more life as the audience, finding itself in and feeling moved by impassioned performance of "the word," urges the speaker on. Tapes of King's sermons reveal performer and audience forging ecstatic identification by sharing the pleasure of giving and receiving sacred speech.

Lischer thus emphasizes the *joy* created by the sound and beat of syllables, the rhythm of words, the music of sentences. King's sermons create an event by poetic devices of simile, metaphor, alliteration, and repetition; by pacing, tone, and pitch; by question, declaration, accusation, and plea. *Pleasure* in language moves people as much as intensity of identification with the suffering and aspiration of characters in the stories he retells. No wonder the preacher, bearing God's word and making it present in the moment, is seen as a sexual figure—a cockerel?—called to arouse (not only berate) others.[18]

As Emerson argues in his Divinity School Address, to depict God's word as if it were a dead letter, or Christ's passion as if a historic event, is to fail at the vocation of preacher. Only one who makes the word live demonstrates election to (and enacts) the office of preacher, and if the office is unfilled, Emerson worries, the wider "faith" is dying. Thoreau goes not to church but to the wilderness to fashion a voice like Chanticleer's, who does not bespeak dejection but brags lustily to wake his neighbors.[19] In contrast, King voices a tradition still alive in his audience, and he awakens it not to dawn as a symbol of possibility in a nature he reads as a new scripture, but to the suffering and redemptive love he locates between scripture and experience.

In this way, King moves from preaching to prophecy. "Any discussion of the Christian ministry must ultimately emphasize the need for prophecy. Not every minister can be a prophet, but some must be prepared for the ordeals of this high calling and be willing to suffer courageously for righteousness." A prophet must address a wider public rather than a local congregation and must preach not only "with his voice" but "with his life." But to what does he awaken his audiences? King lives to demonstrate God's truth in history, the necessity of suffering on its behalf, and the promise that such suffering is redemptive. He demonstrates a *theodicy* to move black audiences to embrace the role of God's protagonist.[20]

Love and Politics I: From Theodicy to Action

In his beautiful essays about the black church tradition and King, Cornel West begins with slavery as social death to identify the "existential strategies" created by people of African descent. With "the death of the Africa gods," they "creatively appropriated a Christian world view" to "come to terms with the absurd in America and as America." They transform an "absurd situation," horrific and senseless, "into a persistent and present tragic one," by imagining themselves "forever on the cross, perennially crucified, continually abused and incessantly devalued—yet sustained and empowered by a hope against hope for a potential and possible triumphant state of affairs."[21]

They "ground" this hope in an "existential encounter" and "personal relationship with Jesus Christ, whose moral life, agonizing death, and miraculous resurrection literally and symbolically enacted an ultimate victory over evil—collective slavery and personal sin." This victory "had *occurred* but was not yet *consummated*." Evil and suffering, love and resurrection, are the twinned axes around which black church theology and prophetic practice revolve. Resistance to conditions of utter domination and dishonor appears as "prophetic thought and action: courageous attempts to tell the truth about and bear witness to black suffering, and to keep faith with a vision of black redemption." Like black music, "the prophetic utterance that focuses on black suffering and sustains a hope-against-hope for black freedom constitutes the heights of black culture."[22]

The political meaning of theodicy changes profoundly when it is a minority strategy against domination. Against those who claim to possess God's blessing, as well as the final meaning of scripture, we assert *our* view of God's universal love, to make every human being worthy, and we imagine this God's covenant with *us*, to make ourselves agents in history. Against those who invoke providence to justify their power, we deny that a just God could support empires and the prideful. Accordingly, social death is not forever, but contingent, subject to change. Because "we were not meant to survive," as Audre Lorde says, we imagine redemption so that we can claim that horrific conditions do not last and can be changed. As Joanna Brooks sees, our ideas of resurrection or rebirth "are not hopeful abstractions but existential imperatives." Thoreau imagines such possibility in (human) nature by dawn's recurring availability, whereas King imagines providence opening history to rupture. Providential history does not decree a fate; on the contrary, in the face of social death as a seemingly unchangeable decree, it asserts contingency as a fact of life: A theological dogma here works pragmatically as a truth needed to live.[23]

For King, therefore, the Bible is not illustrative, nor does it narrate merely past events. Rather, he folds the present into a biblical story of captivity that is ongoing in (and about) the present. He "enrolls" people in a story about the present that discloses (we secularists would say imagines) the transcendent in the particular: Dingy southern towns become theaters of divine revelation, as God's truth is enacted here and now in struggles against captivity. Identification with Hebrews in Egypt and Christians in Rome makes each local march an instance, no mere symbol; every local struggle is magnified, made universal. Whereas for Thoreau spring symbolizes a political energy he cannot find in society, for King the Bible is literally, not only figuratively, the transcendent meaning of particular, local struggles.

By showing how God is active in history, a prophetic King performs God's presence and calls blacks to become a collective protagonist and political subject, a people willing to sacrifice for their emancipation. To place whites into this story is to cast them as a guilty people who worship idols rather than God and betray their founding covenant, but who bear capacities for repentance and renewal. Of course, blacks who choose docility over struggle or murmur in the wilderness are complicit in sin by accepting their subordination, while whites who sacrifice for equality bear a wider redemption in their own redeeming practice.

Accordingly, King identifies whites with Hebrews settled in Canaan and narrates a jeremiad to elicit repentance, but he identifies blacks with Hebrews as slaves in Egypt and exiles in Babylon. Like his prophetic fore-bears, he asks why people suffer in God's universe, but he must address the suffering caused by social death and the suffering entailed in resist-ing it. He rejects the idea of early Hebrew prophecy that dispossession is God's punishment of unjust conduct: Slavery and exile do not signal a guilt for which we must seek pardon by repentance. Black people are not oppressed *because* of their sin or conduct; their suffering is "un-merited." King thus uses other strands in prophecy to address his people. He invokes Isaiah's image of the prophet as God's "suffering servant," whose love for his God and people requires sacrifice on their behalf but whose suffering will be redeemed. He also depicts a dispossessed rem-nant whose suffering signifies the test of a piety that God will vindicate. Prophecy thus enables the other persona he invokes, a "Christ" whose crucifixion symbolizes both unmerited suffering and loving sacrifice and whose resurrection guarantees that remnant's redemption.

King thereby bears witness to the agonizing *fact* of unmerited human suffering, its gross *injustice,* and the *faith* that this suffering is worthwhile. Partly, prophecy finds a pedagogy in suffering: "The purpose of evil is to reform or test" the faithful. Partly, prophetic vocation means willing-ness to "suffer courageously for righteousness" against unjust suffering. Partly, prophetic faith appears in the repeated assertion that "unearned suffering is redemptive." But how so? Is he promising a final salvation by which suffering is made right and ended? Or is he redeeming suffering now by making it fruitful now?[24]

Love and Politics II: Suffering and Redemption

Thoreau speaks as a cockerel to awaken propertied white men to capaci-ties for action. Like Nietzsche, he seeks a subject who, by relinquishing investment in self-denial and life as "penance," can will something other than suffering. King risks investment in suffering in the effort to redeem it because unmerited suffering is the defining—absurd—condition of those he addresses. Thoreau links dawn to action from principle, as if nature underwrites our "essentially revolutionary" capacity to begin anew, while King lodges this capacity in "love," which suffuses God's creation and enables people to redeem unmerited suffering. Thoreau's move from despair to possibility intersects King's witness to suffering and redemption because for each, despair bespeaks fate, not faith in rebirth. Both seek in faith an antidote to rancor at life. But the crux of King's prophetic practice is unmerited suffering as a worldly condition and the power of love to redeem it. Thoreau affirms redemptive sacrifice to defend John Brown, but suffering and love are not the ground of the "freer and less desponding spirits" he cultivates, whether by conscience or nature. So the question remains: What is the political meaning of a prophetic voice that redeems unmerited suffering by love?

"I still believe that standing up for the truth of God is the greatest thing in the world. This is the end of life. The end of life is not to be happy. The end of life is not to achieve pleasure and avoid pain. The end of life is to do the will of God, come what may." King here answers the prophetic question of authority, but what is this will and truth by which he orients? "I think I have discovered the highest good. It is love. This principle stands at the center of the cosmos." He quotes John: "Let us love one another, for love is God; and everyone that loves is born of God and knows God; he that loves not knows not God; for God is love. . . . If we love one another God dwells in us and his love is perfected in us" (1 John 4:7–8, 12). In King's gloss: "He who loves is a participant in the being of God." He thus answers the question of authority by making love the central commitment in his life: To be oriented by God is to be animated by love; to enact love is to identify with those who suffer unjustly and to embrace suffering on their behalf. By "love" he says he means not eros as carnal passion, not the reciprocal love between friends called philia, nor anything "sentimental" or "affectionate," but "agape."[25]

"Agape means recognition of the fact that all life is interrelated. All humanity is involved in a single process and all men are brothers. To the degree I harm my brother, no matter what he is doing to me, to that extent I am harming myself." He embraces ahimsa, doing no harm, because he *is* the other. Ego is an illusion, as is any racial (or substantial) identity. Identity—as Jew or Roman, male or female, black or white—is part of the material (say "fallen") world, but identity and inequality do not hold in the realm of the spirit because all human beings are God's children.[26] All humans are beloved of God and interrelated, but also, each bears a latent potential, and agape is love not so much for what a being is or does now as for (its capacities to develop into) what it could become. King's favorite poem, by his namesake Martin Luther, reads:

This life therefore
Is not righteousness
but growth in righteousness,
not health but healing,
not being but becoming,
not rest but exercise.
    We are not yet what we shall be
but we are going toward it.
The process is not yet finished
but it is going on.
This is not the end
but it is the road.
    All does not gleam in glory
but all is being purified.

"Salvation does not await the believer at the end of the journey but is the journey itself," Lischer says, as if redemption is an ongoing "march," an abiding practice of love. Suffering is made creative by "love" conceived as acting, learning, healing, becoming. Redemption then is an act, not a substance to possess or a final destination. Still, King depicts *the road*, a telos that "bends" toward justice."[27]

"When you love on this level you begin to love men not because they are likable, not because they do things that attract us, but because God loves them." Agape does not distinguish friend and enemy or worthy and unworthy, because "disinterested love" seeks "not [one's] own good but the good of his neighbor." Unlike eros and philia, agape is impersonal and universal: One "loves" others not as erotic partners or friends, nor by approving of their conduct, but by seeking their good. To "love the person who does the evil deed while hating the deed the person does" is to seek that person's good despite his or her conduct, because we are siblings who partake of the oneness of God's being, and we harm ourselves if we harm others. But how does "redemptive good will for all men" make unmerited suffering politically fruitful?[28]

There are several notable criticisms of "love" in and as politics. For Freud, demands to universalize love exceed human capacities and inflict too high a cost in guilt and hypocrisy. Love cannot be separated from exclusion and aggression: As any Jew could testify, constitutively "Christian" claims to love universally still mean loving some rather than others, and loving some by displacing aggression onto scapegoats. As David Nirenberg thus argues, by "the vocabulary of love" we "fantasize overcoming those very exclusions that the history of its use has generated." In Nietzsche's related account, idealization of love bespeaks resentment not only of the powerful but of power, not only of domination but of difference, not only of stigma but of mortal particularity. For Arendt, then, "love" is hostile to politics because it devalues the in-between space necessary to plurality, unless our love is for "the world" itself beyond any other attachment. But King means to answer such concerns, and his practice of agape arguably has political features that Arendt in particular favors, albeit in other terms.[29]

First, agape is an egalitarian political theology: It avows a space *together* to cast "sin" as a disavowal of connection by exclusion or domination. Among members of one body, differences in talent and social position are undeserved contingencies, and investment in them is idolatry. At the founding convention of the Student Nonviolent Coordinating Committee (SNCC), James Lawson thus says, "The Christian favors the breaking down of racial barriers because the redeemed community of which he is already a citizen recognizes no barriers dividing humanity."[30] Willful oppression and fortuitous difference divide one from another, but love means sharing each other's fate and redressing inequality to the greatest extent possible. For King as for Blake before him, such a commitment—to risking the self for others and for the world—emerges not from rational self-interest, even rightly understood, or from aggregation of interests, but from their transformation by another kind of "power" he finds in (human) being.

Second, agape is for King a public ethos seeking what Arendt herself calls *respect:* "a regard for the person from the distance which the space of the world puts between us," an impersonal regard "independent of qualities we may admire or achievements we may highly esteem." Agape thus seeks what she calls *impartiality:* We acknowledge the reality of plural others because we are called to imagine how the world appears to them and to imagine their good. For King, agape is a *moral* achievement, but it entails the "enlarged mentality" and "representative thinking" that Arendt links to sound *political* judgment about adversaries and consequences.[31] Like Arendtian respect or liberal forms of public reason, King's agape is impersonal in its aspiration toward impartiality, but it is "thicker" than prevailing notions of what is public (and civil) as opposed to what is private or intimate. For agape reaches across such lines to engage the other; "love" names a struggle with inherited identities that reconfigures the very meaning of public and private. Love means, not safety, but risking the self and challenging the other, a testing of limits that at once intensifies and elevates life in its worldly and personal dimensions.

King sees that human (all-too-human) love is entwined with rivalry, so that brotherhood and inequality are stitched into the fabric of human life, but third, he believes that agape love turns against both domination and resentment on behalf of mutuality. What he calls love is a form of action that transforms suffering into a creative power that resists domination without repeating it. Because agape indicts evil in social structures rather than in demonized adversaries, and because self-reflection follows the injunction to seek others' good, agape is an ethos orienting people to see domination as a structure that harms even those it privileges. For "the white man's personality is greatly distorted by segregation and his soul greatly scarred."[32] If domination denies connection, love addresses this denial of (our) reality by waking in our oppressors their own capacity for connection. Agape is not just a moral mandate to put the other first, for by prudential political logic, black emancipation means addressing white racism; by King's Christian practice, this means reanimating *whites'* capacity to acknowledge the reality of their conduct and of those they dominate.[33]

As he says in his "Letter from Birmingham Jail," by "using our very bodies as a means" we will bring "to the surface the [racial] tension that is already alive" and "lay our case before the conscience of the local and national community." Our protests elicit, even provoke, and so dramatize the racial violence at American origins; by demonstrations that disturb the public order of apartheid, protesters compel whites to engage them; but their nonviolence reveals whites' own (human) capacity to act otherwise. Agape thus recognizes that political means are ends in the making: "The non-violent resister seeks to attack the evil system rather than the individuals who happen to be caught up in that system" because the point is to engage and transform, not embitter, them. To sustain democratic ends, subalterns *must* resist domination by nonviolence and must *embrace* the suffering they thereby undergo. King thus quotes Gandhi: "Though rivers of blood may have to flow before we gain our freedom, it must be our blood."[34] For King,

We must risk our lives to become witnesses to the truth as we see it. . . . this approach will mean suffering and sacrifice. It may mean going to jail. . . . It may even mean physical death. But if physical death is the price a man must pay to free his children and his white brethren from a permanent death of the spirit, then nothing could be more redemptive. This is the type of soul force I am convinced will triumph over the physical force of the oppressor.

"Do to us what you will and we will still love you. . . . But we will soon wear you down by our capacity to suffer. And in winning our freedom we will so appeal to your heart and conscience that we will win you in the process." A boycott, then, "is never an end in itself," for the goal is not the reification of friends and enemies but "reconciliation and the creation of beloved community."[35]

Fourth, by seeking to "redeem not humiliate" the other, nonviolent resisters break the chain of blows constituting history, and not only by "going to any length to restore community." For King knows the crowning injustice of injustice is that those who suffer it must suffer still more to resist it. They must struggle doubly to address the "violence of spirit" that is the internal legacy of "unearned suffering." Chosen suffering in nonviolent resistance, he claims, regenerates subalterns by "purifying" them of rage and despair. For those who "channel discontent through the creative outlet of non-violent direct action" put hatred of injustice into political form, not self-destructive conduct. Defensive about Nietzsche's claim that nonviolence bespeaks the resentment of the weak, who lack the power to act otherwise, King (like Gandhi) repeatedly casts nonviolence as a willfully *chosen* path that means courageously facing (fear of) death. "No man is free if he fears death," King declares, but this fear *is* faced by "suffering servants" who bear witness to God's truth.[36]

As a practice of creative nonviolence, King consider agape *redemptive* not only because it makes suffering purposeful and creative but because it enables freedom. Partly, he affirms how worldly action moves people from deference and self-hatred to assertion and self-respect. Facing the police, he says, marchers "for the first time dared to look a white man in the eye. . . . The marchers, many of them on their knees, unafraid and unmoving, stared back [at police holding fire hoses]. Slowly, the Negroes stood up and began to advance. Connor's men, as though hypnotized, fell back, their hoses sagging uselessly in their hands." The phallic power of white men is deflated by another power—King calls it love—that needs no inflation.[37]

Experiences of "collective self-respect" enable freedom's internal dimension:

The Negro will only be free when he reaches down to the inner depths of his own being and signs with pen and ink of assertive manhood his own emancipation proclamation. . . . With a spirit straining toward true self-esteem, the Negro must boldly throw off the manacles of self-abnegation and say to himself and to the world, "I am somebody. . . . I am a man with dignity and honor. I have a rich and noble history. . . . Yes, we must stand up now and say, "I'm black and I'm beautiful" and this self-affirmation is the black man's need, made compelling by the white man's crimes against him.[38]

Partly, of course, King links love to freedom in the sense that protesters exercise capacities for speech and action in public. By protesting legal apartheid, they seek representation and recognition, but they also bring into being a public realm that apartheid had destroyed for all by foreclosing to some. Using the places historically available to black people—churches—as a parallel polis, they organize buses, streets, stores, and jails into spaces truly open to action in concert. Participation as a form of what Arendt calls "public happiness" is a recurring motif in every memoir: The spiritedness of "freedom songs," meetings, and marches, says Richard King, testifies "to the sheer happiness of speaking and acting in public." No wonder activists celebrate Thoreau, whose call for "corporations of conscientious men" and depiction of jail as "freer and more honorable ground" for "freer and less desponding spirits," is uncannily apt.[39]

Lastly, King's agape bears a redemptive meaning in the sense we hear when Arendt links forgiveness to freedom. Love means "restoring community" because it addresses what Arendt calls trespass by way of forgiveness. Without forgiveness, she argues, we are trapped in the consequences of prior acts, from which we must release each other if we are ever to act or begin anew. "King's ultimate significance," Richard King claims, "which remains to be absorbed fully, lay in his effort to incorporate the complex dialectic of forgiving and forgetting into politics." He models an answer to the question of how to "rectify and yet go beyond a history of vengeance, transforming the compulsion to repeat into the capacity to act."[40]

King's "I have a dream" speech is idealized, but perhaps its vision of redemption—sharing a meal at the same table—should not be dismissed hastily. Epochal change appears not by violence or apocalypse; rather, it appears as the unprecedented—equality—becomes an ordinary fact of life. Mutual acts of atonement and forgiveness—or at least organizing that compels whites to sit with those they have disavowed—make redemption not an "end" to politics but its condition of possibility.

For "brotherhood" means not unity but reconstituting membership and terms of conflict. Who cooks? What do we eat? In what portions? Who is excluded? If redemption is not a fully realized "beloved community" but this beginning, King does not script the future; he imagines people gathered around a table, not submerged in a mystic body, free at last to make their future differently. Then, in ways Arendt never imagined, struggle to overcome white supremacy reanimates the "revolutionary treasure" of freedom.[41]

National Identity and American Exceptionalism

We have focused thus far on King's prophetic vocation in relation to the disremembered and uncounted, whose unmerited suffering he would forge into—and redeem as—creative power. To do so he remakes black political subjectivity by calling African Americans to identify themselves as Hebrews in Egypt and as Christians in Rome. But rather than use diasporic identity to unite blacks, he reworks American exceptionalism by a jeremiad to whites as a national subject. Is his dissent then "contained," as Bercovitch argues, by a civil religion that replenishes liberal politics and its national frame?[42]

Against accounts of self-interested racial groups struggling over power, his religious language moves from the local to the transcendent and from the racial to the moral, to give the civil rights movement a universal meaning in democratic terms. In this way he does not so much replace politics by principle as use principle strategically. We hear self-righteous reaching for the high moral ground, as if "politics" were beneath him, but he thereby defeats the racial imaginary that makes morality white and makes black assertion barbaric, and he turns what white critics call a race war into a struggle over principles whites already profess to support. Indeed, he *can* abstract in this way because prophetic language is powerful in the United States, and he seeks legitimacy for his cause by appropriating it. How then does he conceive this nation and foster in whites a "willingness to restore community"?

He seeks political authority among whites by appealing to the hegemonic assumption that American nationhood is supposed to be different, that Americans are a chosen people called to found a promised, exemplary land. King does not reject the aspiration. In his profoundly effective retelling of this story, whites have failed to make good on this aspiration, but blacks can initiate its redemption. He does not say, with

Paul, that Jews forfeited a chosen status that God now transfers to those they excluded. Rather, he defines blacks and whites as children in one house, whose history is a story of some disinheriting others and whose redemption requires overcoming that breach to embody founding national principles. But as oppression invests blacks in worldly freedom, so black agency is critical in this redemption.

King always sought to *compel* change in white conduct through marches, boycotts, and demonstrations, or what Niebuhr calls "nonviolent coercion."[43] Denouncing "the tragic attempt to live by monologue rather than dialogue," King says, "we know through painful experience that freedom is never voluntarily given by the oppressor; it must be demanded by the oppressed." The "we" here bespeaks his unambiguous identification with subalterns who constitute a "people" within a nation, cast down and set apart by others who call themselves white. But "abused and scorned though we may be, our destiny is tied up with the destiny of America."

Before the Pilgrims landed at Plymouth we were here. Before the pen of Jefferson etched across the pages of history the majestic words of the Declaration of Independence, we were here. For more than two centuries our foreparents labored in this country without wages; they made cotton king; and they built the homes of their masters in the midst of brutal injustice and shameful humiliation—and yet out of bottomless vitality they continued to thrive and develop. If the inexhaustible cruelties of slavery could not stop us, the opposition we now face will surely fail.[44]

We will win not only because we will not give up struggling for freedom, says King, but because "the sacred heritage of our nation and the eternal will of God are embodied in our echoing demands."[45] Showing how black people shaped American life, King makes black struggle bear national aspiration and divine will. He affirms the romance of American universalism as he uses it to authorize black struggle, but this universalism is fraudulent because of black exclusion; and without black aspiration to make it real it must remain fraudulent.

Members of the Southern Christian Leadership Conference (SCLC) chose as their motto "To save the soul of America" because, he says, "We were convinced that we could not limit our vision to certain rights for black people, but instead affirmed the conviction that America would never be free or saved from itself unless the descendants of its slaves were loosed completely from the shackles they still wear."[46] Casting "America" as a protagonist whose "soul" cannot be "saved" unless the legacy of slavery is overcome, King quotes Langston Hughes:

O yes
I say it plain,
America was never America to me,
And yet I swear this oath—
America will be![47]

Partly, appeals to a national (and white) audience is a strategic necessity for a political minority—we require and must seek majority support
for civil rights legislation and states' enforcement of the law. Partly, he
exploits the cultural hegemony of the Bible to put black struggle into
moral terms that whites can recognize; likewise, he identifies black aspirations with white consensus ideals of America. As Lischer says, "He
wanted whites to recognize the best of their own values in the mirror of
his message." According to Lischer, King's approach thus enacts what
Kenneth Burke calls "the principle of courtship" in good rhetoric: He
begins with the assumptions of his white audience to elicit their assent
to black aspiration. He "articulates the values of white liberalism, which
he has thoroughly internalized," but "in his own black voice." That voice,
"imbued with the irony, judgment, and genuine hope of the black gospel, modifies liberal values even as it articulates them."[48]

King thus speaks directly within the democratic idealism recurrently
wed to American nationalism: He authorizes resistance to legalized apartheid by appealing to whites' idealized image of themselves as a "democratic" and "Christian" nation. Invoking ideals crucial to what Robert
Bellah calls a consensual "civil religion," King opposes ascribed (racial)
identity because all are entitled to develop their God-given potential.
Protesting the gap between inherited ideals and daily practices, he calls
a special people to make good the founding promise(s) it never has
honored: "Now is the time to make real the promise of democracy," but
also, to make good this promise is to fulfill "the goal of America, which
is freedom."[49]

But as King puts black aspiration into the rhetoric of national promise, he "blackens" this promise. For as blacks invoke the rights that signify (white) manhood in a Puritan and trading nation, they do not only
seek a normative citizenship long denied them. Since a racist culture
makes blackness a mark of embodiment that "stains" the spirit and
the political, black entry into the symbolic defeats the abstraction that
makes equality "white" by making rights disembodied. King also blackens "America" by investing its redemption in African Americans. We will
"save the soul of America" by enabling citizens to "rise up and live out
the true meaning of its creed." Our destiny is tied to the nation's, for

our exploited labor and cultural creativity shape it, and, he goes on, "the sacred heritage of our nation and the eternal will of God are embodied in our echoing demands":

One day the South will know that when these disinherited children of God sat down at lunch counters they were in reality standing up for the best in the American dream and the most sacred values in our Judaeo-Christian heritage, and thus carrying our whole nation back to the great wells of democracy, which were dug deep by the founding fathers in the formulation of the Constitution and the Declaration of Independence.[50]

Linking God's moral law to the "wells of democracy" in the Declaration of Independence and the Constitution, King joins democratic idealism and American nationalism, but he also makes African Americans a redemptive protagonist by virtue of their historical exclusion and continuing faith. Purified by agape and nonviolent practice, and "using our bodies as a means," we expose violent origins to elicit white acknowledgment—of black humanity and of gross violation of the national creed—in a way that reveals their (whites') own capacity to redeem racial hatred. Because of "faith that [our] unearned suffering is redemptive," we can redeem the twinned promises of America and democracy.

When King positions black agency in relation to whites, he says, "We will have to repent in this generation not only for the vitriolic words and actions of the bad people, but for the appalling silence of the good people." His prophetic practice of bearing witness provokes the violence of one in order to provoke the conscience of the other. To "white moderates" who call him an "extremist" he asserts, "The question is not whether we will be extremist, but what kind of extremist we will be." A year before Barry Goldwater will notoriously declare that "extremism in the defense of freedom is no vice," King asks, "Will we be extremists for hate, or will we be extremists for love?" For "maybe the south, the nation, and the world are in dire need of creative extremists." Against those who counsel "all deliberate speed," he warns that if "channeling discontent through the creative outlet of nonviolent direct action" fails, "millions of Negroes, out of frustration and despair, will seek solace and security in black nationalist ideologies," which "will lead inevitably to a frightening racial nightmare."[51]

King, therefore, is not only justifying black agency but shaping it. In defending "creative tension" with white supremacy, he depicts himself "in the middle of two opposing forces" in the African American community. On one side are "Negroes who . . . have adjusted to segregation" and therefore live in passive deference and despair. On the other side are those who have "lost faith in America, who have absolutely repudiated Christianity, and who have concluded that the white man is an incurable 'devil.'" Surely King uses those he calls nationalists to legitimize his own politics, and he stokes white fear of black violence to elicit political concessions. But his motives are complex.[52]

Partly, he believes that violence is never regenerative personally or politically. Partly, he believes that democracy requires dialogue, and that struggle for freedom betrays itself by abandoning dialogue. Partly, he is strategic: A minority needs allies to create a ruling majority, and violence risks a racial apocalypse. Partly, he defends against the racial symbolism in which black means, as Toni Morrison says, "insanity, illicit sexuality, and chaos."[53] Individual forms of despair and political calls for violence confirm a racial imaginary he counters by casting African Americans as redeemers of a national covenant.

Accordingly, his language of rebirth from sin does advance a cultural politics. Against the "idolatry" of individualistic pleasure and conspicuous consumption, King endorses a left Puritanism to promote delay of gratification and dispositions to sacrifice for racial uplift. For the broader civil rights project does entail a patriarchal and middle-class cultural politics: It links self-control and work to proper masculinity and fatherhood, imposes proper femininity on black women, and enforces heteronormative sexual practices to save the black community from decadent (toleration of) deviance. While King invokes consensual culture in Bellah's sense, he shows its hegemonic power as he disciplines black agency and dissent to achieve a normative subjectivity.[54]

But the civil rights project cannot escape the racial symbolic. For the identity of God's good son reiterates the other meaning of black: the unconditional, sacrificial love—Morrison says "benevolence, harmless and servile guardianship, and endless love"[55]—that regenerates whites. Inescapably, therefore, argument—over dialogue, appeals to conscience, nonviolence, coalition, and more broadly over the meaning of American nationalism and the limits of liberal politics—occurred in debates about the related meanings of love, power, and blackness. Does King's language of love mean acquiescence to white power?

Black Power Critics and King's Radicalization

From the early 1960s on, Malcolm X, SNCC organizers, and Black Panthers denounce King's servile attachment to whites and idealization of liberal nationalism. These critics depict the United States as an empire, not a nation, and blacks as a colony, not a minority, subjected to oppression, not discrimination. "America" is not a democratic ideal or a nation of individuals ruled by transcendent constitutional principles but a regime characterized by racial domination and capitalist exploitation. Portraying a state originating in violence rather than consent and a nation defined by whiteness rather than democracy, King's critics speak of group liberation, not equal rights; community control, not desegregation; power, not civil rights. They lodge black aspiration for democracy not in national but in diasporic (transnational and local) attachments. They do not express "disappointment" at white behavior or corruption of a creed; they claim to hold no expectations to disappoint, for an imperial regime warrants no loyalty from colonized subjects.[56]

Accordingly, they reject King's idea of dialogue, which appeals to the "conscience" of whites in the name of brotherhood. On the one hand, they say, agape is *emasculating* without real reciprocity, invoking a phallic manhood we will assess critically in our reading of Baldwin. On the other hand, they say, groups do not have consciences, group power is not formed by aggregating individual consciences, and appeals to conscience (and dialogue) cannot erase structural inequality of resources and power. Since blacks and whites are not one but two nations within a regime structured to benefit whites only, no appeals to brotherhood can compel whites to count blacks' reality and address their interests; only militant assertion, including threats of violence in the name of self-defense, can do so. Only then might coexistence and dialogue be possible.

King's critics do see the pressures that redemptive rhetoric imposes on the excluded: When legitimacy requires piety for a founding legacy, they must redeem its promise to oppose its exclusionary practice; when legitimacy requires speaking to and for everyone in a nation, they must discount the depth of division to redeem it; when legitimacy derives from the moral authority of a redemptive role, actors must disown in themselves the partiality and power that signify corruption in the social body they would purify. King risks these pressures by using consensual language, but his critics incur other risks as they deny the need for broad appeals across racial lines.

King embraces the role of redeemer in a narrative that saves the soul of America, whereas his critics equate that role with Uncle Tom because blacks still serve and save whites. To kill off the good son who internalizes a Christian and liberal identity, they invert the difference and idealize the outcast status that whites invest in blackness. Their identity politics thus enmeshes them in the image of blackness that King refuses, because their assertion terrifies whites who project violence behind the mask of love. But threatened violence becomes a chosen mask for young men claiming what they call their manhood. Denying a redemptive meaning to "America" and refusing the role of redeemer, but using white myths of regenerative violence, they are placed in and take on the role of Bigger, Richard Wright's "native son," whose rage and imminent violence haunt a white republic.

King recognizes how white psychodrama allows only two self-destroying roles for blacks—a sacrificial role or a violent one—yet he denies that nonviolent politics means sacrificing black interests or agency to white redemption. But by 1964 political reality is fueling his critics: White recalcitrance about rights already sanctioned constitutionally feeds growing anger among blacks, squeezing out the political space King would open. Progress until 1964 "misled us," he admits, because "everyone underestimated the amount of rage Negroes were suppressing, and the amount of bigotry the white majority was disguising." Even more urgently defending nonviolence after riots in 1964–65, he also listens to his critics, learns from political difficulty, and radicalizes his politics.[57]

Most importantly, he publicly recognizes the inequality of economic, political, and cultural resources that the law cannot reach: He *announces* the limitation of formal equality and rejects the idea of an American creed that discrimination violates. "We deceive ourselves" if we believe "that the dominant ideology in our country, even today, is freedom and equality, while racism is an occasional departure from the norm." As racialized poverty rather than legal discrimination, inequality is systemic and institutional, not a sign of prejudice but part of political economy. "There are 40 million poor people in America . . . why?" To raise "questions about economic systems, about a broader distribution of wealth" is to "begin questioning the capitalist economy." As Bayard Rustin concludes in 1965, "While most Negroes . . . seek only to enjoy the fruits of American society as it now exists, their quest cannot *objectively* be satisfied within the framework of existing political and economic relations."[58]

Substantive equality is costly: "Why is equality so assiduously avoided?" King asks rhetorically, and he replies, "The practical cost of change for the nation up to this point" has been "cheap," obtainable at "bargain prices" because desegregation, unlike the amelioration of poverty, requires no redistribution of wealth or expensive social programs. Because even marginal improvement for blacks requires radical change, King follows (to a point) the logic of Rustin's famous "from protest to politics" argument.[59]

"What is the value of access to public accommodations for those who lack the money to use them?" Rustin asks. "The minute the movement faced this question it was compelled to expand its vision beyond race relations to economic relations." If we see that the issue "is not civil rights strictly speaking, but social and economic conditions," it is clear that "these interrelated problems . . . require government action—or politics." He focuses on institutions, not conscience: "Social, political, and economic institutions . . . are the ultimate molders of collective sentiments. Let these institutions be reconstructed today," and "the ineluctable gradualism of history" will yield "the formation of a new psychology." All along Rustin used demonstrations to compel whites to "the table," but now he seeks an interracial social movement on class lines to gain and exercise "political power." Against "black nationalism," he argues that "20 million black people cannot win political power alone. We need allies" and must make "a progressive coalition" the "effective political majority in the United States." Dividing "protest" (as moralism) from "politics" (as power), he fashions a strategic but pragmatic argument to radicalize the New Deal coalition, whose hegemony seems assured by Goldwater's defeat.[60]

King always endorsed the political logic of interracial coalition. On strategic grounds, he continues to reject the (rhetoric of) revolutionary violence he hears in his critics:

They fail to see that no internal revolution has ever succeeded in overthrowing a government by violence unless the government had already lost the allegiance and effective control of its armed forces. . . . Furthermore, few if any violent revolutions have been successful unless the violent minority had the sympathy and support of the non-resistant majority. . . . [A] violent revolution by American blacks would find no sympathy and support from the white population, and very little from the majority of the Negroes themselves.[61]

But unlike Rustin, King embraces the cultural concerns of black nationalists and increasingly speaks of community control and black pride to black audiences. Moreover, he directs black agency beyond political party coalition: What he soon calls "the black revolution" is "more than a struggle for the rights of Negroes." By "forcing America to face

all its interrelated flaws—racism, poverty, militarism and imperialism,"
it makes "the radical reconstruction of society . . . the real issue to be
faced."[62]

King also seeks a majoritarian and coalitional politics, but while
this goal drives Rustin to support Lyndon Johnson, the Democratic
Party, and the Vietnam War, King is driven by his nonviolence and anti-
imperialism to oppose the war. Against advisers committed to party politics and "civil rights" leaders anxious to keep Johnson's support, King
alienates Lyndon Johnson, the Democratic Party apparatus, and the
labor movement. But speaking out against (the) war is essential to his
prophetic calling, he says, which must question any national allegiance:

I must be true to my conviction that I share with all men the calling to be a son
of the living God. Beyond the calling of race or nation or creed is this vocation
of sonship and brotherhood, and because I believe that the father is deeply concerned especially for his suffering and helpless and outcast children, I come . . .
to speak for them.[63]

Opposing imperial war in the voice of prophecy, not that of Lenin,
he depicts himself as "bound" by allegiances and loyalties which are
broader and deeper than nationalism, which "go beyond our nation's
self-defined goals and positions. We are called to speak for the weak, for
the voiceless, for the victims of our nation, and for those it calls enemy,
for no document in human hands can make these humans any less our
brothers." He speaks in a universal register of voice, "as a citizen of the
world as it stands aghast at the path we have taken." Still, he also speaks
"as an American to the leaders of my own nation."[64]

In both regards his calling is to make visible and audible the suffering caused by national policy: "I speak for those whose land is being
laid waste, whose homes are being destroyed, whose culture is being
subverted," but also, "I speak for the poor of America who are paying the
double price of smashed hopes at home and death and corruption in
Vietnam." Avowing membership in a national "we" whose acts he owns,
King makes a prophetic demand for decision: "The great initiative in
this war is ours. The initiative to stop it must be ours." Addressing not
the details of foreign policy but "the fierce urgency of the now," he declares, "This madness must cease. We must stop now."[65]

At the same time, though, Vietnam is a "symptom of a far deeper mal-
ady within the American spirit." Partly, it reflects imperial investments
that put us "on the wrong side of a world revolution." Like "moderates"
resisting civil rights, Americans "make peaceful revolution impossible
by refusing to give up the privileges and pleasures that come from im-

mense profits of overseas investment." Partly, the Vietnam War and imperial power reflect the rule of instrumental values. "When machines
and computers, profit motives and property rights are considered more
important than people, the giant triplets of racism, materialism, and
militarism are incapable of being conquered." He calls for "a radical
revolution in values" to bring about a "shift from a 'thing-oriented' to a
'person-oriented' society."[66]

The problem is not that our conduct violates our values, as Myrdal
and Walzer argue, and so the solution is not renewing ideals we have
forgotten or corrupted. Rather, our values and conduct are mutually re-
inforcing. The problem is not political hypocrisy but a "spiritual death"
that deprives people of the capacity to feel and hear the suffering they
cause or allow. Like Jeremiah, King moves from a jeremiad denouncing
the gap between a worthy creed and evil practices, to arguing that values
and practices must be revolutionized. As for Thoreau in *Walden*, the
problem is practices and the spirit or values they enshrine, so that a solution must build and cultivate differently. But what faith enables that?

Since both creed and practices need to be transformed, our founding covenant must be called a failure; the task is not to renew but to
supersede it. He still exhorts, "America, you must be reborn again!" But
"our only hope" for that "lies in our ability to recapture the revolutionary
spirit" itself, that is, faith in capacities to create and initiate. Warning that
a nation inexorably, always, reaps what it sows, he seeks a decision:

Time is deaf to every plea and rushes on. Over the bleached bones and jumbled
residue of numerous civilizations are written the pathetic words: too late. There
is an invisible book of life that faithfully records our vigilance or our neglect. . . .
If we do not act we shall surely be dragged down the long, dark, and shameful
corridors of time reserved for those who possess power without compassion,
might without morality, and strength without sight. Now let us begin. Now let us
rededicate ourselves to the long and bitter—but beautiful—struggle for a new
world. This is the calling of the sons of God, and our brothers wait eagerly for
our response. . . . the choice is ours.[67]

When he asserts that the arc of the universe bends toward justice, he now
foretells not divine support of black struggle but judgment of a nation
unwilling to change its ways.

Assessing King's Personal and Political Crisis

In 1967 and 1968, says Lischer, "King's rage was second to none, neither Stokely Carmichael's nor Malcolm X's, but his commitment to

Christianity offered him no outlet in the rhetoric of violence." His rage appears in his angry denunciations, but it must be *God's* anger. Compelled by his calling to avow, rather, his *own* grief, he quotes Jeremiah: "My grief is beyond healing. My heart is sick within me."[68] Warning that "the judgment of God is upon us today," he asserts that "something must be done quickly," and he pleads for a turn and rebirth: "I pray God that America will hear this before it is too late."[69]

King negotiates his anger by emphasizing his grief, but his anger drives him to embrace suffering as chosen sacrifice. As the good son's faith in the redemptive power of love is sorely tested by our persistence in sin, he reaffirms his effort to redeem evil by suffering without retaliation; but oppression and suffering replenish his anger, and his anger jeopardizes both his persona as a redeemer and the authority of his God. Unable to condemn God for innocent suffering or to break God's law by striking at whites, he follows the logic of the good son, whose disavowed anger fuels renewed willingness to suffer. Unable to reject the authority that justifies him, he embraces sacrifice to redeem it. Unable to redeem the dialogic terms of a democratic faith he cannot let go, he embraces self-sacrifice on its behalf. By 1968 he is using "the crucified savior as the organizing symbol for his own depression, failures, rejection, and impending death." Sermons and speeches rarely invoke Jesus "without indirectly referring to himself" to "convey overtones of the Lord's betrayal and death."[70]

As with Thoreau, these pressures may bespeak an inherent logic in prophetic identity, but that logic is triggered as contingent political realities shut down the space prophets would open. For King was not a central galvanizing figure by 1967; rather, he stood to the side as events spiraled out of control. He was marginalized, Lischer argues, partly because "white American liberalism embraced the victim, but not the prophet" and "the radical changes" he called for. Opposing the Vietnam War had rendered King especially vulnerable to demonization by the nationalism he had tried to infuse with new meaning. Meanwhile, "Black America embraced the threatening prophet who predicted long hot summers in the ghettos, condemned the war in Vietnam, and demanded a radical redistribution of wealth," but it refused "to identify itself as a vessel of redemptive or unmerited suffering" and "grew weary" with the suffering servant who "clung ever more tenaciously to suffering and death as the only means of redemption."[71]

Andrew Sabl claims that King imposes this marginality on himself because he moves from jeremiadic critique—which narrates violation of a core "American" creed—to the narration of a genocidal, imperial history. This shift in stories creates a profound crisis because King can no longer appeal to founding national principles drawing on a larger Judeo-Christian heritage. In the terms of Michael Walzer, King abandons "internal" criticism when he no longer depicts practices violating core values whose authority he defends. In Bercovitch's terms, he moves outside a jeremiadic language of consensus (though canonization later returns him to it). Once King depicts a society that, from chattel slavery to capitalist commodification, has been "thing-oriented," his calls for rebirth, even to recover a revolutionary treasure, lack any evident social basis or historical ground.[72]

By rejecting the exceptionalist framework defining a liberal consensus, Sabl claims, King's new narrative marks a crisis in democratic legitimation:

This is not really an argument about historical interpretation. The two stories about American history differ not regarding the facts or even historical causes, but regarding the meaning of the facts. Whether slavery or the Vietnam War are fundamental to America or anomalous departures from noble ideals is not a question that can be settled empirically. Different groups in society will find one or the other interpretation (or neither) to be compelling, based on their respective experiences.

Neither public reason nor deliberative procedures can resolve this difference. In Sabl's inelegant—and ultimately misleading—formulation: "Those who believed in the currency of equality and liberty had more votes than King, who believed that racism was fundamental." If prophecy presents a people with decision, Sabl says, people also make a decision about prophecy.[73]

Sabl relates this narrative defeat by majority rule to a second crisis: King "dissented from the fundamental assumption, shared by democratic citizens and liberal philosophers, that we are not subject to claims made by sources external to ourselves, but only to those we ourselves acknowledge." Whereas King once believed he needed to offer secular justifications to ground his authority to speak on political matters, Sabl claims, he comes to speak "as a literal prophet whose authority came directly from God and superseded human judgment."[74]

Lischer also sees a dialectic between increasing marginality and rhetoric *reduced* to prophecy: "If every rhetorical strategy implies self-interest and careful weighing of costs and benefits to the audience, then

King's practice of confrontation has taken him to the outer boundary of strategy" because "he is no longer double-voiced. He is past signifying. He knows the prophet is answerable only to God." He surrenders to a "prophetic rage" that no longer appeals to secular as well as sacred authority.[75]

For Sabl, the problem is not in the people but in the critic, not in social practices or imperial wars but in critical standards and how they are used. The challenge of what he calls "moral activism" is to "combat the vices of democracy without contesting its fundamental principles," to "respect Tocqueville's distinction between improving selfish, individualist, and democratic tendencies" and "seeking to abolish them." Likewise, if critics do not translate divinely sanctioned principles into secular terms, they violate the basic rule constituting liberal society in public reason. At best, moral activists can mitigate individualism "and brute, narrow forms of majority rule" in favor of "higher moral purposes," but "excessively high ethical standards" drive critics toward "cursing people—and if necessary the whole people—for not living up to the moral standards that activists believe themselves to exemplify."[76]

Sabl believes that King reinterpreted "in politically viable terms his more uncompromising calls for Christian charity" and that "his grasp of civic principles" tempered "excessively demanding moral ideals." But Sabl's King does not sustain the tension between morality and politics. He chooses a prophetic tradition that fears "insufficient vigilance" about domination, but not a liberal tradition that fears "fanaticism" in those who assume that "matters of justice and injustice *are* clear." In that liberal, pluralist voice, Sabl says, "the question is not whether we would welcome activism based on *our* values, aimed at reforming *others,* but whether we would welcome *other* people's activism, based on their view of moral rightness, aimed at reforming *us.*" In his own moment of decision, Sabl lodges the danger to democracy in fanaticism, making toleration, not militancy, what is needful. He does so not as a white subject defending white supremacy but as a secular subject resisting invasive "moral reform."[77]

Claiming to stand with Tocqueville, Sabl defends a prosaic politics and self-interest rightly understood to honor "the liberal quest for toleration and the democratic desire to live one's life undisturbed by moral scolds." Assuming that others do *not* share our own values, democrats value rights and procedure over any one vision of the good to settle conflicts without appeals to any authority higher than their own reason.

But by the paradox of "democracy in America," these very assumptions enable white supremacy and gross economic inequality.[78]

For as Lincoln argues, "popular sovereignty," toleration of diversity, and private rights can excuse slavery. So in what cases are private rights forms of domination? At what point is toleration complicity in evil? When does pluralism put at risk democratic principles? Because imperial war and grievous injustice are authorized or allowed by formally democratic procedures, American prophets must ask such questions. Because democracy in fact requires seriousness about equality in more than formal senses, and because taking equality seriously means questioning rights and preferences that liberalism sanctifies as private, these critics must live in tension with liberal norms, but on behalf of democratic values like equality and self-determination.

King thus steps outside a liberal frame but not outside a democratic one, whereas Sabl defends, not democracy, but liberal proceduralism. The issue is not King's religious dogmatism or antidemocratic moralism but domination, protected by languages of rights and toleration. King's political marginality, then, results not from "excessive moral standards" but from the sustaining of war and inequality by a nationalism linking "America" to freedom. Nor is King invested in marginality. By declaring God's judgment he does not reject national attachment, but invokes its religious origins to deter its imperial practice. Likewise, he does not reject public reason, but prophetically dramatizes the unreason of state power and its vaunted pragmatism, which make the Vietnam War a moral and political catastrophe.

Even if Sabl is tone-deaf to conditions that generate and even justify King's "prophetic rage," however, does a defense of King's "extremism," now, enable the New Right's religiosity to serve antithetical purposes? How does King's prophetic politics appear if we follow Sabl to judge the moral activism of "other" people, based on *their* values, aimed at *us*? God language is valuable in voluntary associations of the like-minded, Sabl argues, but in politics it trumps public reason, forecloses debate, and devalues the "democratic" expression of interests and preferences. I see two lines of response.

One is that King advances his moral principles in democratic ways because he upholds a faith committed to equality, and so to dialogue and nonviolence. He advances not a fundamentalism or scriptural literalism but an ethos called agape. This principle requires interpretation— what does serve the good of the other?—and is open to translation. It is presented as contestable, and King risks this faith, as every utterance calls forth argument. His example suggests, indeed, that absolute or declarative claims do not end debate but provoke it. Likewise, he puts us in sacred or biblical time, but rather than use scripture to decree fate, he depicts contingency and seeks a "decision" by call-and-response. We remain free to rework or simply rebuff such claims, to deny community with him on the terms they dramatize.

By this line of argument, the substance of a faith, whether it is theist or not, matters less than its elective affinity to democratic practices and whether it can be practiced to enable engagement across lines of difference. Then a political response to the Christian New Right should be, not a rigid defense of liberal distinctions between sacred as private and secular as public, but an effort to rework pervasive religious language to foreground its democratic features and challenge its theocratic interpreters. The problem therefore is not religiosity as such but fundamentalism as a practice and the failure to generate countervailing power by contrasting visions.

By a second line of argument with Sabl, the problem is not that religiosity and moral activism threaten constitutional liberalism by invading privacy and dictating private lives. After all, the civil rights and feminist movements "politicized" private life to contest the "rights" of whites and men to dominate others, to defend the rightful autonomy of blacks and women, and to *redefine* the meaning of public and private and of legitimate conduct. Any project to address gross inequality of social and cultural resources—or imminent environmental disaster—will generate enormous opposition by politicizing the conduct of all and by proposing to curtail the rights of some for the sake of democratization. In this sense King's practice of democratic vision and popular mobilization is unarmed prophecy, seeking a Machiavellian moment to reconstitute a republic. Such moments embody democratic aspiration by threatening the authority of already-constituted laws, precedents, and preferences.

Still, we are left with two concerns about King's project, each addressed by Baldwin. One is King's cultural politics, which not only devalues women in the movement but enforces middle-class morality and heteronormative sexuality on men and women. Second is King's trope of rebirth, which posits a *pure* condition to be reached; an "after" that redeems an injured, subordinated, impure "before"; and a "higher" that redeems a "lower" of particularity, aggression, desire—of sin. He believes that nonviolent action "channels" aggression, just as he sometimes admits (though more often denies) that agape sublimates eros. But as rebirth redeems the sinful by moral spiritualization, splitting occurs. We saw it in Thoreau: He would "redeem" the carnal by incarnating spirit in it, as if it were a "brute" thing requiring elevation. But he also celebrates "the wild" and his attraction to it, which King cannot do. Thoreau experiments in building and cultivating to affirm Dionysian energies in creative tension with Apollonian forms, but a Christian King ever more desperately must affirm love's power to purify what he otherwise abhors as sin.

This is not only a personal issue seen in extramarital sex, a haunting remainder of a spiritualized love ethic. For "human stain" includes political particularity and aggression, which cannot be wholly redeemed by claims to universality. Like sexual desire, they *are* "redeemed"—or made good—as they are enlarged by agape to reach beyond the self to care about the good of concrete others and of the whole. By ideas of brotherhood and redemptive sacrifice, King *does* enable black agency and greater equality. And in some political moments, sacrifice is not only a political necessity but a democratic value and is profoundly regenerative of community, as Danielle Allen shows. Still, an idiom of Christian love moralizes politics and agency in ways that Baldwin will name and move beyond. Rejecting theism, he interprets love as meaning not rebirth from sin but the acceptance of actualities we have denied. Bearing witness to the waywardness of desire, the reality of the other, and the knotted ambivalence binding love to aggression, he makes of "love" a tragic language by which to theorize politics.

4. James Baldwin and the Racial State of Exception
Secularizing Prophecy?

This depthless alienation from oneself and one's people is, in sum, the American experience.
— James Baldwin, "Encounter on the Seine: Black Meets Brown"

It can be objected that I am speaking of political freedom in spiritual terms, but the political institutions of any nation are always menaced and are ultimately controlled by [its] spiritual state.
— James Baldwin, *The Fire Next Time*

From King to Baldwin

Like King, Baldwin is shaped profoundly by his experience in the black church, and he forges a language of love, suffering, and redemption that is both personal and political.[1] Like King, he exemplifies a "double-consciousness" toward both whites and blacks, whose entwined fates he can address partly because he refuses to be wholly defined by either. Like King, he works through a complex attachment to an "American" identity he links both to white supremacy and to a "promise" of overcoming ascription by "race, caste, and class." Like King, he invests in African Americans a special responsibility for voicing and redeeming democratic aspirations and for provoking whites to finally make good on them. Like King, therefore, he raises central prophetic questions: about the commitments we authorize and how we practice them, about whom we identify with and on what basis, about which story we tell to depict the past and its power, and in each regard, about how we conceive and seek redemption.

In what consists the difference? Having identified two registers of prophecy in Thoreau, one theist and moral, the other poetic and libidinal, we heard one register in the abolitionist tradition whose apotheosis is King, while we now hear Baldwin strongly inflect the other. It is tempting to identify one register with King and the other with Baldwin, but

Baldwin surely sustains a powerful "moral" sensibility toward life, and though he affirms unredeemed carnal life rather than theism, he does not so much celebrate desire as witness its vicissitudes. Still, he is a great critic of what is called morality in liberal society and of the bourgeois and Christian forms of racial respectability in African American culture.

He left America because of racism, but he left Harlem because of homophobia. As a result he can say, "The country which is your birth-place and to which you owe your life and identity has not, in its whole system of reality, evolved any place for you."[2] Rejecting a liberal consensus tied to racism and fear of the body, but also rejecting a black church whose theology of sin and redemption mirrors the terror of desire in the white church, he refuses liberal and Christian signifiers of moral virtue and normative citizenship. Taking biblical tropes and King James cadences from the black church, a tragic aesthetic from the blues, a vision of American innocence (and layered syntax!) from Henry James, and ideas of responsibility and bad faith from existentialism, Baldwin fashions a nontheist prophetic voice as an artist bearing witness to human finitude.

I call him nontheistic because he does not announce God's words or point of view as a messenger, but prophetic because, on the avowed basis of experience, social position, and artistic vision, he announces what is disavowed and unsayable and testifies to what he sees and stands against it. I call him nontheistic but prophetic because he announces the vicissitudes of human finitude not by way of God's righteousness in a providentially ordered universe but by way of the exemplary meaning or "truth" of his experience as a human being and as a "sexually dubious" black man.[3] By translating theist prophecy into such secular terms, what does Baldwin achieve? How does his translation both reflect and shape his engagement with white supremacy? Is there sense in the notion of "secularizing" prophecy and redemption?

Let us begin by recalling that King imagines redemption in terms of the "rebirth" of the soul and the nation. This rebirth requires "purification" in order to overcome violence, resentment, and narrow self-interest, signifiers of sin, antitheses of love. The self is reborn by discovering God's love within and for every creature, which binds them together as members of one body. Human beings can fulfill the Golden Rule only by discovering this love, which, by enabling sacrifice for the sake of the other, breaks the repetition of domination that is the mark of Cain, the symptom of sin. To "save the soul of America," then, is to make the nation a subject responsible for conduct it can repent of and overcome, by a love that purifies the predatory partiality that builds the freedom of some on the servitude of others. God gives each subject this capacity for rebirth, supports this freedom by a redemptive telos in history, and calls on prophets to demonstrate it.

It is not for strategic reasons only, therefore, that King closets a sexual life increasingly desperate! For he is a *prophet* who lives and dies for the *redemption* of human desire in the love of the other; his office and persona require him to embody the righteousness that elevates the base into the sublime, the carnal into the moral. But he is driven toward *unredeemed* carnal life as the risk of death makes mortal pleasure precious, and because the flesh that bears the impurity he must purify is also invested with a humanity he cannot forsake. But public admission of carnal impurity discredits the authority of the prophet by reducing him to unredeemed particularity. Such unmasking also subverts King's political project by staining the redemptive universalism he (and blacks) must exemplify. In his effort to infuse nationhood with new meaning, he is vulnerable to being hijacked by its historic meaning, and likewise, he can be unmasked by the historic meaning of prophecy, which requires redeeming the human by the moral.

Baldwin also speaks of redemption, but not of rebirth. We do not *purify* ourselves of corruption (by sinful impulses, unjust conduct, or idolatrous culture) to *recover* a prior purity, first principles, or a lost revolutionary treasure. We do not act "as if" we are beginning history anew, and though we can recover our capacity for initiative, we do not display Arendtian "natality" if it means action unconditioned by history. Baldwin does not use Christian tropes of rebirth, liberal tropes of self-making, or metaphors of nature, like Thoreau's "somewhat excrementitious" rebirth of the base and larval into the winged and noble. Tropes of rebirth suggest before-and-after motion forward in time, as if to leave behind an old condition, and motion upward, as if to separate the higher from the lower, whether the "divine" and "diabolical" separated by Thoreau's "action from principle," or the "revolutionary" spirit of freedom Arendt would redeem from entombing embodiment. Rebirth implies transcending a historical embodiment at once carnal and social, whereas redemption for Baldwin is (generated by) "accepting" (*wrestling with* rather than *purifying*) our incompletion and abiding need for others, our willful partiality toward them and obscurity to ourselves, our suffering as embodied, mortal, historical beings.

In contrast to tropes of rebirth, "acceptance" is Baldwin's conception of redemption as a practice of acknowledging nonsovereignty in relation to the desire and history that he makes the ground of human being. Nonsovereignty must be acknowledged because we author neither desire nor history and instead must come to terms with their constitutive power, to make them into conditions of action rather than conditions we resent, wish to escape, and profess to transcend. Desire and history are a ground not as a justifiable or knowable basis of action but as conditions we must acknowledge or else live in bad faith, which Baldwin calls *innocence*. Echoing Nietzsche's claim that the weak invent true worlds by which they devalue the actual one, Baldwin redeems impure actuality from such schemes of redemption, by a truth-telling that refuses transcendence to reveal a divided subject facing a universe unwritten by symbolic order. Rather than orienting prophecy by a God calling us to overcome our sinful denial of finitude, he orients prophecy directly by finitude as a truth, which means he translates sin as its disavowal.

"Innocence" thus denotes, partly, a denial of the Dionysian that he links to carnal mortality and the "tragic" nature of life; partly, a denial of the reality of others and a disclaiming of this refusal; and, partly, a denial of the past that constitutes our situated particularity. In each regard, innocence is a dream of safety and purity by imagining a sovereignty not subject to sentience and need, history and others, loss and death. But our experience of finitude in these senses is socially mediated, for we undergo "life" through another subjection: to social categories, ascribed hierarchy, domination, and violence. For Baldwin, innocence also means denying this social reality and positioning in it. In his critique of white supremacy, therefore, disavowal creates the blackness that enables whiteness as a form of innocence: One is a specter of what is disclaimed in life and humanity; the other is a purified identity he depicts as idolatry.

For we invest "tribes, races, creeds, and nations" with false reality and reified power, but such "chimeras" are vain, for they inflate some at others' expense, and they are futile, for they cannot deliver the redemption, the safety, or sovereign freedom, they promise.[4] People not only imprison themselves in idols they invent through disavowal; to live within such fictions secures not flourishing but a death-in-life. Baldwin does not speak for a God who mocks the vanity of identity and states, but his testimony returns people to the need and wayward desire, the mortality, nonsovereignty and "human stain" that he calls "the truth" of their condition, which they deny at horrific cost to themselves and others. He thus depicts not God's punishment but the "terrible, inexorable law that one cannot deny the humanity of another without diminishing one's own." In a declarative voice he announces "the price of the ticket," both the cost of innocence and the terms of flourishing.[5]

He thus secularizes prophecy as a practice that, instead of trading on disavowal, names it. He explains its motivation, announces its penalty, laments its price, warns of its consequences, and calls forth a contrary capacity to "accept"—Thoreau says "front" and Cavell says "acknowledge"—disclaimed motives, denied realities, disavowed others. The alternative to innocence, therefore, is not guilt but acknowledgment, because he is provoking people to count as salient what they already know and to count as important what they already feel. His idiom of disavowal and acceptance is a way to address responsibility without the rigid categories and idealized agency of the subject imagined by Christian morality. To move from innocence to acknowledgment is not to embrace moral categorization but to turn to what we have evaded in "life" and inner experience, social practices, political conduct, and national history. To acknowledge disavowal, indeed, is to shift from moral rules to political responsibility and collective action, and if guilt arises partly from not acting on what we already know, then Baldwin's prophecy is not imposing a bad conscience, but showing how we can release ourselves from it. Redemption does not require God's grace or mean an end to history; it is a practice, rather, of "accepting" and "wrestling" by which to make the fatalities of history and desire into conditions of action.

Accordingly, I read Baldwin in Nietzschean terms: He enacts for himself and dramatizes for us a struggle to name and digest his origins in a Christian and slave society. Partly, he shows how a ruling class enacts not nobility but disavowed resentment in its formation of identity; partly, he shows how subalterns struggle with worldly subordination and its internal legacy of self-hatred and rancor. Confronting the dichotomous categories and resentful motives in white supremacy and theological melodrama, in abolitionism and protest novels, but also in black Christianity and nationalism, he does model a kind of Socratic self-reflection or Emersonian self-reliance. But unlike Socrates, he does not invoke reason to authorize the better argument, and unlike Emerson he identifies as a black subject and not only an American individual, to fashion a prophetic language in and for politics.[6]

Against redemption as a "true world" created by those who call themselves "Christian" and "white," he speaks as a prophetic witness who remembers what they forget. And like Nietzsche, he does not give up redemption as an emancipatory practice. He, too, redefines it to mean coming to terms with a problematic history, to make "an illness into a pregnancy," as Nietzsche puts it. But Baldwin also democratizes Nietzsche as he stands with subalterns: He acknowledges how their instinct of freedom is turned inward as a double consciousness both tormented and fruitful, and he endorses worldly action to redeem themselves from captivity. Moreover, as Baldwin casts himself not only as an artist but as a lover addressing his beloved, he speaks both to blacks and to a white republic, mediating the part that has no part and the whole it would reconstitute. What, then, is the politics in translating prophecy as a practice of overcoming disavowal by acceptance?

From Self to Nation and from Lover to Artist

To plot a movement from innocence to acknowledgment, Baldwin builds an analogy between individual and collective subjects by interpreting identities and categories as defenses: We "give a name to the evil without" rather than "locate the terror within," and though "the labels change, the terror is constant." What do we fear? "This terror has something to do with the irreducible gap between the self one invents—the self one takes oneself as being, which is, however, and by definition a provisional self—and the undiscoverable self which always has the power to blow the provisional self to bits." To see "the joke" between reality and appearance is to cross "the barrier between oneself and knowledge of oneself," to front a "wilderness" undiscoverable because we *cannot* know or master it, and terrifying because it defeats identity. An undiscoverable self—wayward in desire, impure of motive, opaque to reason—makes for a "gap" we must "accept" if we are not to make identity an imprisoning idol. Tragic wisdom and prophetic pathos live in this "gap," and Baldwin's stated purpose is to provoke us to face it.[7]

Analogously, Baldwin sees a gap between the identity of a political subject and its undiscoverable "wilderness," which exceeds and disturbs it. "In the same way that to become a social human being one modifies and suppresses, and ultimately, lies to oneself about all one's interior, uncharted chaos, so have we, as a nation, modified and suppressed and lied about all the darker forces in our history." Likewise, "we know in the case of the person that whoever cannot tell himself the truth about his past is trapped in it," and "this is also true of nations." The office of artists, then, is to "tell a truth about ourselves" that is "at variance with what we wish to be" and who we claim we are. While "society must accept some things as real," indeed, artists recognize "that visible reality hides a deeper one, and that all our action and achievement rests on things unseen. A society must assume that it is stable, but the artist must know, and he must let us know, that there is nothing stable under heaven." Baldwin embraces such "grandiloquent claims" for the artist's public vocation, which is to "never cease warring with [society] for its sake and for his own." Indeed, "societies never know it, but the war of an artist with his society is a lover's war, and he does, at his best, what lovers do, which is to reveal the beloved to himself and, with that revelation, to make freedom real."[8]

He means love not "in the infantile American sense of being made happy, but in the tough and universal sense of quest and daring and growth." As this love impels us to "take off the masks we fear we cannot live without and know we cannot live within," so artists are lovers who block "the door to the spiritual and social ease" of their beloved other by acting as a "disagreeable mirror." This visual metaphor for the way his prophetic voice reverses the white gaze also signals one aspect of "the enormous contribution the Negro has made to this otherwise shapeless and undiscovered country." For Baldwin, then, "love" names the transforming engagement that moves an individual or collective subject not from ignorance to knowledge but from innocence to acknowledgment, and so from sterile repetition into the unknown.[9]

Baldwin's prophet-as-artist, like Thoreau's Chanticleer, would arouse his neighbors—both to a violent history they deny and to a "wilderness" alterity whose possibilities they dare not credit. But Thoreau, so anxious that faith in possibility is crushed by despair at the weight of history, excludes from his poetry of the dawn the doubts we hear at midnight. In contrast, Baldwin awakens us not to dawn as a symbol of possibility, but to a denial of history that leaves us in darkness, since facing our historical constitution is the basis of any credible faith in possibility. And when he looks from "Four AM" toward the dawn, what he sees is the likelihood of repetition and the certainty that "a day is coming which one will not recall, the last day of one's life," when "one will *oneself* become as irrecoverable as all the days that have passed." How is one to face this prospect?[10]

Baldwin thus makes death a condition of life: "The whole root of . . . the human trouble" is that we "sacrifice all the beauty of our lives" and "imprison ourselves in totems, taboos, crosses, blood sacrifices, steeples, mosques, races, armies, flags, nations in order to deny the fact of death," whereas one "ought to rejoice in the fact of death—ought to decide, indeed, to earn one's death by confronting with passion the conundrum of life. One is responsible to life: it is the small beacon in that terrifying darkness from which we come and to which we shall return. One must negotiate this passage as nobly as possible, for the sake of those coming after us."[11] Whereas Thoreau folds death into regenerative nature, then, Baldwin redeems death by the "miracle of love," which alone lights the darkness. For "some deep and ineradicable instinct causes us to know that it is only this passionate achievement which can outlast death, which can cause life to spring from death."[12]

Personal confession, however, memorializes collective struggle. "In the church I come from—which is not at all the same church to which white Americans belong—we were counseled . . . to do our first works over," that is, "re-examine everything. . . . travel your road again and tell the truth about it. Sing or shout or testify or keep it to yourself, but *know whence you came*."[13] And his abiding question, to himself and to those he addresses, is, "How can this past be used?" He surely draws from it the example of love's power:

I have . . . felt that no fire would ever warm me and no arms would ever hold me. I have been, as the song goes, "buked and scorned" and I know I always will be. But in that darkness, which was the lot of my ancestors . . . what a mighty fire burned! In that darkness of rape and degradation . . . terror and . . . helplessness, a living soul moved and refused to die. We really emptied oceans with a home-made spoon and tore down mountains with our hands.[14]

His forebears bequeath "a mighty heritage" he identifies with, but the love they exemplify is also "the human heritage, and it is all there is to trust":

For nothing is fixed, forever and forever. . . . the earth is always shifting, the light is always changing . . . the sea rises, the light falls, lovers cling to each other, and children cling to us. The moment we cease to hold each other, the moment we break faith with one another, the sea engulfs us and the light goes out.[15]

Endurance and self-overcoming are impossible demands to place on any human being, but "the impossible is the least that one can demand," for "the spectacle of human history in general, and American Negro history in particular . . . testifies to nothing less than the perpetual achievement of the impossible."[16]

Baldwin's essential political claim is that democratically authorized racial domination and its disavowal constitute the regime of liberal nationalism and shape every aspect of American life. What is needed to suspend the racial state of exception that sustains the liberal rule, the American ordinary? We see the template of his answer in his typical form of address as one who bears witness. On the one hand, he analogizes self and nation as divided entities, at once defenses forged by disavowal and achievements open to remaking. On the other hand, he analogizes lover and artist to secularize prophecy: As the lover reveals the beloved to himself, so the artist reveals to a collective subject its disavowed otherness—as well as its capacities to accept what is disavowed and reconstitute itself.

Correspondingly, we can anticipate the patterned ways he is criticized by whites and by blacks. Many whites are outraged at his claim that they live by a willful blindness about race and domination: He makes an interpretation of history into a truth they must accept, or he insists they live in self-denial. Resenting the aggression and judgment in his view, his white critics typically say that effective critics must use other registers of voice to persuade by argument, not self-righteous testimony. Inversely, black critics object that he acquiesces to white power by investing in dialogue; and by casting blacks as a collective truth-teller who redeems a beloved, his idiom of love sacrifices black political autonomy in a vain effort to free people who cannot listen and to change a regime invested in racial rule. In the ways that Baldwin translates prophecy, he provokes such criticisms, which in turn can be translated into questions guiding our analysis.

First, Baldwin exercises prophetic authority by invoking fidelity, not to a god or a (transcendent) principle but to actuality, to what is. Announcing what is, testifying about the world as it opens to *him*, he claims to reveal a human condition of finitude and a political condition defined by white supremacy. He exercises authority, then, by announcing the truth about conditions—not only death and domination but love—that people deny at great cost to others and themselves. He therefore depicts not the constitutive blindness of actors embedded in discourse, nor a contest among the different and valid perspectives these actors advance, but a prophetic struggle to overcome an innocence he casts as willful, and so as culpable—and remediable. What, then, is the status of claims about innocence or disavowal: What kind of truth is this? Does it moralize white supremacy, or politicize it? Does this idiom devalue dialogue, or might it clarify how people know something, say about torture or inequality, and yet do not acknowledge or count as salient, and so cannot act on, what they know? Does his mode of address replace the politics of consensus building with a single truth, or state the conditions of moving beyond pluralism within white supremacy? In turn, does the idiom of acknowledgment suggest people achieving reconciliation in beloved community, or beginning to wrestle with their real differences, to take on an avowedly political life?

Second, his narrative of acceptance overcoming disavowal raises questions about political identification. We recall that Jeremiah lives a double consciousness forged in conflicting identifications with God and people, whereas Baldwin mediates black and white; lodging authority in a black voice that "sentences" the conduct of whites, he testifies to the imbrication of one in the other and to their entwined fate. In an idiom of "love" as eros and not only as agape, he depicts a history of mutually constitutive connection: Freedom for whites requires accepting rather than disavowing their "wedding" with blacks, and black emancipation also depends on reworking rather than repudiating it. Does Baldwin romanticize national identification and bind blacks to it by giving them a prophetic vocation? Or, by depicting the gothic ambivalence that weds white and black, does he announce the only terms on which democratic politics can even begin in the United States?

In narrative terms, third, Baldwin does not deliver a jeremiad to return citizens to first principles or a founding "event"; rather, he tells a story of black creativity in the face of white domination and its disavowal. Only by coming to terms with what is tragic, not progressive, in their history can white citizen-subjects move beyond repetition and open spaces to act otherwise. And he narrates black redemption not as an exodus from captivity but as a coming-to-terms with captivity's complex, haunting legacy. For Baldwin, as for Nietzsche, we must "redeem" the past because we cannot change or escape it; we must change our relationship to it, its meaning for us, to make it a condition of action. Both insist on the haunting power of the past, not to produce despair, but as the only way to open a possibility for new possibilities. To quote Jonathan Lear, they seek not "an ordinary possibility, like all others only new," but "an alteration in the world of possibilities." Such a transformative possibility, for Baldwin, is not inherently emergent in the process of becoming, but entirely contingent on coming to terms with the past.[17]

Baldwin thus creates an analogy of self and national subject, despite its obvious faults and risks, because he requires a subject of attribution to take political responsibility for white supremacy in Arendt's sense, and because whites and blacks—apart and together—must "redeem" their entwined history in this Nietzschean sense. Still, what does "coming to terms" with or "accepting" the past mean politically? Does the prophetic critic call people to mourn a history whose crimes and suffering they must relinquish to move on, or does he rather call them to live *with* death and loss, from which they must draw new life? In what consists redemption for Baldwin, and how does this prophet bear witness to it?[18]

Disavowal: Race and American Nationhood

Baldwin translates prophecy by using a language of disavowal to name what people turn away from and refuse to count as real, which he calls them "to accept" as a condition of their freedom. By bearing witness to what is disremembered and who is uncounted by a liberal nationalist regime, he reveals its racial construction, disrupts its innocence, and seeks its reconstitution. Invoking his personal experience as a black man, his testimony as a witness diagnoses dimensions of disavowal in this regime by relating the domination of racialized others, the symbolic meaning of blackness, and whites' "innocence" about their conduct and history.

American nationhood originates, he argues, in democratic idealism and white supremacy, both tied to Europe. As a result, "founding democracy on the American continent was scarcely as radical a break with the past as the necessity . . . of broadening this concept to include black men."[19] Like literary radicals from Thoreau to William Carlos Williams, he laments an America still Old World, and he uses a trope of New World possibility to imagine moving beyond a history of racial domination: "America of all the Western nations" could "prove the uselessness and obsolescence of the concept of color," but "it has not dared to accept this opportunity or even to conceive of it as an opportunity."[20] As a result, Baldwin testifies,

If we, who can scarcely be considered a white nation, persist in thinking of ourselves as one, we condemn ourselves . . . to sterility and decay, whereas, if we could accept ourselves as we are, we might bring new life to Western achievements and transform them. The price of this transformation is the unconditional freedom of the Negro; it is not too much to say that he . . . must now be embraced and at no matter what psychic or social risk.[21]

"The Negro" is the key figuratively, not only literally, because he bears the meaning of an "undiscoverable" blackness symbolically linked to death and desire, whose disavowal subjugates actual African Americans while imprisoning whites in sterility. For whites to "embrace" him is redemptive because by "accepting" what (and who) they disavow in life and in their history, they free not only him but themselves.

By this argument, Baldwin depicts racial domination as (being like) the original sin of American politics: Democratically authorized racial domination constitutes "American" identity but makes democratic possibility stillborn. Because racial domination is no unfortunate anomaly but rather is central to American liberalism, he denies that it is an exemplary civic nationalism unlike European nationalisms of blood and soil. To this day, rather, the liberal freedom of those calling themselves white depends on the material domination and cultural exploitation of racially marked others. Accordingly, Baldwin rejects a story of a providentially chosen people, and he refuses national jeremiads that redeem this people from corruption by making good their liberal creed. Unlike Lincoln, he does not invoke an ideal America to be made real by acts of dedication and sacrifice. Unlike Thoreau in his antislavery lectures, Baldwin neither returns to '76 to oppose '87 nor recovers a revolutionary treasure. Unlike King, he does not declare that the goal of America is freedom or depict black Americans as the true heirs of that promise. He does not undertake to remake—and so to blacken—the ostensibly national principles by which African American sons and daughters can authorize oppositional practices.

Rather, he depicts a nation founded in genocide and slavery, whose ideals have never been practiced, or have been practiced only in exclusionary ways. Denying that progress is the telos of American history, he narrates a *tragic* story in which a nightmarish racial past imprisons everyone in barren repetition. But imprisonment signifies differently for whites and blacks, and to mediate parts and whole, a prophet must address both the persistence of racial domination among whites who celebrate democratic ideals, and the traps that white supremacy creates for those marked as black.

In the first part of *The Fire Next Time* he speaks openly as an African American in a "letter" to his young nephew, so that whites must, in effect, overhear his account of them:

The crime of which I accuse my countrymen, and for which neither I nor history will ever forgive them, [is] that they have destroyed and are destroying hundreds of thousands of lives and do not know it and do not want to know it. One . . . must strive to become tough and philosophical concerning destruction and death. . . . But it is not permissible that the authors of devastation should also be innocent. It is the innocence that constitutes the crime.[22]

He initiates the moral and political education of his nephew by saying, "This innocent country set you down in a ghetto in which, in fact, it intended that you should perish. You were born where you were born and faced the future you faced because you were black and *for no other reason*." He urges his nephew to "remember that what they do and cause you to endure does not testify to your inferiority but to their inhumanity and fear." Indeed,

there is no basis for their impertinent assumption that they must accept you. The really terrible thing . . . is that you must accept them . . . with love. For these innocent people have no other hope. They are trapped in a history they do not understand and until they understand it they cannot be released from it.

Accordingly, "we, with love, shall force our brothers to see themselves as they are, to cease fleeing from reality and begin to change it." To grasp Baldwin's revision of prophecy, then, we must unpack the meaning of disavowal and innocence, and trace how "we" move "them" to "acceptance."[23]

What constitutes the innocence he calls the crime? Baldwin uses the moral category of innocence ironically, to denote not excusable ignorance but a blindness that is culpable because it is willful. At issue is not a lack of knowledge but a "refusal to acknowledge" the reality of others and of our conduct toward them. To render others invisible, in Ralph Ellison's sense, is an injustice built into human life by hierarchy and power; Baldwin also acknowledges that destruction is commonplace in human life. But *disavowal* of domination is the innocence he denounces as criminal. Innocence means refusing not only to acknowledge the other but to acknowledge that we enact this denial; it is disowning (our connection to) social facts we in some sense know, such as the exercise of power, the practice of inequality, or their benefits.

Innocence is likely, therefore, in a society professing but violating democratic norms. We can continue to believe in our fidelity to equality, and so in national claims as the bastion of democracy, as long as we deny the existence of white supremacy, which means denying the meaning of our history, the impact of our conduct, the truth of our intentions, and the reality of those we racialize. "Innocence" is thus a moral and political catastrophe that shapes a distinctive American culture—and prevailing forms of democratic theory. As a prophetic witness, Baldwin's office is to name its causes and consequences.

At one level, disavowal reflects how American life is founded on a cross constituted by egalitarian ideals and slavery. "Confronted with the impossibility of remaining faithful to one's beliefs, and the equal impossibility of becoming free of them"—because one at once violates and values the principle of equality—"one can be driven to the most inhuman excess."[24] Excess is the very idea of blackness: Race and blackness are invented to justify slavery and inequality, by racializing subalterns in demonic and debased terms. But masters are haunted and crazed:

It was impossible for Americans to accept the black man as one of themselves, for to do so was to jeopardize their status as white men. But not to accept him was to deny his human reality, his human weight and complexity, and the strain of denying the overwhelmingly undeniable forced Americans into rationalizations so fantastic that they approached the pathological.[25]

While "Europe's black possessions" were "at a remove," blacks in the United States were "an inescapable part of the social fabric," and on-going efforts to "make an abstraction of the Negro" only "reveal the tremendous effects the presence of the Negro has had on the American character." This "spectacle, at once foolish and dreadful," warrants the joke that "the Negro-in-America is a form of insanity that overtakes white men."[26]

Partly, then, whites invent fictions of race and sustain melodramas of black pathology to justify domination and protect an innocence expressed in repeated claims to moral virtue and an exceptional—liberal—nationalism. Also, whiteness is reinvented by generations of immigrants: Entering a society divided by a racial binary and at first positioned by "Americans" as not-white, they typically seek political—racial—identification as white to gain access to rights in the national house. They must seek political rights by undergoing the cultural rites that racialize American citizenship. "No one was white before he or she came to America. It took generations, and a vast amount of coercion, before this became a white country." Immigrants pay "the price of the ticket" and become white, or suffer exclusion by identification as a racial (not "ethnic") group. Marking blacks as a "race" with a fixed symbolic meaning and fixing them in social space enables the "mobility" we link to ethnic pluralism, which Baldwin depicts as a form of passing. Indeed, as social mobility entails anxiety about identity, blackness is reinvested with social meaning as a defining "bottom" by which to stabilize identity.[27]

But the symbolic meaning invested in blackness also signals another kind of denial:

The racial tensions that menace Americans today have little to do with real antipathy—on the contrary, indeed—and are involved only symbolically with color. These tensions are rooted in the very same depths from which love springs, or murder. The white man's unadmitted—and apparently, to him, unspeakable—fears and longings are projected onto the Negro.[28]

Blackness is created by disavowing and projecting impulses that people fear in themselves, which means blackness is also a site of attraction and longing for the very qualities whites split off. Partly, blackness is linked to death: "White Americans do not believe in death, and this is why the darkness of my skin so intimidates them."[29] But "death" does symbolic work for Baldwin, bearing the meaning of a finitude he links to time, change, and mortality, to separateness and incompletion, to embodiment and desire, and thus to vulnerability, loss, and disappointment but also to violence. Partly, "there is a sense in which it can be said that my black flesh is the flesh that Saint Paul wanted to have mortified," for in the name of spirit Christianity "splits itself into dark and light."[30] Partly, a liberal culture idolizes self-mastery as sovereignty, a wish constantly referenced to the license, irrationality, and failed discipline, the dependence and childishness, the passion and violence, and the chaos and insanity lodged in racialized others, who signify what normative citizens must rule in themselves. "White" thus denotes not skin color but a "moral choice" to "opt for safety instead of life" through an ideology of disavowal that both justifies and entails violence.[31]

When Baldwin tells his nephew that whites "set you down in a ghetto" where they "intended that you should perish," accordingly, "innocence" means disclaiming that intention: Those calling themselves white dissociate from their own destructiveness by projecting it onto those they destroy. Loading onto others the license or willfulness they deny in themselves, they invoke morality as they exorcise specters of darkness, as if to triumph over their own impulsive life by controlling the symbolically charged bodies of others. Blackness symbolizes the Dionysian, then, and innocence is the bad faith that racializes and moralizes it.

In his diatribe against "the protest novel," Baldwin finds in *Uncle Tom's Cabin* "what might be called a theological terror, the terror of damnation," which once "sought to exorcise evil by burning witches" and which more recently "activates lynch mobs."[32] Terror fuels the moralism that dichotomizes good and evil in the way it dichotomizes white and black, and, in America, *as* white and black. As the abolitionist Harriet Beecher Stowe shows, this theology also sentimentalizes love as long-suffering service that overcomes the stain of blackness as evil. Moral dichotomy and racial categorization, wed by a story of damnation redeemed by love, make the "American" conception of life abstract and rigid. Baldwin writes,

The American vision of the world—which allows so little reality, generally speaking, for any of the darker forces in human life, which tends to paint moral issues in glaring black and white—owes a great deal to the battle waged by Americans to maintain between themselves and black men a human separation which could not be bridged.[33]

Terror of blackness, perhaps especially among reformers whose prophetic theology is inflected by Christianity, creates a worldview hostile to a life unforgivably stained by carnal embodiment, willful particularity, and moral ambiguity. But "people who shut their eyes to reality simply invite their own destruction, and anyone who insists on remaining in a state of innocence long after that innocence is dead turns himself into a monster."[34]

Race and morality (whiteness and goodness) are twinned idols, defended as political theology; Baldwin's response is countertheology, though by a prophecy artistic rather than theistic in form. For prophets warn that to flourish, we must turn from idols, or "true worlds," toward the actual world we devalue. *How* Baldwin argues is therefore crucial to *what* he says. For he speaks to those calling themselves white by using a purposely ambiguous "we," not only a "they." Just as Hebrew prophets speak to and from different social positions, as if with the poor and to the rich, and yet apart from each and to both by way of God's perspective, so Baldwin—not always, but distinctively—uses a "we" that is mobile and ambiguous. He marks out a racially divided terrain and moves through it as if, like Machiavelli's landscape painter at the outset of *The Prince*, he represents the key positions in the social geography created by the color line. As if he were not fixed in place, he identifies (with) and moves through different positions, giving each a voice and so bringing them into relationship. By a mobile "we" he speaks both what is unspeakable *by* whites, whiteness itself, and what has been unsaid by African Americans *to* whites. Baldwin's textual dialogue models, and perhaps thereby enables, a worldly dialogue that would be unprecedented.[35]

Baldwin's "Many Thousands Gone," an early and perhaps his greatest essay, suggests the value in this rhetorical strategy. He begins by depicting "the Negro" as a "he," so that his use of "we" defeats the racial binary and a wish to fix him in it:

It is only in his music, which Americans are able to admire because a protective sentimentality limits their understanding of it, that the Negro in America has been able to tell his story. It is a story which otherwise has yet to be told and which no American is prepared to hear. As is the inevitable result of things unsaid, we find ourselves until today oppressed with a dangerous and reverberating silence; and the story is told, compulsively, in symbols and signs, in hieroglyphics; it is revealed in Negro speech and in that of the white majority and in their different frames of reference.[36]

The first "we" is Americans, black and white, subject to a condition of silence in a world divided by race. But his location shifts:

The ways in which the Negro has affected the American psychology are betrayed in our popular culture and in our morality; in our estrangement from him is the depth of our estrangement from ourselves. We cannot ask: what do we *really* feel about him—such a question merely opens the gates on chaos. What we really feel about him is involved with all that we feel about everything, about everyone, about ourselves.[37]

The "our" and "we" seem to imply that Baldwin speaks from a white subject position about "the Negro." But if "the Negro" is symbolic, a figure of blackness, "we" also bespeaks an African American subject position, for everything "we feel" is also connected to "him." Baldwin thus says,

The Negro in America, gloomily referred to as that shadow which lies athwart our national life, is far more than that. He is a series of shadows, self-created, intertwining, which now we helplessly battle. One may say that the Negro in America does not really exist except in the darkness of our minds.[38]

This "we" can be whites and blacks, Americans, but when he shows how this darkness is externalized, he stands with whites:

To think of him is to think of statistics, slums, rapes, injustices, remote violence. . . . In this arena the black man acquires quite another aspect from that which he has in life. We do not know what to do with him in life; if he breaks our sociological and sentimental image of him we are panic-stricken and we feel ourselves betrayed.[39]

Baldwin depicts a society ruled by a racial imaginary that casts "the Negro" as a figure both sentimental and sociological: a problem reduced to statistics and a melodramatically split image of superhuman, self-sacrificing, unconditional love on the one hand and chilling deception, vengeful violence, and hypersexuality on the other. Since apprehension of life is mediated by racial symbolism, whites are like Br'er Rabbit, stuck to a tar baby whose meanings mark every aspect of life. But by speaking whites' view of "the Negro," Baldwin *can* then say, "Our dehumanization of the Negro is indivisible from our dehumanization of ourselves; the loss of our own identity is the price we pay for our annulment of his." Indeed, if "we" demonize "him," or seek "to make his face blank if we cannot make it white," he adds, we remain attached to him because "it is we who, every hour that we live, reinvest the black face with our guilt, and we do this—by a further paradox, no less ferocious—helplessly, passionately, out of an unrealized need to suffer absolution" and gain redemption.[40]

Accordingly, "in our image of the Negro" breathes the past, "not dead but living yet and powerful, the beast in our jungle of statistics." No wonder "wherever the Negro face appears a tension is created" by a "silence filled with things unutterable" about "the meaning of the past we deny." Innocence appears, then, not only as the disclaiming of domination and the disavowal of the Dionysian, but also as the denial of history.

It is a sentimental error . . . to believe that the past is dead. . . . it is not a question of memory. Oedipus did not remember the thongs that bound his feet; nevertheless the marks they left testified to that doom toward which his feet were leading him. The man does not remember the hand that struck him, the darkness that frightened him as a child; nevertheless, the hand and the darkness remain . . . indivisible from himself forever, part of the passion that drives him wherever he thinks to take flight.[41]

To address a people invested in Christian ideas of rebirth and in the liberal romance of self-making, Baldwin invokes the image of Oedipus, whose claim to make his own destiny assured he blindly acted out his fate, whose effort to start over sealed his doom, whose insistence he could escape the past tightened its grip, and whose claim to know himself assured misrecognition of his identity. Like Sophocles, Baldwin uses Oedipus to signal the power of history to citizens blind to the self-defeating vanity of their self-making.

White man, hear me! History . . . does not refer merely or even principally to the past. On the contrary, the great force of history comes from the fact that we carry it within us, are unconsciously controlled by it in many ways, so history is literally *present* in all that we do. It could scarcely be otherwise since it is to history that we owe our frames of reference, our identities, and our aspirations.[42]

American culture is resolutely antihistorical: Each must escape the past or annul its power, to achieve the status of subject, of freedom as self-determination. But for Baldwin, freedom begins only in recognizing that the past is not past or dead: We trap ourselves if we deny its power; we repeat it by efforts to escape.

What is the alternative to Christian and liberal languages of rebirth and to jeremiadic tropes of renewal? In his view, we are constituted by history, and our freedom appears not by renewing origins construed as a resource but, paradoxically, by accepting and wrestling with origins conceived as a problem. In "great pain and terror" he grasps the extent of his historical constitution, but then he can

enter into battle with that historical creation, Oneself, and attempt to recreate oneself according to a principle more humane and liberating; one begins the attempt to achieve a personal maturity and freedom which robs history of its tyrannical power and also changes history. But obviously, I speak as a historical creation which has had to bitterly contest its history, to wrestle with it, and finally accept it in order to bring myself out of it.[43]

While Baldwin's reference to Oedipus suggests the gravity of the past as a fate we cannot escape but must bear, he at once "accepts" and "wrestles" with history, and he repeatedly refers to human capacities for self-overcoming and transformation, which he links to the miraculous. He cannot escape his past or fix what went wrong with it, as if to change it. He precludes redemption in these senses, but an unredeemed past is a disaster. For if we submit to a wounding past passively, we are driven to self-blame or rancor, and if we (resignedly or resentfully) submit to the future that seems dictated by this past, we also relinquish our freedom. If we "accept" our historical constitution as a reality, however, we can rework it in a spirit less ruled by rancor. By accepting history, we diminish the power it accrues from denial; if we are ruled less by resentment of the past or fantasies of escaping it, we can act rather than react as we "wrestle" with it.

Baldwin's testimony thus models what Nietzsche calls "my redemption." Partly, argues Nietzsche, redemption is a practice of *amor fati*: He would "transform every 'it was' into 'I wanted it thus,'" to alter, not his past, but his relationship to it. By accepting (or willing) the past that constituted him, he can revise who he might become now, actively making what he once resented a condition of possibility. Baldwin also models a second aspect of Nietzschean redemption: "the art and aim to compose into one and bring together"—to organize and endow with meaning—"what is fragment and riddle and dreadful chance." By narrative the "poet" is a "redeemer" of contingency and injury, or as Baldwin says, of the "cosmic joke" of being born black in America.[44]

By narrative art and acceptance, the heir of slaves would redeem himself from rancor and "redeem" the past in the sense of making it fruitful. Likewise, he would impel whites to come to terms with the disclaimed history in which they are imprisoned. As wrestling connotes an agon with others, so Baldwin politicizes what Nietzsche calls "my redemption," but his analogy of self and nation obscures as well as clarifies the challenge. For partly, there is no one "it was," but multifaceted sides of many pasts whose meaning is not self-evident and whose relationship involves power as well as vision. Partly, there is no centering "I" to redeem the "it" of a past, but a "we" whose very existence is a political artifact contingent on speech and action by unequal subjects. Still, Nietzsche signals the question Baldwin must answer: What political "art" can "compose and bring together" fragment (divided subjects), riddle (the meaning of their histories), and dreadful chance (the joke of race and its legacy)? By what political arts can divided subjects fashion a "we" and transform "it was" into a "we will it so"? Baldwin draws on prophecy to address whites and blacks, each as a separate "we" yet also as an "American" we, about the price of redemption.

From Disavowal to Acceptance

Baldwin's prophetic practice links disavowal to idolatry and both to innocence. As the weak invent true worlds or fixed categories to seek an impossible kind of protection from life, and as "those who cannot suffer cannot grow up," so "freedom and innocence are antithetical." He confronts innocence for the sake of freedom by a nontheistic prophecy that "turns" people to (accept) what has been split off. Baldwin thus echoes Freud's "where it was I shall be," if "it" is disavowed reality, and "I" is not a masterful ego knowing itself but a subject acknowledging internal division and historical constitution. Calling the normative citizen both "the American boy" and an Oedipus, Baldwin creates scenes of tragic recognition to front the history and conduct, the drives and forces whose disavowal plagues the republic.[45] As a truth-teller he might have been Tiresias, but in a biblical culture he is "a kind of Jeremiah."[46] Let us rewind his argument about disavowal to identify what he calls us to accept.

Partly, the freedom of those who call themselves white depends on accepting the centrality of white supremacy in their history, which means seeing their national origins in violence and slavery, not consent, and seeing their abiding investment in inequality, not equality. Partly, they remain trapped by this history unless they accept how racial domination and black agency have shaped American culture in every regard. "What happened to the Negro . . . is not simply a matter of *my* memory and *my* history, but of *American* history and memory." For "the history the Negro endured . . . was endured on another level by all the white people who oppressed him. . . . I was here, and that did something to *me*. But you were here on top of me, and that did something to *you*." Right now, "whatever is happening to every Negro in this country at any time is happening to you," and what "this republic does to the Negro, it does to itself." If whites were to count the reality of black testimony and accept the fact of connection, he imagines "a fusion between what I remember and what you remember; then there will be no question about our separation. We are really one people and—this is part of our problem in fact, we spend all our time denying it."[47]

But this means facing disavowal not only of actual people but of blackness. Like Thoreau, Baldwin testifies that "the white man is himself in sore need of new standards, which will release him from his confusion and place him . . . in fruitful communion with the depths of his own being." To contact such "depths" is "to become black himself, to become part of that suffering and dancing country that he now watches wistfully from the heights of his lonely power."[48] If whites can "accept and love themselves" by learning to accept the "dark stranger" within "—which will not be tomorrow and may very well be never—the Negro problem will no longer exist for it will no longer be needed."[49]

Becoming "black" is risking the fiction of racial identity, not by minstrelsy but by turning toward the Dionysian:

It is the responsibility of free men to trust and celebrate what is constant—birth, struggle, and death are constant, and so is love, though we may not always think so—and to apprehend the nature of change, to be able and willing to change. I speak of change not on the surface but in the depths—change in the sense of renewal. But renewal becomes impossible if one supposes things to be constant which are not, safety for example, or money or power. One clings then to chimeras, by which one can only be betrayed, and the entire hope—the entire possibility—of freedom disappears.[50]

Whites can escape sterility only if they accept mortal finitude, the tragic character of their history, and connection to disavowed others. But what of these others? Where is their agency in this redemptive story?

Acceptance and Black Agency

Like King, Baldwin imagines black people as a prophetic protagonist. He, too, believes a history of domination invests black people in the worldly defense of freedom, but he identifies what—in themselves, their history, and life—they must *accept*, not purify, as a condition of fruitful action.

Using his mobile "we," he begins with hegemony: "It is exceedingly difficult for most of us to discard the assumptions of the society in which we were born, in which we live, to which we owe our identities." Subalterns do not live in a separate reality: "Oppressed and oppressor are bound together within the same society; they accept the same criteria, they share the same benefits, they both alike depend on the same reality." Indeed,

it is the peculiar triumph of society—and its loss—that it is able to convince those people to whom it has given inferior status of the reality of this decree; it has the force and weapons to translate this dictum . . . so that the allegedly inferior are actually made so insofar as societal realities are concerned. . . . We find ourselves bound, first without, then within, by the nature of our categorization. . . . We take our shape . . . within and against that cage of reality bequeathed to us at our birth; and yet it is . . . through our dependence on this reality that we are most endlessly betrayed.[51]

Such categories "betray"—reveal and imprison—"we" whites, but what of "we" blacks? We must "take our shape" in relation to a racial imaginary that proposes either the unconditional and sacrificial love of Stowe's Uncle Tom or the phallic sexuality and enraged violence of Wright's Bigger, either the endless good humor and abiding nurturing of Aunt Jemima or the hypersexuality of the welfare queen. Facing "the absurd in and as America," what must we "accept"?

Baldwin indeed uses Wright to argue that African Americans must *not* believe these images of blackness, especially the "living image, living yet" of "the 'nigger,' black, benighted, brutal, consumed with hatred . . . 'the native son' . . . the monster created by the American republic."[52] He depicts Stowe and Wright, "the one uttering merciless exhortations, the other shouting curses," locked in a battle dictated by the same categorical "theology." To expose it, Baldwin enacts a this-worldly turn:

Bigger's tragedy is not that he is cold or black or hungry, not even that he is American, black, but that he has accepted a theology that denies him his life, that he admits the possibility of his being sub-human and feels constrained, therefore, to battle for his humanity according to those brutal criteria bequeathed to him at his birth. But our humanity is our burden, our life; we need not battle for it; we need only do what is infinitely more difficult—that is, accept it.[53]

If he accepts "that it is his categorization alone which is real" and "surrenders to the image," his "life has no other possible reality" than self-hatred and hatred. Yet "bitter railing" at a category is "the only motion needed to spring the trap on us," for we reinstate it in our protest.[54] To "accept" our humanity and elude the trap, paradoxically, we also must *accept* that "the American image of the Negro lives in the Negro's heart."[55] We must accept *doubleness:*

> There is no Negro living in America who has not felt, briefly or for long periods, with anguish sharp or dull, in varying degrees and to varying effect, simple, naked, and unanswerable hatred . . . no Negro finally, who has not had to make his own precarious adjustment to the "nigger" who surrounds him and to the "nigger" in himself. Yet the adjustment must be made—rather, it must be attempted, the tension perpetually sustained—for without this he has surrendered his birthright as a man no less than his birthright as a black man.[56]

Of the legacy of white supremacy for blacks, Baldwin thus says, "No American Negro exists who does not have his private Bigger Thomas living in his skull." But he narrates this legacy in terms of freedom: The black man *must* "accept that this dark and dangerous and unloved stranger is part of himself forever" because, paradoxically, "only this recognition sets him in any wise free," and it is "this necessary ability to contain and even, in the most honorable sense of the word, *to exploit* the 'nigger' which lends to Negro life its high elements of the ironic." To "accept" this stranger within is to credit, at once, our carnal humanity and our internalization of its estranged white image, and in this way gain the tragic insight, and freedom, that enable cultural creativity.[57]

Rejecting a protest that reifies racial categories, Baldwin seeks a precarious adjustment that "accepts" their power but does so to disable their authority and assert his own. This authority, he claims, is one of the great gifts of African American life: "This past, this endless struggle to achieve and reveal and confirm a human identity . . . contains, for all its horror, something beautiful. I do not mean to be sentimental about suffering . . . but people who cannot suffer never grow up, can never discover who they are," while those who forge identity despite the "cruelty that rages to destroy it," if they survive, "achieve [their] own authority" by "hewing out of the mountain of white supremacy the stone of their individuality." By "surviving the worst that life can bring" they also "cease to be controlled by fear of what life can bring; whatever it brings must be borne." An overcoming of resentment appears to Baldwin, then, not in a future overman, but in black children facing white mobs and in parents who teach them "not to hate the hater whose foot is on your neck." They "come out of a long line of aristocrats—the only genuine aristocrats this country has produced. I say 'this country' because their frame of reference was totally American."[58]

Baldwin's critique of categories, therefore, does not deny identification as African American but makes it a culturally paradoxical rather than racially authentic act. Indeed, people of African descent in America must *accept* that they are entwined with Anglo-Europeans. Their relationship is "more terrible, more subtle, and more meaningful than the relationship of bitter possessed to uncertain possessor" or of "master to slave." It is "literally and morally a blood relationship, perhaps the most profound reality of the American experience, and we cannot begin to unlock it until we accept how very much it contains of the force and anguish and terror of love."[59] The "interracial drama," by literal and figurative miscegenation, has created "a new black man" and "a new white man, too."[60]

To shape black agency as nonviolent prophetic witness, King "purifies" African Americans of willful particularity, to model agape love as a democratic practice. Baldwin models a black subject that affirms its impurity and provokes whites to accept what they disavow by shifting prophecy from transcendence to immanence. For King's prophetic actor invokes the universality of moral law and declarations of independence to redeem their contamination by a violent history, but Baldwin's prophetic actor derives a voice by descending to that ground on which domination and love are not easy to separate. One actor seeks authority by proving universality of intent and purity of motive; the other earns authority by refusing transcendence, *and* its guilty alter ego, to accept a space of impurity. King's prophet enacts agape, then, while Baldwin's is a lover facing a beloved in an erotic and agonistic relationship. But does Baldwin therefore endorse the romance of American nationhood, does he revise it in a political way, or does he do both?

Nationhood and Political Identification

Baldwin sees whites and blacks undergoing (and shaping) a constitutively "American" (nation-building) historical process:

The one thing all Americans have in common is that they have no identity apart from the identity being achieved on this continent. This is not an English . . . Chinese . . . or French necessity, but . . . the necessity of Americans to achieve identity is a historical and a present personal fact and this is the connection between me and you.[61]

Baldwin here paraphrases Perry Miller's claim—which founds what has come to be called American studies—that "American" identity is "achieved" rather than "given." This "new" nation is sustained not by blood, soil, or ancient tradition, Miller argues, but only by ideas about identity; nationhood is ideological, at once anxious and rigidly imposed, because chaos seems the only alternative. McCarthyism is typical "Americanism" in this sense, even as it denies the contingency that Miller makes the true lesson of "our history." Indeed, Miller contrasts the anxiety of an achieved (or truly American) identity to the "given" identity of native people and those of African descent: They live by cultural habit or natural instinct, he says, free from "our" anxious burden of contingency and invention.[62]

In response, Baldwin reads race as Miller reads McCarthyism: Racial identity is a form of bad faith, an anxious effort to end the "problem" of identity. The flux of American life generates "race" as its defining injustice and compensatory anchor. Baldwin also makes blacks into "Americans" in Miller's sense: Defined by "natal alienation," they undergo the loss of a given identity and face the necessity to "make" a new one. Racism shows that acts of identity making are not equivalent: Social power makes all the difference, for whites repeatedly appropriate black cultural forms while leaving actual blacks fixed in social place. Still, interaction produces "an entirely unprecedented people, with a unique past." Yet "the truth about that past is not that it is too brief or superficial, but only that *we*, having turned our faces so resolutely away from it, have never demanded from it what it has to give." What does "turning" toward it yield?[63]

Like Ellison, Baldwin identifies distinctively "American" experience with the presence and agency of blacks. But Ellison emphasizes that the endless play of masks makes one people, whereas Baldwin joins white and black by prophetic tropes. On the one hand, by saying, "My ancestors are both black and white," he depicts one familial "house" divided as some disown others. In this sense nationality is unchosen kinship, and the "sins of the fathers" shape and haunt the lives of black and white children, who may yet confound the color line they inherit. Indeed, on the other hand, he uses prophecy to depict the nation as an erotically charged yet troubled marriage:

Love does not begin and end in the way we think it does. Love is a battle, love is a war; love is a growing up. No one in the world . . . knows Americans (i.e. whites) better or, odd as it may sound, loves them more than the American Negro. This is because he has had to watch you, outwit you, deal with you, bear you, and some-times even bleed and die with you, ever since . . . both of us, black and white, got here—and this is a wedding.[64]

By describing nationhood as a wedding, Baldwin makes blacks and whites "members of one body" in the Mosaic and Puritan sense of collective liability while repeating the recurring claim that European contact with racial others creates a distinctive "American" culture. But do meta-phors of carnal marriage, which connote voluntarism, only obscure the politics of nationhood?[65]

Surely, Baldwin is unlike Gunnar Myrdal, or Michael Walzer and Richard Rorty more recently, who define American nationhood by its quasi-transcendental "creed," incarnated to varying degrees. Whereas this universalizing move abstracts from racial ground to posit a true America, Baldwin does not invoke a true America to criticize the ac-tual one. He knows that exclusion and stigma are seen by many citizens not as violations of American ideals but as legitimate or even necessary ways to practice them. The bond of American freedom to slavery is not anomalous because enfranchised citizens proudly practice their ideals in exclusionary ways: Worthy ideals and egregious practices cannot be neatly separated. "Americans like to think we are getting better all the time," but few "have the courage to recognize that the America of which they dream and boast is not the America in which the Negro lives." Bringing universalist language down to tainted racial ground, Baldwin depicts a nation invested in domination and inequality, not in equality or democracy. Yet he uses the metaphor of a wedding rather than dis-avowing national attachment.[66]

His conception of the nation attributes not an essence to a charac-ter, or a transcendent ideal to a substantial identity, but a history to a relationship. "Our nation" is the historical relationship of those consti-tuted by their encounter with each other and this place. Identification "as American" means "owning" not a transcendent ideal to be incar-nated but a constitutive history and relationship with others. "Ameri-can" names who people have become, contingently, through choices, conflict, and dependence; like any relationship it is an artifact partly independent of their wills, a reality they have created over time but can change now only with difficulty.

Baldwin thus moves between metaphors of family, in which one brother confronts another, and metaphors of a wedding, in which a lover confronts a beloved, as he tries both to register and engender investment in a bond readily disavowed but impossible to escape. "We, the black and the white, deeply need each other if we are really to become a nation—if we are really, that is, to achieve our identity, our maturity, as men and women. To create one nation has proved to be a hideously difficult task: there is certainly no need now to create two." Criticizing white disavowal of the wedding and denying divorce to blacks, he depicts an unchosen bond each must choose—accept and rework—now. But what is there to "achieve"?[67]

If American history is a wedding one party disowns, surely the achievement is acknowledging its—charged, gothic, perhaps fruitful—reality. To accept *this* means naming white supremacy as a problem to be overcome, partly by refusing its black nationalist mirror. "We" would accept and use, rather than deny, what we *already* are. For "accepting" *racial domination* as central in our history is the condition of also finding a *wedding* that, if embraced, discredits the color line and allows democracy for the first time. Baldwin inflects prophecy, then, by translating the biblical "turn." Accepting that American history is shaped by (disavowal of) domination and miscegenation is to reconstitute a "we" and initiate a nation building (in antiracist and so democratic ways) never before undertaken. We do hear romance, not only in the trope of a wedding but in Baldwin's echoing of the poetry of a new world finally slipping the grip of the old. Still, he privileges a national frame for politics, not because he loves an ideal America but because he believes that freedom means wrestling with the actual America to move politics beyond repetition. He answers white disavowal not with refusal, then, but with ambivalent engagement.

Ambivalence may render too passively his *investment* in an attachment he knows is grievously—many say irredeemably—flawed. Still, we should not forget the clarity of his critique or his keen sense that the fruitfulness of his investment is contingent. But in the early sixties, he sees a transforming engagement moving blacks and whites, and so the national subject, into *the unknown*. We will "undergo the torment of being forced to surrender more than we ever realized we had accepted," for we are "overhauling all that gave us our identity." Indeed, "any real change implies the breakup of the world as one has always known it," and with it "the end of safety." Yet "only when a man is able to surrender a dream he has long cherished or a privilege he has long possessed" is he "set free—he has set himself free—for higher dreams, for greater privileges."[68]

Baldwin's imagination of blacks and whites as a national subject is another instance of how critics of white supremacy draw on prophecy to raise the issue of identification: With whom do you identify, and on what basis? Hebrew prophets give vertical and horizontal answers, while Baldwin sustains this-worldly tensions in several dimensions. His central claim is that identificatory bonds are inescapable in human life, at once costly, valuable, and open to reworking. In one dimension, he sees attachments divide some from others, which means negotiating the relation of particular and universal. For "inheritance" is "particular, limited and limiting" compared to a "birthright" that is "vast, connecting me to all that lives and to everyone, forever," but no one "can claim the birthright without accepting the inheritance." In turn, to "accept" an inheritance means seeing how attachment bears "love and murder," or ambivalence, for attachment entails disappointment and anger. Fratricide is the inescapable double of fraternity; romance entails gothic shadows. Ambivalence also shapes another dimension of identification, because its most powerful forms are unchosen and coercively ascribed yet invested with value and subjected to remaking by politics. Indeed, freedom appears as we remake the meaning of inherited, constitutive, and knotted attachments.[69]

Like Jeremiah and Jesus, therefore, Baldwin engages those (whites) with whom he identifies (as "American") even as they disavow him. He does not choose another particular attachment or, like Paul, reject a particular "inheritance" in the name of a universal "birthright." He sees the imperialism of "the West," but unlike Richard Wright or W. E. B. Du Bois, he does not form an antinational diasporic identity. Paul and Wright would repudiate a central, inherited attachment in order to establish another (ostensibly more universal) identification. In contrast, Baldwin depicts the fatality of bonds we cannot really repudiate, and he makes the political judgment that we can rework them in fruitful ways— but he may be mistaken and he may change his judgment.

Still, for Baldwin as for Wright, for Jesus as for Paul, the central work in politics is judging and recasting identificatory bonds. In these terms, indeed, he depicts a fateful moment of decision: With whom will you stand, on what basis? *The Fire Next Time* ends, therefore, with him speaking as a watchman warning of "a vengeance"

that does not really depend on, and cannot really be executed by any person or organization, and that cannot be prevented by any police force or army: historical vengeance, a cosmic vengeance, based on the law we recognize when we say, "whatever goes up must come down." And here we are, at the center of the arc, trapped in the gaudiest, most valuable, and most improbable water wheel the world has ever seen. Everything now, we must assume, is in our hands; we have no right to assume otherwise.

To forestall danger, he shows the choices resting in our hands—we have no right to assume otherwise. If "we" do not "like lovers, insist on or create the consciousness of the others"—"if we do not dare everything" to "end the racial nightmare and achieve our country"—then "the fulfillment of that prophecy, re-created from the Bible in song by a slave, is upon us: God gave Noah the rainbow sign, No more water, the fire next time!"[70]

Queering Prophecy and Dishonoring Prophets

In his essays between 1948 and 1962, Baldwin enters the cultural imaginary of white supremacy, partly to bear witness to the danger of innocence and partly to disable the theology and categories driving dramas of black pathology. He prefigures black power argument by unmasking the white power in liberal claims to universalism and a language of formal equality, but he depicts the fatality of a miscegenated national subject. The nation, if not defined transcendentally, can be reconstructed politically, he believes, by a redemptive practice of coming to terms with its racially constituted history. This possibility may not materialize, but it depends on the collective agency of blacks, cast in a prophetic role, and on their living *as if* whites can move beyond repetition.

By 1963, however, Baldwin is being attacked less by the whites he professes to redeem and more by the blacks who reject "the truth" he announces as a self-evident ground of political renewal. His story of disavowal overcome by acceptance, and the mobile "we" by which he tells it, are interpreted as acquiescence in white power, evasion of commitment, and avoidance of politics. Partly, his critics argue, he puts blacks in a morally superior position, but he requires them to love and redeem whites, the historical and subordinate role they must refuse. Partly, he sacrifices black autonomy to a dream of reconciliation with people who will never recognize them. He weds blacks to an "American" frame when their political power requires nation building against and beyond it. Lastly, he adopts a white perspective in his texts, not because he practices "visiting" to form valid political judgments but because self-hatred drives him to self-betrayal. For these reasons, indeed, his critics claim, whites increasingly reward him with prominence![71]

White media cast him as a spokesman, and he claims to speak, rather, as a witness, but critics depict his trope of acceptance as an abdication of (black) aggression, autonomy, and politics. The critique is often coded in homophobic ways: As he is being called Martin Luther Queen on the street and is being portrayed as distinctly effeminate in white media, younger black activists and writers reduce his art and politics to "loving the white man." By naming his sexuality explicitly, his critics invalidate his authority: Denying that he can be black and queer and reducing him to his sexuality, they reject his testimony as a witness and cast him as a false prophet. We need to explore this reduction, but without in turn reducing his critics to homophobes.[72]

White literary critics also struggle to interpret Baldwin's novels, which dramatize interracial romance and (homo)sexuality, in relation to essays that reject "the protest novel." In "Black Boys and Native Sons," Irving Howe inverts Baldwin's critique of Wright: "To assert his humanity," Howe declares, "the Negro must release his rage." Linking rage to politics and denying any political import to novels exploring the difficulty of love, Howe dismisses Baldwin as a cosmopolitan aesthete and defends Wright as a revolutionary and a prophet.[73] Norman Mailer goes one step further, celebrating black masculinity as a phallic model for white men emasculated by mass society.[74]

Baldwin ridicules Mailer for succumbing to a racist myth, but Eldridge Cleaver endorses black rage and phallic sexuality—both Wright and Mailer—against Baldwin and his "Martin Luther King–type of self-effacing love for his oppressor." Baldwin's work joins "the most grueling, agonizing, total hatred of blacks, particularly of himself, and the most shameful, fanatical, fawning, sycophantic love of the whites." For "the black homosexual" has submitted to being "castrated at the center of his burning skull," and by "taking the white man for his lover . . . turns the razor edge of hatred against 'blackness' in himself."[75]

Baldwin assumes that his testimony (from personal experience and perspective) tells a larger truth about white racism, black experience, and the human condition: This is the premise of prophetic witnessing. But these critics reject his authority as a witness; he cannot stand in for absent blacks because he does not testify to a representative experience. Indeed, sexual perversity entails the "American" identification that betrays racial solidarity: A man who loves (white) men is a false prophet, for true prophets stand up to authority rather than acquiesce to it, separate slaves from Egypt rather than reconcile them to it, and defend rather than disable the markers of difference on which identity and power depend.

If love means castration or effeminacy, then power is phallic sexuality, but for Baldwin this very equation only inverts the sexual politics of white racial domination:

That men have an enormous need to debase other men—and only because they are *men*—is a truth which history forbids us to labor. [But] it is absolutely certain that white men, who invented the nigger's big black prick, are still at the mercy of this nightmare, and are still, for the most part, doomed . . . to attempt to make this prick their own.[76]

But for his critics, same-sex desire *means* subordination; those "open" to penetration are failed men, effeminized because they are penetrated and penetrated because they are self-castrating.[77] As proper masculinity signifies agency, so possessing the phallus means being a subject rather than an object, seminal rather than inseminated, self-possessed rather than possessed by others. Paradoxically, bell hooks argues, an equation of freedom and manhood "forged a bond between oppressed black men and their white male oppressors. They shared the patriarchal belief that revolutionary struggle was really about the erect phallus."[78] To allow penetration is self-hatred, unless one is female, but neither these men nor women can make credible claims to, about, or for a community. Baldwin's critics, therefore, use sexuality "to renounce him," while his defenders "minimize his sexuality to redeem him."[79]

Such arguments about sexuality and prophecy return us to the debate between Bellah and Bercovitch about "consensus" in "a Puritan and trading nation." For codes of racial and sexual difference underwrite normative citizenship as a manliness both white and heterosexual. Projects of racial uplift, therefore, are shaped in relation to sexual and not only racial norms. Bourgeois projects of *respectability*, like the civil rights movement, link sexual propriety—reproductive sex and family values—to the work ethic to justify citizenship. Black power turns proscription toward a counternationalism defending racial *authenticity* from corruption. In either form, sexual policing is crucial to nation building. Such projects do not exorcise white supremacy but, rather, repeat phobic conceptions of black sexuality in denigrated images of queer sexuality. Facing homophobia not only in white racism but in the black church, melodramas of protest, and projects of racial uplift, Baldwin queers prophecy as he fashions another idiom for masculinity.[80]

Emerson declared that society "is a conspiracy against the manhood of its members" and instituted an individualism forever juxtaposing the erect to the castrated, but Baldwin testifies to the truth denied by the fear of castration: Each human is incomplete, because separated from the (m)other, but men deny incompletion (and establish sexual difference) by claiming the phallus, or what the (m)other lacks. In refusing this claim, he renounces not agency but *false* power, not aggression but its defensive character. Selfhood remains for him a criminal act, a self-authorization that steals agency to "achieve" an identity otherwise imposed by society. Aggression is crucial in making claims about and on the world, in our sense of entitlement to speak, and in any act that resists domination. But we protest domination to be recognized as subjects, which means counting others as subjects, too.

If this agon is entailed by the truth of nonsovereignty, Baldwin finds in it a second truth, central to the way he queers prophecy, and also used to deny his authority as a prophetic witness. This second truth is that categories are fictions. Norman Podhoretz summarizes its implications:

> Baldwin's intention is to deny any moral significance whatsoever to the categories White and Negro, heterosexual and homosexual. He is saying that the terms . . . refer to two different conditions under which individuals live [and] pursue love, but they are still individuals . . . governed by the same fundamental laws of being. . . . He is saying . . . that the only significant realities are individuals and love, and that anything which is permitted to interfere with the free operation of these is evil and should be done away with.[81]

If assertions of sovereignty deny the truth of incompletion, categories of identity deny the truth of desire, whose opacity defeats our demand for intelligibility, whose perversity betrays any category, whose intensity condemns us to vulnerability, and whose waywardness means moral imperfection. Those who live by reified categories defend against the messy imperfection of carnal attachment to protect the illusion of normative identity. Because Baldwin's critique of bad faith explodes categories of racial and sexual identity, of course he is attacked on political grounds: He seems to valorize individual desire at the expense of (racial) solidarity, to reject the historical inheritance carried by the racial sign in favor of a miscegenated cosmopolitanism. His political critics agree with Podhoretz: As a *liberal* who sees social categories "interfering" with the "free operation" of individuals and love, Baldwin is also a *cosmopolitan,* and in both regards he seems to seek emancipation from ascribed identities.

But Baldwin's view of categories is more complex—and political—

than this liberal translation: Categories are constitutive of subjectivity, not merely external obstacles to it. In Lee Edelman's words, just as "the operation of cultural histories and libidinal rhetorics produce us," so "the histories we produce in turn are the judgments we pass" on those forces, and that is why there is no clear distinction between inside and outside or between active and passive. "Active agency is itself produced within, and determined by, the particularity of a history." For Baldwin, history "is the source of contradictions so profound" that "we ourselves are their expression, their effect. . . . He recognizes a doubling or division in the very nature of self-consciousness, which is constantly constituted by the other." In his view of the subject, "the integrity of identity is violated by the presence of the other within it," while "that otherness is also needed for the constitution of identity." Baldwin's redemption thus means "wrestling" with, not transcending, categories and their constitutive legacy.[82]

For Eldridge Cleaver or Imiri Baraka, a queer Baldwin is too impure to serve as a mediator with whites or a prophet bearing witness to "black" experience. For King, too, prophets must strive to be pure vessels, or they dirty the word they bear. But Baldwin queers prophecy by abandoning the purity entailed in the logic of fidelity to God, principle, or people. He practices a prophecy whose authority is earned by "accepting" impurity, and this prophecy is political precisely by troubling pure identity and the domination it entails. Still, he troubles racial and sexual categories while "achieving" identity as a *nation;* he imagines a national frame for a democratic project that disrupts reified identity in other forms. The nation he envisions is "another country" because he makes national attachment an investment in impurity, but is there social ground for his prophecy of renewal? Does he, in fact if not in intention, acquiesce in white power?

Narrating the Crisis in Baldwin's Prophetic Vocation

Baldwin is uneasily situated in relation to the major ideological formations of his day. Though he defends a complex individuality, he tightly ties liberalism to white supremacy. Yet he argues that blacks and whites must "accept" that they are stuck together and must seek redemption in this fatality. As a result, he is misrecognized as an integrationist by critics who would accept that separation is a fact and a fatality. His language of love thus becomes a foil in a moment of black assertion because it seems too bound to whites, too congenial to individual expression but not political power, too bound to dreams of communion and not enough to exigencies of conflict. As homophobic attacks imposed on him a kind of marginality even by 1965, so recent critics have made this moment pivotal to tell stories of his decline and self-betrayal.[83]

Most notably, Henry Louis Gates begins with what he calls the "puzzle" that when Baldwin wrote *The Fire Next Time*, "he was exalted as *the* voice of black America," and yet his "richly nuanced and self-consciously ambivalent" arguments "were far too complex to serve straight-forwardly political ends." Opposing ambivalence and irony not only to liberal nationalism or racial essentialism but also to any political ends, Gates's Baldwin is not a "Gramscian organic intellectual"; rather, he models the competing ideal of "the alienated artist or intellectual, whose advanced sensibility entailed his estrangement from the very people he would represent." Gates thus separates a Jamesian (1950s) Baldwin from politics and ideology, which Gates associates with the late 1960s: By then, "Baldwin-bashing was a rite of initiation for a younger generation of intellectuals and activists." Gates's initial "puzzle"—that irony once was linked to politics—is resolved reassuringly by separating the antithetical elements in a story about Baldwin's crisis.[84]

Gates's Baldwin does not answer his critics by defending irony against ideology but instead seeks "to reclaim his lost authority by signaling his willingness to be instructed by those who had inherited it." (Hilton Als speculates that Malcolm X, Baraka, and Cleaver were "reincarnations of his withholding and judgmental preacher father" and returned Baldwin to his childhood position as a son desperately seeking approval.) As he became "simplistic" and "strident" to "chase" the new vanguard, Gates laments, "we lost his skepticism, his critical independence." He "succumbed" to black power ideology: In his desperation to be loved, he "allowed himself to mouth a [black nationalist] script that was not his own," yet young blacks "wanted nothing from him." Unable to tolerate marginality as an estranged intellectual testifying to complexity, he became a false prophet "performing" black anger. Because he sought love more than truth, he replaced irony with ideology and abandoned the anti–identity politics that Gates finds in the ironic, mobile voice of the early essays. Yet Gates, stunningly, mirrors Cleaver: Baldwin's problem is his need for love, which subjects him to white power—or black ideologues.[85]

Did Baldwin betray himself by performing a script not his own, or did he change his script to register changing political judgment? Might he have been disillusioned and radicalized by the assassinations of Malcolm X, King, and Black Panther leaders, by the failure of the civil rights movement in the North, by invasive spying on political opposition, by the violence linking the Vietnam War to the repression of black and student radicalism, and by the ascendancy of white backlash, an emerging Republican majority, and the election of Nixon twice? How *does* one digest the bloody, hysterical termination of the second American Reconstruction by a repressive regime invoking "law and order?" As his political hopes confront white recalcitrance after 1965, does his mobile "we" seem insupportable? Does he simply lose irony and "succumb" to ideology, or does he face political realities that Gates evades?

To begin with, a psychologizing account of Baldwin's need for love is surely inadequate as a description, let alone an explanation, of his trajectory. Moreover, Gates's story of self-betrayal is dubious because it suppresses Baldwin's early militancy to create an unconvincing break between salutary irony early and lamentable stridency later. It is more persuasive to read Baldwin in prophetic terms, to bring irony and stridency into relationship all along. Then we can analyze Baldwin's crisis time—and a crisis it was!—by relating the pressure of political circumstance to the internal pressures dictated by his prophetic form of understanding.

Irony, Prophecy, and Politics

For Gates, Baldwin's pre-1965 writing is too "complex" and "ambivalent" to serve "straight-forwardly political ends." But this miscasts Baldwin's politics. Simply, Gates never credits the way Baldwin speaks about white supremacy. Baldwin uses a mobile "I" to inhabit different positions in the social landscape so that he distances himself from positions he voices, but he thereby utters what had been unspeakable about race and whiteness. He creates a dialogue within his texts to name white disavowal of racial domination and its constitutive role in "American" life. For Baldwin, we "accept" this truth or live in denial. Like Douglass, then, he speaks by scorching irony.

His testimony presents not an interpretation of history open to debate, a claim whose validity he redeems, or an alternate background narrative to liberal individualism, but a truth whites willfully refuse to acknowledge. He testifies to social facts we already "know" but do not *own* that we know: We do not count his experience as real, nor do we credit what it means to and for us, which would change our judgment of our conduct and history. He creates a textual "space" in which what we know but disown can become real or salient, both personally and politically. So he uses self-exposing personal testimony as well as "humble" irony—sympathetically rendering positions he does not endorse—but to elicit acknowledgment, and never without "scorching" irony to expose our bad faith as an outrage. His irony always bespeaks "firm persuasion" about truths unspeakable by us.[86]

Accordingly, Baldwin does not ask people to credit the way their identity (as white, say) depends on difference (say, blackness.) "Whiteness" must be abolished as an identity because it is a form of domination entwining every aspect of ordinary life. "Politics" thus names not the mediation of plural identity positions but a structure of rule and struggle against that rule. He speaks, then, not only as an alienated intellectual but as an abolitionist: Moving beyond white supremacy is a condition of democratic possibility, period; the alternative is fraudulent pluralism among whites. Baldwin's politics—his value to we who theorize politics—lies precisely in this antipluralism, which depicts the institutional power and cultural authority of a regime, renders visible the subordination on which it rests, and seeks to reconstitute it.

The *political* office of prophecy is to shift how people judge the meaning of pervasive practices long deemed legitimate, to provoke a decision to act otherwise. In the useful terms of Jacques Rancière, Baldwin engages in "politics" through "speech acts" that show how a regime is constituted by exclusion. He stands with "the part that has no part," which is neither legible in the "field of the visible" nor counted as a part by those who say "we" and consider themselves whole. This part is not, in itself or necessarily, a political subject, and its injuries do not in themselves signify politically. Rather, it is speech that transforms a demographic category into a political subject and injury into a claim about "wrong" or injustice, which advances a standard the enfranchised can recognize.

On the one hand, then, "the part that has no part" becomes a political subject only by making claims about justice. On the other hand, because a regime is constituted by disavowed exclusion of a "part," its visibility disrupts "the partition of the sensible" structuring the regime. But speech about wrong also addresses the enfranchised about the good and fate of the whole. What Baldwin calls "love" thus enacts what Rancière calls "dis-agreement," engagement across difference, not a movement beyond it. Like Rancière, indeed, Baldwin sees that violence may be part of this engagement and that efforts to sustain the relation of parts to whole may fail.[87]

Baldwin shifts how enfranchised people judge the meaning of their history and present conduct by articulating experiences and perspectives they silence or evade. As a result, the American exceptionalist story of immigrant mobility and ethnic pluralism is not invalidated but recast as racial innocence—if it evades the fact that the color line premises mobility for some on fixity for others. His experience, which teaches domination, is no longer pathologized by a story of mobility that makes ghettos signify black inferiority rather than white supremacy. But neither the ruling story of white mobility (and black pathology) nor his story of white supremacy (and pathology) can be "proven" because each precedes what we even count as "facts," let alone how we endow them with meaning. Critics—whether Amos recasting normative worship as idolatry or Baldwin recasting American democracy as white supremacy—take up prophecy, then, to undertake a shift in perspective at this deep level.

As Sabl argued about King, the meaning of "the facts" (black fixity and ethnic success) depends on persuasive arts and political struggle, which reconstitute political judgment. Partly, then, Baldwin voices (to question) the unsaid perspective of those who disavow his reality; partly, he makes claims about injustice in ways they might recognize; partly, he supports the part that has no part as a political movement of speaking and protesting bodies who reject invisibility, demand acknowledgment, and contest prevailing social practices. Partly, his prophetic—poetic and political—task is to shift the fundamental narrative by which parts and whole mediate their histories and conceive their possibilities. In these ways, prophecy does not decree a fate but demands a decision.

Still, what is the nature of the judgment he makes about white supremacy? Is he a moral absolutist, or moralistic, about what Rancière calls wrong? Unlike moralists proclaiming universal norms, he denies that it is possible to separate pure principle from practice. He sees, rather, that people give principles divergent meanings through their worldly practices: Moral and political ideals that seem common or self-evident are practiced in different, even antithetical ways. How else could a society committed to equality and self-determination undergo profound conflict about slavery, abortion, and same-sex desire? He thus denies the faith, in Kant or liberalism, that universality is an answer; he does not justify universal ideals and apply them to particular cases. Rather, he testifies that principles are always "betrayed" in practice, by necessarily partial (some say sinful) actors, and "exposed" in their inherent imperfection. He does not close the gap between principle and practice but makes it the inevitably impure space of politics.[88]

Accordingly, when he criticizes "the protest novel" he rejects a "theology" that juxtaposes pure moral ideals to actors contaminated by embodiment, and that invests redemption in a quest for purity. But he also rejects the alternative he hears in Max's final speech in Richard Wright's *Native Son,* which seems to say, "Though there are whites and blacks among us who hate each other, we will not; there are those who are betrayed by greed, by guilt, by blood lust, but not we; we will set our faces against them and join hands and walk together into that dazzling future when there will be no white and black." This humanism, Baldwin concludes, is "the dream of all liberal men, a dream not at all dishonorable but nevertheless, a dream," for it would rise above "the real battle," which "proceeds far from us in the heat and horror and pain of life itself, where all men are betrayed by greed and guilt and blood lust, and where no one's hands are clean." Any faith in "good will" is another form of innocence.[89]

In his vision of politics, then, Baldwin does not imagine pure principles or pure hands. He does not invoke a Kantian universalism that puts morality over nature or a Christian universalism demanding saintly nonviolence. He does not invoke human rights. No moral rule is commanded by God, anchored in nature, validated by reason, or entailed by human communication. He only affirms our sentient human dignity and bears witness to the "inexorable law" that "whoever debases another debases himself." At issue, though, is not only a personal refusal to acknowledge the reality of an other, but a worldly and political struggle over power, membership, and values. In what spirit? He seeks a "tension" between

two ideas which seem to be in opposition. The first idea is . . . acceptance totally without rancor, of life as it is and men as they are: in the light of this idea it goes without saying that injustice is a commonplace. But this does not mean that one can be complacent, for the second idea is . . . that one must never in one's life accept these injustices as commonplace, but must fight them with all one's strength.[90]

Hebrew prophets, who also see injustice as both ordinary and unacceptable, suggest the difficulty of sustaining this tension, which can be called tragic in character.

Baldwin depicts as real the possibility that whites could acknowledge the injustice of white supremacy, but he also claims that "injustice is a commonplace." To "accept ourselves as we are,"[91] therefore, is to accept that politics is inescapable, because we humans are partial and motivated, because no common good is truly common in a community both unstable and heterogeneous. Baldwin thus lives a second tension that is constitutive of prophecy and difficult to negotiate: What about those who commit injustice and refuse to acknowledge it? Are they to be accepted "without rancor" as an inevitable part of life, and yet also resisted, even redeemed? Can he sustain his faith in their capacity to change and yet also accept their grievous limitations, as the second Reconstruction collapses in violence and reaction?

Between Jeremiah and Job

To address this question and conclude this chapter, consider *No Name in the Street,* a memoir and essay Baldwin began in 1967 and published in 1972. For Gates it is an aesthetically failed retelling of experiences in the civil rights movement, failed partly because it performs a script (and anger) not his own. But it is truer to say the text struggles to come to terms with the defeat of a second Reconstruction. The tone *is* different: Earlier hopes for social change now seem illusory, and he rarely says "we" about Americans; there are "the blacks" and "the whites," and he stands with one judging the other. Yet he also shows the cost of his fame, his dislocation from any black "we," and his difficulty regaining his bearings. Does he abandon irony for stridency and ambivalence for self-promotion, or does he use irony to at once register and endure a catastrophe?

The title, from the book of Job, is quoted as an epigraph:

His remembrance shall perish from the earth, And he shall have no name in the street.
He shall be driven from light into darkness, and chased out of the world.
    (Job 18:17–18)

Who is "he"? The words are spoken by Bildad, one of Job's false comforters: Whoever does evil will suffer in a universe ruled by a just God. Does Baldwin address this to whites as "evil-doers"? Or rather, does he invert Bildad's "prophecy" to depict not only the nameless invisibility and homelessness of social death under white supremacy, but also the obscurity to which triumphant evil consigns the dishonored prophet? The essay suggests that both views are true. Does he endorse Bildad's theodicy of an ethically rational world—in which people do pay for what they do, by who they become—or like Job himself, does Baldwin depict absurdity to mock this faith? Again, the essay sustains each view by an exemplary performance of irony. Raising questions about faith and justice by the naming (and practice) of his text, he suspends himself—and us—between Jeremiah and Job.[92]

His overt political argument depicts a crisis. On the one hand, he portrays desperate white Americans:

For a very long time, America prospered. . . . Now, the people who are the most spectacular recipients of this prosperity . . . cannot or dare not assess or imagine the price paid by their victims, or subjects, for this way of life, and so they cannot afford to know why the victims are revolting. They are forced, then, to the conclusion that the victims—the barbarians—are revolting against all established civilized values—which is both true and not true—and, in order to protect these values, however stifling and joyless these values have caused their lives to be, they desperately seek out representatives who are prepared to make up in cruelty what they lack in conviction.[93]

In an uncannily timely way, he depicts Americans using violence to defend a way of life they equate with civilization itself, but partly because they will not assess its cost to themselves and others. On the other hand, he celebrates the increasing self-assurance of American blacks: "To be liberated from the stigma of blackness by embracing it is to cease one's interior agreement and collaboration with the authors of one's degradation." But "blunt open articulation of self-affirmation . . . has frightened the nation to death."[94]

Unable "to believe that the grievances of others are real" because "they cannot face what this fact says about themselves and their country," white Americans endorse violence. He does not only analogize ghettos and Vietnam: "Now, exactly like . . . the Third Reich, though innocent men are being harassed, jailed, murdered in all the northern cities, the citizens know nothing and wish to know nothing of what is happening around them."[95] No longer able to call blacks to transform the "achievements of the West" and save America from sterility, he depicts—and voices—the enraged contempt of subalterns. Baldwin does not mediate but insists on this abyss: "That is why, ultimately, all attempts at dialogue between the subdued and subduer break down."[96]

After King is assassinated and the Black Panther Party is violently repressed, Baldwin witnesses how a movement made up of a plurality of voices in cacophonous conflict is silenced and simplified. He had inhabited and voiced different (black as well as white) positions on the political landscape. His account of the Nation of Islam in *The Fire Next Time* is exemplary: He *uses* Elijah Muhammad to criticize white supremacy, even as he distances himself from the conclusions Elijah draws, just as he uses sanguine voices to invoke hopes on which he then casts doubt. Moving among such voices, Baldwin gains his own authority by bringing out and mediating their truths. But this plurality is disappearing by the early 1970s as militant voices are jailed and killed. He always drew on their anger, even as he criticized rancor; now, perhaps, he feels required to take on rage in less mediated ways, even as he has lost access to and faith in other registers of voice.

Accordingly, Baldwin cannot sustain a tension between redemption and "the fire next time" to express the contingency, or dramatic possibility, in his narrative of "decision" on the fate of the nation. He no longer publicly discusses whether whites can "accept themselves as they are." Rather, "if the American people are unable to contend with their elected leaders for the redemption of their own honor and the lives of their children, we, the Blacks, the most rejected of the Western children, can expect very little help at their hands." Since "we cannot awaken this sleeper, and God knows we have tried," we "must do what we can do" to "fortify and save each other." We are *not* "drowning in apathetic self-contempt"; we *are* committed "to change our fate and the fate of our children."[97]

But that fate no longer involves saving or "awakening" whites. Correspondingly, in a 1972 interview, Baldwin calls John Brown a "true American prophet" because he tried to free, not black slaves as such, but "a whole country from a disastrous way of life." At issue is "not what white people had done to black people, but what white people are doing to themselves. It's not a question that has anything to do with me at all. Because you're doing it . . . only you can undo it. Nobody else is going to save you. You've got to save yourselves."[98]

But he did not *begin* with this perspective, by which he now looks back on the early sixties: "Many of us believed or made ourselves believe that the American state still contained within itself the power of self-confrontation," the power to "change itself in the direction of honor and knowledge and freedom, or as Malcolm put it, to atone." "It says a great deal about the black American experience both positively and negatively, that so many should have believed so hard, so long" in this capacity to change, and "paid such a price" to sustain it.[99] "Even a skeptic like myself" was moved by the faith demonstrated in and by the March on Washington:

One very nearly dared, in spite of all one knew, to hope—to hope that the need and passion of the people, so nakedly and vividly, and with such dignity, revealed, would not be, once again, betrayed. . . . For a moment, it almost seemed that we stood on a height, and could see our inheritance; perhaps we could make the kingdom real, perhaps the beloved community would not forever remain the dream one dreamed in agony.[100]

Looking back, though, he recounts how "Martin's death forced me into a judgment . . . I have always been reluctant to make." The judgment is that "most people, in action, are not worth very much," but he is reluctant to make it because he also believes that "every person is an unprecedented miracle." To "treat them as the miracles they are while trying to protect oneself from the disasters they've become" is "an act of faith" once demonstrated by "all those marches and petitions when Martin was alive."[101] But "hope—that we, human beings, can be better than we are—dies hard; perhaps one can no longer live if one allows that hope to die." His "life-style," indeed, is "dictated" by his "reluctance" to conclude that people cannot change.[102]

What he means becomes clearer because he addresses Cleaver's judgments:

Naturally, I didn't like what he had to say about me at all. But . . . I thought I could see why he felt impelled to issue what was, in fact, a warning: he was being a zealous watchman on the city wall, and I do not say that with a sneer. He seemed to feel that I was a dangerously odd, badly twisted, fragile reed, of too much use to the establishment to be trusted by blacks. I felt that he used my public reputation against me both naively and unjustly, and I also felt that I was confused in his mind with the unutterable debasement of the male—with all those faggots, punks, and sissies, the sight and sound of whom, in prison, must have made him vomit more than once.[103]

He makes Cleaver the prophetic watchman warning of danger, lodged in those too identified with the establishment—or in queers. Baldwin denies he is "of . . . use to the establishment," and he denies he belongs among those queers he marks off as abject.[104] Linking Cleaver and prophecy to "the revolutionary," he links queer to the category of "the artist." But revolutionaries and artists are *related* because each is "possessed by a vision and they do not so much follow this vision as find themselves driven by it. Otherwise, they could never endure much less embrace the lives they are compelled to lead." The revolutionary's vision judges incapacity to change, while the artist's vision celebrates faith in human being as a miracle, but "we need each other, and have much to learn from each other, and now more than ever."[105]

Baldwin does not criticize Cleaver or abandon irony to rival his militance, but he seems to abandon politics, judgment, and prophecy to him; still, a "badly twisted" (ironic?) figure can inhabit the legitimate office of the *artist*. While some construe Baldwin's reluctance to relinquish faith as a mark of weakness, Baldwin depicts the artist's commitment to our miraculous capacities as needful. In this way, he seems at once to affirm and yet split generative tensions in prophecy about human (in)capacity to change, about judgment and faith, about speech and action.

In the concluding passages of *No Name in the Street,* however, he again sustains these tensions in his own voice as he returns to the trope of the lover critically engaging the beloved:

To be . . . an American black is to be in a situation, intolerably exaggerated, of all those who have ever found themselves part of a civilization which they could in no wise honorably defend—which they were compelled, indeed, endlessly to . . . condemn—and who yet spoke out of the most passionate love, hoping to make the kingdom new, to make it honorable and worthy of life.[106]

It is as if he cannot resist investing in black Americans the voice of the God (and prophet) who loves a wayward people while remaining committed to the aspirations by which he judges them. Here Baldwin again identifies himself and the African American community with judgment wed to "passionate love." He displaces both his black critics and his sexuality as he again merges his prophetic voice and the black community into a protagonist that is "mocked and detested" by *whites*. Their ridicule and hatred "is moving" to witness "because it is so blind: it is terrible to watch people cling to their captivity and insist on their own destruction." Indeed, "black people have always felt this about Americans" and "[have] seen, spinning above the thoughtless American head, the shape of the wrath to come."[107] Not divine punishment, or a projection of his own rancor, "wrath" names the relentless consequences of conduct. The one law in Baldwin's universe is that every "ticket" has its price, every act its cost. Affirming that we always "pay" for what we do by what we become, he leaves us with our choices and their legacy. "Everything now, we must assume, is in our hands; we have no right to assume otherwise."[108]

5. Toni Morrison and Prophecy
"This Is Not a Story to Pass On"

*This society is not likely to become free of racism. Therefore it is necessary
for Negroes to free themselves by becoming their idea of what a free people
should be.*
—Ralph Ellison, "Working Notes for a Second Novel"

*We tell stories because in the last analysis human lives need and merit being
narrated. This remark takes on its full force when we refer to the necessity to
save the history of the defeated and lost. The whole history of suffering cries
out for vengeance and calls for narrative.*
—Paul Ricoeur, Time and Narrative

*If I am getting ready to speak at length about . . . ghosts, which is to say about
certain others who are not presently living . . . it is in the name of justice.*
—Jacques Derrida, Specters of Marx

I INITIALLY conceived a book about "prophetic narrative"
because I was so profoundly affected by Toni Morrison's novel *Beloved*.
More effectively than any other text in my experience, it dramatizes the
redemptive language and longing that has driven American culture
and that has twinned white and black. As its themes led me to reread
Sacvan Bercovitch's *American Jeremiad*, which depicted the hegemony of
redemptive rhetoric in American liberal nationalism, I conceived this
book, which here returns to its origin. For *Beloved* still seems at once
to address and end, though not simply end, a story that entwines the
machinery of racial domination and the redemptive narratives by which
people have justified or opposed it.

As Bercovitch argues, Puritans revised Hebrew prophecy, and their
jeremiads provided the narrative form by which subsequent political actors imagined and produced a nationhood that sacralized liberal origins. But while Bercovitch speaks an Americanized Marxism to argue
that the redemptive rhetoric of "the jeremiad" has "contained" dissent

in liberal terms and in a national form, I focus on race and draw on Nietzsche to emphasize the hegemony of redemptive language beyond a liberal frame.

For genocide, slavery, white supremacy, nativism, anticommunism, and wars on terror, but also abolition and other American social movements, are justified by a rhetoric of special American nationhood and its specifically redemptive promise. Likewise, literary artists who condemn the domination of American life by acquisitive liberalism (or by white supremacy) still "speak their defiance as keepers of the dream" of a special (democratic) nationhood. In response to these prophetic voices, I have asked, Must rhetorics of redemption devalue the conditions that make politics necessary and valuable, or can redemption be conceived in ways that sustain vibrant political life?[1]

Beloved seems significant by contrast to most voices and texts in the American political and literary tradition. For it dramatizes the power of the idea of redemption, exposing redemption as a problem in ways that lead readers (if not characters) to work through (if not move beyond) it. Making the wish for redemption and the ways we practice it a problem we must face for the sake of our freedom, *Beloved* performs a complex and political view of redemption.

For by focusing on a community of ex-slaves, *Beloved* fosters critical distance from American nationhood, whose "promise" is never mentioned, let alone criticized, while it troubles the redemptive meaning of any counternationalism. Still, a story of ex-slaves confronting the haunting power of the past, the wish to redeem it, and the difficulty of freedom is exemplary of the challenge that both white and black Americans must face to create a more democratic politics. And the novel's literary form—in which multiple voices struggle to understand the meaning of their entwined histories—seems to model a *democratic* politics that resists a coercively unifying nationhood. Bercovitch and Michael Rogin state the problem: the twinned hegemony of liberal nationalism and redemptive language in a society constituted by white supremacy. *Beloved* seems to dramatize a way to name and perhaps move beyond it.

Most scholarship about the novel since its publication in 1987 addresses the issue of redemption in multiple dimensions. But not surprisingly, most commentators read the novel as narrating a story of the redemption of the main character, Sethe, and the black community around her. Of the small cohort of critics who say the novel does not redeem its characters, most still argue that it enables the redemption of

readers presumed to be black, female, or both. In either view, the novel
is said to demonstrate the redemptive power of love or of narrative to
"heal" people traumatized by their histories and to free them to create
a future on different terms.

Few commentators depict the text as troubling, let alone defeating,
such dreams of healing and redemption. At the same time, *Beloved* is
read in terms of mother–daughter bonds and gender, psychoanalysis
and narrative, trauma in black culture, and "black" or postmodern aesthetic practices. With notable exceptions, it is not typically read as engaging African American *political* life, let alone "American" politics. But I
will read it that way. The novel's place in this book is thus clear: As it explores the necessity and (im)possibility of coming to terms with the past,
it dramatizes the issues of redemption, narrative, and nationhood that
are central in my analysis of prophecy's bearing as a genre in politics.[2]

But my reasons for ending with Morrison have been enriched since
the appearance of *Beloved* in 1987. Especially noteworthy are her address on receiving the Nobel Prize and her essays on race and the literary imagination, which address the issue of prophecy directly. In her
commentaries on the Clarence Thomas–Anita Hill episode and on the
O. J. Simpson trial and in numerous interviews, she also voices a project
of racial consolidation in cultural and aesthetic terms while engaging
a national public about race and politics. Most famously, perhaps, she
entered national politics by publishing a piece in the *New Yorker* (and
headlining a major rally in New York City) to defend then-president Bill
Clinton from impeachment. The piece calls him "our first black president," and the rally ends with Morrison and Odetta holding hands on
stage, leading the crowd in "God Bless America."

Did Morrison's continuing engagement with our post–civil rights
era draw her into a prophetic language she had abjured? The point
of this chapter is not to condemn a contradiction but, on the contrary,
to assess the different registers of prophecy she uses to imagine both
African American community and American nationhood and thereby
to explore her ways of mediating the relations of parts and wholes. To
set up my reading of *Beloved,* therefore, I visit several texts in which she
depicts prophecy, evokes the redemptive power of language, imagines
black community, and narrates its post–civil rights crisis. In turn, *Beloved*'s ambivalent relationship to redemption and nationhood illuminates the Clinton episode.

From Baldwin to Morrison I

In her 1987 essay on the American canon, "Unspeakable Things Un-spoken," Morrison asks Baldwin's question: "What intellectual feats had to be performed by the author or his critic to erase me from a society seething with my presence, and what effect has that performance had on the work? What are the strategies of escape from knowledge?" The "unspeakable" names "the ghost in the machine," she says, the way American literature (like its politics) is formed by disavowing the bond between freedom and racial domination. Quoting Tocqueville's claim that poets in America, "not finding the ideal in the real and true," would "flee to imaginary regions," she notes that critics depict an affinity between American culture and the genre of romance rather than the realist novel. Like him, they see a literature of "monsters" and ghosts, but rather than attribute such "fantastical creatures" to a literary imagination vitiated by its flight from social reality, she asks, "[Where] is the shadow of the presence from which the text has fled?"[3]

As she uses Melville's *Moby-Dick* to show how white writers do register race, she puts aesthetic questions in prophetic and political terms. For Melville recognizes "the moment when whiteness becomes ideology." Indeed, "if the white whale is the ideology of race, what Ahab has lost to it is personal dismemberment and . . . his own place as a human in the world." As a result, Ahab shows that if someone "took on not abolition, not the amelioration of racist institutions or their laws, but the very concept of whiteness as an inhuman idea, he would be very alone, very desperate, and very doomed. Madness would be the only appropriate description of such audacity."[4]

But audacity or madness can be prophecy, for she selects Father Mapple's "thrilling" sermon on Jonah as her exemplary chapter in *Moby-Dick*. Jonah is saved from the whale's belly for a single purpose, as Morrison quotes Mapple:

To preach the Truth to the face of Falsehood! That was it! . . . Delight is to him . . . who against the proud gods and commodores of this earth, ever stands forth his own inexorable self. . . . Delight is to him who gives no quarter in the truth and kills, burns, and destroys all *sin* though he pluck it out from under the robes of Senators and Judges. Delight . . . is to him who acknowledges no law or lord but the Lord his God, and is only a *patriot to heaven*. [Morrison's emphasis][5]

In her own voice, she adds,

No one, I think, has denied that this sermon is designed to be prophetic, but it seems unremarked [in the literary scholarship] what the sin is . . . that must be destroyed regardless [of the cost]. Nature? A sin? The term does not apply. Capitalism? Perhaps, but capitalism is not in itself sinful to Melville. Sin suggests a moral outrage within the bounds of man to repair. The concept of racial superiority would fit seamlessly.

Ahab is thus the only American "heroic enough to try to slay the monster that was devouring the world as he knew it."[6]

Many scholars see Mapple as Melville's way of voicing Theodore Parker's abolitionism, which weds moral truth to destruction in the name of overcoming sin. In this view, Melville recoils from the violence Parker justifies, and he depicts Ahab as captive to the monster making by which he bewitches his crew. In this view, the novel creates critical distance from the resentful, demonizing rhetoric whose destructive impact is the sinking of the *Pequod*. But Morrison weds Melville to the abolitionism running from William Lloyd Garrison and Parker to John Brown; her Melville embraces Ahab's monster-killing project. They voice antiracist prophecy: Attacking whiteness "was dangerous, solitary, radical work. Especially then, especially now. To be 'only a patriot to heaven' is no mean aspiration in Young America for a writer—or for the captain of a whaling ship." Rather than note the resentment that contaminates Ahab, she imagines a prophet addressing people whose blindness dooms him to marginality and them to destruction.[7]

Is Morrison endorsing a theistic language of sin and so a moral absolutism? Does she idealize Ahabian rage as prophetic audacity? Consider her December 1987 eulogy for James Baldwin. She depicts him as one she calls an ancestor, a seminal or generative source, and she identifies three gifts he bequeathed. First, he gave her "a language to dwell in" by "making English honest"; he "de-colonized" what had been "forbidden territory" so that black people could "enter it, occupy it, and restructure it to accommodate our demanding beauty, tragic knowledge and lived reality." Second, he gave black people "the courage to appropriate an alien, hostile, all-white geography." Tellingly, she casts that courage in prophetic terms when she quotes him: "A person does not lightly elect to oppose his society. One would much rather be at home among one's compatriots than be mocked and detested by them. But the mockery of the people, even their hatred, is moving because it is so blind: it is terrible to watch people cling to their captivity and insist on their own destruction." Because he voices a prophetic pathos about choices he failed to change and suffering he cannot forestall, she credits his third gift as a "tenderness" whose lesson is that "though I stand on moral ground . . . it must be shored up by mercy."[8]

Thoreau eulogizes Brown as a martyr to memorialize his own prophetic persona; Morrison memorializes Baldwin not so much to establish a canon as to identify the space he created by making over a language that "has never been able to recognize us." Does her invocation of loss register her vocation not only as a writer but also as a prophet? Does she forewarn a people who self-destructively cling to their idols? Does she address blacks as a protagonist in a story of collective liability and decision? She dramatizes the hold of prophetic language on others, but is she herself gripped by it?

Surely, she recognizes an elective affinity between antiracism and prophecy in her analyses of Melville and Baldwin. In what does this affinity consist? First, critics of white supremacy are drawn to prophecy to announce that people, at great cost to themselves and others, deny the meaning of their history and present conduct. Such messengers make unequivocal claims not because of theism but to undertake the constitutively political act of remaking the passionate frame of reference that orients the self-reflection and action of their audiences.

Correspondingly, and second, critics of white supremacy are drawn to prophecy because it offers them a language of collective liability. They denounce what Morrison calls "sin," which "injustice" fails to translate, for the wrong is not only the exclusion by which a republic at once constitutes and betrays itself but the ongoing disavowal that this is the case. The judgment is entailed not by theism or moral absolutism but by what Cavell calls the difference between knowledge and acknowledgment. In this sense, it is the office of prophets not only to announce but to bear witness, by saying what they see and standing against it.

Facing a refusal of acknowledgment, critics of white supremacy draw on prophecy to seek the "turn" that is translated as repentance. A "turn" toward those we have not counted as real is the other side of acknowledging how disavowal has constituted community. To provoke such political judgments is to recast first principles and reconstitute community. Critics of white supremacy are drawn to prophecy, therefore, not to depict a pluralism of valuable perspectives but to name a willful blindness and reconstitute the whole. Like Hebrew critics of idolatry, they warn that the alternative to "turning" is political self-destruction.

Accordingly, and third, critics of white supremacy are drawn to prophecy because it bears an idea of freedom: When Baldwin warns of "the fire next time," he speaks in prophetic terms because the office of the prophet is to serve as a watchman who warns of danger to forestall it. Baldwin depicts an ever-present capacity for choice, he knows that choices (including inaction) are fateful, he identifies grave dangers in our conduct, and he fears that repentance can come too late, after the accumulating consequences of prior choices have already overwhelmed agency. Though crediting the power of fear, narrow self-interest, and vanity, prophetic critics like Baldwin still affirm a capacity to act otherwise, a capacity that they interpret as the miraculous and link to redemption.

Still, does prophecy, by a trope of blindness, deny openness to a plurality of perspectives, which must be an axiomatic principle of democratic life? By identifying fateful choices about constitutive practices, does prophecy enable political dialogue, or does it conflate compromise and self-betrayal? By advancing urgent claims, prophets would provoke self-reflection and action, but do they generate recrimination and fear? By linking formal democracy to domination, do they name the gap that endangers a republic, or do they encourage violence?

But Morrison voices no such political anxieties about patriots to heaven, whose audacity seems like madness. Rather, she depicts prophecy as a political office whose purpose is to shift how whites judge the meaning of pervasive practices they have deemed legitimate—so they can act otherwise. Indeed, Morrison registers every step of this book's argument thus far: She sees how critics turn to prophecy to confront the racial state of exception that at once constitutes and betrays American liberal society, for she sees how prophecy gives them rhetorical resources by which to name disavowal of domination, but also of our capacity to act otherwise. Rather than demand obedience to a moral-political command, then, critics draw on prophecy to seek acknowledgment—of realities we deny, of conduct we disclaim, of people we do not count as real, but also of our own best commitments and of our authority as citizens. In Rancière's terms, critics of white supremacy draw on prophecy to enact politics in a constitutive sense: Standing with "the part that has no part," they make claims about constitutive wrong to demand the restructuring of the whole.

Inescapably, then, prophets recast people's relationship to the past, their understanding of its meaning. Rancière presumes constitutive exclusion, and it is but a step to see amnesia as its symptom and prophecy as the office of those who remember origins people too readily forget. The jeremiads of Frederick Douglass or Martin Luther King Jr. thus return to origins in a Machiavellian sense, by reinterpreting first principles long practiced in viciously exclusive ways or idolized in reified forms. In contrast, however, Baldwin and Morrison reject a jeremiadic narrative: Like Nietzsche, they depict coming to terms with a past that is haunting and imprisoning because it is horrific and because it has been denied.

History and narrative thus reveal another reason why critics of white supremacy are drawn toward prophecy. For uprooting, exile, and subjugation shout the question of redemption and generate prophetic responses, which in turn can acutely energize and yet also endanger political life. Here is one way to represent the shift from Baldwin to Morrison and to suggest how she *herself* assumes a prophetic office. She does not cast herself as a patriot to heaven or as a critic mocked by people whose doom she would forestall but must witness. She works another strand in the tradition of black prophecy in America: She speaks to those she calls "my people" about the terms on which to hold together as a community. She bears witness to "the unspeakable"—the horror and suffering they have veiled to survive but must remember to flourish—while she also celebrates the cultural and aesthetic forms that have enabled their solidarity.

In this she echoes Hebrew prophets after invasion, uprooting, and exile. For they asked, How can we go on after this violent catastrophe and historical rupture? In effect, they answered, By transfiguring sorrow into narrative form, we at once redeem our past and reconstitute our community. But that narrative also promised a national vindication that overcame Gentile adversaries in the name of redeeming them. Since Nietzsche, commentators thus ask, Does resentment fuel such prophecy? Do prophecies of redemption promise an impossible deliverance from history and so from politics? Correspondingly, we ask, Does Morrison redeem her people *from* a traumatic past? Or does she seek the redemption *of* that past by accepting it as a fatality and making it a condition of action? In either case, does she, unlike her biblical forebears, trouble the redemptive promises she makes?

When Nietzsche's Zarathustra defines "my redemption," he argues that since we cannot change or escape the past, we must redeem it, partly by narrative art to make it meaningful and partly by working through loss and resentment. Freud argues similarly as he tries to distinguish mourning and melancholia. The problem is an unredeemed and therefore haunting past, and the issue is not how to get free *from* it but how to come to terms *with* it. Baldwin speaks this way to provoke a national dialogue among blacks and whites about a history he depicts as tragically repetitive. But after a failed second Reconstruction, Morrison inflects this redemptive language, and the relation of parts and whole, differently.

For Baldwin and Morrison there is no exodus from Egypt: We cannot leave masters in Egypt; nor can we leave behind the dead in the wilderness. But for Baldwin, overcoming white supremacy means accepting— in full gothic ambivalence—a "wedding" with former masters we cannot divorce. Morrison, however, does not call whites to a decision about national fate or urge blacks to "accept" a bond whites disown. Her view of black life, rather, is postcolonial and diasporic. On the one hand, she depicts African Americans as haunted by a traumatic past they would forget but must redeem. She too emphasizes disavowal, but of the dead by the living. Those she calls "my people" forget trauma rather than principles and ancestors rather than covenants, but facing the past and forging the "we" whose past it is remain the central collective project. On the other hand, therefore, Morrison writes to create a space apart—a linguistic and cultural space, not a different place—for the part that has no part. Her project takes prophetic form as she asks, Which stories do we let go, and how do we retell the ones we pass on? Consider her Nobel lecture in this regard:[9]

Narrative has never been merely entertainment for me. It is, I believe, one of the principal ways in which we absorb knowledge. I hope you will understand, then, why I begin these remarks with the opening phrase of what must be the oldest sentence in the world, and the earliest one we remember from childhood: Once upon a time . . .

Recalling and initiating a scene of instruction, she refuses the authority of "in the beginning," instead choosing to link storytelling to the plural possibilities (and temporalities) of "once upon a time." She begins, "Once upon a time there was an old woman. Blind but wise." She has heard many versions of this story, but

in the version I know the woman is a daughter of slaves, black, American, and lives alone in a small house outside of town. Her reputation for wisdom is without peer. . . . Among her people she is both the law and its transgression. The honor she is paid and the awe in which she is held reach beyond her neighborhood to places far away, to the city where the intelligence of rural prophets is the source of much amusement.

Blind like Tiresias we might say, but female and black, a daughter of slaves and an American, this "ancestor" is a prophet mocked by "the city" but esteemed by "her people," who share a pastoral life that is passing away. Several young people go to her house, and one says, "Old woman, I hold in my hand a bird. Tell me whether it is living or dead." After a long silence the old woman says, "I don't know whether the bird you are holding is dead or alive, but what I do know is that it is in your hands."

Beginning her explication, Morrison specifies her choice to interpret the bird as language and the old woman as a writer. "Being a writer she thinks of language partly as a system, partly as a living thing over which one has no control, but mostly as agency—as an act with consequences." Morrison's first reading of the tale imagines the old woman "worried about how the language she dreams in, given to her at birth," is used. It dies if it becomes "statist language, censored and censoring," or "official language . . . dumb, predatory, sentimental," or a means to enable or sanitize domination. She protests, "Oppressive language does more than represent violence; it is violence." A "policing language of mastery" does not "permit new knowledge or encourage the mutual exchange of ideas." Invoking collective liability, "she is convinced that when language dies . . . not only she herself but all users and makers are accountable for its demise."

In contrast, "the vitality of language lies in its ability to limn the actual, imagined, and possible lives of its speakers, readers, writers. Although its poise is sometimes in displacing experience, it is not a substitute for it. It arcs toward the place where meaning may lie." Morrison herself offers Lincoln's words as an example of living language:

When [he] thought about the graveyard his country had become, and said, "the world will little note nor long remember what we say here, but it will never forget what they did here," his simple words are exhilarating in their life-sustaining properties because they refuse to encapsulate the reality of 600,000 dead men in a cataclysmic race war. Refusing to monumentalize, disdaining the "final word," his words signal deference to the uncapturability of the life it mourns. It is the deference that moves her [the old woman], that recognition that language can never live up to life once and for all. Nor should it. Language can never "pin down" slavery, genocide, war. Nor should it yearn for the arrogance to be able to do so. Its force, its felicity is in its reach toward the ineffable.

Morrison identifies with Lincoln on the prophetic question of how, or whether, crime, violence, and suffering can be redeemed. If language's authority depends on granting its limits, is prophecy the office of those who work the line between language and the violence or suffering it would redeem? Is false prophecy the violation of this limit?

But then Morrison offers a second reading of the tale, by imagining that the young people *hear* "it is in your hands" *as* "it's not my problem. . . . the future of language is yours." Morrison imagines, "Suppose the visit was only a ruse, a trick to get to be spoken to, taken seriously." They feel abandoned by her, and their accusation is a plea:

Is there no context for our lives? No song? No literature . . . no history connected to experience that you can pass along to help us start strong? You are . . . the wise one. . . . Make up a story. . . . Forget your name in the street; tell us what the world has been to you in the dark places and the light . . . What it is to live at the edge of towns that cannot bear your company. . . . Tell us about a wagonload of slaves, how they sang so softly their breath was indistinguishable from the falling snow.

As the young people imagine a story about those slaves, the old woman can respond, "Finally, I trust you now . . . with the bird that is not in your hands because you have truly caught it. Look. How lovely it is, this thing we have done—together."

Morrison's speech represents different aspects of prophecy than does her essay on the American canon and her eulogy for Baldwin. Partly, prophecy is directly about (the fate of) language: Redemption is a practice of meaning making whose vitality depends on accepting *limits* to what words and humans can do. Partly, prophecy is about authority in a generational relationship conceived in rhetorical and political terms. For the old woman names a responsibility in our hands, while we want salvation from her, though we may mock her rather than admit our wish. Morrison shows that expectations of prophets are a material fact and political reality that the old woman (and Morrison) must reckon on. By refusing to dispense solace, do they free us to narrate? By taking on meaning making, do we enable them to become allies, interlocutors? Showing how prophet and audience are differently positioned, Morrison shares the old woman's hope to enable a successor generation. Having "passed on" the redemptive work of narrative, they together affirm the collaborative bond—of author and reader, prophet and people, and among citizens—whose initiation is their deepest wish. Does her lecture, then, model a nontheist, post–civil rights prophecy?

What is the office of a (black) prophet in America *now*? Morrison does denounce the idolatry of those who call themselves white and profess allegiance to democratic principles, but she does not play that prophetic and redemptive role *for* them, on their behalf. She sustains Baldwin's image of the artist speaking to her beloved, but casts that love as the ancestor's solicitude for her people. The office of the prophet, as she avows it at least, is not to "achieve our country" but to sustain a black nation subjugated and exiled in an American Egypt or Babylon. Since Baldwin would wed black and white and wrote before civil rights fully made its complex impact, he did not conceive a project to sustain black solidarity, whereas she presumes the failure of his dream of one nation and draws from a tradition of nation building in black prophecy beginning before David Walker's 1828 *Appeal*.[10] But on what basis does Morrison assert and sustain black solidarity?

Partly, she calls for fidelity, not to a god or to principles but to what she calls a "black aesthetic" rooted in traditional and vernacular cultural forms, which she tasks the novel to embody. Partly, she sustains solidarity by memory of history: Uprooting, death, and subjugation are cast as a traumatic legacy whose narration is a constitutive collective project of redemption. Partly, she imagines solidarity in Arendtian senses, as the action and judgment of a community of African American interlocutors; by "laying stories next to each other," as she says in *Beloved*, their plural voices forge and recast a collective subject.[11]

Her concerns—with history and haunting, mourning and healing, acknowledgment and dialogue among the living and with the dead— echo not only prophecy but African spirituality, Greek tragedy, and psychoanalysis. But prophecy is crucial. For it is but a step from Hosea's forgiving God saying, "I will betroth thee unto me forever . . . and I will say to them which were not my people, thou art my people" (2:19–23), to *Beloved*, whose epigraph is Paul quoting Hosea—"I will call them my people, which were not my people; and her beloved, which was not beloved" (Rom. 9:25). Morrison quotes not Hosea, whose God seeks covenant renewal with a wayward people, but Paul, who invokes the experience of slavery as social death to depict both faith in resurrection and its constitution of a new chosen people from an unloved remnant. As Morrison herself takes up the office of those who mediate between death and life as well as part and whole, so I also ask, In what ways does she enact, and in what ways does she trouble, this story and promise of redemption?

From Baldwin to Morrison II

If we join Morrison's eulogy for Baldwin to the story in her Nobel address, we can imagine him as a forebear like the old woman, one whose example and language enable her own vocation as a writer. She echoes his critique of disavowal and innocence but revises his view of the artist as a lover whose truth-telling redeems the beloved. It is not that he emphasizes the redemptive power of love, while she emphasizes the redemptive power of language; both depict a horrific past we cannot escape or change and must redeem through narrative and love. Yet she emphasizes the intergenerational: Though he repeatedly says we must act with "the children" in mind, his artist-as-prophet typically addresses a lover, while she typically imagines ancestors and mothers passing on stories to and undertaking narration with daughters as cultural heirs and collaborators.

Morrison thus needs to be positioned in relation to a post–civil rights and feminist era: She would come to terms with the legacy of a second Reconstruction, and not only a slave past, which means digesting profound political disappointment in the civil rights era and its "American" promise and taking in enormous change in the world of those she calls my people. Acute disjuncture defines this moment: an enlarged black professional class but a growing "underclass" and staggering rates of black incarceration; political consensus against overt racism but a national culture that still uses black bodies symbolically. Jesse Jackson competed in the Democratic primaries in 1984, though no one believed a black could be elected president—for reasons revealed in 1988, when George Bush used the image of Willie Horton to defeat Michael Dukakis. In an intersecting universe, academic Afrocentrism and Louis Farrakahn's Nation of Islam rejected integrationist ideals, while black conservatives used civil rights rhetoric and ideas of "color-blindness" to attack programs addressing racial inequality.[12]

Morrison emphasizes the continuing reality of white supremacy: In a post–civil rights era, whites use legislative milestones to deny the continuing reality of racial categories and racialized domination, while "race has assumed a metaphorical life . . . more necessary and more on display than ever before." Asking, "In what public discourse does the reference to black people not exist?" she offers critical literacy to "avert the critical gaze from the racial object to the racial subject."[13] "In a society with a history of trying to accommodate both slavery and freedom, and a present that wishes both to deny and exploit the pervasiveness of racism," literacy is also decoding the racial symbolic. "Black people as a group are used to signify the polar opposites of love and repulsion. On the one hand, they signify benevolence, harmless and servile guardianship, and endless love. On the other hand they represent insanity, illicit sexuality, and chaos." Thus, "the exorcism of critical national issues" is "situated in the miasma of black life and inscribed on the bodies of black people."[14] By using black bodies in "official stories," whites forge a *national* culture. "It is *Birth of a Nation* writ large—menacingly and pointedly for the 'hood.'"[15]

Standing in that social place, she questions the civil rights project and its national frame. "Deep within the word 'American' is its association with race. To identify someone as South African is to say very little; we need the adjective 'white' or 'black' or 'colored' to make our meaning clear," while "American means white."[16] In a 1988 interview, Paul Gilroy notes her "consistent refusal to identify herself as an American": "My childhood efforts to join America were continually rebuffed. . . . America has always meant something other to me—them."[17] Despite Clarence Thomas's claim that the integration project presumed black inferiority, she portrays him as Friday in Daniel Defoe's *Robinson Crusoe:* Each renounces his culture of origin to accept "rescue" by another; escaping from a culture experienced as life-threatening, each denies that it also loved and protected him. Sometimes "it is easier, emotionally and professionally, to deny, ignore, erase, even destroy" one's culture than to endure ambivalence. But "if the language of one's culture is lost or surrendered," one must "describe it in the language of the rescuing one." To lose the "mother tongue" is to "internalize" a "master's tongue" that demeans one's origins.[18]

Morrison situates Thomas in a geography of two nations with different languages, one a clearly bounded colony ruled by another whose power can (by language) be taken inside. The colony is not unitary; indeed, her essays and fiction emphasize division by gender and class, not to mention the actuality of plurality. Still, essays and interviews in the 1980s depict black society as a "tribe" and "village," figures of gemeinschaft that submerge division in a rhetoric of community, if not homogeneity. These metaphors perform crucial work as she tells a story about a community thrown into crisis when it undergoes a migration from "village values" and solidarity to "the city." In this jeremiad, traditional forms of solidarity are jeopardized because "my people, we 'peasants,' have come to the city, that is to say, we live within its values. There is a confrontation between the old values of the tribe, and the new urban values."[19] Cornel West too argues that "our black foremothers and forefathers" created "powerful buffers" and "cultural armor to beat back the demons of hopelessness, meaninglessness, and lovelessness," but the forms "that once sustained black life in America are no longer able to fend off the nihilistic threat."[20]

Because preliterate cultural forms are failing as rituals of solidarity and healing, other forms must be devised. "For a long time the art form that was healing for Black people was music." Now that it "is no longer exclusively ours" because of mass culture, "another form has to take that place, and it seems to me that the novel is needed by us now in a way that it was not needed before."[21] Seeking "a mode to do what the music did for blacks, what we used to be able to do with each other in private and in that civilization . . . underneath the white civilization," Morrison writes "what I have recently begun to call village literature, fiction that is really for the village, for the tribe. Peasant literature for *my* people."[22]

Morrison thus attacks theories that deconstruct race:

Suddenly . . . "race" does not exist. For three hundred years black Americans insisted that "race" was no usefully distinguishing factor in human relationships. During those three hundred years every academic discipline . . . insisted "race" was *the* determining factor in human development. When blacks discovered they had shaped or become a culturally formed race, and that it had specific and revered difference, suddenly they were told there is no such thing as "race," biological or cultural, that matters, and that genuine intellectual exchange cannot accommodate it.[23]

Refusing the skeptical move that denies the "truth" of race, she instead depicts a community of interlocutors who refigure its meaning. Insisting on the reality of "Afro-American culture," she asserts, "We have always been imagining ourselves. We are the subjects of our own narrative, witnesses to and participants in our own experiences, and, in no way coincidentally, in the experience of those with whom we have come in contact."[24]

Thus, "in Afro-American literature itself the question of difference, of essence, is critical." The key is language: "The most valuable point of entry into the question of cultural (or racial) distinction, the one most fraught, is its language—its unpoliced, seditious, confrontational, manipulative, disruptive, masked and unmasking language."[25] Reading race as cultural, Morrison defines difference aesthetically. She claims repeatedly that a "black" aesthetic guides her writing; she is trying to "develop a way of writing that is irrevocably black . . . not because I was, or because of its subject matter." It would be linked to "the sentences, the structure, texture, and tone."[26]

Her "parallel is always the music, because all the strategies of the art are there," but the music bears broader oral traditions whose improvisational and participatory features she would "translate into print."[27] Her language must "provide spaces and places" so readers can "work *with* the author in the construction of the book."[28] Accordingly, "my compact with the reader is not to reveal an already established reality [we] agree on beforehand. I don't want to assume or exercise that kind of authority."[29] Rather, the text must be "like jazz," which

always keeps you on the edge. There is no final chord . . . and it agitates you. Spirituals agitate you, no matter what they are saying about how it is all going to be. There is something underneath them that is incomplete. There is always something else you want from the music. . . . I want that feeling of something held in reserve and the sense that there is more."[30]

She would emulate the great black musicians whose performances have "the ability to make you want it, and remember the want. . . . They will never fully satisfy—never fully."[31]

D. H. Lawrence is surely right that we should trust the tale, not the teller. But rehearsing the vocational identity and aesthetic aspirations of the teller helps contextualize the tale Morrison tells in *Beloved*. For she invests the novel with the political responsibility of nation building by a literary aesthetic that bridges between urban-literate and village-vernacular cultures. Modeled on jazz to elicit reader participation in the production of meaning, this aesthetic has political resonance in "democratic" and not only "black" terms. But her "racial" intention is crucial to her redemptive purpose. A "speakerly" text makes present the racial community and oral tradition whose loss is the condition calling forth the novel as a genre.[32]

As Morrison laments an endangered way of life, judges what can be saved, and seeks a way forward, we hear registers of prophecy. After all, the book of Jeremiah is not a historical record but a literary form whose illusion of speakerly immediacy preserves the antiphonal exchanges of a lost oral culture, and thus of a "nation" no longer territorial. Biblical authors do not so much sustain as constitute "a people" through attachment to a text. Does Morrison use her novel similarly? *Beloved* commemorates the "Sixty Million and more" lost in the middle passage and slavery, to whom the book is dedicated. It dramatizes a wish to redeem unspeakable suffering by retelling a story of destruction and endurance. But its form also comes to terms with more recent losses, as if it returns to aesthetic origins, to renew cultural forms that both signify and enable black solidarity.

Morrison's novel, therefore, needs to be read in the context of the identity politics emerging in response and reaction to the civil rights movement. On the one hand, she witnesses the advance of a nation-

alist jeremiad in which innocent whites are victimized by a state serving only blacks and middle-class women. This story of a demonic love
triangle achieves ascendancy in 1980, when a Ronald Reagan smiley
face replaces a scowling George Wallace—though Reagan announces
his campaign in Oxford, Mississippi, where brutal violence founded its
racial meaning. Holding an MX missile in one hand and a budget axe
in the other, he forms national identity in a wounded innocence seeking vindication against groups and practices demonized as subversive
threats to the "American way of life." On the other hand, politicized
women and minorities after 1968 are narrating not jeremiads redeeming American ideals but captivity stories about nonnational subjects defined by colonial captivity and sisterhood. *Beloved* is written at the peak
of this moment, as identity politics is first criticized in the academy. In
Wendy Brown's seminal critique, subalterns create politicized identity
by investing in a subject position that is a "wounded attachment" fixing
them in injury and in the past, while overvaluing sameness rather than
difference in politics.[33] But Morrison conceives "wounded" attachment
very differently.

Like advocates of Afrocentric identity politics, Morrison seeks anti-
colonial solidarity, but they anchor it in a pure, uninjured African past,
while she commemorates a traumatic history and the vernacular forms
that transfigure it. Black identity is "wounded" because it originates in
social death, but attachment also names signifying practices that remake
race and redeem a horrific past. She practices politicized identity to confront rather than endorse investment in resentment and sameness. Indeed, though Morrison avows animus toward "American" identity, her
novel bears witness that a hyphen binds not only wound to attachment
but African to American. She avows animus but performs ambivalence,
for though she addresses "my people" and "the village," her art opens
the canon of American literature and enters the national public sphere
while crossing the racial sign by gender and sexuality. She avows animus
toward American nationhood and avows a project of racial consolidation in aesthetic and therapeutic terms, but she still works the line of
nation/hood, mediating a part that has no part and the whole constituted by its disavowal.[34]

By one critical view, however, a focus on trauma and mourning is a
symptom of disappointment, displacing "politics" onto culture. Is cultural consolidation around memory a surrogate for political struggle
over the inequality of a regime? Does redemption as *amor fati* avoid

engagement across difference over the fate of the whole? It seems truer to say that the character of racial power and a history ruled by it invest politics in cultural work. Moreover, it is no mere displacement of politics to seek redemption not in rights from the state but in openly "political" relations among those marked as racial others, and in practices of association and speech that rework the meaning of race, partly by working through the meaning of past. Still, there remains the question of how Morrison uses prophecy to mediate the relation of part and whole.[35]

Framing *Beloved*

Morrison denies an investment in redeeming whites or an American nation, but the problematic of redemption is central in her view of black life and the role of art. One hundred years after the last slave narrative, in the shadow of the civil rights and black power movements, during a second post-Reconstruction resurgence of white racism, black disappointment, and Afrocentric revivalism, Morrison uses the genre of the novel, and the novel *Beloved*, to address "my people" about our history and suffering, our current crisis, and the way forward.

I will focus on the meaning of the plot centered on Sethe, a woman who escapes from the plantation Sweet Home, the white father's household, and settles in a community of escaped slaves across the Ohio River. In this community without whites, she creates for herself and her children a home without husbands and fathers, and for twenty-eight days they celebrate their redemption through rituals of prayer, song, and dance initiated by the community's spiritual leader, her husband's mother, Baby Suggs, Holy. Yet the past and the white world invade this refuge when her former owner, Schoolteacher, appears. In what she sees as a supreme act of love, she tries to kill her four children but can send only one "through the veil . . . where she would be safe" (163). Prevented from killing the others, Sethe is jailed and then released. Selling herself sexually to buy an inscription from a white stonecutter, she can afford only "Beloved" for her dead child's tombstone.

Readers learn these and other elements of her story in flashbacks from her present, nineteen years later, in 1876, the year Reconstruction is abandoned by sacrificing black freedom to reunify whites. By then, her two sons have run off and Baby Suggs has taken to her bed and died; willfully isolating herself from a community that also shuns her and intent on "beating back the past," Sethe lives with her remaining daughter, Denver, in a family home haunted by a "spiteful" baby ghost. When Paul D, an ex-slave from Sweet Home, arrives and tries to open Sethe to the idea of a reconfigured family and a future, this ghost apparently becomes flesh, as a nineteen-year-old woman with no lines on her hands.

In Sethe's effort to redeem her deed by seeking, and sacrificing herself to gain, Beloved's forgiveness, and in Beloved's effort to guarantee Sethe's love and punish her, we witness both the haunting of a formally emancipated ex-slave who barely knew her own mother and an understandable but destructive symbiosis between mother and child. But as Sethe nears self-sacrificing death, Denver leaves home to get help; neighbors who had refused to warn Sethe nineteen years earlier because they envied her great good fortune at her family's gaining freedom, now resolve that the ghost and past should not possess her or "invade" the present. They gather in front of her house to exorcise the ghost by creating "a sound that broke the back of words" (261).

Mr. Bodwin (the abolitionist benefactor of this black enclave, who owns Sethe's house, his own childhood home) arrives at this moment to take Denver to work in town. Seeing again a white man on a horse coming into her yard, a hallucinatory Sethe relives the terror that once drove her to murder. But this time, rather than destroy what she loves, she directs her rage at the white man—though the wrong man. Running to stab him, she is disarmed by the crowd, and Beloved, left alone on the porch, disappears. Utterly bereft, Sethe takes to Baby Suggs's bed, lamenting, "She was my best thing." But Paul D insists, "You your best thing, Sethe, you are" (272–73). The narrator, having retold a devastating ghost story and captivity narrative, does not tell us Sethe's future or indicate whether she finds a way to live and love again.

An epilogue, though, describes the characters—even Sethe, presumably—forgetting the resurrected ghost, as if to bury the past it made flesh:

It was not a story to pass on. . . . They forgot her like a bad dream. After they made up their tales, shaped and decorated them, those that saw her that day on the porch quickly and deliberately forgot her. It took longer for those who had spoken to her, lived with her, fallen in love with her, to forget, until they realized they couldn't remember or repeat a single thing she said, and began to believe that, other than what they themselves were thinking, she hadn't said anything at all. So, in the end, they forgot her too. Remembering seemed unwise. . . . It was not a story to pass on. . . . So they forgot her. Like an unpleasant dream during a troubled sleep. . . . This is not a story to pass on. . . . By and by all trace is gone . . . the rest is weather. Not the breath of the disremembered and unaccounted for, but wind in the eaves, or spring ice thawing too quickly. Just weather. Certainly no clamor for a kiss. (274–75)

"Pass on" means "transmit" but also "let [something] go by": The story is not to be passed by or ignored, and yet it is not to be repeated either. It is not to be ignored, and it is not to be bequeathed. It must be confronted but not repeated in the way it is retold. As if to reject willful forgetting and confirm this ambiguity, these passages are followed by a space and a last word: "Beloved."

The novel's protagonists are almost all African American men and women. While Beloved's delirious monologues voice the anonymous death and horror of the middle passage, the other characters struggle to narrate and digest their experiences of slavery and to make sense of Sethe's traumatic act, while the novel experiments with literary form to dramatize the episodic temporality, fractured subjectivity, and multiple perspectives that characterize their meaning making. The novel thus renders the ambiguity of memory, for remembering slavery and the dead seems both essential and imprisoning; the ambiguity of narrative, for narrative seems necessary to life but dangerously misleading in its promises of coherence and closure; the ambiguity of maternal love, for that love means life but also self-sacrifice and murder; and the ambiguity of redemption, for the deliverance sought by men and whites has enslaved others, while they risk self-imprisonment in their struggles to escape slavery and redeem their history. Aspirations to achieve freedom and make meaning are admirable but readily go awry as domination and self-defeat.

To explore these ambiguities, begin with the deed that inspired the novel: Margaret Garner, who killed her infant daughter rather than see her returned to slavery, became a key symbol both for slavery apologists and for Frederick Douglass and white abolitionists. Douglass used Garner to symbolize the horror of slavery, arguing that "every mother who . . . plunges the knife into the bosom of her infant to save it from the hell of our Christian slavery should be . . . honored as a benefactress."[36] While Douglass's "our" bespeaks an openly ambivalent identification with the ideals of the whites he criticizes, the novel inverts Anglo-American versions of jeremiadic prophecy. New World and Christian origins are not deliverance from despotism but hell on earth, Egyptian servitude. By narrating founding and freedom from the position not of fathers and sons but of slaves as mothers and daughters, Beloved also inverts the origins of culture from white to black and from paternity to maternity.

By beginning with captivity in Egypt, Morrison does not only counter the master's jeremiadic discourse. She also reworks the Exodus story framing the genre of slave narrative. For it "drops a veil" over "proceedings too terrible to relate," as if survival requires forgetting. The "struggle to forget" is indeed important to survival, Morrison says in an interview, but it is "fruitless, and I wanted to make it fruitless."[37] She would "rip that veil and expose a truth about the interior life of a people who didn't write it."[38] Using Du Bois's image of a veil separating the speakable and unspoken, she notes how slave narratives sever physical and formal emancipation from the psychic and cultural legacy of servitude, as if excluding internal life could put the past irrevocably behind the present.

In this regard, ex-slaves repeat the repression in liberal narratives of self-making and political emancipation. "We live in a land where the past is always erased and America is the innocent future" where "immigrants" can "start over. The culture doesn't encourage dwelling on, let alone coming to terms with, the truth about the past." So she would "rip" the veil between the unspeakable and spoken that not only separates but also joins whites and blacks, for their emancipatory stories—albeit for different reasons—entail a "national amnesia" about a past and "interior life" that "no one wants to remember."[39]

Like a prophet, Morrison remembers what her people would forget, and she frames her novel by a simple dedication, "Sixty Million and more." Garner and her dead daughter are exemplary, signifying "the disremembered and unaccounted for." As Morrison elsewhere says, there is "no suitable memorial or plaque," not even a "small bench by the road" to "summon the presence of or recollect the absence of slaves," of "those who made the journey and of those who did not [survive]."[40] To overcome "a silence within the race," to confront "things that are repressed because they are unthinkable," she "inserts this memory that was unbearable and unspeakable into the literature."[41] A storyteller, then, must summon the dead—these "unburied or at least unceremoniously buried people"—to "properly, artistically, bury them."[42] We say that biblical prophets are called by God, but do they not also summon, call into life and language—conjure—realities otherwise lost to us?

That is why ghost stories or "romances" are the disavowed genre of American *political* thought: Liberal theory since James Madison and Alexander Hamilton depicts pragmatic conflict of rights and interests, but split off from the highly charged psychological, racial, and sexual conflicts that literature depicts in both frontier and domestic spaces.

Literary art is the return of the repressed; it makes visible what is made absent by a discourse of contractual relations. Rather than flee "the real and true," such literary art represents the monstrous but disavowed actuality of racial domination. A symptom of the violence that made it and of the disavowal that sustains it, a ghost is a messenger seeking a reckoning.[43]

"Not a house in the country ain't packed to the rafters with some dead Negro's grief," says Suggs in *Beloved* (5). Every house, and the American house, is haunted: Though Morrison conjures a particular black community, family, and ghost, the figure of Beloved derives its emotional force from being not only Sethe's dead daughter but "the symbolic compression of innumerable forgotten people into one miraculously resurrected" being, "the remembering of '60 million and more' in one youthful, indeed ageless body." By a story whose characters are haunted by ghosts who are themselves haunted, a prophet-as-writer addresses "my people," haunted by the disremembered millions for whom these characters and ghosts stand in.[44]

How does Morrison "properly" bury the disremembered? First, we see, by "summoning" and resurrecting them: She tells a story of a mother who kills her daughter to protect her from slavery, of a ghost-daughter who returns to feed hungrily on her mother's stories, and of a community whose members tell and compare stories to make sense of their own lives and of that traumatic event, whose meanings are entwined. The prophet-as-writer raises the dead and puts unspeakable trauma and unspoken interior lives into words. Arcing toward meaning, those words defeat black-and-white moral categories, defy linear temporality, refuse conventional narrative closure, and shatter fictions of coherent subjectivity. But such storytelling—a "talking cure"?—is needed to "bury the dead" and "heal" the living, even if the dead are not simply buried and the living not simply healed.

Accordingly, there are two ambiguities in the "work" of storytelling. Following Freud, we could imagine the task as "mourning" the dead in the sense of letting them go, so that, as the past no longer haunts or rules the present, the bereaved can make new attachments in and to the present, can even create a tradition of the new. But who is "the race"—who is any "we"—without its dead? Perhaps, then, the living must not so much bury the dead as change demonic ghosts into ancestors by avowing rather than disavowing loss. Judith Butler thus imagines community engendered "in and through a common sense of loss," which refuses to let go of a loved object the wider world has disparaged. Such a community "does not overcome the loss"; indeed, it "cannot overcome the loss without losing the very sense of itself as a community." This tension, between mourning and attachment called melancholic, is paralleled by a tension about storytelling. For proper burial of the dead seems to require meaning making among multiple voices, especially ones dis-remembered. In this sense, we must not "pass on," must not let go by, a story of the middle passage and slavery. But "this is not a story to pass on" because proper burial also means laying some stories to *rest*, to make a space for *other* and *new* stories.[45]

A dedication to "Sixty Million and more" raises questions—about forgetting and memory, resurrection and burial, storytelling and healing—but for whom? Consider the epigraph: "I will call them my people, which were not my people; and her beloved, which was not beloved." Paul quotes Hosea, whose God would heal his estrangement from his chosen people by saying, "You are my people" as he imagines them saying, "You are our God." Hosea represents community as a chosen, erotic covenant, subject to failure but capable of renewal. Imagining the wife unsatisfied by her promiscuous idolatry, and the husband "wooing" her as he once did "in the wilderness," Hosea dramatizes redemption as covenant renewal. It makes community anew, though as perfect union rather than as space of politics, for the Hebrews *completely* repair their relationship with God and each other—as if, erasing not only a wound but any scar, community is seamlessly sutured, begun wholly anew. Still, Hosea imagines rebirth through remarriage, while Paul imagines God choosing another people as his beloved.

The passage is worth quoting—and is quoted often—because Paul claims that those who invest their faith in Christ's resurrection will *super-sede* the Jews as God's chosen people. Membership is not a matter of kinship or descent: "It is not the children of Abraham by natural descent who are children of God; it is the children born through God's promise who are reckoned as Abraham's descendants" (Rom. 9:8). To say that "not all the offspring of Israel are Israel" is to repeat the anti-ethnic origin of "Hebrew" as a chosen, not inherited, identity. Paul quotes Isaiah: "Only a remnant shall be saved" (Rom. 9:27). A new "people" are formed by God's call and their choice:

We are those objects of mercy whom He has called from among the Jews and Gentiles alike, as he says in Hosea: "Those who were not my people I will call my people, and the unloved I will call beloved." In the very place where they were told, "you are no people of mine," they shall be called sons of the living God. (Rom. 9:24–26)

Paul states the lesson: "That Gentiles who made no effort after righteousness nevertheless achieved it, a righteousness based on faith, whereas Israel made great efforts after a law of righteousness but never attained to it. Why was this? Because their efforts were not based on faith but, mistakenly, on deeds" (Rom. 9:30–32). What faith? "If the confession 'Jesus is Lord' is on your lips, and the faith that God raises him from the dead is in your heart, you will find salvation" (Rom. 10:9). Gentiles once excluded from God's grace—by gatekeepers presuming to own redemption—now manifest it, if they have faith in resurrection.

While Hosea imagines redemption as a remarriage that begins anew, Saul of Tarsus imagines redemption as rebirth by faith: Renamed Paul, he depicts God's new beloved, once outcast but elected by their faith in *resurrection*. To assert this faith is to move from the position of outcast to the identity of sonship and the privilege of inheritance: Israel, living by "the law," is superseded by those whose faith in resurrection makes them God's beloved. What does it mean to use *this* passage to name and frame a novel about slavery and its legacy in America?[46]

Orlando Patterson offers one illuminating answer. Just as "the slave experience was a major source of the metaphors that informed the symbolic structure of Christianity," so Jesus and the Resurrection, not Moses and the Exodus, dominate slave theology in America. Because "slavery is social death," ideas of "redemption, rebirth and resurrection were not hopeful abstractions, but existential imperatives." As "emancipation from sin" draws on the social fact that "redemption quite literally means release from enslavement," so "justification by faith" draws on manumission, which restores the natality and honor of one once dishonored. Just as an outcast is elevated to sonship and becomes "an heir through God" to salvation, so a manumitted slave is reborn as a member of a community from which social death had excluded him.[47]

Morrison's epigraph thus evokes every dimension of argument about the spiritual and worldly meanings of redemption. In *what* does redemption consist? Is it an impossible plenitude, or a worldly movement from being nameless, uncounted, and dishonored? *When* does redemption occur? Is "I will call her beloved" a promise and a *future,* or is her redemption enacted *now* by *calling* her beloved, by now bestowing on her a reality and value once withheld? *Who bestows* this redemption? The "I" in Hosea and Paul is God, but does Morrison invest redemption in herself as an artist, and in "my people" as collaborators? *Who receives* redemption? Outcasts bear a redemptive promise—*if* suffering, and an agonal relation to law, imbues them with faith in resurrection—but what future between whites and blacks does Morrison thus imagine?

By its dedication and epigraph, *Beloved* inflects a prophetic idiom of redemption by identity politics and a therapeutic discourse of healing. Not surprisingly, most commentators read the novel as making good— not also troubling—the redemptive promises it seems to make. Indeed, most critics read *Beloved* as a redemptive story in Christian terms, though they use the trope of rebirth to redeem subaltern subjects defined by race and gender.

To declare with Paul that "I will call . . . her beloved, which was not beloved," Mae Henderson argues in the best of such arguments, is to announce both a promise of redemption and who is to be redeemed. As Paul figures "the law" as a "schoolmaster" holding prisoners, so Morrison creates a scientific and cruel slave owner, Schoolteacher, to cast law and literacy as forms of domination. But, argues Henderson, Paul also announces

that the doctrine of justification by deeds under the Old Dispensation of the Law is to be revised through justification by grace under the New Dispensation of the Spirit. Engaging the Scripture as a kind of intertext, Morrison enacts in her novel an opposition between Law and Spirit, redeeming her characters from "the curse of the law" as figured in the master's discourse. In her rewriting of Scripture, Morrison ushers in an ironic new dispensation figured not by the law of the (white) father, but by the spirit of the (black and female) child, Beloved.[48]

No more than Jeremiah (or Paul) does Henderson's Morrison trouble this promise. Indeed, as Sethe achieves redemption through her encounter with Beloved, so she (and the other characters) models redemption for readers who are presumptively black, female, or both.

Sethe's redemption unfolds in two dimensions, Henderson argues. In the sense of redemption as deliverance, "Sethe must discover some way of regaining control of her story, her body, her progeny, her milk, her ability to nurture her future" (71). She must seek "redemption from the law," from the whip and the pen that constitute paternal and white authority, if she is to enter into self-determination. But this redemption depends on redemption *from sin,* figured by her bloody act, which can only come through the spirit, not the law. Beloved represents that spirit, which "possesses" Sethe to enable her redemption. Like Paul, Henderson links "the spirit" to love and forgiveness, which redeems Sethe *from* captivity to the paternal rule of law, and so from her sense of haunting sin. "It is not through the law . . . but the spirit (its reclamation and relinquishment) that the individual achieves 'deliverance' from the 'sins' of the past." Thus *Beloved* "(re)inscribes the conditions of the promise in the New Testament" (82).

Henderson also translates glad tidings into psychoanalytic terms. For Sethe is "possessed" by what she calls "re-memories," which Henderson calls "unconfigured and literally disfiguring images" from a traumatic past (68). Sethe must "imaginatively re-constitute or re-member her history" to change the "meaning of those events and their significance" for her life as a whole. To redeem her past she must "learn to represent the unspeakable and unspoken in language—and more precisely as narrative" (67). Beloved compels this "working-through," which "enables Sethe to achieve redemption through the creation of a cohesive psychoanalytical and historical narrative" (82). Indeed, her encounter with Beloved teaches Sethe "to regard her problematic past as an enemy worthy of her mettle . . . out of which things of value for her future life have to be [and can be] derived" (74).

Sethe's redemption *from* slavery, law, and sin, as well as her redemption *of* the past, is achieved most obviously by the love and stories she shares with Beloved. When Bodwin enters her yard, she also reenacts her trauma with a difference, attacking the man rather than killing her child. Her rebirth is consummated in her "reclamation by the community" and its exorcism of Beloved. "Not only is Sethe 'delivered' from the 'errors' of her past," says Henderson, "but her discourse is 'delivered' from the constraints of the master('s) discourse" (81).

I quote extensively from Henderson to identify key elements in the gestalt shaping most readings of the (redemptive) meaning of the novel. First, slavery shapes the worldly meaning of redemption as freedom from captivity, but also, slavery makes the past a problem and thus poses the problem of how to live in relation to horrific loss and suffering. Second, those who evade the past are haunted, but a ghost-become-flesh figures the way confronting the past enables healing as rebirth. Third, that redemptive possibility is actualized by storytelling and love, which heal a fractured psyche and community, translate trauma from symptoms into coherent narrative, and "free" the present from "possession" by the past.

Contra Nietzsche, redemption in these senses is seen not as solitary but as dependent on community. Jennifer Fitzgerald states a typical view when she identifies "not only the psychic damage of slavery but its therapeutic alternative, the cooperative self-healing of a community of survivors."[49] Indeed, the gestalt I am describing depicts redemption not only by loving intimacy or eros but also by communal ritual, such as the celebrations Baby Suggs sponsors in the "Clearing" before the traumatic crisis and the exorcism of Beloved climaxing the novel. "When Sethe is taken back to the Clearing by the women's song in the yard, it is a sign of both personal and community redemption," Susan Bowers claims, for the exorcism "returns them all to a new beginning where, cleansed, they can create a new life." She concludes:

The suffering of the "black and angry dead" is the inescapable psychologi-cal legacy of all African-Americans, [but] they can rescue themselves from the trauma of that legacy by directly confronting it and uniting to loosen its fear-some hold. *Beloved*'s redemptive community of women epitomizes the object of salvation in biblical apocalyptic literature: the creation of a new society.[50]

Despite other differences, then, many critics also argue that ritual *in* the text makes the text itself a ritual to "heal" its readers.[51]

Surely, Morrison makes redemption central to the novel. That con-cern appears not only in its title, dedication, and epigraph, but also in the naming that is crucial to and in the novel: "Sethe" evokes Seth, the third son of Adam and Eve, who replaces Abel and whose name means "anointed by God"; and "Paul," a name associated with rebirth, is given to every male slave at Sweet Home by their deluded "liberal" owner, Gar-ner. But Garner unwittingly desecrates the promise of redemption in Paul, and it is an understatement to say the novel makes the epigraph's promise less secure.

If redemption means complete deliverance from servitude and cap-tivity once and for all, the novel defeats this hope. If redemption means rebirth into a life or self wholly cleansed of the old, the novel defeats this wish. If redemption means fixing what went wrong in the past, as if to free people from the past by erasing its wounds or their impact, the novel defeats this promise. If redemption means creating a coher-ent narrative to endow the past with meaning, as if to fix for sure the meaning of our suffering, the novel defeats this yearning. Indeed, no character in the novel is healed, not by love or by narrative. No wounds really heal, though scars impossible to erase *may* be transfigured by love and art. But Sethe never concludes this, and we readers miss an insight if we do not acknowledge our need to redeem her evident failure by such wise, belated reflections.

By my reading of *Beloved,* then, no arc unfolds from servitude to freedom, injury to healing, suffering to wholeness, sin to rebirth. It emplots no symmetry of a stained before and a cleansed after, nor even a clear break between then and now. No exodus offers redemption in a promised land, whether the American North or some subaltern countercommunity. No resurrection offers a decisive rebirth from old to new; and resurrecting ghosts does not assure their proper burial. We close a book whose title and last word we speak as if gathered around an impossible-to-close grave. Like its characters, we have not understood, let alone mastered, the trauma of slavery or the meaning of Sethe's bloody deed. This novel about possession rebuffs our need to know, resists our claims to possess understanding.[52]

But does the novel offer a kind of "working through?" By allowing us to contact the trauma of slavery, it dramatizes the meaning of redemption as making free and making meaningful, and it depicts redemption in these senses as a necessary aspiration and impossibly difficult undertaking. We are left feeling the urgency and political necessity of a redemption people must seek but cannot guarantee, must not preclude but cannot possess. This reading can be supported by revisiting crucial moments in the story: slavery, emancipatory community in the North and its traumatic crisis, Sethe's haunting, and Beloved's exorcism.

Retelling *Beloved*

The story originates in the plantation Sweet Home, which white men create in pursuit of freedom through the right to own property and through limited government. This first moment, which conditions all that follows, depicts the emancipatory masterlessness mythically and politically sought by those Anglo-American men whom D. H. Lawrence calls escaped slaves: Fleeing mother and despotism, they define freedom as the absence of dependence and seek redemption in sovereignty. Their freedom requires others' servitude, for if dependence is slavery, a free man must control those on whom he depends. But because fathers and sons depend on those they call Hagars and Ishmaels, they are haunted by specters; the masters' dependence gives an estranged power to their slaves.

For Morrison, "modern life begins with slavery," by fatefully joining Enlightenment ideas of reason and liberal ideals of self-determination to an emerging racial science that cloaks exculpatory rationalization in a language of civilization, morality, and hygiene.[53] The cartoonish School-teacher, who inherits the plantation after Garner dies, represents this regime, coldly invoking science to distinguish the human and animal in Sethe, while his nephews gorge on the milk they force from her breasts. To the enslaved, therefore, servitude means exploitation and objectification by language. Their milk and labor are "stolen"; slaves are forced to provide to others a recognition and nurture they lack the power to demand or the right to receive. Masters, says Sethe, do not only "work, kill, or maim you"; they "dirty you . . . so bad you couldn't like yourself anymore" (251).

But whites thereby dehumanize themselves. Stamp Paid, whose name also signifies on redemption, describes the dialectic:

Whitepeople believed that whatever the manners, under every dark skin was a jungle. Swift unnavigable waters, swinging screaming baboons, sleeping snakes, red gums ready for their sweet white blood. In a way, he thought, they were right. The more coloredpeople . . . used themselves up to persuade whites of something Negroes believed could not be questioned, the deeper and more tangled the jungle grew inside. But it wasn't the jungle blacks brought with them to this place from the other (livable) place. It was the jungle whitefolks planted in them. And it grew. It spread. In, through and after life, it spread, until it invaded the whites who had made it. Touched them every one. Changed and altered them. Made them bloody, silly, worse than even they wanted to be so, so scared they were of the jungle they had made. The screaming baboon lived under their own skin; the red gums were their own. (198)

A culture founded in slavery engenders the very barbarism it imagines in those it exploits, while its achievements depend on them. Recognizing that she "made the ink" by which Schoolteacher enacts a literacy dividing the human and animal, Sethe is proud of and yet horrified by her estranged power. Culture as language and law thus derives not from the primal crime of sons' killing the father who monopolizes the women, but from sexual violence, exploited reproduction, and appropriated labor, which empower both fathers and sons.[54]

To gain redemption from the dependence signifying captivity and shame, Southern and Northern men affirm political self-determination and property rights, but they disagree about property in slave labor. Mobilizing Northern men against "the slave power conspiracy," leaders of the Republican Party invoke the emancipatory promise of liberalism to redeem the sin of slavery and bring a rebirth of freedom to the father's house. It is with these promises in mind that we should imagine Sethe fleeing northward to join a community of escaped slaves in Ohio, as if she were making an exodus to reach a promised land. But from the perspective of ex-slaves in Morrison's retelling, free labor in the father's house means wage labor, ongoing subjection to racism, and subordination in a despotic home writ large. Still, formal rights do enable ex-slaves to form a countercommunity, whose vicissitudes make up a second moment in Morrison's story of captivity and the problem of redemption.

Her depiction of slavery illuminates by contrast what ex-slaves consider the central constituents of freedom: control of one's labor in its many senses; being able to love and protect what one loves; political voice and representation. The characters link freedom to power: Being an agent of one's own desire is at first a legal entitlement, but it means gaining the sense of authority Paul calls "justification." For people forbidden to desire and unable to protect those they love, the power to love and to be loved is crucial to freedom as redemption from captivity. Claiming she has "enough milk for all" (100), Sethe imagines a community in which nurture, as love and labor, is not devalued and coerced but chosen, reciprocal, and effective.

Freedom thus depends not only on rights to self-determination but also on bonds of love, which promise to redeem a captive people. As escaped slaves invoke rights, but to found a "beloved" community, they repeat with a difference a recurring, perhaps distinctively "American," rhetoric that joins emancipatory (liberal) rights to (biblical) visions of regenerated community. This dream, of a community in which law is superseded by love, is movingly expressed by Sethe's mother-in-law, Baby Suggs, Holy. Literally redeemed from captivity by her son's labor, she had awaited the rest of the family, and meanwhile she assumed the vocation of "unchurched preacher." Letting "her great heart beat" in the presence of her peers, Suggs led healing rituals of celebration in a space called "the Clearing," calling the men to dance, the children to laugh, and the women to cry "for the living and the dead" (88–89).

Some critics construe her as a heretical Christian because her language seems biblical in tone, but she never mentions God, sin, Christ, or resurrection. "She did not tell them to clean up their lives or to go and sin no more. She did not tell them they were the blessed of the earth, its inheriting meek, or its glorybound pure." Rather, "she told them that the only grace they could have was the grace they could imagine. That if they could not see it, they could not have it." After they laughed, danced, and cried, she declared, "Yonder they do not love your flesh. They despise it. . . . *You* got to love it, *you!* . . . This is flesh I'm talking about here.

Flesh that needs to be loved" in every organ and aspect, but most of all "the beating heart, love that too. More than eyes or feet. More than lungs that have yet to draw free air. More than your life-holding womb and your life-giving private parts, hear me now, love your heart. For this is the prize" (88–89).

Suggs voices and practices a wholly this-worldly redemption by loving flesh despised by whites and so by their slaves too. Redeeming flesh from devaluation and redeeming human beings by affirmation, Suggs celebrates as holy bodies that were once commodified and abused. This redemption depends not on a transcendent God but on self-authorization; to be loved they must bestow grace on themselves, or lack it. In the arc of the story, as Sethe is remembering it nineteen years later, Suggs gives this sermon during the twenty-eight magical days, paralleling the generative menstrual cycle, that separate Sethe's arrival with her new baby and the arrival of Schoolteacher. We can imagine these twenty-eight days as a redemptive moment within the book, when history is ruptured by grace, when "the law" is suspended by the power of a love. In a self-created protected space, ex-slaves can begin to experience self-regard, desire, and freedom. The promise of this moment is clearly stated: "To get to a place where you could love anything you chose—not to need permission for desire—well now, *that* was freedom" (162). But the moment itself is short-lived; in fact, the book's meaning depends on the defeat of Suggs's vision, though its hopes are reaffirmed in its final word: "Beloved."[55]

Suggs's vision is defeated partly because Schoolteacher appears: Morrison invokes the book of Revelation to depict "the four horsemen" arriving. Since these figures join knowledge to power, legal ownership to coercion, formally democratic authority to violence, she transforms biblical figures of divine wrath into agents of human evil. Indeed, as James Berger argues, "The scene reveals a political and social history whose entire duration—which has not ended—is traumatic and apocalyptic." Apocalyptic because the scene "un-veils" the nature of power in America. Traumatic because their appearance is "a world-ending event," a "pivotal moment" that makes previous history seem "premonitory" to a future defined by a somatic symptom, compulsive repetition.[56]

The traumatic event itself is two-sided. Partly it is the crushing recognition that, as Baby Suggs repeatedly says, "they came into my yard," for even in the "free" North ex-slaves cannot protect those they love. Partly, the trauma is Sethe's response: She protects her children from the reach of evil in the only way she can, even by killing them. Her intense violence follows from seeing the horsemen as human evil rather than as divine wrath: Because no god judges sinners and redeems the oppressed, her only way to protect her children rests in her hands, even if that means killing them. Claiming maternal right against a slave system that denies it, Sethe at once suffers love's powerlessness and exercises the frightful power love can justify. "Whites might dirty *her* . . . but not her best thing" (163), the "parts of her that were precious and fine and beautiful"; she gathers "every bit of life she had made," to "drag them through the veil where no one could hurt them; where they would be safe" (163). Claiming subsequently that her act was "right because it came from true love" (251), she asserts the meaning of a maternity that slave women were forbidden.[57]

Baby Suggs feels defeated and chooses to die, partly because "they came into my yard" to destroy the love she defended, partly because "a community of other free Negroes" let envy subvert solidarity by not warning Sethe, and partly because Sethe's love had meant murder. "Baby Suggs, Holy, believed she had lied. There was no grace—imaginary or real—and no sunlit dance in the Clearing could change that." Confronted with the reality of white power and the choice it exacted, "her faith, her love, her imagination and her great big old heart began to collapse" (89). As Stamp Paid argues, the problem that drove her to her bed and then to her death was that "she could not approve or condemn Sethe's rough choice. One or the other might have saved her, but beaten up by the claims of both, she went to bed" (180). If she could approve, she would reaffirm a grace that encompasses everything, even cutting a child's throat to save her from slavery. Or if she could judge Sethe's act out of bounds, unwarranted pride, as Ella does, she would recover a voice, though not the Clearing's voice.

If the dream of love first voiced by Suggs is defeated by the power of whites and by Sethe's bloody choice, Morrison restages this dream in a third moment, the relationship between Sethe and the ghost, she believes, of her dead child. Released from jail, she is rejected by neighbors judging her "pride" and her refusal to repent of it. With Denver, the daughter born during her escape, she retreats to her house, now haunted by a "baby" ghost both "spiteful" and "needing a lot of love." Sethe lives a half life, until the arrival of Paul D provokes a crisis. Once her responsiveness to him compels the ghost to return in the flesh, Sethe and it seek a seamless union to repair their wounds. Their relationship dramatizes the motives, appeal, and dangers in the wish to make love redemptive and use love as a model for politics.

In psychoanalytic terms, Beloved is a pre-Oedipal fragment of every self, seeking its lost other, but she also condenses the countless, uncounted, disremembered dead of the middle passage. Beloved is thus Sethe's daughter and Sethe's own murdered mother: The symmetry in their bond thus suggests two child-women coming to terms with the meaning of maternity and abandonment under slavery. As daughter and mother, Beloved enacts the claims of the past on the present, as if to embody the past as a burning desire to be recognized by, even to possess, the living. They inscribe a circuit of grief: The living mourn the dead, and the dead mourn lost life and (m)others. The plot turns on the murder of a child but is fueled by grief for lost mothers. If Beloved returns to redeem her wounds as a daughter, Sethe resurrects her beloved other to redeem her own abandonment as a daughter, not only her murderous act as a mother. By nurture and storytelling, each would make good what went wrong in the past.[58]

Many critics thus depict Beloved's resurrection as the condition of Sethe's redemption because the daughter compels the mother to remember and retell rather than "beat back" the past. At the same time, the daughter "feeds" on Sethe's stories, which are for her the food of life, as if storytelling is the "sincere milk" that Isaiah's God offers his children. Entwining storytelling and loving as practices that redeem people wounded by violence, their bond also signifies the bond between readers and Morrison, whose recuperative storytelling reimagines *our* (lost) history and recoups its losses. But this picture of mutual nurture excises what is deeply troubling in their dyad.

Whether a literal resurrection of Sethe's dead daughter, an embodied fantasy, or a figure of an entire people under slavery, Beloved is what Sethe calls a "re-memory," not only existing in the past and in the mind but possessing the worldly present. Resurrecting the past seems crucial to the health of the living, who would forget, and at first Sethe is revitalized, drawn from the death-in-life she has imposed on herself. But Sethe is possessed; her house becomes a tomb as she insists, "the world is in this room" (183). And Beloved nearly kills any who "rememory" her. From the novel's first sentence she is a "spite ghost" who freezes history at the moment of her own disappearance. Her spite is inseparable from her longing: She seeks the face of her (m)other, without whom she is shattered, as if to recover a fantasized union before separation, subjectification, and language.

Sethe makes herself captive to this ghostly other because she, too, dreams of perfect union to repair the past and the wound that at once binds and separates them. In the name of maternal love, indeed, she would sacrifice her mortal being, as she once sacrificed the mortal being of her daughter. She never accepted her separateness from her children: She experiences her children and her love for them as the best parts of herself. Morrison offers a tragic view of (maternal) love: As she says of Margaret Garner, by loving "something other than herself so much" and placing "all the value of her life in something outside herself," she shows how "the best thing in us is also the thing that makes us sabotage ourselves."[59] Sethe became "like a chastised child" as Beloved "ate up her life," and "the older woman yielded it up without a murmur" (250). Sethe would "make up for a handsaw," and Beloved is "making her pay for it" (251), but both enact a "longing" that is "bottomless" (58).

Bound to a past each would fix by gaining wholeness and vindication from the other, Sethe and Beloved create a familial prison drained of life. For loving, knowing, and remembering, Emily Budick reminds us, "are activities that depend on leaving open the spaces between people—even between lovers or between parents and children"—while it is this very space that Sethe and Beloved close down in their "desperate and ultimately doomed effort to resurrect, compensate for, or replace an irrevocably lost past." For Budick, "memory of the past must include the idea of loss" because "what the past has taken from us no present or future reality can restore." The lesson of their destructive dyad is that we must mourn irrevocable loss if we are to create a space of plurality in the present.[60]

Masters seek redemption in domination, and ex-slaves seek redemption from it, but masters and ex-slaves both make family a model of politics, and redemption its purpose. In turn, Morrison tells their stories of captivity and deliverance as a tragically imprisoning attempt to make community a home that redeems its members. Life and freedom *do* require the love that signifies food and reciprocal recognition. Still, nurture is problematic, no answer to all ills, because it is entwined with power, abasement, and resentment and because it can jeopardize, not only enable, the "space between" of plurality and politics. Moreover, nurture is not all of life, and freedom requires more than its mutuality. Though Suggs's "love ethic" is profoundly attractive in its self-affirming and all-embracing grace, Sethe and Beloved dramatize its dark side. Against the identity politics of her day, therefore, Morrison does not derive moral superiority from oppression or innocence from love, for oppression generates envy and resentment while love can mean both domination and self-sacrifice. Redemptive countercommunity imposes captivities whose costs she dramatizes for the sake of freedom.

Consider lastly, then, the exorcism, or fourth moment, which climaxes Morrison's ghost story. Made aware by Denver of Sethe's mortal danger and feeling guilty about her moral(istic) judgment, Ella leads the neighbors to exorcise, for the sake of life in the present, a ghostly "invasion" by the past. On the grounds that Beloved has enabled Sethe to act differently and that the exorcism then restores Sethe to the community, many critics assert that Sethe achieves redemption and that Morrison's story fulfills its promise by raising and then burying the dead. But is this reading credible?

Start with Morrison's description of the exorcism: "It was as though the Clearing had come to her with all its heat and simmering leaves, where the voices of women searched for the right combination, the key, the code, the sound that broke the back of words." Once they found that key, Sethe "trembled like the baptized in its wash" (261). But how are we to understand this? For Mae Henderson, spirit annuls law, female community displaces male power, and the semiotic ruptures the master's discourse. But this wordless sound, which Madhu Dubey calls "the sonic sublime," subverts the claim that *narrative* is redemptive.[61] The exorcism may display the power to reject the master's language, but it is no model for *speaking* the unspeakable. The women break the back of language but cannot represent the ghost as *part* of the community they reconstitute. Their repudiation of the ghost is confirmed by the epilogue, in which everyone forgets her. Even still, is Sethe redeemed?

Claims about Sethe's rebirth depict her reliving her primal terror but redoing her primal deed, as if redemption is a second chance. Surely this is the American dream, but is it possible only in fiction? The moment *does* suggest that humans are free because, or to the extent that, they can begin to act rather than react. Sethe cannot change the past, and her life is conditioned by embodiment and human bonds, by poverty, patriarchy, and white power, but she *can* make choices differently, to direct rage at its proper target. If psychologically credible, however, this argument avoids the reality principle. For as Stamp Paid notes, Bodwin is no enemy: He "never turned us down. Steady as a rock. I tell you something, if she had got to him, it'd be the worst thing in the world for us" (265).[62] Meanwhile, Sethe is "delivered" from possession into depression, not into new life. Having willed Beloved's presence, she feels loss, not liberation; her loss might be pregnant with change, but we only see her bereft and silent. Without her beloved other and "best thing," her identity is not bound to a nightmarish past, and we imagine her freed to remake it, but *she* cannot imagine who she is without this trauma and her effort to redeem it.

Since the Garden of Eden, freedom is a gift often experienced as loss. The loss of Beloved is that painful gift if Sethe could enter the present and will a future rather than suffering and self-denial. She could *become* her *own* "best thing," as Paul says, defined by accident of birth, child-rearing, and circumstances, but also by her ongoing re-creation of herself, servitude, sins, and all. To say she could become her own best thing is to imagine she doesn't need redeeming, but isn't *this* a wish, repeating the redemptive move of redeeming her from (the need for) redemption? Better to credit that Sethe requires redemption in Baldwin's sense: Because she can neither change nor escape the past, she must "redeem" it in the sense of changing her relationship to it, shifting its meaning by accepting its fatality as a condition she must make fruitful. Redeeming the past in this (meaning-making) sense might help redeem her in the other (making-free) sense: She might free herself to create a future on terms other than those the past dictated when she was wholly possessed by it.[63]

Redemption in this sense is transfiguration of a legacy rather than transcendence of history. Sethe did not create the horrible wounds on her own back, but as the white girl, Amy, described them to Sethe as a chokecherry tree, and as Sethe shares that metaphor with Paul D, we witness a creative practice of resignifying, which transfigures the markings inflicted by history. In this parable of renaming, which also crosses racial and gendered lines, we see how she might become her own "best thing" in relation to scars she cannot efface, but whose beauty others can help her affirm. Indeed, scars illegible to us are made meaningful by the love and art of our interlocutors: As Paul's friend Sixo also says of his lover, "The pieces I am, she gathers them and give them back to me in all the right order" (272). As such stories turn "accident, riddle, and dreadful chance" into "I will it thus," so community is re-formed by practices of gathering stories no one authors alone and laying them next to each other.

The novel represents the impossibility of redemption as an effort to fix what went wrong in or escape the scarred legacy of the past, but it also represents the necessity of redemption as a coming-to-terms with this legacy. Still, even this argument is a wish the novel also undercuts. For the exorcising of Beloved is followed by characters embracing amnesia. Or is "forgetting" a necessary part of redemption as *amor fati*?

Perhaps the characters in the epilogue enact mourning in Freud's sense: Accepting the loss of a beloved—burying the dead—enables new attachments, indeed, enables a present. In this sense, "forgetting" seems a necessity and an achievement, just as Morrison is concerned to bury the dead "properly." To turn "a clamor for a kiss" into "the weather" then seems a needed disenchantment and letting go, not "amnesia." Yet the epilogue depicts even such forgetting, even "successful" mourning, as problematic, albeit understandable. For as James Berger says, "the absent place where Beloved stood is another scar in the symbolic order, sutured by repression." Sethe and Denver are reclaimed for the community by exorcising Beloved, but this "resolution" seems to repeat what came before, if forgetting means disavowal. To imagine successful forgetting is to repeat the denial of trauma in post–civil rights amnesia, which means the ghost will return, "to inhabit each succeeding present until the crimes that repeat themselves are worked through in every organ of the body politic."[64]

Because the forgetting of Beloved is problematic, we can see why the narrator ends the epilogue with a last word. As a plea from the past, "Beloved" bespeaks a pain and loss that forgetting can never erase and that no language or art, act or story can fully redeem. As a reminder or even rebuke, "Beloved" bespeaks the disremembered we must *never* forget, an attachment we must not get over, dead generations whose weight we must bear. It is unclear whether we could but should not forget, or whether we simply cannot move beyond this past because it always "returns." But the novel ends with the word signifying a past we are told we derive from, but from which we also must struggle to spring.[65]

As a noun the last word resists (and calls us to resist) amnesia, but it also is a verb in the imperative voice, "Be loved," calling readers to take up the work Baby Suggs initiated in the Clearing, to make a space in which to cultivate grace. Then readers themselves commemorate the dead and make themselves count. By saying the word that, in "Dearly Beloved," begins funerals and weddings, readers gather as "we the living," congregated to carry on what the characters hardly could imagine. By a story of rebirth retold as tragedy, we readers reach a generative moment whose "issue" is in our hands. Still, who is this "we"?

From Part to Whole I

Accept for a moment Morrison's declaration that "my people" are her audience and construe her as *addressing* the part that has no part about "our" haunting history. As Kathleen Brogan argues, "Writers conjure ghosts to solve a single problem: how to reframe the narrative organization of ethnic experience. Ghosts . . . figure prominently when people must re-conceive a fragmented, partially obliterated history, looking to a newly imagined past to redefine themselves for the future." For Caroline Rody, Morrison takes on "the function of narrative love," which is "to repair the violation of love wreaked on her characters by slavery, separation, and death." Does such "narrative love" enable (African American) readers to accept their past as a condition of action? And what kind of community does this love enable them to constitute?[66]

The novel brings readers to an open grave: Dearly Beloved, we are gathered here today. Hailed as "beloved," called together as mourners, we ourselves say "beloved" to hail the disremembered and to rejuvenate the living. By performing the epigraph, we make good on its redemptive, value-bestowing promise. Reading that we must, and yet must not, close this grave or lay this story to rest, we repeat this contradictory promise as a last demand and prayer. We thus acknowledge that *this* past, entwining the noble and horrific, cannot be represented fully, digested finally—or relinquished. By calling we the living to commemorate a newly imagined history, perhaps the novel opens a space between amnesia on one side and possession by re-memories on the other side.

We constitute ourselves as a community by sharing the space of loss, which we commit to preserving rather than overcoming, because without it we are not a community and lose our ground of creativity. Who are we? We are those who hail the disremembered and count the unaccounted for; we are those who contact this traumatic history by becoming present to its unredeemed absence, by undertaking the necessary but impossible task of redeeming it, as a condition of our lives together. Who is a member of this community? Those who place themselves in this history, around this grave, are joined together and count as being among us. Several obvious questions follow.[67]

First, do we gather as an unmediated (racial) community unified by grief? Morrison does re-member a *people*, forming a collective subject, by calling them beloved. We gather *together* around the grave of our history, but we lay our stories *next* to each other: We may elicit from each other a wish for more perfect union and for stories to seal it, but the exposure to different stories chastens this wish, whose dangers we also have witnessed in the novel. We imitate its dialogic form, in which characters reinterpret Sethe's choices differently, narrating a history that binds them and judgments that distinguish them. Their practices of making sense constitute a political space; in it, authority lies not in origins, revealed truth, or even consensus but in plural speakers and in language. By it they endow their pasts, experiences, and choices with meanings not self-evident, authored singly, or produced once and for all. In its form, a novel *about* the effort to redeem the past undercuts redemption as narrative closure, while suggesting a dialogic community beyond the text.[68]

But second, if we are constituted as those who gather around the grave, are we bound to a wound and to its repetition? Rather, having impelled narration by readers she situates as heirs, she echoes her prophet-as-writer: "Look. How lovely it is, this thing we have done—together." The lovely thing is making meaning by narration, which constitutes us as a community. As a last word, "Beloved" says language cannot erase the sorrow it voices or annul the meaninglessness it momentarily suspends. But as a demand, "be loved" also calls forth redemptive energies in our capacity to narrate together, itself a form of action that bears an abiding possibility of initiating the unprecedented. This possibility cannot be predicted, let alone guaranteed, but it cannot be precluded either.

In gathering around we fashion ourselves as a political subject, an identity that also is a politics, though it does not exhaust all that politics can be. But third, does our politicized identity lead beyond itself? The teller claims to speak to (and for) the part that has no part, but does the tale also cross difference to foster "dis-agreement"? Does it, as Rancière says true political speech must, articulate wrong to reconstitute the whole? Morrison's text avows animus toward the nation, but does it perform ambivalence? Does it mediate the relationship of part and whole? (Is it a failure or a liability if it does not?)

One tempting way to mediate part and whole is to make Sethe stand in for a generic white American citizen who must redeem the violent and haunting history. Likewise, it is tempting to say that characters laying stories next to each other is a model of dialogue across reified racial differences. *Beloved*'s "black" aesthetic then becomes a democratic ethos and political parable: By laying stories next to each other, racially divided Americans might come to terms with the past and create a multivoiced political space. But such claims of exemplarity seem to sacrifice black particularity.

Deliberative theories of democracy imagine that every actor seeks meaningful inclusion, which never requires the dominant to defer their right to speak, while always sacrificing difference to canons of rationality and universality. For surely, Sethe is no generic citizen: Coming to terms with the past is different for her than for, say, Mr. Bodwin, though their pasts entwine, and treating her *as* generic repeats the erasure of particularity founding the liberal regime. Morrison thus suspends aspirations to inclusion: My characters, she seems to say, are not speaking *to* you, white America, as if seeking inclusion in *your* conversation; nor is my novel a prophetic performance *for* you, who are not "chosen" by its overt terms of address. Her refusal seems to say, We black Americans bear witness to each other, but we will not testify against racism on *your* behalf; we fashion political judgments about and for ourselves, but will not serve as your conscience, or serve your republic by our critical testimony. You must redeem yourselves; we will not (and cannot) do it for you.[69]

But, unlike black nationalist arguments that openly exclude whites, Morrison's novel speaks to her beloved *in public* and in a way that invites whites to listen (in). It is as if she says, We blacks are not in the same one (unified) community as you whites, but blacks and whites are not sealed off from each other, either; we, blacks and whites, can "listen in" on each other. Or rather, as subalterns we blacks have had no choice about hearing your white voices, but in this venue I am inviting you to overhear *our* stories and think about them. In this way, perhaps Morrison allows for differences in audience and experience that are erased by theories of deliberation.[70]

To the question of who is gathered around the open grave, then, the answer is politically contingent, not racially given, depending on who responds to her public invitation. Just as Morrison sees an *American* literature in which race is the ghost in the machine, and enters and revises the canon, so her novel tells a *national* story by way of African American protagonists. What could be learned by whites who listen in? Whites listening in to the novel's black conversation go behind the veil, to make contact with the unspeakable—the horror of the middle passage and slavery and the interior lives of those who underwent it, but also whiteness as violence. We are implicated in it, whether as perpetrators, like Schoolteacher, in more complex but still disturbing ways, like Bodwin, or as the unnamed, uncomprehending "white" world—though there is also Amy, who plays a crucial and wholly supportive role in Sethe's life. At issue is not how we as individuals relate to specific African Americans, but whether we confront whiteness as power and innocence, to reposition ourselves toward a regime of racial domination. For as Rancière argues, the question of who counts, and who is of no account, is the fundamental political question, and the constitutively political act restructures "the field of the visible" by changing who counts and how. To acknowledge *that* these others exist, and recast how they exist *for us,* is to reconstitute who "we" are.

Though Morrison avows animus toward the nation, therefore, she performs ambivalence: Her beloved is Americans of African descent, and through them she narrates the constitution of an American past, which does not erase a black past but which cannot be erased, either. She speaks in a resonantly American, not "English," language. Her tale shows how freedom depends on naming captivities that bespeak an *American*—not only a human or black or diasporic—condition. Since a transformed relation to the past, self, and others is central to the imagination of freedom *in America,* the novel is a work of political education engaging a national culture it uses and resists, illuminates and changes.

Against her overt animus, but in the spirit of the ambivalence she performs, I credit a broader meaning than she directly avows: By going below contractual surfaces, behind liberal origins, and outside redemptive symmetries, *Beloved* does represent the idea that a haunted people can face the history (and redemptive story) holding them captive to achieve not solace or unity but authority as speakers and citizens. Poetry is not politics, but the grip of this history can be confronted only by a retelling that also takes redemption seriously as a problem. Only such a retelling can move American politics from racial stalemate and rhetorical repetition.

On its face this claim may seem absurd. At the least it seems to overinvest in the power of narrative. And arguably, the very idea of facing history and its legacy seems politically impossible now: For on the one hand, the ideology of self-making invests people in denying history and generates resentment of those who signify failed sovereignty, while on the other hand, a focus on historical wrong and its legacy seems difficult to separate from a moralism of recrimination or vindication. Pressures to assert mastery and deny history, and resentful energies around historical judgment, are symptoms of our racial history, and they are intensified in post-9/11 culture. Though Morrison shows the possibility of telling stories that use the past to foster "acceptance" rather than to prove guilt or vindicate innocence, many scholars and activists have concluded that any political way forward requires forgetting slavery and its legacy, requires folding African American difference within a wider "progressive" emphasis on social justice within an inclusive nationalism. This view is credible but obviously repeats the very disavowal that has constituted national politics. If that disavowal drives Morrison's overt animus, confronting it remains the truth in the ambivalence she performs.[71]

Refusing to step into the office of prophecy for or to whites, Morrison's post-*Beloved* essays in effect invite whites to bear witness for (and against) themselves. No wonder those essays also defend Melville, Ahab, and Lincoln as prophetic voices! Partly, she defends actual black bodies and refashions a collective black subject, while partly, she praises prophetic white critics who testify against the disavowal constituting a racialized nation. It is incredibly instructive, then, to analyze the moment Morrison herself takes up national language and uses "black" to signify "American."

From Part to Whole II: Clinton's Impeachment

I have argued that *Beloved* speaks one register of voice in black prophecy: Morrison's story dramatizes the problem of redemption and the terms for sustaining solidarity as a people, even as the novel also creatively mediates part and whole in a nation constituted racially. In turn, her post-*Beloved* essays recognize the nation as a crucial symbolic center in politics and expose its danger both as a persistent practice of white supremacy and as a fantasy of full inclusion or perfect union. If redemption in American politics means endorsing racial exclusion to purify national corruption or seeking national reconciliation to heal this wound, she refuses such symmetries. Morrison thus undertakes a complex mediation: She would avoid being a Friday who embraces the master's discourse, a translator speaking for the natives, or a conscience for whites. But her positioning, avowed identification, and register of voice shift dramatically in her intervention against Clinton's impeachment.

She calls him "our first black president" in a locution whose "our" doubles her meaning: The Right's racialization of his body shows both how black particularity is demonized and how it dramatizes the fate of the Republic as a whole. Clinton mediates black experience, democratic politics, and national attachment in ways Sethe could not without erasing her particularity; Clinton, paradoxically, mediates part and whole without sacrificing the part, indeed by showing its centrality to the whole. To defend his (black) body is to protect democratic traditions she calls a national treasure. But by narrating a crisis of the Republic, does she uncritically retell the nationalist *jeremiad* she once complicated by her literary art? Does her intervention signal acknowledgment that, though grievous exclusions constitute an American Republic, its survival remains a condition of democratic possibility? Do certain political moments require—and dignify—a narration of nationhood?[72]

Morrison's now famous *New Yorker* piece of October 1998 follows the thematic structure of her Clarence Thomas and O. J. Simpson essays: She dismisses an "official story" to disclose the real one:

African-American men seemed to understand it right away. Years ago, in the middle of the Whitewater investigation, one heard the first murmurs: white skin notwithstanding, this is our first black President. Blacker than any actual black person who could ever be elected in our children's lifetime. After all, Clinton displays almost every trope of blackness: single-parent household, born poor, working class, saxophone-playing, McDonald's-and-junk-food-loving boy from Arkansas. And when . . . the President's body, his privacy, his unpoliced sexuality became the focus of the persecution, when he was metaphorically seized and body-searched, who could gainsay these black men who knew whereof they spoke? The message was clear: "No matter how smart you are, hard you work . . . we will put you in your place or put you out of the place you have somehow, albeit with our permission, achieved. . . . Unless you do as we say (i.e. assimilate at once) your expletives belong to us.[73]

As if retelling a story pervasive among blacks but unknown to whites, she deploys racial meanings in three ways at once.[74]

First, by "reporting" how African American men view Clinton, Morrison exposes the unvoiced racial subtext of the Right's hatred for and attack on Clinton: The racial meaning of Clinton's body for the Right exposes the racial meaning of—and so debunks—their claim to moral virtue. Projection of blackness explains conservative hatred of Clinton and African American sympathy: Morrison reports how Clinton is identified as one of "us."

Second, she seems to buttress racial solidarity by reporting (and repeating) a story of racial victimization, which draws from and sustains a deep investment by African Americans in the notion that the white psyche is profoundly pathological. She focuses not on Clinton's policies as president but on who he is as a symbol: He is "blacker than any actual black person who could ever be elected in our children's lifetime." She reads Clinton as the victim of what Clarence Thomas called a high-tech lynching: She attacks Thomas for fleeing his blackness, but she defends O. J. Simpson and Clinton to suggest the stakes that "we" have in saving "our" men from victimization by the racial sign. In other contexts she observes that this story discounts the predatory sexual behavior of these men and that the victimized bodies of men, not women, are used to sustain the solidarity of a racial or national "we," and she notes who is excluded and what is veiled by such identificatory language. Still, she here voices the stories of African Americans living as a second nation within an "American" nation ruled by white supremacy.[75]

But third, Morrison uses a story of racial victimization to compose a story of *American* nationhood. Clinton stands in for blacks, and his humiliation signifies a *national* crisis:

Certain freedoms I once imagined as being in a vault somewhere, like ancient jewels kept safe from thieves. No single official or group could break in and remove them, certainly not in public. The image is juvenile of course, and I have not had recourse to it my whole adult life. Yet it is useful now to explain what I perceive as the real story. For each bootstep the office of the Independent Counsel has taken smashes one of those jewels—a ruby of grand jury secrecy here, a sapphire of due process there. Such concentrated power may be reminiscent of a solitary Torquemada on a holy mission of lethal inquisition. . . . But [this is] a sustained, bloody, arrogant coup d'etat. The Presidency is being stolen from us. And the people know it.[76]

The key word is the "us," now denoting not only African Americans but an inclusive national community. Treasured national jewels—freedoms never before, in her writings at least, visibly possessed by blacks or protecting them—are now a possession being stolen by thieves. Here, the nation is neither an imagined community promising democracy nor an instrument of white supremacy, but a Republic, however flawed, whose continued existence enables all other goods.

Its fate rests, indeed, on how citizens—black and white—respond to Clinton's victimization by a power whose pathology, tied to whiteness and religious persecution, threatens us all. Here, a language of citizenship does not erase black particularity but, rather, is rooted in it, for the (black) experience of lawless power signifies a Constitution put in jeopardy as rights are smashed and the presidency stolen. Using black particularity to dramatize national belonging in a Republic constituted by rights, she names a "we" she calls "the people," whose interest in such rights trumps even other profound differences.

In December 1998, I attended a rally at New York University Law School, organized by Toni Morrison among others. During three hours speakers included Elie Wiesel, Gloria Steinem, Alec Baldwin, Ronald Dworkin, E. L. Doctorow, Arthur Schlesinger Jr., Sean Wilentz, and Mary Gordon—and the last speaker was Morrison herself. From my notes I can quote her words:

We live in the greatest, the leading, democracy in the world, and justifiably proud of itself. But if we let this process go on, we will show how a great democratic power can reduce itself to an arrogant theocracy . . . controlled by a political cabal that allows no debate or dispute. . . . The majority of Americans now oppose this process but are completely disenfranchised. We have lost public spaces and no public body is obliged to pay us attention. . . . Whatever your race, age, sex, or class, this is not an entertainment. If you think so, you are deceived. . . . When this Constitution . . . of this particular country is suspended, we *all* go down. So from our hearts, let us beg God to bless America.

Then, Odetta and Jesse Norman, standing next to Morrison, led the crowd in singing "God Bless America."

How shall we assess her performance of American nationalism? Her work has twinned the meaning of America with white supremacy, not democracy, to voice a counternational politics, even while troubling its redemptive promise. Here she seems to embrace American nationalism: Her defense of democracy is not abstract or universalist but constitutional and national, about covenants binding a specific people. She still gives critical testimony about the nation, but now that testimony concerns rights and victimization, not constitutive disavowal, and she seeks God's blessing to secure a worthy but jeopardized civic legacy. The first question, then, is what triggers this shift from violent origins to first principles, from amnesia to a coup, from tragedy to jeremiad?

Any answer must begin with the meaning of Clinton's personal and political bodies to the Right, so that the vicissitudes of his personal body signify both an African American and a national community threatened by the Christian Right. The logic is simple: The Right reads him as black; Morrison takes up their projection and identifies a blacked-up Clinton with both a besieged black community and an endangered nation. These intersecting fantasies, which invest political meaning in Clinton's body, are best read by way of cultural conflict since Wallace and Nixon in 1968.

Surely, the Right has linked sex and race in jeremiads against the sixties, whose corrupting legacy appears in Clinton and his "morals," his presidency, and the people who elected him. In Clinton, Dan Quayle intones, "The nation is finally coming to grips with the consequences of what we have tolerated"—"moral collapse."[77] Partly, the phrase "what we have tolerated" bespeaks how prophetic language defines an ideal center against subversive threats: The Christian Right is a beleaguered minority speaking truth to power, testifying that a dominant secular liberalism causes moral collapse. Juxtaposing fidelity to core values and moral law, and identifying adultery as a literal sin and a trope of deviation, this prophetic actor returns the nation to its authentic core.[78]

Partly, "what we have tolerated" bespeaks the sexual and racial imaginary of possessive individualism. If release from state control is to produce "liberty" rather than "license," self-control must be implanted, which is why economic liberalism (a.k.a. neoconservatism) repeatedly endorses religious sanctions and female domesticity. These are racialized: Sexual austerity, disciplined labor, and antistate politics are sustained by images linking demonized dependence to fertile welfare queens and infantilized, hypersexual men. But by the logic of splitting in minstrelsy, these racialized others are objects not only of aversion but of envy, voyeuristic desire, and political nostalgia.[79]

Kenneth Starr thus follows in the footsteps of his father, a resolute segregationist whose hellfire preaching used prophecy to figure sin in sexual metaphors of impure (racial) mixing. To them, Elvis means miscegenation: White appropriation of black cultural forms is sin, not minstrelsy. The child of minstrelsy, Clinton, is empowered but also rendered vulnerable by proximity to blackness, which draws the pornographic gaze of his critics. The Right does not directly call Clinton a "black" president, but its language, linking immorality to sexual appetite and loss of control, does bespeak the racial subtext that Morrison names outright. Yet Clinton escapes political punishment, despite repeated exposure. For cultural changes since the sixties endorse as "toleration" what remains complicity in immorality. In the Right's view, therefore, unwillingness to punish Clinton shows the nation's moral corruption. By persuading people to punish him on "moral" grounds and seeking a repudiation of the legacy joining sexual freedom, civil rights, and toleration, the Right would initiate a national redemption.[80]

In contrast, one *Times* article is headlined "Blacks Stand by a President Who 'Has Been There for Us.'" African Americans widely praise "the guiltless and unpatronizing egalitarianism" in Clinton's relationship with blacks, the author reports, but they also believe that a *racial* agenda—to reverse black gains since the 1960s—is being pursued by driving Clinton from office. The author reports anger at his political compromises but quotes Christopher Edley, a black professor at Harvard Law School: "Faith in redemption cuts the other way," against the angry will to punish. "In the face of painful circumstances, you have to believe that faith will not only heal your [own] wounds but reform the master." As another respondent notes, "Forgiveness is part of [our] culture. . . . we couldn't survive with all that pent-up hatred and fear, so we've had to forgive and move on." Punishment is not the means of redemption, but the (unstated) pathology requiring redemption by forgiveness.[81]

To many blacks, according to both Morrison and the *Times,* Clinton signifies what the Right says, and therefore, stands in for the civil rights movement, for civil rights more broadly, and for a culture valuing forgiveness rather than punishment. Views of Clinton on the right and left are mediated by mirrored allegories relating the fate of the nation to the sixties and the culture wars since. But these intersecting versions of a blacked-up Clinton distort the meaning of his presidency. How so?

On the one hand, he never openly defended any affirmative legacy of the sixties, whether antiwar sentiment, sexual freedom, skepticism toward corporate power, or recasting morality as social justice rather than propriety. Symbolic proximity to blacks—and to other special-interest groups—allowed him to sacrifice their interests, repeatedly, to prove his allegiance to a New Right discourse he did not contest. By conceding New Right discourse (on issues of welfare, crime, and so-called family values), he became its hostage. To say he defended a liberal legacy in adverse circumstances is an idealization, unless one also acknowledges the way he contributed to those circumstances by both his silences and his own rhetoric. On the other hand, as Kenneth Warren notes, while Clinton "pursued a policy agenda that undermined the well-being of significant portions of the nation's minority population," his "personal trials and déclassé tastes managed to secure his blackness." He "could nonetheless 'represent' the constituency he had spurned by becoming a victim rather than a wielder of political power."[82]

Even if his defenders engaged in a kind of idealization, though, context is all in politics: At issue is not (only) the meaning of Clinton as a symbol but (also) the meaning of the Right's effort to impeach him. Partly, he had to be defended to resist the broad cultural and political project of the Right. Partly, the Right's success in the Senate would have been like a putsch removing a democratically elected president. Partly, the entire process endangered due process and privacy protection, which are important to all of us, though most pressingly to gay rights activists, minorities in the criminal justice system, and "enemy combatants" denied any access to redress. In ways that many of us at that rally did not recognize in our political radicalism thirty years earlier, procedural safeguards and privacy rights are essential to personal and political freedom—a lesson even more obvious after 9/11. But radical insights of thirty years ago remain pertinent. For constitutional piety and privacy rights, as theorists from Catharine MacKinnon and Karl Marx to Sheldon Wolin argue, can evade the issue of power and separate democracy from practices of *public* freedom. Morrison herself invokes this other vision of freedom when she says a majority of Americans are "disenfranchised" because they have "lost public spaces."[83]

Accordingly, Morrison declares a crisis in the Republic, as a *national* community, a "we" on which *every* "I" depends. She evokes a nationality she anchors in constitutional membership rather than blood and soil, repeating ideal elements of a civic nationalism enfolding other attachments or loyalties. She does not speak as a prophet to a black nation within the "American" nation. She does not call upon the idiom of Marx's "On the Jewish Question" and Malcolm X's "The Ballot or the Bullet" to condemn the constitutive inequality that mocks the inclusionary poetry of liberal nationalism. She does stand with the excluded, but on the line of nation/hood, making a series of associations: Clinton stands in for blacks, and his victimization signifies a national crisis caused by the Right's attack on constitutionally protected (and customary) rights, from due process and privacy to speech, assembly, and democratic elections. Rights historically denied to blacks—and again in the 2000 election—are "jewels" whose possession by all is endangered.

Morrison thus inverts the typical left critique of the nation and nationalism: Rather than decry the false universality of a nation that erases black particularity, it signifies the national fate because it bears a democratic universality. Like Douglass, King, and Baldwin, she often unmasked the language of American nationhood to reveal how a purportedly universal "we" is the exclusionary voice of white supremacy. But here she echoes their other claim: African American victimization and resistance are at once the barometer and the bearer of an *American* freedom by revealing both a dangerous default on and a redeeming commitment to *democratic* principles.

Her intervention collapses too much the difference between Clinton and the Right's image of him, but it thereby takes on a side of politics she earlier devalued. She depicts a constitutional republic as the basis of other goods, including political freedom; as a frame that enables other conflicts over erasure and power, it must, despite its defects, be defended if it is jeopardized. Her jeremiad, voiced from the position of black subjects whose rights are disposable, shows those defects, but does so to claim both that any threat to the rights of some threatens all and that rights historically denied to blacks are a legacy essential to all.

We should affirm such efforts to articulate a national "we" in constitutional and political terms. Her intervention shows how the nation remains the organizing center of American life, and why we should refuse not only the fantasy of full inclusion by that identification but also the fantasy of escaping it. Likewise, we should affirm her effort to mediate the experience of the part and claims about the whole, for political power depends on it. That projection of meaning, that is, by which a part makes claims and tells stories about a whole, is necessary if one interpretation—of history since the sixties, of social movements, democracy, and nationhood—is to be advanced against others. Politics in a democratic form is precisely such claim making, by which some speak on behalf of others—who can speak back.

To protect a legacy of rights she avows as her own, she strategically uses jeremiadic rhetoric—for political ends. Her jeremiad does risk sentimentalizing the relationship between democracy and the Constitution by speaking of the nation only as a republic, not also as an imperial power, corporate regime, and racist state. But of course, it was *Toni Morrison* speaking: Her appeal to defend the Republic in crisis had authority (on the Left, among other blacks) precisely because of her history as a counternational witness whose critical testimony she could leave *unstated* to a left-liberal audience. Considerations of timing—of crisis—also could warrant idealizing rhetoric, which knowingly leaves to another moment a more critical story.

I therefore find myself contrasting Morrison's literary art and this example of political rhetoric. It is not that one is critical and the other is not, but the character of the criticism is different. Rather than confront amnesia and constitutive exclusion by a tragedy that grieves for irredeemable losses, her jeremiad narrates constitutional jeopardy to defend treasured jewels under attack. Vulnerable (black) bodies and persecuting power remain the site of injustice, but now she avows attachment to—and seeks God's blessing for!—the Republic that is at once the guarantor of rights and the political form within which apartheid has flourished. I find myself asking, Is it more effective to use a jeremiad for political ends, without troubling those purposes and exposing the assumptions behind them? Or is it politically essential to always complicate the claims we make in political speech?

Her jeremiad is not simple; rather, it is complex and ironic, because it begins from the position of blacks who have yet to secure the rights whose violation they protest through Clinton's personal and political body. Evoking the racial violence linked to the Republic whose jewels she defends, her jeremiad does not simply idealize the legacy it avows. Still, those who link religious truth and moral self-righteousness to racial rule are *threatening the Republic,* not a central voice shaping its history. As their "ecstasies of sanctimony," to quote Philip Roth, are seen to jeopardize but not animate it, Morrison can seek God's blessing without referring to a history of violence in God's name.[84]

Whereas the Clinton speech performs national avowal by underplaying ambivalence, I find myself wishing that Morrison had overtly performed her ambivalence about nationhood, despite the tacit knowledge of her audiences, as if to avoid even the appearance of repeating jeremiadic nationalism. I find myself wishing she had fought the New Right not with constitutional patriotism only but with counterprophecy in the mode of her Melville or Baldwin. For at stake in the ascendancy of the New Right, of which the Clinton impeachment is one episode, is not only constitutional liberalism but the shape of every fundamental institution in American society, of the terms governing thought and action— and so of the world our children inherit. In the prophecy I imagine, her adversaries might well appear as false prophets who, in the name of saving the nation, ensure its destruction; but surely, her story would have to depict both the haunting consequences of a history whose meaning we have denied and the fateful choices on which our freedom and flourishing now depend.

But my wish for counterprophecy hides another: that *Clinton* had taken on, not tried to mollify, his adversaries and their discourse. In turn, this disappointment in Clinton reveals another wish, expressed best as a question: Would a more powerful challenge to the Right, speaking out loud what Clinton left unstated, have shifted political discourse? Could a story about American nationhood voice the critical testimony whose negativity Morrison elided at the rally *and* the avowal of attachment that makes critique into politically generative speech?

The prescience of Morrison's jeremiad, and the resonance of these wishes, seems confirmed by events since the impeachment. First, public opinion never accepted the Right's case against Clinton, and indeed it turned against Starr. Second, the Christian and congressional Right took this famous "disconnect" as evidence of the very moral corruption they lamented, which confirmed their culture "war." But third, Democrats offered no narrative to explain, let alone politically exploit, this disconnect. The story of moral failure from the sixties to Clinton was not challenged, and the impeachment episode, which controlled the 2000 election, was never narrated to shift political judgment of its meaning. Fourth, when a "cabal" of judges on the Supreme Court elected George W. Bush by disenfranchising black (but also Jewish) voters in Florida, Democrats hurriedly confirmed the "legitimacy" of government in the name of constitutional piety. Fifth, Bush's lackluster and widely criticized administration was salvaged by 9/11, which created an opportunity to reauthorize a national security state by once again joining the Puritan and the liberal in a countersubversive project.

These highlights suggest how elements in Morrison's account of constitutional jeopardy and national crisis became more pertinent and literal than anyone in 1999 might have imagined. Constitutional usurpation on one side, and a failure to narrate on the other side, remained two sides of one crisis, even as the phobic object has shifted from Clinton to terrorism. Amnesia, enabled by fear of confronting the meaning of the past in politics, and racialized violence, enabled by fear of confronting the question of whose reality we count and how, made "democracy" the justification of state power, not its countervailing antagonist. After eight years, this marriage of the evangelical, the neoliberal, and the punitive seems to have lost credibility, but it remains to be seen if the disavowals that have animated it can be named or confronted.

In Democratic Party primaries in the spring of 2008, the prose of Hillary Clinton's managerial competence was trumped by Barack Obama's avowedly nationalist "poetry" of hope, whose premise is that progressive change means turning away from a divisive past and from the partisanship originating in the sixties, to seek instead an inclusive future. Partly, his success depended on emphasizing his immigrant story, not his blackness, even as he delicately mediated racial part and national whole and drew endorsements from many prominent Americans, black and white, including Toni Morrison. Partly, to become "our first black president," he narrated neither a tragic retelling of American nationalism nor a jeremiad calling for fateful choices about practices long deemed legitimate, but a poetry of the future that repeats the redemptive promise of American exceptionalism. This nationalist narrative may generate electoral support, but the question remains: Does democratic political possibility depend, rather, on narratives that address the ghosts haunting the American house?

Conclusion

Prophecy as Vernacular Political Theology

This is not a story to pass on.
—Toni Morrison, *Beloved*

The bird is (not) in your hand.
—Toni Morrison, "Nobel Lecture"

The final belief is to believe in a fiction, which you know to be a fiction, there being nothing else. The exquisite truth is to know that it is a fiction and that you believe in it willingly.
—Wallace Stevens, *Opus Posthumous*

The blues is an impulse to keep the painful details and episodes of a brutal experience alive, in one's aching consciousness, to finger its jagged grain, and to transcend it, not by the consolation of philosophy but by squeezing from it a near-tragic, near-comic lyricism.
—Ralph Ellison, *Shadow and Act*

I HAVE sought in this book to bring together political theory and a version of American studies by placing central concerns of the European canon into conversation with a politics organized by racial domination and biblical language. This has meant displacing philosophical modes of apprehending politics by rhetorical practices and literary genres. Bringing political theory into conversation with an American modernity shaped by race, religion, and genre, and not only by capital, normalization, and disenchantment, also expands the vocabulary of references and theories for analyzing politics. I then could trace how prophecy is reworked by critics of white supremacy to revitalize politics in ways both needful and dangerous, and how their reworkings expose the racial innocence in prevailing forms of democratic theory but also illuminate issues that theorists now address through other discourses. As the figures in this book suggest not only the dangers but the value of this language, they bring readers to a question: Are its risks worth it? As prophecy demands a decision rather than decrees a fate, so I have argued, in all ambivalence, that the risks are worth taking.

But these claims need to be unpacked as a conclusion. I begin by highlighting the central claims of the book through a contrast with Tocqueville, the one canonical theorist who addresses every issue I raise about America, race, and politics in revealingly different yet resonant ways. Then I clarify one of the fundamental purposes of this book, which is explaining the capaciousness of prophecy as a language not only *in* but *of* politics. Lastly, I clarify my other purpose, using the examples of prophecy in this book to enter current debates in political theory about "political theology" and politics.

Seeing Prophecy through Tocqueville

Tocqueville has been a silent presence throughout this book, which has inflected his view of religion and politics to rewrite his account of race and "democracy in America." Without losing focus, but to gain focus, consider how the case for prophecy is clarified through the lens of Tocqueville's central concerns.

First, Tocqueville typifies how political theory tends to separate theorizing democracy from race: In the last chapter of the first volume of *Democracy in America,* he says that the relation of "Europeans" to native people and slaves concerns America, not democracy. He never theorizes the paradox that race both joins and tears apart "democracy" and "America," even as he narrates how democracy in America is founded on genocide and slavery. Never grasping the racial origins of modernity, he never theorizes the raced constitution of democracy. In volume 2, indeed, race disappears in his dark vision of "democratic despotism," a modern form of power that retains the "outward forms of freedom" but makes participation in power an archaic custom.[1]

Second, therefore, Tocqueville identifies but separates the two major critiques of liberal society that my figures join: While his chapter on race shows how the fluid freedom of Anglo-Europeans depends on fixing (destroying or enslaving) racialized others, his chapters on majority tyranny and democratic despotism show how the enfranchised engender a nightmarish imprisonment. In shorthand, he separates mass society and racial domination, which haunt the democratic idealism of "America" as a special site of possibility. In contrast, Thoreau sees entombment as the penalty of racial domination; King sees conformity as the other side of racism; Baldwin links whiteness to cultural sterility and political docility; Morrison sees white supremacy as the script of mass culture and black bodies as exciting democratic despotism.[2]

Third, Tocqueville's account of "democracy" is oriented toward agency, but his account of race denies it in ways prophetic critics contest. He would cultivate "the art of freedom" to resist "instincts" toward docility and withdrawal that are engendered by a culture of individualism, but he does not speak of cultivation or agency to address or reconstitute the racial foundation of that individualism. In volume 1 he calls equality a "providential fact," a fact we cannot change, but to draw freedom from it, and volume 2 warns of democratic despotism to forestall it. But he reifies race as intractable difference. Does his deeply political sense of contingency fail him? Is he, rather, crediting political intractability?

"These two races are fastened to each other without intermingling," unable "to separate entirely or combine. The most formidable of all the ills that threaten . . . the Union arises from the presence of a black population upon its territory." The threat to freedom appears in the novel forms of despotism that democracy produces internally, but the threat to national union is the legacy of its racial founding. The problem is that "the abstract and transient fact of slavery is fatally united with the physical and permanent fact of color. The tradition of slavery dishonors the race and the peculiarity of race perpetuates the tradition of slavery." If inequality in France, rooted "solely in the law," is difficult to "root out," how can "distinctions be destroyed which seem based on the immutable laws of nature herself? . . . I despair of seeing an aristocracy disappear which is founded upon visible and indelible signs. Those who hope the Europeans will ever be amalgamated with the Negroes," he says, "delude themselves."[3]

He denies to both whites and blacks any possibility of self-overcoming—the redemptive promise of biblical prophecy: "An isolated individual may surmount the prejudices of religion, of his country, or of his race; and if this individual is a king, he may effect surprising changes in society, but a whole people cannot rise, as it were, above itself." Tocqueville calls the defense of freedom a "holy (because redemptive) task" and sees "the art of being free" as transformative, but he sets impassable limits on collective agency in regard to race. In contrast, the voices in this book bear witness to what Buber calls "prophetic faith." Prophets since Jeremiah ask whether the leopard can change its spots, and they acknowledge that power and privilege, fear and shortsightedness are obstacles to change, but their faith casts self-overcoming as a possibility that cannot be precluded, though it cannot be produced at will, either.

There is, therefore, a fourth way that Tocqueville sharpens the claims I am making. For he calls the United States a "Puritan and trading nation," depicts a republic founded by joining the "spirit of liberty" to the "spirit of religion," and argues that "republican religion" is its "first political institution." By relating "faith" to "freedom" and "religion" to liberal politics, he engages current concerns with the theo-political. We note that he uses religion to stabilize political culture, but also that he theorizes the "utility," not the "truth," of faith, echoing Machiavelli and perhaps prefiguring theory after the linguistic turn. The paradox is that he celebrates the "spirit of religion" in Puritan origins, but he stands outside of, even ignores, the prophetic language that is its living legacy.[4]

Accordingly, Tocqueville's exclusion of both race and prophecy from his theorization of democracy seems paradigmatic for political theorists since. Drawing on prophecy to revitalize politics, in contrast, my figures take on the reification of race. For them, race is an idol to be smashed in the name of equality, while for him, equality is the idol he resists in the name of freedom. But for them, the defense of freedom is inconceivable without addressing the racial domination he takes as given. They use the prophetic idioms he ignores to rethink democracy as a political form, a cultural ethos, and a social practice.

Surely, the elasticity and limits of prophetic speech can be seen by contrasting Tocqueville to these figures. After all, he is typically called a prophet too. Just as he does, the figures in my book voice a tension between the intractable and the contingent, announcing what we cannot change to incite decision and action about what we can. But they differ not only about race but in language. To mitigate "instincts" toward docility and conformity, he defends the utility of faith in cultivating an "art" of being free, while they are invested in (or inhabited by) the "faith" in equality and redemption from which he stands apart. I do not mean that "prophets" are unreflective compared to ambivalent, equivocating theorists, for "prophecy" as a genre and reiterative practice has always problematized itself, as those standing "within" it *remake* it. I mean, rather, that we theorists may be Tocqueville's heirs in our own distance from this language, which others inhabit, even ambivalently, and rework.[5]

The Capacious Inside of Prophecy as a Genre

My first purpose in this book, then, was simply to retrieve prophetic voices that Tocqueville and Eurocentric political thought do not register. To show the capaciousness of prophecy as a political language has meant stepping inside "the spirit of religion," even as we saw our figures translate and move beyond that spirit. In turn, to discover that "the spirit of religion" is not just antithetical to "the spirit of liberty" is to take seriously the ways biblical idioms are used not only in politics but to revitalize it.

Variation and fruitful contest are manifest even among the monotheistic voices, as displayed by the primal conflict between John Winthrop and Anne Hutchinson: about the bearing of faith on worldly political authority, as its adversary or justification; about the practice of faith in austere and purifying forms of social control or in ecstatic forms of enthusiasm among a widening "priesthood of all believers"; about faith in relation to causality and contingency; and, as William Connolly argues, about the "disposition" by which people *live* their faith and relate it to others. Rather than reify prophecy, we trace its reiteration in practice, its availability to inflection by performance. Prophecy thus includes figures as opposed as Winthrop and Hutchinson, or Falwell and Blake, who rework a semantic field to cultivate their tropes.[6]

Even in its theistic forms, I have also argued, prophecy does not found a law of laws or seek obedience to one, though there is scriptural evidence to justify why figures like Leo Strauss, Norman Podhoretz, and Jerry Falwell defend that view. But if we follow William Blake instead, prophecy bears an ever-renewing uncontainable "word" in a visionary practice of reimagining the world. And if we follow Martin Buber, prophecy is a rhetorical practice and political "office" that recasts how people judge the past and their choices, to incite their action now. By shifting focus from law to vision, decision, and action, we do not avoid the issue of "dogmatism." But rather than bind dogmatism to theism, we can redescribe it as inhering in imperative and conditional registers of voice, which are entailed by any claim making about the character of the whole, the consequences of conduct, and the conditions of flourishing.

I have argued, therefore, that we should interpret prophecy as an "office" that involves making certain kinds of claims in certain registers of voice: as a messenger bearing truths we deny at great cost, as a witness giving testimony about the meaning and costs of conduct, as a watchman who forewarns of danger to forestall it, as a singer whose lamentations redeem the past for the present. In these ideas of office, biblical prophecy made available a genre of speech for translation and use. Capacious itself, biblical prophecy thus enables extraordinary elasticity of use, as moderns "translate" theistic idioms to put these kinds of claims and registers of voice in "secular" form.

From Blake to Thoreau, as we saw, prophecy is recast as "poetry" as "the poet" assumes (and revises) a special "office" with great political ramifications. Literary artists from Thoreau to Morrison thus depict themselves assuming a public office entailing certain practices. Romanticism is "severely displaced Protestantism," Harold Bloom says, because divinity is invested in nature, and because poesis, the world-transforming capacity of "the word," is invested with public significance. Baldwin and Morrison suggest how far translation and revision (or "secularization") can go, and how contested the passage is.

If we imagine Jesus announcing that the meaning of the law is to love God and to love one's neighbor as oneself, we also can imagine Blake announcing that "God becomes as man is so that we may become as God is." One path from biblical prophecy is opened by this logic of incarnation, which inspires Blake's Dionysian Christianity as well as Baruch Spinoza's democratization of reason as the voice of God in each. Baldwin models a related path, which translates theism into an ethos of finitude that "accepts" the mortality and interdependence of human creatures neither self-sufficient nor sovereign. While Thoreau translates redemption as the idea of awakening to a dawn incarnated in (human) nature, Baldwin and Morrison shape a nontheistic prophecy in which *amor fati* replaces deliverance from captivity as the this-worldly and political meaning of redemption.

Because translation is so extensive, one has to ask, What is *not* "prophetic" or "prophecy"? Yet borders to the semantic field surely are visible. In theoretical terms, prophetic language contrasts with "democratic theory" as communicative rationality, deliberation, or self-interested action by rational actors. As public discourse, compare Thoreau to the *Federalist Papers,* or abolitionist rhetoric to the languages of interest-group liberalism, constitutional procedure, or *raisons d'état.* Imagine, conversely, the civil rights movement without prophetic language: We would hear interest-group bargaining by quid pro quo or rights claiming, but no vision of internal and worldly transformation.

No wonder Ronald Reagan reduced social movements to "special-interest groups" seeking narrow material benefit at the expense of a common good: Denying a prophetic role to the part that has no part, whose language of wrong exposed a whole constituted partially, he invested redemption in a national whole by denying its partiality, not by reconstituting it. While "Morning in America" thus invokes a people innocent rather than collectively liable, his appeal also contrasts prophecy to individualism as acquisitive self-making, which invests moral value in material success. Indeed, Reagan exemplifies how individualism and nationalism are mutually entailed idioms, as tropes of rebirth signify regeneration of one in terms of the other, whereas prophetic critics draw on other biblical tropes to evoke the impossibility of individual sovereignty, the inescapability of interdependence, the wounding in attachment, and the need for accountability.

I have emphasized the capaciousness of this genre, partly to undo its reification but also thereby to say, with Morrison in her Nobel lecture, that "language" is a bird (not) in our hands, at once at our disposal and beyond our grasp, a gift we can keep alive only if we surrender (to) it. But in the United States, *prophecy* is this bird (not) in our hands. It remains the only legitimate public language for addressing the character and fate of the whole. No one owns it; it is available for reworking in politics. Bob Dylan and James Baldwin took up prophecy—"A Hard Rain Is Gonna Fall" echoes *The Fire Next Time*—and are canonized now, but the fact that the office remains open to *anyone* is registered when Simon and Garfunkel sing that "the words of the prophets are written on subway walls and tenement halls."

Prophecy in this culture is not esoteric speech or an idiom we learn at school; rather, it is vernacular and vulgar, the currency of spoken-word poetry. The fruitful question is not, Who counts as a true prophet? Rather, it is, What shall we do with this language, which is (not) in our hands? Poets and prophets are active now, writing on subway walls; do we notice their signs, read their warnings? "The word" is spoken all around us; are we listening? Which words will we remember? As you read this very sentence, prophecy is being spoken nearby, about our larger fate. And the bird flutters in your hands, too.

I unfreeze reification, however, to recover the ways critics of white supremacy cultivated prophecy for political purposes, to political effect. While Tocqueville decrees the impossibility of reconstituting a republic whose citizens he calls a racial aristocracy, figures like Douglass, Thoreau and King, Baldwin and Morrison use prophecy not to decree a fate but to demand a decision about conduct that can be changed and to redeem a past that cannot. Critics of white supremacy use prophecy, in either mode, as a resource to conceive and pursue democratic projects.

From Capaciousness to Race and Politics

By interpreting prophecy as both an office and a genre, I have identified in it registers of speech unavailable in liberal discourse but needful in politics. I have focused especially on three recurring registers, involving authority, identification, and narrative. One is the imperative voice of "firm persuasion," as Blake puts it: It announces the unspeakable or unsaid, the consequence of conduct and the conditions for flourishing; it bears witness not only against our conduct (by saying what it sees and standing against it) but also on behalf of a faith that we can act otherwise, a faith (not in God, but in action) that is essential to democratic practices. Second, as critics use prophecy to raise such issues of commitment and judgment, the genre entails tropes of membership and solidarity that critics draw on to ask who "we" identify with and on what basis. Reworking the relation of part and whole by counting what has been denied reality, they recast political identification and reconstitute community. Third, they use prophecy to retell the history of this "we." Whether rendering the past as a resource or as a traumatic loss, prophecy voices the necessity of coming to terms with the constitutive power of the past as a condition of agency in the present. In these ways, prophecy bears "redemption" not as an escape from politics, but as an aspiration both to achieve freedom and to make suffering meaningful.

But critics of white supremacy, especially, demonstrate the political value, not only danger, in these registers of speech. Simply put, they draw on prophecy to suspend the racial state of exception that constitutes the liberal rule, the American ordinary. The challenge they face is not "justifying" claims to rights or personhood; the problem is that enfranchised people profess democratic principles they practice in viciously exclusionary ways, while disavowing the meaning of their conduct, the reality of those they dominate, and the possibility of practicing their principles differently. Critics depict willful blindness not to moralize but to politicize domination, by clarifying how people may know something, say about torture or inequality (and so also about dignity and equality), and yet do not acknowledge or count as salient, and so cannot act on, what they know. Critics of white supremacy draw on prophecy because they seek not an absolute form of justification but forms of authority and modes of address that shift in visceral ways who and what people count as real, while enabling them to affirm avowed commitments in new ways.

These critics thus assume the prophetic office—of messenger, witness, watchman, and singer—not to found a law of laws or to predict the future but to provoke acknowledgment of what citizens disavow, both domination and a history shaped by it, as well as their own authority to remake their commitments and reconstitute community. In the face of white supremacy, their acts of declaration, judgment, and witness seem less like symptoms of dogmatism and more like aspects of political action, which entails claim making about conduct and its impact, about flourishing and its conditions, about the reality of others and the partiality of community, and about fateful choices between commitments not readily reconciled. They draw on prophecy, then, not only as the bird already in their hands, but to undertake constitutively political—albeit always dangerous—speech acts.

Even if we were to accept that these kinds of claims are necessary and not only dangerous in politics, however, there is no denying the specific legacy and repressive weight of how prophecy has been practiced historically in the United States. It is no empty signifier, a purely performative practice critics can make to mean, now, whatever they wish. Better to recall that this book began with Sacvan Bercovitch's critique of Robert Bellah: Prophetic speech typically reiterates the axiomatic framework and exceptionalist narrative of liberal nationalism. As Michael Rogin thus argues, prophetic figures end up demonstrating the traumatic racial origins they would overcome.

By arguing that Bercovitch reduces variation to repetition of the same, however, I have defended the value of *retelling* as a way to work through a story not to "pass on." Against Rogin's view of white supremacy as an original sin, a constitutive condition impossible to escape, I have defended capacities to initiate rather than repeat what theology calls a miracle and prophecy calls redemption. Yet even if Bercovitch and Rogin reify origins, do my prophetic figures refute their view of hegemony and repetition? After all, my chapters end with violence, self-sacrifice, and bitter estrangement—or with "God bless America"—as if to confirm the fated orbit within which even great critics are confined, partly by the persistence of white supremacy and partly by their longing to redeem the culture they criticize.

Is Tocqueville entitled to the last word about the intractability of white supremacy? After two Reconstructions, his denial that a people "can rise above itself" seems less like an anxious refusal of redemption by a theorist ambivalent about equality, and more like a reminder of agency's intractable limits in a republic constituted racially. Bercovitch and Rogin reject the American exceptionalism he created, and they aspire to a radical democracy he feared, but they echo his sense of a fatality against which no "scorching irony" or literary art can prevail, as if no speech or "action in concert," no trumpets blasting and pitchers smashing, can shake the walls of race.

Assertions of intractability seem undefeated, yet no guarantee secures these walls or precludes contest. Indeed, to say "this is not a story to pass on" is to credit both the power of this history and the need to redeem it, to voice an imperative both to remember and overcome it. Intractability does not justify relinquishing the truth—or should I say faith?—that change remains a possibility we cannot preclude. Baldwin thus says, "I know that what I am asking is impossible. But in our time, as in every time, the impossible is the least one can demand—and one is, after all, emboldened by the spectacle of human history in general, and American Negro history in particular, for it testifies to nothing less than the perpetual achievement of the impossible." Redemption—necessary to dream and (im)possible to realize—names the bent bow of democratic desire.[7]

From Prophecy to Political Theology

At issue in prophetic language is not only the resiliency of white supremacy despite repeated reconstructions promising democratic rebirth. The example of American prophecy also speaks to current debates among theorists about "political theology" in a postsecular world. Most obviously, to interpret prophecy as vernacular speech is to view religion less as theology and more as culture, to view theology less as philosophy and more as rhetoric. In this sense I have turned to prophecy not because it is an "answer" to the question of political theology but because it is the bird (not) in our hand, and what are we going to do with it? We have seen critics use the vernacular of prophecy to depict landscapes involving not only identity and difference but inequality, not only plurality but domination. Since it is tied to race, and so to power, prophecy in America emphasizes the adversarial as well as the rhetorical.

How then does a vernacular rhetoric of domination and redemption enrich current arguments about religion and political theology?

In liberal political theory the defining act—from Thomas Hobbes to John Rawls—is dividing public and private, to protect property from state power and conscience from coercion, but also to privatize religious discourse because conflict between "comprehensive doctrines" cannot be settled by reason. The key theoretical and political move is to establish the sovereignty of "public reason" by alienating citizens from conscience and faith.[8] The defining act of "communitarian" political theory—from John Winthrop to Robert Bellah and Michael Sandel—is the inverse: to expose property (or ostensibly private rights and conduct) to public forms of judgment or accountability and to (re)politicize religious faiths and moral doctrines. That is why criticism of liberalism in the United States often takes a "left Puritan" cast: By politicizing "comprehensive doctrine," critics judge conditions of servitude and privilege in workplaces and families to reconfigure a range of rights and prohibitions and redraw the boundary between public and private. It is understandable, then, if readers assume a book about prophecy bears a communitarian political agenda. But for me, prophecy clears a space neither "liberal" nor "communitarian."

Many liberal and left thinkers wish religion and religious discourse would go away: "Religion" is the name of irrationality and submission to authority, whereas "enlightenment" means escaping from tutelage into self-determining reason. But religion will not go away, and redemptive investment in rationality poses its own threats to political life. Better to acknowledge, with Tocqueville, that "prejudice" or culture is anterior to reason. Better to see what William Connolly calls "the ubiquity of faith" in every optic. Better to credit how "comprehensive doctrine" or "political theology" underwrite every political position, including a "secular" liberalism disavowing theology. Attempts to reject or escape "political theology" only reproduce it in other forms. The issue is how to conceive and practice it. To assess the alternatives that emerged in this book, though, we must first return to Tocqueville and his communitarian heirs.

Though many liberals place Tocqueville in the "liberal tradition" because he endorses the constitutional privatization of religion, he also declares it the first political institution of the American republic, and he empowers it culturally and politically. Seeking to enable and yet contain the "spirit of liberty" while giving coherence to a fragmented social body, he relies not on public reason but on "the spirit of religion" and "the family." Making theist faith (and family) conditions of liberal agency, he openly raises issues of authority and faith typically precluded by liberal political thought. Yet he protects the authority of this faith by putting it beneath political life, as though to underwrite a culturally constitutional order enabling political conflict and innovation. William Connolly thus calls him an "arboreal" pluralist: He does not insist on unity as Jean-Jacques Rousseau does; rather, he depicts one faith as the trunk of a tree whose branches express a bounded range of differences.[9]

In turn, Bellah argues that liberal constitutionalism depends upon but ideologically disavows culturally thick and historically rooted forms of subjectivity. For "religion" names not irrationality or dogmatism, but culture. "Public theology," he says in 1968, offers "substantive vision," not "technical reason," to address the interiority of subjects whose preferences liberalism only aggregates, and to address a common good not reducible to individual rights. "Religion" offers moral ballast and cultural coherence, but it also justifies and enables forms of dissent. Defending this vision thirty years later, Sandel attributes fundamentalism to the ethical disengagement liberalism imposes: "A politics that brackets morality and religion too completely soon generates its own disenchantment. Where public discourse lacks moral resonance, the yearning for a public life of larger meaning finds undesirable expression. . . . Fundamentalists rush in where liberals fear to tread." But if the sovereignty of public reason requires citizens to alienate "private" judgments and "comprehensive doctrines," does repoliticizing them create irreconcilable conflict?[10]

Because the authority or theology that Tocqueville makes extrapolitical is (re)politicized by Sandel, we see a Schmittian element in his communitarian politics: if Carl Schmitt's political moment is the decision constituting friend and enemy, and if the sovereign is the holder of that power, then Sandel is endorsing political contest in which "the people" claim sovereignty to decide the "theology"—or vision of the good—by which they live. He is not endorsing one vision of the good over another but arguing that issues must be addressed substantively rather than procedurally, by a political "decision" constitutive of the character and fate of the whole. As he echoes Schmitt, so we can see Buber return Schmitt to biblical origins by depicting the moment of "decision" when a "primordial religiosity" constitutes a "kingdom of God" against every other way of life or authority in Hebrew society.[11]

The attraction of this charismatic and antinomian, self-authorizing and generative moment ("it is written," but "I say unto you") is obvious to radical democrats seeking to enable political action against a constituted order or institutional reification. For Buber, Arendt, and Wolin, this extralegal energy overturns the worldly (state) sovereignty in which Schmitt (idolatrously) had invested it. But what of the friend–enemy distinction in the formation of a collective subject? Fidelity to one god's sovereignty seems to translate as worldly identity demonizing the difference on which it depends. Does not the language of fidelity (to one god or principle) pose its own threat to democratic politics? This question seems to regenerate liberal logic, but it need not.

Because human beings pursue multiple goods and visions of the good, pluralism must be a core principle of a democratic politics. The challenge in politicizing faith, as Chantal Mouffe argues, is avoiding the sovereignty of one, partly by turning "antagonism" between conflicting faiths into an "agonism" that enables their coexistence within a political framework. If a counterhegemonic project is to be democratic, she argues, an ethos of citizenship is needed to frame conflict. At issue is not only what faith people avow, but how (in what spirit, by what cultivated dispositions) they practice it in relation to people bearing other faiths. In contrast to Sandel's view of a community governed by one centering faith, *and adversaries competing to define it,* William Connolly thus offers a "theo-political" ethos that pluralizes as well as politicizes faith.[12]

Connolly seeks a politics in which people bring different faiths or visions of the good into public life, but the condition of their contest is that actors recognize the contingency of every faith, for on the basis of that recognition as a common ethos, they can form relations of "critical responsiveness" and "agonistic respect." Faith is ubiquitous and political theology is inescapable, but if adversaries recognize that each faith is contingent on others to define itself, and that no faith can be (dis)proven definitively, then constituencies can engage rather than demonize the differences on which their identities depend, to create a culture fostering generosity rather than bellicosity. As Connolly rejects a sovereignty that "centers" a nation as a collective subject with an identity to (re)define, he diffuses the friend–enemy distinction in shifting "assemblages" of association, partial and temporary intersections of purpose and interest that cut across rather than presume a national frame.[13]

My reasons for focusing on prophecy begin with the critique of liberal politics that joins Sandel and Connolly, but I diverge from each.

Like them, I presume that culture is anterior to reason and that faith is inescapably a condition of politics. But unlike Sandel, my prophetic figures relate rather than oppose the liberal and the communitarian. We recall that for Schmitt, liberalism is antipolitical because a pluralist and inclusive creed defers decision and refuses the friend–enemy distinction; he therefore seeks a political—populist or communitarian—moment of reconstitution. But for prophetic critics of white supremacy, "political theology" recurrently defines the constitutive outside (and internal other) of American liberal nationalism. What Rogin calls counter-subversive politics is Schmittian decision in American drag: A liberal regime reconstitutes sovereignty and normative citizenship by enforcing a racial and sexual frontier. That is the paradoxical role of race in America, which at once defines and violates an ostensibly liberal creed. When Jerry Falwell objects to "liberalism" as toleration, therefore, he politicizes the faith it had privatized, but he does so to sustain the other exclusions on which it was founded. In sum, race exposes the operation of power and exclusionary logic that is the "communitarian" reality of *liberalism* as political theology.[14]

It is true that, historically, biblical prophets stood with "the people" against outsiders, though also with the poor against the privileged. But my American figures typically stand with the enemy or subversive against which "the people" has constituted itself as a political community unified by its core commitments and defining boundary. I stand, says Douglass, with God and the slave against a people constituted by disavowal and idolatry; I stand, says Thoreau, with fugitive slaves, Mexicans, and Indians (and with "true Puritans" like Brown) on "the freer and more honorable ground" of the jail. Mindful that race and sexuality are knotted in what Tocqueville calls a "Puritan and trading nation," Baldwin and Morrison also see civil religion as complicit in domination, and they refuse a unifying creed. We thus count as prophetic Garrison and Debs but also Ginsberg and Baldwin, who queer prophecy by Dionysian energies that de-center identity. Making counterclaims, not only about the authority we (could) live by but also about who we (could) identify with and on what basis, each politicizes faith to "demand a decision" about the fate of the Republic. But how do they respond to the friend–enemy distinction by which Schmitt secularizes the biblical idea of fidelity to God and covenant? What defines the "political" in their "theology"?

It is here that my prophetic figures diverge not only from Sandel but, in certain ways, from Connolly, too. The animating ethical energy in

Connolly's theo-politics is to foster self-reflective receptivity by showing how a faith or identity depends on difference to articulate itself and by affirming how life's manifold energies of becoming exceed any form we give to human being. The animating political aspiration of this ethos is to disturb the consolidation of identity, while creating spaces in which the exclusions it harbors can achieve visibility and reconfigure an entire field of action. To disrupt the reified border between friend and enemy is to challenge identity as a form of power, as well as the other forms of power in which it is imbricated. Against collective subjects invoking identity to claim sovereign power, Connolly seeks pluralization as a democratic political project.

When Thoreau and King avow a theist faith, they practice it in this way, to cultivate dispositions Thoreau calls wakefulness and King calls love; likewise, Baldwin's nontheist prophecy seeks "acceptance" of fatalities we do not invent and cannot master, as a condition of action animated neither by prideful disavowal nor resentful bitterness. Each embodies an "ethos" to foster democratic contestation; each confronts existential resentment to resist demonizing their adversaries. Yet they focus political energy differently than do theorists of ethos and cultivation.

These prophetic figures do not so much thematize identity and difference to capture issues of power and subordination. They see the ways slavery, legal apartheid, and institutional racism signal an identity constituted by denying its "contingent foundations," but they see race as a regime of domination and subordination cutting across *every* subject position and register of identity. White supremacy is not a valid identity to reconcile with others, but a social practice empowering some by subordinating others. No wonder that Thoreau, Douglass, King, and Baldwin are cast as invasive moral fanatics opposed to democratic norms: Working not within a democratic frame but confronting the state of exception that at once founds and violates it, they must live in a vexed relationship to the democratic ideals they value. Accordingly, they do not so much pluralize faiths that they teach are contingent as confront a refusal of acknowledgment; they proceed less by chastening dogmatism and more by unrelentingly judging conduct, less by advancing an ethos of receptivity to difference and more by calling for decision and conflict about constitutive practices we must end, not privatize, learn to appreciate, or work to pluralize.

In a way, these contrasts approach the same issue but in different aspects and ways. Connolly might be seen as addressing ways to prevent beliefs from being practiced in ways oppressive to others; King and Baldwin, say, address what to do in relation to others already oppressing them. We surely hear registers of receptivity and forbearance in them, just as we hear registers of judgment in Connolly, but distinctively, Baldwin announces willful innocence, enacts judgment, and seeks abolition in the face of domination. Neither approach to domination is universal, though Baldwin can sound that way; each may warrant emphasis depending on political context and theoretical purpose. But the issue of race in the United States, it seems to me, calls us to face the issue of power in ways that seem to elude both postidentity thematization and an Arendtian language of plurality.

In many ways, indeed, "race" in this book has served as a kind of trope for the issue of power, to suggest why politics, while it always must concern modes of being and becoming that emerge among interlocutors in dialogue about plural identities and faiths, also must be something else: adversaries struggling to reconstitute regimes that privilege some by subjugating others. In common is an agonal rather than consensual view of democracy that Connolly and I both endorse. But it may be that the angle of vision provided by racial politics intensifies the issue of domination and foregrounds a kind of response whose very intensity— of commitment, judgment, and grief—is an abiding (dangerous, terrifying, but sometimes needful) aspect of prophecy.

An adversarial engagement with domination, on the one hand, and intensity of judgment, on the other hand, distinguishes the genre of prophecy from prevailing forms of theorizing democratic politics. A kind of affinity, therefore, links Buber and Schmitt not only to abolitionism and King's defense of extremism, but also to Baldwin's denunciation of the innocence and equivocation of a racially constituted liberalism. They turn to prophecy and embrace the scorching irony that is a recurring—and dangerous—feature of the office, because they are confronting the racial exception that at once defines and violates the democratic ordinary.

These prophetic American figures do not invert a reified or absolutized friend–enemy distinction, but they do not defuse or diffuse it, either. Partly, they see a worldly adversary in constituencies invested in domination, but partly, the "enemy" is internal to each person as capacities for pride, or conformity, or disavowal. They therefore stand with some against others, but also in an agonal relation to every neighbor and citizen, which means drawing a boundary within the self to identify the terms of self-overcoming. Yet they do not chasten their judgment of white supremacy, which remains an evil fundamentally at odds with a democratic life whose possibility they doubt but whose value they do not question. They avowedly stand with some against others, therefore, but argue that ending white supremacy will truly benefit those others, who call themselves white, though they cannot now perceive how. Changing that judgment of benefit is a central goal of prophetic rhetoric. Instead of polarization or pluralization, so to speak, prophetic figures work a mediating position between part and whole to reconstitute a regime.[15]

In distinguishing prophecy as a form of political theology I have emphasized so far its features as an office, not only its characteristic modes of address but therefore its adversarial view of power, intensity of judgment and language, and mediation of part and whole. For these reasons, I can now say, prophecy is not epistemological in character; biblical prophets and American exemplars do not address "knowing" God as a problem to be solved; nor do they engage politics by replacing illusion or ideology with knowledge, as if truth would secure agreement. We are blind, but it is a moral and political rather than an epistemological problem.

The "message" of prophecy—when Elijah chides Ahab's pride, or Amos remembers the poor, or Douglass testifies as a slave, or Morrison bears witness to the disremembered dead—is that our relation to the world and to others depends not on knowledge but on acknowledgment. Indeed, Cavell bespeaks a prophetic tradition by making this shift, which originates in the biblical claim that what God requires of us is not esoteric but common, not abstract but "carnal," not a remote Archimedean point to reach but a "turn" toward what is nearby, to become present to it.

While Cavell sees disavowal as a human "drive" in skepticism and its metaphysical "answers," however, my figures see disavowal as white supremacy; if Cavell (re)turns us from metaphysics to the ordinary, they (re)turn us to a history of horrific racialized violence. Still, the problem each confronts is not that we posit absolute instead of contingent foundations to faith or identity but that we refuse to count the other or the past as real—a problem of disavowal, not error or ignorance. As a result, they do not emphasize faith's contingency as a basic truth—though Thoreau, Baldwin, and Morrison see this—but address what and who we acknowledge as real, and how. For this reason, to recall the idea of office with which we began, prophets speak in registers of announcing, bearing witness, and warning to address crucial dimensions of politics.[16]

Judgment and Aggression in Prophetic Claim Making

To reimagine political theology through prophecy is to rethink the meaning of authority as a practice of claim making, not justification. I am emphasizing in prophecy especially the declarative and imperative registers of voice that announce the reality of the truths we disavow, bear witness to the meaning of the past we forget, name the conduct for which we are accountable, and assess its penalty. We hear such registers of voice when Baldwin testifies that "it is not permissible that the authors of devastation also be innocent. It is the innocence that constitutes the crime." Likewise, when he reports black expectations of divine vengeance, he adds, "The intransigence and ignorance of the white world might make that vengeance inevitable—a vengeance that does not really depend on, and cannot really be executed by any person or organization . . . historical vengeance, a cosmic vengeance."[17]

He acknowledges contingency in the "might," for we *make* vengeance inevitable by choosing inaction, and so he seeks a decision to forestall what *might* be a fate. But he still speaks in imperative terms: "Everything now, we *must* assume, is in our hands; we have no right to assume otherwise" (emphasis added). He thus announces the conditions we *must* accept to flourish:

It is the responsibility of free men to trust and celebrate what is constant—birth, struggle, and death are constant, and so is love, though we may not always think so—and . . . to be able and willing to change. I speak of change not on the surface but in the depths—change in the sense of renewal. But renewal becomes impossible if one supposes things to be constant that are not—safety, for example, or money, or power. One clings then to chimeras, by which one can only be betrayed, and the entire hope—the entire possibility—of freedom disappears.

Stipulating the conditions of "renewal in the depths" is one side of insisting that "the *price* of the liberation of white people is the liberation of the blacks—the total liberation, in the cities, in the towns, before the law, and in the mind."[18] No matter the currency, he always is stating the "price of the ticket."

Such assertions—about how we must see our history if we are to bring ourselves through it, about how we must see life if we are not to serve death, about how we must see our circumstances to begin doing justly—feel coercive or inarguable, as if any counterargument is mere "denial." At issue, though, is not a dogmatism deriving from theism or from interpreting morality as a law commanding obedience. At issue rather, is speech acts and claim making about the nature of reality, the entailment of commitments, the meaning of the past, the cost of conduct. These claims enact an authority in assertion and judgment that bears unmistakable aggression. I want to assert the necessity of these kinds of claims in politics, which means defending the authority exercised by making them and the aggression they entail.

On the one hand, as prophets demonstrate, the authority to speak (and act) is exemplary: As Baldwin says, we must assume it is in our hands, and we have no right to assume otherwise. "Authority" names not a truth we must justify but a commitment we must own and enact. For it is only by living out a god or first principle, a truth or table of values, that we "test" its authority, both its capacity to elicit the assent of others and its generativity in life. Norman Mailer calls Martin Luther King Jr. an "existential hero" for this reason: He lives out a myth (of equality or democracy) that may be dead in us; its fruitfulness cannot be discovered except by enacting his faith into an unknown, exposing it and himself to the risk of failure. This testing of authority by the example of a life, the testing of our lives by the example of authority in one who bears witness, is what prophets do; it is their office.[19]

On the other hand, when Jesus announces glad tidings, he declares, "I bring not peace but a sword." Why is a gospel of love, the word he carries, also a sword? Partly, it speaks of (God's) anger at injustice. Abraham Heschel thus says, "Admittedly, anger is something that comes dangerously close to evil, yet it is wrong to identify it with evil. It may be evil by association, but not in essence. Like fire, it may be a blessing as well as a fatal thing—reprehensible when associated with malice, morally necessary as resistance to malice." Indeed "the great contribution" of prophecy "was the discovery of the evil of indifference. . . . the wrath of God is a lamentation. All prophecy is one great exclamation: God is not indifferent to evil." That is why Blake says, "Honest indignation is the voice of God." That is why, when prophetic figures declare, "Here I stand; I can do no other," they do not move when we feel offended.[20]

The word is also a sword, however, because it demands a decision about how to live, and any such decision divides before and after, and some from others, opening new paths by forgoing others. The word is a sword in our hands *especially* if it announces a gospel of love requiring us to renounce familial bonds and ethnic identities to form a new (kind of) community. The aggression lodged in commitment and judgment, and the conflict they entail, are part of the glad tidings, the "love" that reconstitutes community by recognizing "the least" among us.

In our assessment of postsecular politics, then, the issue is not whether speakers—say, Jeremiah, Jesus, or Falwell—are dogmatic and aggressive rather than receptive or loving. As King himself argued, the issue is how they give form to aggression—in the service of what values or commitments, articulated in what spirit, on behalf of whom, in what relation to others. As Cavell argues, moreover, claim making (even by "extremists," King would add) is always an invitation to community— which can be rebuffed:

> To speak for oneself politically is to speak for others with whom you consent to associate, and it is to consent to be spoken for by them—not as a parent speaks for you, i.e. instead of you, but as someone in mutuality speaks for you, i.e. speaks your mind. Who these others are, for whom you speak and by whom you are spoken for, is not known a priori, though it is in practice generally treated as a given. To speak for yourself then means risking the rebuff—on some occasion, perhaps once and for all—of those for whom you claimed to be speaking; and it means risking having to rebuff—on some occasion, perhaps once and for all— those who claimed to be speaking for you.[21]

As Ralph Ellison's protagonist concludes *Invisible Man*, "Who knows but on the lower frequencies I speak for you?"[22]

Who knows, because he cannot know in advance who will assent to his words: Community—with whom we identify and on what basis— is in question not given, achieved (if at all) by claim making that risks rebuff. Democratic politics requires such claims—and counterclaims by adversaries and interlocutors—to discover what matters and who counts, if community is, or what it might be. Firm persuasion in such claims need not foreclose politics but can provoke it, does not end dialogue but initiates responses that cannot be predicted in advance. In contrast, the rejection of prophecy, and the avoidance of authority, is governed by a view of politics that imagines there could be a political claim that would not be totalizing because it would not be exclusionary. But to adopt that view is in fact to refuse a *political* claim as such, that is, as a judgment (about conduct and commitments) that at once speaks on our behalf and invites our response—indifference, outraged refusal, revision, or assent. The problem is not *doxa* as dogma, then, but the absence of a public in which such claims can be contested, and the properly political response to such claims is counterclaims, not admonitions to be less attached to our convictions.

Yes, claims about disavowal bespeak anger and entail conflict, but as Baldwin says, every accusation contains a plea because it addresses an other, as if anticipating the very community it would (but may fail to) reconstitute. To read political theology through prophecy, then, is to rethink democratic authority not only as a kind of claim making that entails judgment and aggression, but also as a kind of rhetorical practice, for the political task is engaging an actual audience, a "concrete" rather than a "generalized" other.

From Theology to Rhetoric: Rethinking Redemption

I began to study prophetic language simply because politics involves persuasion, and persuasion requires starting with how one's audience thinks and speaks. In this sense philosophy, and not only politics, is rhetorical, for Socrates "goes down to the Piraeus" to solicit, engage, and rework the opinions, or *doxa,* of fellow citizens. This view of rhetoric illuminates Thoreau's reworking of the "keywords" of his culture, King's mediation of the scriptural and constitutional, Baldwin's practice of "visiting" to hear and then voice the unsaid perspectives both of people who call themselves white and of those they silence, and Morrison's retelling of the redemptive narrative that has twinned (and not only divided) black and white in American life. We can say that prophecy has been crucial to the rhetorical practice of great American critics because it is the passionate frame of reference of so many Americans—hegemonic, yes, but thus a vernacular "political theology" already in our hands, the ordinary language even of those who (believe they) are secular.

What I mean is illustrated by a revealingly unexceptional episode: Trent Lott, Republican senator from Mississippi, was forced in 2003 to resign as majority leader because at a birthday dinner for Strom Thurmond he expressed regret that Thurmond's white supremacy agenda had not been made national policy; when he was reinstated by the Republican caucus in November 2006 after they lost control of the Senate, John McCain commented, "We all believe in redemption, thank God." This "we" thanks a God of atonement who stands for mercy if we repent, but also, "thank God" we believe in redemption because otherwise, Arendt argues, we would be trapped by our history, by acts whose wayward and injurious consequences are boundless and binding. But in a way that Arendt does not discern and that Thurmond and Lott exemplify, practices of domination generate, for master and slave, rhetorics of redemption.[23]

That McCain says "we" unreflectively in a way that collapses the national and the human, and that he seems not to doubt the promise of redemption, is my simple point: "Religion" is itself the surface of what Tocqueville calls an "involuntary agreement" or "grammar" beneath argument, indeed, beneath every aspect of American life. Surely "redemption" is a commodity to be acquired, as celebrity figures and politicians perform obviously hypocritical rituals to "apologize" for and "put behind" them racist outbursts and other kinds of injurious or self-exposing conduct. But the idiom of redemption can work as a commodity, and it is available for debasement, because it remains alive in the culture; both New Right rage at and black support for Bill Clinton were voiced in terms of redemption, and the concept continues to relate adversaries across other profound differences.

Prophecy appears here not as articulated doctrine but as the common sense and narrative condensed in a word, "redemption." If this conclusion began by comparing Tocqueville on intractability to Baldwin on miracle, we end it by unpacking the issues McCain's word bespeaks and the unreflective "we" it mediates. Lott's unthinking endorsement of Thurmond's white supremacy and his all-too-easy "redemption" surely confirm the view of racial intractability. When McCain—himself baited in 2000 for having a black baby—defends "redemption," he knows that Lott stands in for a white nation, whose redemption from racial sins McCain and Lott also accredit too readily. By moving from ethics to narrative, from teaching the contingency of faith to living a faith in redemption, from a generalized to a concrete other, and from theology to rhetoric as a political practice, we again ask, What shall we do with the bird (not) in our hand?

Through the figures in this book, I have explored two different idioms of redemption, each originating in relation to domination. One depicts redemption *from* captivity or oppression, then also from sin, and from history. (Redemption *from* captivity can thus mean recovering or repossessing a prior condition of freedom, purity, or wholeness.) "Redemption" then seems like a noun denoting final freedom "from" one condition, and sure achievement of another, but for King, say, "redeeming from" is also a verb, an ongoing practice of making free by action. This idiom can be heard in the exodus from Egypt, in Christian rebirth from sin, in millennial prophecy of an end-time, but also in Puritan captivity narratives and recurring hostage dramas.

The other idiom depicts redemption *of* history: To "redeem" suffering or crime means to endow it with meaning, to atone for it or heal it, to make it justified, worthwhile, of value. In this idiom, masters and slaves, from reverse perspectives, seek to "redeem" domination—the crime or the injury. By this idiom we identify ourselves as guilty agents to redeem shameful acts and restore our worthiness. As subalterns subject to power, we also redeem a history of suffering or a wounding experience of oppression by drawing value from it, by making it meaningful, by seeking vengeance, reparation, or vindication. Lincoln invokes this cluster of meanings when he narrates a story in which the sin of slavery is redeemed by Civil War deaths, which in turn "we the living" must redeem by our own dedication to the principles for which those people died—or their death and suffering are in vain. King invokes Moses to depict redemption *from* white supremacy, but when he calls on whites to "redeem" the American promise, he means make good on it; and by making amends for conduct that violates the promise of equality, whites "redeem" themselves and "make whole" a union rent by injustice.

The idioms of redemption *from* (oppression) and redemption *of* (past suffering or crime) form a grammar; in individual and collective senses, redeeming involves both making free and making meaning. Arendt deems politics redemptive and Nietzsche calls *amor fati* "my redemption" because they grasp this double meaning. But we can see why redemption readily goes awry, as Nietzsche most acutely analyzes. For if we seek deliverance from conditions in fact fundamental to life, which we must wrestle with rather than devalue or escape, our practice of redemption bespeaks "ressentiment" and enacts violence. And if we imagine an "unconditional truth," as if to solve the *problem* of the meaning of our suffering, then we erase the gap between art and life and create a "true world by which to devalue the actual one."[24]

The damage wrought by redemptive language is indeed staggering, and by no means only in American history. Clearly, overt violence is authorized by promises of redemption as deliverance: As redemption from Egypt dispossesses Canaanites, so the saved are produced by marking the preterits, the pagans and racialized others who embody unredeemed life. Violence thus bridges the avowedly redemptive practices of Christianity and liberalism as emancipatory projects. For Weber, the quest for redemption generates worldly asceticism. For heirs of Nietzsche, redemptive rhetoric in religious and then secular forms justifies resentment, generates herd morality, and entails nihilism.

On the one hand, rhetorics of redemption as deliverance always seem to identify the saved by marking the damned, to forge virtue by demonizing impulse, to seek harmony by devaluing conflict, to imagine freedom by erasing history. Redemptive rhetorics disown or purify conditions seen to stain life rather than wrestle with conditions seen to constitute it. On the other hand, when we lodge redemptive hope for meaning in our future or children, in our work or possessions, in community, art, or politics, we impose an unfeasible burden and enact an imprisoning investment. Any reckoning impels the question, What must people do to themselves and others to gain redemption as they understand it? What is the price of the ticket?

As Talal Asad has argued, the discourses of late-modern power are authorized by this aspiration to forge a "we" and "redeem" it. The danger is intensified since 9/11, which has enabled ruling American elites to revitalize the myth of America as a redeemer nation called to free the unredeemed from captivity to nonliberal practices. This emancipatory promise *is* the redemptive meaning of American liberal nationalism, whose fruit has always been violence and repressive unity. It seems credible to conclude that a democratic life depends on disenchanting redemptive myths layer by layer, from liberal internationalism and human rights to teleological narratives in providential or progressive forms.[25]

If so, the "office" of theorist is to drain communities and political action of redemptive meaning, to chasten dogmatism, unmask power, and foster reverence for endangered human diversity. The task is not to justify resistance but to reveal the practices by which every justification is a form of power. De-idealization of language, especially of redemptive and democratic rhetoric, is the only way to expose how ideals, taken up in the logics and ruses of power, are practiced at human expense. Secularism is an ideology, but from this perspective, its distinguishing disillusionment is the best—or perhaps the only—resource against disciplinary power.

This disillusioning practice need not be gloomy. Just think of the nonredemptive Marxism, Groucho's, the voice of irreverent play, endlessly fertile and disruptive, standing against every form of order and authority, every piety and virtue. Such iconoclastic yet inventive negativity sees meaning making itself as a coercive imposition of order and propriety, and it sees any specific form of meaning as a vanity to be ridiculed. If we arrogantly devalue life in the effort to bestow meaning, and if we are imprisoned by the forms of meaning we make for ourselves and impose on others, the only way to escape self-defeat is shameless irreverence.

A kind of liberatory antipolitics is performed by those jesters who unmask the promises and mock the arts that elicit our involvement in schemes of redemption. Against "the teachers of the purpose of existence," Nietzsche defends those whose laughter undermines all convictions and motivational frameworks, as if we could protect life against the violence entailed by meaning making if only we could de-idealize the human and revalue the unredeemed matter we are. No wonder that jesters from Groucho to Philip Roth find in desires, sex acts, and pleasure what Roth calls a "redeeming corruption," a blessed release from the tyranny of meaning.[26]

Such a tension between the Apollonian and Dionysian suggests a tragic (Cornel West says "tragi-comic") rather than redemptive vision. When I began this book, indeed, my thought was to invoke a tragic ethos to both highlight and counter the dangers of redemptive rhetoric. I was looking for a vocabulary to oppose: teleological narrative in the form of theodicy or providential design; dreams of communitarian fullness; longings to purify "the human stain." In contrast, tragedy teaches the impersonal forces and fatalities that defeat any version of sovereignty; the inevitable misrecognition that defeats any idea of an identity transparent to itself; the contingency that haunts every faith; the incompletion that makes us motivated actors, always partial, if not predatory; the plurality that generates multiple goods and views of the good, incommensurable conflict among them, and so the necessity of choice and loss. In response to the political question—What kind of language is needful now?—the idea is to counter neoliberalism and its evangelical alter ego by a tragic (rather than theistic) ethos of finitude.[27]

But perhaps another genre is not necessary; perhaps a tragic perspective on redemption has already been fashioned in American culture, of course as a minority voice, partly by way of the African American tradition of the blues and partly by way of literary artists and critics who retell (as tragedy) the stories of redemption driving the culture. The great writers about redemption are critics of the motives and worldly consequences of practices their audiences call redemptive. They show how "redemption" entails brutally violent as well as self-denying and bewilderingly self-defeating forms of action. Indeed, with the exception of Morrison, but only because she is still alive, each not only tells a tragic story but is a tragic figure. But they also redefine rather than renounce redemption.

Whereas Jeremiah, Douglass, and King do not narrate redemption as tragedy, and whereas Thoreau remains ensnared by the redemptive logic whose costs he partly sees, Baldwin and Morrison (like Nietzsche) present more complex visions. They are distinguished from other prophetic voices because they question rather than expound the idea of deliverance from captivity, trouble rather than avow the idea of a redemptive promise in politics, dramatize what is problematic and not just needful in efforts to redeem the past, and mark the limits of language's ability to redeem suffering and not only its power to do so. They stage redemption as a problem, but they make it impossible "to pass on," as they try to redeem the history whose crimes and horrors they unblinkingly narrate. In sum, they forge a tragic perspective on redemption by the way they confront both (American) language and history.

Why is this preferable to directly unmasking justificatory schemes? To recall Bercovitch, why *retell* rather than simply renounce stories of redemption? Partly, Baldwin and Morrison, like Nietzsche and Arendt, retell prevailing redemptive stories to dramatize both their grip and their dangers. But partly, they rework redemption because human beings require a sense of purpose or meaning: Redemption is a problem, but human beings cannot flourish unless, by creating ways to make life (seem) worthwhile, they resist the wisdom of Silenus—better not to have been born. Likewise, human beings *must* "redeem" the past because they cannot escape or change it: They must fashion a fruitful relationship to the past, or they live by amnesia, resentment, and repetition. As Arendt's engagement with Silenus so beautifully shows, meaning making is one side of the freedom that makes politics redemptive.

We retell rather than renounce stories of redemption because redemption is so intimately tied to freedom and to meaning. What, then, makes life worthwhile? For Nietzsche, it is making riddle, chance, and accident "cohere" by *narrative,* so that we become not only subjects but authors and actors. For Arendt, it is *action,* a capacity for initiative and generativity she associates with miracles and attributes to faith. That she turns to biblical exemplars to depict this "natality" is no more coincidental than is Morrison's quoting Paul citing Hosea, though Morrison thereby emphasizes *love,* which is devalued by Arendt and Nietzsche but is central to prophecy's view of redemption.[28]

Capacities to narrate, act, and love are here invested with redemptive possibility of freedom making and meaning making. This possibility can never be precluded, though we can lose faith in it, perhaps the greatest political disaster, because freedom depends on faith in it, and we are likely to lack that faith when we most need it. Still, moments of initiative or meaning can neither be foreseen nor guaranteed. Like Arendt and Nietzsche, then, Baldwin and Morrison depict a capacity (not) in our hands, a promise available to us but not at our disposal. Correspondingly, redemption is no longer an exodus moving decisively from Egypt to a promised land. Redemption is partial, never complete(d), an ongoing practice of making free and making meaning, not an all-at-once or once-and-for-all transcendence. It has been the office of prophecy to *conjure*—to represent and summon—capacities for redemption by love, art, and action, which we bear as actors if we have faith in it. Still, even if we have faith in redemptive possibility, it is an impossible burden.

In Steven Spielberg's *Saving Private Ryan,* the figure (played by Tom Hanks) who "saves" Ryan (Matt Damon) says to Ryan with his dying words, "Earn this." Forty years later, Ryan, now a grandfather, stands at his savior's grave surrounded by his uncomprehending family as he helplessly weeps, undone by the feeling that his conventional middle-class life has not redeemed that death. Is Spielberg berating baby-boomer America? Saying, rather, that bourgeois normality in its very ordinariness does redeem the horror of war? Or is he showing how hard it is to will *amor fati,* for what life could possibly "earn" this death? Prophecy is the office that asks the question of redemption, and every answer entwines blessing and burden.[29]

Crucial to how Baldwin and Morrison rework redemption, then, is the demand that we acknowledge rather than disavow the darkness surrounding us, which action or art can momentarily illuminate but never banish. To shift emphasis in Baldwin's assertion: "Everything now, we must assume, is in *our* hands" (emphasis added)—not in God's—and "we have no right to assume otherwise." If he thus echoes Nietzsche's sense of *amor fati* as the greatest weight, necessary yet impossible to bear, he also politicizes what Nietzsche calls "my redemption." To assume providential design is bad faith, but to assume it is in *my* hands alone avoids the politics signaled by the "our." We hear again the imperative voice of "must," which leaves everything in the hands of a community not pregiven but conjured into being, if at all, by redemptive language.

From Race and Redemption to Post-9/11 Politics

But whose hands? Is it any longer credible to answer that question by invoking a national "we"? Indeed, it seems credible to say, rather, that my story about prophecy is a symptom of left melancholy, idealizing a political rhetoric that arguably had its place, conceding regretfully that that was then and this is now. Partly, a focus on race seems misleading, for post–civil rights politics seems characterized by a proliferation of wrongs and critics, not by the constitutive fault that Karl Marx called "wrong in general."[30] Partly, narratives of crisis and fateful decision seem to serve only those who simplify and polarize, to enact countersubversive politics. Partly, ideas of reconstituting a regime seem dangerous, because regimes monopolize violence, nations center identity, and the language of democracy is the rhetoric of empire. Democratic energies are self-defeating unless practiced insurgently and episodically, between nation and empire. Such arguments are credible, but they cede too much.

First, liberal nationalism as an imperial project can be challenged politically, at least from within the United States, *only* by coming to terms with the historical amnesia that enables elites to repeat manifest destiny in the name of liberty. To narrate a counterhistory of American empire is to take on a project of "redeeming" the past, and to fashion an alternate legacy from which to creatively spring means reconstituting (both troubling and reimagining) a collective national subject that claims responsibility and acts otherwise. An anti-imperial politics, or a challenge to "the war on terror," if any such is to emerge, depends on narrating a story of nationhood and empire in ways that are politically resonant and therefore energizing.

Second, power can only be resisted by power, power requires solidarity, and solidarity depends on narratives that, in a present marked by domination, dislocation, and despair, project a better future to solicit desire and motivate action. If democracy is the ideology of state power, perhaps it is necessary to take on—not cede—democracy's mythic meaning as an experiment bearing a redemptive significance. The survival even of constitutional forms, let alone directly democratized practices and culture, may depend on prophetic poets and mobilized constituencies to dramatize democratic possibility in redemptive terms.

What position should such constituencies and prophetic voices take toward nationhood? Who is this "we" who believe in redemption, thank God? For biblical prophets, human beings approach the universal only through a community trying to embody it by making a claim to exemplarity. The danger here is manifest in a "redeemer" nation whose democratic promise authorizes imperial monomania. My prophetic figures call this false prophecy, but they do not simply refuse the language of promise or its national framing.

Partly, they turn democratic principles against the practice of American nationalism. Partly, they invest democratic promise in African Americans as a political protagonist bearing America's "only consistent universalism" because experience of domination leads to demanding freedom for all. Still, they do rework ideas of nationhood to authorize democratic practices, though Thoreau, Baldwin, and Morrison consistently resist what Lauren Berlant calls "the deep and serious claims the nation has to the love and obligation of its citizens." Invoking a constellation of (local, ethnic, diasporic, cosmopolitan) attachments, they displace (but do not and cannot erase) the nation as "the fundamental reference point of collective political identity, fantasy, and practice."[31]

What matters is not "believing" again in "America" as the name and literal site of (democratic) possibility. What matters rather, as Thoreau argues, is tracing the fateful connection of domination and disavowal and provoking the action and art that resist and redeem it. That tracing confounds what he ironically calls "native" and "foreign" forms of servitude to expose what is strange nearby and to discover kindred at a distance. Some of us may repeat his discovery that "I have lost my country." But to "front" our allegiances, to count what they cost us and others, and to say what we see and to stand against it, is to clear "freer and more honorable ground" on which strangers and kindred can reconstitute political community. If prophetic traditions of abolition and black solidarity bespeak this ambivalence about how and in whom to locate democratic promise, just these mediations—between parts and whole, between specific communities and aspirations toward universality, between conscientious incorporations and national fantasy—seem a fruitful legacy of prophecy in America. What could it mean now?

Notes

Preface

1. See Paul Boyer, *When Time Shall Be No More: Prophecy Belief in Modern American Culture* (Cambridge: Harvard University Press, 1992); Melani McAlister, "Prophesy, Politics, and the Popular: The *Left Behind* Series and Christian Fundamentalism's New World Order," *South Atlantic Quarterly* 102, no. 4 (2003): 773–98.

2. Chapter 1 elaborates the claims in these paragraphs and the scholarship that supports them.

3. Robert N. Bellah, "Civil Religion in America," *Daedalus* 96 (1967): 1–21; Michael Rogin, *Ronald Reagan, the Movie, and Other Episodes in Political Demonology* (Berkeley and Los Angeles: University of California Press, 1987).

4. An enormous body of scholarship explores the presence of prophetic language in American life, but few scholars directly theorize prophecy as a "political" and specifically "democratic" language. Among striking exceptions, the most notable is Cornel West in all his work, but especially in *Prophesy Deliverance!* (Louisville, Ky.: WJK, 1982) and *Prophetic Fragments* (Grand Rapids, Mich.: William E. Eerdmans, 1988); many essays from these two works are collected in *The Cornel West Reader* (New York: Basic Books, 1999). Also notable are James Darsey, *The Prophetic Tradition and Radical Rhetoric in America* (New York: New York University Press, 1997); David Gutterman, *Prophetic Politics and Christian Social Movements* (Ithaca, N.Y.: Cornell University Press, 2005); David Howard-Pitney, *The Afro-American Jeremiad: Appeals for Justice in America* (Philadelphia: Temple University Press, 1990); and Theosophus Smith, *Conjuring Culture: Biblical Formations of Black America* (New York: Oxford University Press, 1994). In *The Shape of Things to Come* (New York: Farrar, Straus and Giroux, 2006), Greil Marcus brilliantly embeds American prophecy in mass culture.

5. Alasdair MacIntyre, "Epistemological Crises, Dramatic Narrative, and the Philosophy of Science," *Monist* 60, no. 4 (1977): 453–72.

6. Toni Morrison, *Beloved* (New York: New American Library, 1987), 274.

1. Introducing Jeremiah's Legacy

1. William Blake, "There Is NO Natural Religion" and "Marriage of Heaven and Hell," in *Blake: Complete Writings,* ed. Geoffrey Keynes, 97–98 and 148–58 (New York: Oxford University Press, 1972); Percy Bysshe Shelley, "In Defense of Poetry," *Norton Anthology of English Literature*, vol. B (New York: W. W. Norton,

2003), 744–62; Ralph Waldo Emerson, "The Poet," in *Selected Essays,* ed. Larzer Ziff, 259–85 (New York: Viking/Penguin, 1982).

2. I do not recover the truth about Hebrew prophecy as a template to impose on subsequent figures; rather, I identify the resources that biblical prophecy provides for figures struggling to engage *their own* present. My reading of Hebrew prophecy is, therefore, deeply informed by these later figures, who cast themselves as its heirs and critics. To define prophecy in literally biblical terms is to reify a historical practice that has changed enormously. To define prophecy functionally, as prediction or social criticism, is to ignore how it has been understood and is now practiced in *specific* communities and times.

3. In the Bible, prophets are also called *ro'eh,* or seers. For contrasting arguments about the history and development of prophecy, see Joseph Blenkinsopp, *A History of Prophecy in Israel* (1983; rev. Louisville, Ky.: Westminster John Knox Press, 1996); Martin Buber, *Kingship of God* (New York: Harper and Row, 1967) and *The Prophetic Faith* (New York: Harper and Row, 1949); Frank Moore Cross, *Canaanite Myth and Hebrew Epic: Essays in the History of the Religion of Israel* (Cambridge: Harvard University Press, 1973); George Mendenhall, *The Tenth Generation: The Origins of the Biblical Tradition* (Baltimore: The Johns Hopkins University Press, 1973); Herbert Schneidau, *Sacred Discontent* (Berkeley and Los Angeles: University of California Press, 1976); Eric Voegelin, *Order and History,* vol. 1, *Israel and Revelation* (Baton Rouge: Louisiana State University Press, 1956); Max Weber, *Ancient Judaism* (New York: Free Press, 1952). History aside, "the prophets" are a rhetorical citation: The book of Isaiah, for example, is formed from speeches by at least three figures over one hundred years; Isaiah is a literary construct created from historical persons. See Margaret Zulick, "The Agon of Jeremiah: On the Dialogic Invention of Prophetic Ethos," *Quarterly Journal of Speech* 78, no. 2 (May 1992): 125–48.

4. Weber, *Ancient Judaism,* 293; Alasdair MacIntyre, "Epistemological Crises, Dramatic Narrative, and the Philosophy of Science, " *Monist* 80, no. 4 (1977): 453.

5. Buber, *Prophetic Faith,* 2–3, 103.

6. Prophets are quoted from the King James Bible.

7. Weber, *Ancient Judaism,* 305.

8. Weber, *Ancient Judaism,* 303–5; Friedrich Nietzsche, *On the Genealogy of Morals,* trans. Walter Kaufman (New York: Vintage, 1969), 57. For Voegelin, prophetic narrative "established the standards of order by which defection could be measured." Prophets fashioned not a "pragmatic history" of events chronologically narrated but a "paradigmatic history" in which all action is interpreted as "obedience to or defection from the revealed will of God." *Israel and Revelation,* 331. The *meaning* of life explains the "pragmatic existence" of a nation in history. The great rejoinder to this theodicy is Nietzsche's *On the Genealogy of Morals,* but see also Susan Neiman, *Evil in Modern Thought* (Princeton: Princeton University Press, 2002); William E. Connolly, "Letter to Augustine," in *Identity\Difference,* 123–58 (Ithaca, N.Y.: Cornell University Press, 1991), and "Pluralism and Evil," in *Pluralism,* 11–38 (Durham, N.C.: Duke University Press, 2005).

9. Weber, *Ancient Judaism,* 284. The attack on idolatry is directed not only against imperial states but also against matriarchal religion and fertility cults that celebrate nature's autonomy. Cf. Herbert Schneidau, *Sacred Discontent;* Moshe Halbertal and Avishai Margalit, *Idolatry* (Cambridge: Harvard University Press, 1992).

10. Toni Morrison, *Beloved* (New York: New American Library, 1987), 275.

11. Recent historiography suggests that prophets were innovators. First, they revised the monarchical view of an unconditionally supportive warrior God. Second, they demanded monotheism in a way that was unprecedented in Hebrew history because Hebrews had consistently worshiped fertility goddesses as well as Yahweh. Third, they did not inherit but in fact developed the language of covenant. Fourth, they predated the law codes. For Blenkinsopp, therefore, "those whom we refer to as 'the' prophets formed only a small and in several respects anomalous minority of prophets." *History of Prophecy in Israel,* 25. "Misunderstood and hated by the mass of their listeners," says Weber, "the pathos of solitude overwhelms their mood." *Ancient Judaism,* 292. Yet Isaiah and Jeremiah hailed from prominent families and persuaded their kings to pursue reform, though both kings failed.

12. Hannah Arendt, *On Revolution* (New York: Viking, 1971), 217.

13. Pride is "vanity" because sovereignty is falsely inflated, and it is *futile,* doomed to defeat. To Jeremiah, Babylon is a symbol of pride in both senses: "Babylon has been a golden cup in the Lord's hand, that made all the earth drunken: the nations have drunken of her wine; therefore the nations are mad. Babylon is suddenly fallen and destroyed: howl for her; take balm for her pain, if so she may be healed. We would have healed Babylon, but she is not healed; forsake her and let us go everyone into his own country; for her judgment reaches heaven" (51:7–9).

14. The grammar of redemption involves the idiom of *deliverance from* a condition of captivity—a worldly Egypt or sin—but also a second idiom: to "redeem" suffering or the past by making them meaningful. Redemption thus means making free and making meaning. See George Shulman, "Redemption, Secularization, and Politics," in *Powers of the Secular Modern: Talal Asad and His Interlocutors,* ed. David Scott and Charles Hirschkind, 154–79 (Stanford: Stanford University Press, 2006).

15. Harold Rosenberg, *The Tradition of the New* (New York: McGraw-Hill, 1965).

16. Here, all peoples accept one God, rather than each walking with its own. Moreover, the "holy remnant" creates a new Jerusalem partly by "taking captive" those "whose captives they were." Indeed, the last lines of Isaiah promise, "[They] shall look upon the carcasses of those who have transgressed against me; for their worm shall not die, neither shall their fire be quenched, and they shall be an abhorring unto all flesh" (66:24). Do the carcasses of sinners memorialize what must be vanquished for this home and holiness to be?

17. Hannah Arendt, *Men in Dark Times* (New York: HBJ, 1968), 21; Philip Roth, *The Human Stain* (New York: Houghton Mifflin, 2000). Visions of a new

covenant are reworked four hundred years later by Jesus, who continues the prophetic practice of resisting the worldly authority of states, law, and priests. He asks their key question—What does God require of us?—and condenses their answer: To love God means to love thy neighbor as thyself. He thus seeks God in the other, but now in Gentiles and not only in the Hebrew poor. Scholars thus ask, How does Jesus revise, reject, and affirm the tradition he inherits? For the controversies interpreting Jesus, see Paula Frederickson, *Jesus of Nazareth: King of the Jews* (New York: Vintage, 1999).

18. Voegelin, *Israel and Revelation;* Leo Strauss, "Jerusalem and Athens: Some Preliminary Reflections," in *Studies in Platonic Political Philosophy,* 147–73 (Chicago: University of Chicago Press, 1983), and the preface to *Spinoza's Critique of Religion,* 1–31 (Chicago: University of Chicago Press, 1997).

19. Since Spinoza's prophet "interprets the revelations of God to those who are unable to attain sure knowledge of the things revealed by God," his prophecy is Immanuel Kant's tutelage, but Brown argues that philosophy democratizes prophecy by using reason to end tutelage. Spinoza quoted in Norman O. Brown, *Apocalypse and/or Metamorphosis* (Berkeley and Los Angeles: University of California Press, 1991), 97; for Dionysian Christianity, see his *Love's Body* (New York: Vintage, 1966), 196.

20. See Michael Walzer, *Interpretation and Social Criticism* (Cambridge: Harvard University Press, 1987) and *Exodus and Revolution* (New York: Basic Books, 1985). For the inverse view, linking prophets (and Jewish particularity) to universalistic revelation, see Norman Podhoretz, *The Prophets: Who They Were, What They Are* (New York: Free Press, 2003).

21. Weber, *Ancient Judaism,* 268. For Hobbes, "enthusiasm" marks those "possessed" by the delusion that they possess God's word, but some *use* prophetic speech strategically to authorize self-interested ends. They are either lunatics or charlatans, and their "spirited" speech incites seditious action, while sovereignty depends on creating public reason. Are we heirs of Hobbes in how we "read" prophecy? See Brian Garsten, *Saving Persuasion* (Cambridge: Harvard University Press, 2006).

22. Jerry Falwell, quoted in Laurie Goodstein, "After the Attacks: Finding Fault; Falwell's Finger-Pointing Inappropriate, Bush Says," *New York Times,* September 15, 2001; Falwell's other sermons are quoted from and available at http://www.juntosociety.com.

23. Lincoln is quoting Matthew 18:7 or Luke 17:1.

24. All passages quoted from Frederick Douglass, "The Meaning of July Fourth for the Negro," in *The Life and Writings of Frederick Douglass,* ed. Phillip S. Foner, vol. 2 (New York: International Publishers, 1952), 181–204. On Douglass, see James A. Colaiaco, *Frederick Douglass and the Fourth of July* (New York: Palgrave Macmillan, 2006), and William Andrews, *To Tell a Free Story: The First Century of Afro-American Autobiography, 1760–1865* (Urbana: University of Illinois Press, 1988).

25. Jacques Rancière, *Disagreement: Politics and Philosophy,* trans. Julie Rose (Minneapolis: University of Minnesota Press, 1999).

26. For a parallel argument, see Bonnie Honig, "Declarations of Independence: Arendt and Derrida on the Problem of Founding a Republic," *American Political Science Review* 85, no. 1 (1991): 97–113.

27. Prophets must come to terms with this past and make it meaningful or redeem it because they cannot change or escape it. And because slavery is a form of social death, they must negate its assumed finality, to imagine redemption as rebirth into life: Despair is never warranted because servitude is contingent and transformation is possible. Since capacities to act depend on just this faith, which is needed most when it seems least credible, prophets insist on faith in redemption. See Orlando Patterson, *Freedom in the Making of Western Culture* (New York: Basic Books, 1991), 5–11, 319–29; Joanna Brooks, *American Lazarus: Religion and the Rise of African-American and Native American Literatures* (New York: Oxford University Press, 2003); Theosophus H. Smith, *Conjuring Culture: Biblical Formations of Black America* (New York: Oxford University Press, 1994); Cornel West, "Black Strivings in a Twilight Civilization," in *The Cornel West Reader*, 87–118 (New York: Basic Books, 1999).

28. Kimberly K. Smith, *The Dominion of Voice: Riot, Reason, and Romance in Antebellum Politics* (Lawrence: University Press of Kansas, 1999); see also Lynn Sanders, "Against Deliberation," *Political Theory* 25, no. 3 (1997): 347–76.

29. Stanley Cavell, *Must We Mean What We Say?* (Cambridge: Cambridge University Press, 1976), 238–64.

30. Douglass ends his 1845 autobiography by quoting Jeremiah's God ("Shall I not visit for such things? Saith the Lord") and then Jeremiah himself ("Shall not my soul be avenged on a nation such as this?").

31. Hartz echoes Tocqueville's view of an uncontested consensus about possessive individualism and popular sovereignty. Louis Hartz, *The Liberal Tradition in America* (New York: Harvest, 1955). Miller echoes Tocqueville's view of America as a "Puritan and trading nation." But Miller narrates a shift from conscience to interest, from collective liability to individualism, from Jonathan Edwards to Emerson and Horatio Alger. Perry Miller, *Errand into the Wilderness* (New York: Harper, 1964). On the relationship of Puritanism and liberalism, also see Robert Bellah, *The Broken Covenant: American Civil Religion in Time of Trial* (New York: Seabury, 1975); Sacvan Bercovitch, *The American Jeremiad* (Madison: University of Wisconsin Press, 1978) and *The Rites of Assent: Transformations in the Symbolic Construction of America* (New York: Routledge, 1993); Michael Rogin, *Ronald Reagan, the Movie, and Other Episodes in Political Demonology* (Berkeley and Los Angeles: University of California Press, 1987); Richard Slotkin, *Regeneration through Violence: The Mythology of the American Frontier, 1600–1860* (Middletown, Conn.: Wesleyan University Press, 1973).

32. Bellah, *Broken Covenant,* 172. Sounding like Falwell, Bellah declares that republicanism and liberalism are "antithetical" because one is oriented by virtue and the other by interest. But Falwell attacks what he calls liberalism while endorsing free enterprise and representative government.

33. Michael Rogin, *Blackface/White Noise* (Berkeley and Los Angeles: University of California Press, 1996), 23–27.

34. Herman Melville, *White Jacket*, chapter 36, quoted in Bellah, *Broken Covenant*, 38. Melville goes on to say, "God has predestined, mankind expects, great things from our race, and . . . the rest of the nations must soon be in our rear. We are the pioneers of the world; the advance-guard, sent on through the wilderness of untried things, to break a new path. . . . Long enough have we been sceptics in regard to ourselves, and doubted whether . . . the political Messiah had come. But he has come in us, if we would but give utterance to his prompting. And let us remember that with ourselves, almost for the first time in the history of the earth, national selfishness is unbounded philanthropy, for we cannot do good to America, but we give alms to the world."

35. Michael Rogin, *Fathers and Children: Andrew Jackson and the Subjugation of the American Indians* (New York: Alfred A. Knopf, 1975), 312.

36. Bellah, *Broken Covenant*, 3, 14, 50, 130.

37. Ibid., 153.

38. Sheldon Wolin, "America's Civil Religion," *Democracy* 2 (April 1983): 7–17.

39. Regretting the antinational turn taken by the academic Left, these figures use prophetic language (and often the example of Martin Luther King Jr.) to argue that *democratic* norms can be made the test of national existence. Also see Rogers Smith, *Civic Ideals* (New Haven: Yale University Press, 1999).

40. Bercovitch, *American Jeremiad*, 9.

41. Sacvan Bercovitch, *American Jeremiad*, 179, 187, 205, and "Rights of Assent: Rhetoric, Ritual, and the Ideology of American Consensus," in *The American Self: Myth, Ideology, and Popular Culture*, ed. Sam Girgus (Albuquerque: University of New Mexico Press, 1981), 5–6, 13, 20. Biblical prophecy is "at war" with "secular" society and a "grossly inadequate" present, says Bercovitch, opening a gap between God and secular society, between "vision and fact" as well as between tradition and the present. That jeremiad is "Americanized" by closing the gaps.

42. Bercovitch, *Rites of Assent*, 2, 20, 29, 65.

43. Bercovitch, *American Jeremiad*, 179–81.

44. I owe the formulation of the Marxian and the Nietzschean to Mark Reinhardt. "Fundamental pre-requisites of life" from Nietzsche, *On the Genealogy of Morals*, 120.

45. Among the postidentity theorists to whom my own view of political theory is especially indebted are Wendy Brown, *States of Injury* (Princeton: Princeton University Press, 1995) and *Politics out of History* (Princeton: Princeton University Press, 2001); Judith Butler, *The Psychic Life of Power* (Stanford: Stanford University Press, 1997); William Connolly, *Political Theory and Modernity* (London: Basil Blackwell, 1988) and *Identity\Difference;* Bonnie Honig, *Political Theory and the Displacement of Politics* (Ithaca, N.Y.: Cornell University Press, 1993); Ernesto Laclau and Chantal Mouffe, *Hegemony and Socialist Strategy* (London: Verso, 1985); Claude Lefort, *Democracy and Political Theory* (Minneapolis: University of Minnesota Press, 1988); Linda Zerilli, *Feminism and the Abyss of Freedom* (Chicago: University of Chicago Press, 2005).

46. See especially William Connolly, *Why I Am Not a Secularist* (Minneapolis:

University of Minnesota Press, 1999) and *Pluralism* (Durham, N.C.: Duke University Press, 2005). For the European referents, see Giorgio Agamben, *Remnants of Auschwitz* (New York: Zone Books, 1995); Walter Benjamin, "Theses on the Philosophy of History," in *Illuminations*, 253–64 (New York: Schocken Books, 1969), and "Theologico-Political Fragment," in *Reflections*, 312–13 (New York: HBJ, 1978); Jacques Derrida, "Force of Law: The 'Mystical Foundation of Authority,'" in *Cardozo Law Review* 11 (1990): 919–1045; Emmanuel Levinas, *Entre-Nous* (New York: Columbia University Press, 1998); Carl Schmitt, *Political Theology* (Chicago: University of Chicago Press, 1985).

47. Among noteworthy exceptions to my overly broad—arguably unfair or even false—generalizations about political theory and race, see Lawrie Balfour, *Evidence of Things Not Said: James Baldwin and the Promise of American Democracy* (Ithaca, N.Y.: Cornell University Press, 2001); William Connolly, "Tocqueville, Religiosity, and Pluralization" and "Fundamentalism in America," both in *Ethos of Pluralization*, 105–34 and 163–98 (Minneapolis: University of Minnesota Press, 1995); Thomas L. Dumm, *United States* (Ithaca, N.Y.: Cornell University Press, 1994); Eddie Glaude, *In a Shade of Blue: Pragmatism and the Politics of Black America* (Chicago: University of Chicago Press, 2006); Bonnie Honig, *Democracy and the Foreigner* (Princeton: Princeton University Press, 2001); Charles Mills, *The Racial Contract* (Ithaca, N.Y.: Cornell University Press, 1999); and the entire corpus of Cornel West.

48. Ralph Waldo Emerson, "The American Scholar," in *Selected Essays*, ed. Larzer Ziff, 83–106 (New York: Penguin, 1982); Stanley Cavell, *In Quest of the Ordinary* (Chicago: University of Chicago Press, 1988).

49. John H. Schaar, "Legitimacy in the Modern State," in *Legitimacy in the Modern State*, 15–51 (New Brunswick, N.J.: Transaction, 1981).

50. Wallace Stevens, *The Necessary Angel: Essays on Reality and Imagination* (New York: Vintage, 1951).

51. Weber, *Ancient Judaism*, 281.

52. For Kenneth Burke, "true irony, humble irony is based upon a sense of the fundamental kinship with the enemy, as one *needs* him, is *indebted* to him, is not merely outside him as an observer but contains him *within*." Because a "we" is often made by violent scapegoating of an other, "kinship with the enemy" is a crucial democratic value: By irony actors credit that commitments they hold absolutely are one among other possible "tables of value." Burke quoted in Stephen Hartnet, *Democratic Dissent and Cultural Fictions* (Urbana: University of Illinois Press, 2002), 16–35; cf. Beth Eddy, *Rites of Identity* (Princeton: Princeton University Press, 2002), which reads Burke in relation to race and religion.

53. Michael Walzer, *Interpretation and Social Criticism;* Michael J. Sandel, *Democracy's Discontent: America in Search of a Public Philosophy* (Cambridge, Mass.: Belknap Press, 1996). For William Connolly's critique of Sandel, see "Civic Republicanism and Civic Pluralism: The Silent Struggle of Michael Sandel," in *Debating Democracy's Discontent: Essays on Politics, Law, and Public Philosophy*, ed. Anita L. Allen and Milton C. Regan, 205–11 (New York: Oxford University Press, 1998).

54. Before the linguistic turn, the danger in "identity" was scapegoating, as

Kenneth Burke and Ralph Ellison argued. In contrast to "bad faith," though, "achieving" an "authentic" identity remained the existential project. In psychoanalytic terms, that meant differentiating from "identification" with parental authority. But once "identity" means "sameness," politics is aligned with difference. Claims to identity then appear as fictions that deny the fluid, fragmented, and crosscutting multiplicity of actual attachments and differences. When "identity" is constituted—by subjection to a sign or category—then the point, as Foucault says, is not to discover what we are but to refuse it. Michel Foucault, "The Subject Is Power," in *Essential Works of Foucault*, ed. James D. Faubion, vol. 31 (New York: New Press, 2000), 336.

55. Hannah Arendt, "Collective Responsibility," in *Responsibility and Judgment*, ed. Jerome Kohn, 147–58 (New York: Schocken Books, 2003); also see Judith Butler, *Precarious Life* (London: Verso, 2004).

56. James Baldwin, *The Price of the Ticket* (New York: Macmillan, 1985), 395.

57. The erotic and familial language that bridges biblical prophecy and the work of Baldwin and Morrison, if we read it generously, does not (only) misconceive politics but also tells a truth about it. The truth is that there is no politics without libidinal energy and psychic fantasy, which lead us to others, and generate disappointment, aggression, conflict. In epochal political moments, fundamental fantasies are reconstituted, and abiding attachments are repudiated or significantly reworked—as we see by contrasting Jesus to Paul or Baldwin to Richard Wright.

58. Victoria Hattam, *In the Shadow of Race: Jews, Latinos, and Immigrant Politics in the United States* (Chicago: University of Chicago Press, 2007).

2. Thoreau, the Reluctant Prophet

1. Edmund Wilson, *Patriotic Gore: Studies in the Literature of the American Civil War* (New York: Farrar, Straus and Giroux, 1962); for material on Brown, see n45.

2. Page numbers for quotations from Henry David Thoreau, *Walden* (New York: Holt, Rinehart and Winston, 1961); "Civil Disobedience," "Slavery in Massachusetts," and "A Plea for Captain John Brown," all in *Civil Disobedience and Other Essays* (New York: Dover, 1993); and "The Last Days of John Brown," in *Reform Papers*, ed. Wendell Glick (Princeton: Princeton University Press, 1973) are given parenthetically in the text.

3. Søren Kierkegaard, quoted in Erik H. Erikson, *Young Man Luther: A Study in Psychoanalysis and History* (New York: Norton Library, 1962), 71. On Protestantism and abolition, see Robert Abzug, *Cosmos Crumbling: American Reform and the Religious Imagination* (New York: Oxford University Press, 1994); Donald M. Scott, "Abolitionism as a Sacred Vocation," in *Antislavery Reconsidered: New Perspectives on the Abolitionists*, ed. Perry Lewis and Michael Fellman, 51–74 (Baton Rouge: Louisiana State University Press, 1979); John Stauffer, *The Black Hearts of Men: Radical Abolitionists and the Transformation of Race* (Cambridge: Harvard University Press, 2002).

4. I accept the arguments of George Kateb and Jane Bennett that Thoreau

moves beyond possessive individualism and the idea of a unitary or stable subject. Jane Bennett, *Thoreau's Nature* (New York: Rowman and Littlefield, 2002); George Kateb, *Inner Ocean: Individualism and Democratic Culture* (Ithaca, N.Y.: Cornell University Press, 1992). But their readings exclude Thoreau's religiosity and the profound ways he retells *national* myths in which he is invested. My "prophetic" Thoreau is thus deeply indebted to Stanley Cavell, whose Thoreau engages his neighbors, their worldly circumstances, and language. Stanley Cavell, *Senses of Walden* (New York: Viking, 1972). But Cavell sanitizes Thoreau by eliding his abolitionist orthodoxy and his infatuation with John Brown. These readings *secularize* Thoreau in ways that are very appealing, even redemptive, but meanwhile his religiosity and abolitionism remain at once disturbingly and profoundly connected to the meaning of race in American political life.

5. Thanks to Bonnie Honig for help on these ideas and passages.

6. Melville's *Moby Dick* appeared in 1851; Stowe's *Uncle Tom's Cabin,* in 1852; Thoreau's *Walden,* in 1854; Whitman's *Leaves of Grass,* in 1855.

7. Albert J. von Frank, *The Trials of Anthony Burns: Freedom and Slavery in Emerson's Boston* (Cambridge: Harvard University Press, 1998), quoted in David Reynolds's review of that book, "Slavery on Trial," *New York Times,* March 8, 1998.

8. Thoreau, *Journal,* ed. John C. Broderick and Robert Sattelmeyer, vol. 2 (Princeton: Princeton University Press, 1981), 264. Responding to vigilante violence against abolitionists in 1838, Lincoln's so-called Lyceum Address ("The Perpetuation of Our Political Institutions," speech before the Young Men's Lyceum of Springfield, Illinois, January 27, 1838) warned American men that their republic was in danger *only* if passion were to lead them to reject the authority of the law and of constitutionally mandated ways to amend it. "Let reverence for the laws be breathed by every American mother to the lisping babe. . . . let it become the *political religion* of the nation." For Thoreau, this is entombment: He says "patriotism" is "a maggot in their [Americans] heads" because they are already dead (*Walden,* 19).

9. In "Civil Disobedience," Thoreau imagines a state that truly recognizes "the individual as a higher and independent power from which all its own power and authority are derived" (18). Such a state would "cherish" its critics as "neighbors" and "wise minorities" rather than "crucify" or "excommunicate" them as enemies (7).

10. Simon Critchley, "Metaphysics in the Dark: A Response to Richard Rorty and Ernesto Laclau," *Political Theory* 26, no. 6 (1998): 803–17.

11. William Blake, "Marriage of Heaven and Hell," in *Blake: Complete Writings,* ed. Geoffrey Keynes (New York: Oxford University Press, 1972), 153.

12. Frederick Douglass, *Narrative of the Life of Frederick Douglass, An American Slave* (New York: Anchor Press, 1973), 74; see also Sadiya Hartmann, *Scenes of Subjection: Terror, Slavery, and Self-Making in Nineteenth-Century America* (New York: Oxford University Press, 1997); Karen Sanchez-Eppler, "Bodily Bonds: The Intersecting Rhetorics of Feminism and Abolition," *Representations* 24 (1998): 28–59.

13. Hannah Arendt, "Civil Disobedience," in *Crises in the Republic* (New York:

Harvest, 1972), 60–62. On Lincoln, see David Greenstone, *The Lincoln Persuasion: Remaking American Liberalism* (Princeton: Princeton University Press, 1993); Harry Jaffa, *Crisis in the House Divided: An Interpretation of the Issues in the Lincoln–Douglas Debates* (Chicago: University of Chicago Press, 1982). Views of Lincoln often echo Weber's two ethics in "Politics as a Vocation."

14. The critique of moralism is developed best in Wendy Brown, "Moralism as Anti-Politics," in *Politics out of History*, 18–44 (Princeton: Princeton University Press, 2001), and Jane Bennett, "Moraline Drift," in *The Politics of Moralizing*, ed. Jane Bennett and Michael Shapiro, 11–26 (New York: Routledge, 2002). For distinctions between "moral" and "political" judgment, also see Hannah Arendt, *Lectures on Kant's Political Philosophy* (Chicago: University of Chicago Press, 1992), and Sheldon Wolin, "Plato: Political Philosophy versus Politics," in *Politics and Vision: Continuity and Innovation in Western Political Thought*, 28–68 (Boston: Little, Brown, 1960). On dirty hands, see Maurice Merleau-Ponty, "Notes on Machiavelli," in *Signs*, 211–23 (Evanston, Ill.: Northwestern University Press, 1964).

15. The two best defenses of abolitionism against such arguments are Eileen Kraditor, *Means and Ends in American Abolitionism: Garrison and His Critics on Strategy and Tactics, 1834–1850* (New York: Vintage, 1969), and Joel Olson, "The Freshness of Fanaticism: The Abolitionists and the Democratic Uses of Zealotry," *Perspectives on Politics* 5, no. 4 (December 2007): 685–701.

16. Kraditor, *Means and Ends in American Abolitionism*, 276.

17. Hannah Arendt, "Collective Responsibility," in *Responsibility and Judgment*, ed. Jerome Kohn (New York: Schocken Books, 2003), 153–55; Arendt, "Civil Disobedience," 95–99. Thoreau and Arendt both split the moral and political, but he engages the political in Arendt's sense of "action in concert" and "association," and she at her best sees a moral dimension transfigured by speech to others.

18. Jonathan Schell, introduction to *Letters from Prison and Other Essays*, by Adam Michnik (Berkeley and Los Angeles: University of California Press, 1985), xvii.

19. Henry Abelove, "From Thoreau to Queer Politics," *Yale Journal of Criticism* 6, no. 2 (1993): 17–27. On the difference between democracy as a form of rule and as episodic insurgency, see Sheldon Wolin, "Fugitive Democracy," in *Democracy and Difference: Contesting the Boundaries of the Political*, ed. Seyla Benhabib, 31–45 (Princeton: Princeton University Press, 1996).

20. Peter Euben, "Democratic Accountability and Socratic Dialectic," in *Corrupting Youth*, 91–108 (Princeton: Princeton University Press, 1997). To link Socrates and Thoreau, see Dana R. Villa, "Socrates, Lessing, and Thoreau: The Image of Alienated Citizenship in Hannah Arendt," in *Liberal Modernism and Democratic Individuality*, ed. Austin Sarat and Dana Villa, 47–63 (Princeton: Princeton University Press, 1996).

21. Thoreau negotiates different "perspectives" rather than invoking one: "Seen from a lower point of view, the Constitution, with all its faults, is very good. . . . even this State and the American government are, in many respects, very admirable and rare things to be thankful for . . . ; but seen from a point of

view a little higher, they are what I have described them; seen from a higher still and the highest [point of view] who shall say what they are or that they are worth looking at or thinking of at all?" ("Disobedience," 16).

22. Henry Thoreau, "Life without Principle," 75–90, in *Civil Disobedience and Other Essays,* 87. Cavell's response to Emerson's use of the word "slavery" applies here: Is it "merely a weak, metaphorical way of feeling and speaking, one that blunts both the fact of literal slavery and the facts of the particular ways in which we freely sell ourselves out?" Cavell, *Philosophical Passages: Wittgenstein, Emerson, Austin, Derrida* (Cambridge, Mass.: Blackwell, 1995), 16.

23. Cavell, *Senses of Walden,* 112.

24. Thoreau, "Reform and Reformers," in *Reform Papers,* 182–83. However "afflicted by the sight of misery around him and animated by the desire to relieve it," any reformer would "instantly and unconsciously sign off from these pure labors" if he had "righted some obscure and perhaps unrecognized private grievance" (184).

25. In Thoreau's view, therefore, a true reformer would "not stay to be an overseer of the poor, but endeavor to become one of the worthies of the world" (*Walden,* 64). He seeks exemplary rather than missionary reform: "Be sure that you give the poor the aid they most need, though it be your example which leaves them far behind. If you give them money, spend yourself with it." Cf. Thoreau, "Reform and Reformers," 184, 191–92.

26. Thoreau, "Walking," in *Civil Disobedience and Other Essays,* 73.

27. Blake, "There Is NO Natural Religion," in Keynes, *Blake: Complete Writings,* 98; Emerson, "The Poet," in *Selected Essays,* ed. Larzer Ziff (New York: Viking/Penguin, 1982), 279. On the exalted idea of "the poet" among transcendentalists and its literary and cultural context, see Laurence Buell, *New England Literary Culture* (Cambridge: Harvard University Press, 1986). On the shift from Puritanism to romanticism, see Perry Miller, "From Edwards to Emerson," in *Errand into the Wilderness,* 184–203 (Cambridge: Harvard University Press, 1956), and "International Romanticism," in *Nature's Nation,* 175–84 (Cambridge: Belknap Press/Harvard University Press, 1967). On the disenchantment of romanticism, see Simon Critchley, *Very Little . . . Almost Nothing: Death, Philosophy, Literature* (New York: Routledge, 1997).

28. Alfred Kazin, *God and the American Writer* (New York: Vintage, 1998), 118; Harold Bloom calls romanticism "severely displaced Protestantism" because redemption is not undone but invested in nature. Bloom, *Anxiety of Influence* (New York: Oxford University Press, 1997), 152.

29. George Kateb, *The Inner Ocean: Individualism and Democratic Culture* (Ithaca, N.Y.: Cornell University Press, 1992), 73, 75, 93; Emerson, "The Poet," 279–80.

30. For Chanticleer, indeed, "whoever fronts a fact, even if it be his neighbor, faces a wilderness between him and it." Signifying on the "wildness" in wilderness, Thoreau also sees "an instinct toward a higher or as it is named spiritual life" and "another toward a primitive, rank and savage one, and I reverence them both. I love the wild not less than the good" (*Walden,* 176). Against the moral binary of monotheism, he sustains the tension of a Blakean "contrary," for he

affirms both the need to endow life with meaning and the value of unredeemed life in itself. The "wildness" of Chanticleer's voice is not a "savage" antithesis to morality but whatever resists or exceeds our efforts at signification. On Thoreau's terrifying experience on Katahdin, the Maine mountain whose sublimity exposed the limits of language, see Ronald Wesley Hoag, "The Mark on the Wilderness: Thoreau's Contact with Ktaadn," *Texas Studies in Literature and Language* 24, no. 1 (1982): 23–46.

31. On Thoreau defeating the idea of unchanging ground, see Walter Benn Michaels, "Walden's False Bottom," *Glyph* 1 (1977): 132–49.

32. Drafts of *Walden* show him deleting the self-pitying first version of the epigraph: "I could tell a pitiful story respecting myself, with a sufficient list of failures, and flow as humbly as the gutters, but I do not propose to write an ode to dejection."

33. For such critiques of Thoreau, see Sacvan Bercovitch, *The American Jere-miad* (Madison: University of Wisconsin Press, 1978), 186–88, and Leo Marx, "The Two Thoreaus," October 26, 1978, 37–44; "The Struggle over Thoreau," June 24, 1999, 60–64; and "The Full Thoreau," July 15, 1999, 44–47; all in *New York Review of Books*.

34. Cavell, *Senses of Walden*, 33, 92, 85–86. The parallel between the author-ity of language and that of God is that we are lost if we repudiate the criteria for using our words in their ordinary contexts, but we must be free to refuse if we are to consent truly. Turning people from skepticism to ordinary language, Cavell echoes the prophets' turning people from idolatry to a God near at hand.

35. Thoreau, "Walking," 65; Norman Mailer, *The Presidential Papers* (New York: Berkley Medallion, 1963), 210.

36. William Carlos Williams, *In the American Grain* (New York: New Direc-tions, 1956), 111, 136. Thoreau's retelling initiates a chorus of artists and critics, from William Carlos Williams, Randolph Bourne, and D. H. Lawrence in the 1920s, to Norman Mailer and Allen Ginsberg in the 1950s and early 1960s. They take up Chanticleer's poetic voice—ecstatic, libidinal, and aesthetic. They tell stories of rebirth from the death-in-life enfranchised men impose on themselves. They recast the nationalist rhetoric of a "new" world to support countercultural and democratic projects. See also D. H. Lawrence, *Studies in Classic American Literature* (New York: Seltzer, 1923), and Mailer, *Presidential Papers*.

37. "I went to the woods because I wished to live deliberately, to front only the essential facts of life, and see if I could not learn what it had to teach, and not, when I came to die, discover that I had not lived. I did not wish to live what was not life, living is so dear; nor did I wish to practice resignation, unless it was quite necessary. I wanted to live deep and suck out all the marrow of life . . . and if it proved mean, well then to get the whole and genuine meanness of it and publish its meanness to the world; or if it were sublime, to know it by experience and be able to give a true account of it in my next excursion. For most men, it seems to me, are in a strange uncertainty about it, whether it is of the devil or of God, and have *somewhat hastily* concluded that it is the chief end of man here 'to glorify God and enjoy him forever'" (*Walden*, 74).

38. Building from inside-out is sacramental—an "outward and visible sign

of an inward and spiritual grace." A worldly dwelling and a self are two sides of one experiment in answering the question of authority. For builders must ask, "What do we want most to dwell most near to?" And Thoreau answers, "Not . . . where men most congregate, but to the perennial source of our life," which "will vary with different natures." For "nearest to all things is that power which fashions their being. *Next* to us the grandest laws are continually being executed. *Next* to us is not the workman whom we have hired . . . but the workman whose work we are" (*Walden*, 110). Indwellers are not Prometheans; rather, they build in relation to a generative "source," which they must reverence to flourish. Thoreau thus transforms conscience from a slavedriver to a neighbor and workman "next" to the "I."

39. Cavell, *Senses of Walden*, 85–86. On the necessity of solitude for politics, see Hannah Arendt, "Philosophy and Politics," *Social Research* 57, no. 1 (Spring 1990): 88–90. If we discover the "strangeness" within, we can "promote the togetherness of those foreigners we all recognize ourselves to be." Julia Kristeva, *Strangers to Ourselves* (New York: Columbia University Press, 1991), 3.

40. Thoreau, "Life without Principle," 88.

41. Thoreau's view of cultivation betrays his abiding attachment to a purity that dichotomizes higher and lower: "The spirit" must "pervade and control every member and function of the body and transmute what in form is the grossest sensuality into purity and devotion." To "treat himself with increasing respect," he must "practice some new austerity, to let his mind descend into his body and redeem it" (*Walden*, 184, 186).

42. See Michael Warner, "*Walden*'s Erotic Economy," in *Comparative American Identities: Race, Sex, and Nationality in the Modern Text*, ed. Hortense J. Spillers, 157–74 (New York: Routledge, 1991).

43. Herman Melville, *Moby Dick* (New York: W. W. Norton, 2002), 165, 140.

44. See Michael Rogin, *Subversive Genealogy: The Politics and Art of Herman Melville* (New York: Alfred A. Knopf, 1993).

45. David Reynolds, *John Brown, Abolitionist: The Man Who Killed Slavery, Sparked the Civil War, and Seeded Civil Rights* (New York: Alfred A. Knopf, 2005), 334, 346. Also see Stephen Oates, *To Purge This Land with Blood: A Biography of John Brown* (Amherst: University of Massachusetts, 1984); David M. Potter, "Harpers Ferry: A Revolution That Failed," in *The Impending Crisis: 1848–1861*, 356–84 (New York: Harper Colophon, 1976); and Stauffer, *Black Hearts of Men*.

46. Reynolds, *John Brown, Abolitionist*, 346–47; Bob Pepperman Taylor, *America's Bachelor Uncle: Thoreau and the American Polity* (Lawrence: University Press of Kansas, 1996), 150.

47. Reynolds, *John Brown, Abolitionist*, 300.

48. Lawrie Balfour, "The Argument of John Brown" (paper presented at the American Political Science Association annual meeting, San Francisco, August 30–September 2, 2001).

49. Russell Banks, "John Brown's Body: James Baldwin and Frank Shatz in Conversation," *Transition* 9, nos. 1–2 (2000): 250–66.

50. For such assertions, see Kazin, *God and the American Writer*, 55–56, 72–73; Michael Meyer, "Thoreau's Rescue of John Brown from History," in *Studies in*

the American Renaissance, ed. Joel Myerson, 301–16 (Boston: Twayne, 1980); Gilman M. Ostrander, "Notes and Documents: Emerson, Thoreau, and John Brown," *Mississippi Valley Historical Review* 39 (1952–53): 713–26; Lewis Hyde, "Henry Thoreau, John Brown, and the Problem of Prophetic Action," *Raritan* 22, no. 2 (2002): 53–61. For an account emphasizing the performative, but to other conclusions than mine, see Jack Turner, "Performing Conscience: Thoreau, Political Action, and the Plea for John Brown," *Political Theory* 33, no. 4 (August 2005): 448–71.

51. Balfour, "Argument of John Brown"; Emerson quoted in Reynolds, *John Brown, Abolitionist,* 366; Lincoln, "Cooper Union Address," in *Abraham Lincoln, Great Speeches* (New York: Dover, 1991), 45–47.

52. See especially Stauffer, *Black Hearts of Men.*

53. Emerson, "Courage," in *Complete Works,* vol. 7, *Society and Solitude,* quoted in Reynolds, *John Brown,* 366. See also Wendell Phillips, "John Brown and Harpers Ferry," in *Wendell Phillips on Civil Rights and Freedom,* ed. Louis Filler, 95–113 (New York: Hill and Wang, 1982).

54. Frederick Douglass, quoted in James Colaiaco, *Frederick Douglass and the Fourth of July* (New York: Palgrave Macmillan, 2006), 81–85.

55. *The Life and Writings of Frederick Douglass,* ed. Phillip S. Foner, vol. 2, *The Pre-Civil War Decade, 1850–1860* (New York: International Publishers, 1952), 93, 458.

56. Quoted in Colaiaco, *Frederick Douglass and the Fourth of July,* 136–37.

57. Foner, *Life and Writings of Frederick Douglass,* 2:460.

58. Baldwin quoted in "Interview with Frank Shatz, 1973," transcribed in Banks, "John Brown's Body," 263, 254.

59. Eugene V. Debs, "John Brown: History's Greatest Hero," in *Writing and Speeches of Eugene V. Debs* (New York: Hermitage Press, 1948), 280–81. Nick Salvatore argues, in *Eugene V. Debs: Citizen and Socialist* (Urbana: University of Illinois Press, 1982), that Debs offers himself in this role of Christ/Brown. Sacvan Bercovitch, *The American Jeremiad* (Madison: University of Wisconsin Press, 1978), 160. I am indebted here to Lawrie Balfour's concern that "the truth of Brown's life should not be read as an American truth" (ibid.).

60. Before Brown's death, Thoreau delivered "A Plea for Captain John Brown," and after Brown's execution, he delivered "The Last Days of John Brown."

61. Greeley quoted in Reynolds, *John Brown, Abolitionist,* 335. In Kansas Brown was involved in the Pottawatomie massacres, a vicious raid to retaliate for a bloody attack on antislavery proponents.

62. According to Alfred Kazin, "only Thoreau, among New England writers, identified his life and his looming early death so wholly with the liberation of the slaves as John Brown did. Of course John Brown becomes Thoreau's saint, his idea of perfect holiness in action." That identification "impaled" each "on a single idea, an exclusive view of life, that permitted no compromise with what the rest of the world might think." But they lived "this holy narrowness" differently. Echoing Arendt's distinction of the moral and the political, Kazin's Thoreau wanted "to be eternally right with himself," while Brown, a "true revo-

lutionary," wanted to "do right, cost what it may." Kazin, *God and the American Writer,* 70. I have tried to trouble this distinction.

63. Thoreau is gripped by the idea of joining the transcendental and the manly in a heroic purity that redeems what is base: "When a man stands up serenely against the condemnation and vengeance of mankind, rising above them . . . even though he were of late the vilest murderer who has settled that matter with himself—the spectacle is a sublime one" ("Plea," 40). Thoreau may refer here to Brown's involvement in the bloody murders of Pottawatomie, but to psychoanalytically inclined readers, his insistence on the necessity both of violence and of Brown's execution signals a profound conflict about (his own) aggression toward the state and his neighbors. He consciously justifies why "my thoughts are murder to the state" ("Slavery," 30), but he *unconsciously* feels guilty about his aggression and atones for it by endorsing self-sacrifice. Open aggression, without atoning self-sacrifice, is not an option. See Raymond Gozzi, ed., *Thoreau's Psychology* (Lanham, Md.: University Press of America, 1983).

64. Oates, *To Purge This Land with Blood,* 318–20. Reynolds does not emphasize this irony.

Interlude

1. Richard Rorty, *Achieving Our Country: Leftist Thought in Twentieth-Century America* (Cambridge: Harvard University Press, 1998); Michael Walzer, *Interpretation and Social Criticism* (Cambridge: Harvard University Press, 1987), 87; Gunnar Myrdal, *An American Dilemma: The Negro Problem and Modern Democracy* (1944; repr., New York: Harper and Row, 1962); Sacvan Bercovitch, *The Rites of Assent* (New York: Routledge: 1993), 29.

2. My formulation of their relationship to American liberal nationalism is indebted to Nikhil Singh, *Black Is a Country: Race and the Unfinished Struggle for Democracy* (Cambridge: Harvard University Press, 2004).

3. Henry David Thoreau, *Walden* (New York: Holt, Rinehart and Winston, 1961), 272; Martin Luther King Jr., "The Drum Major Instinct," sermon delivered February 4, 1968, in *Testament of Hope: The Essential Writings and Speeches of Martin Luther King,* ed. James M. Washington (New York: HarperCollins, 1986), 259.

4. James Baldwin, *The Price of the Ticket: Collected Nonfiction, 1948–1985* (New York: Macmillan, 1985), 458.

5. Friedrich Nietzsche, *Thus Spake Zarathustra,* trans. Walter Kaufman (New York: Vintage, 1966), 141; Stanley Cavell, "Knowing and Acknowledging," in *Must We Mean What We Say?* (Cambridge: Cambridge University Press, 1976), 238–66.

6. What Uday Mehta calls "liberal exclusion" occurs because normative manliness and citizenship are forged through codes of racial and sexual difference that give women and blacks a *symbolic* meaning that fixes them in a subordinate *social* place. On the one hand, white men (like Thoreau) can cross over to appropriate the meaning of red or black: To declare independence of the fathers by identifying with racial outcasts is the masquerade repeatedly

refounding America—not in legislatures but in tea parties, frontier violence, antebellum minstrelsy, and youth culture. Dissent and generational revolt are inconceivable without the cross-racial identifications that often—not always—leave actual others fixed in place. On the other hand, these others (like King and Baldwin) must negotiate the symbolic meanings written on their bodies as they struggle to forge agency on their own terms. Uday Singh Mehta, *Liberalism and Empire* (Chicago: University of Chicago Press, 1999).

7. King, *Testament of Hope*, 165.

8. James Baldwin, "Everybody's Protest Novel," in *Price of the Ticket*, 27–41; "The Creative Process," in *Price of the Ticket*, 318.

9. Jacques Rancière, *Disagreement: Politics and Philosophy*, trans. Julie Rose (Minneapolis: University of Minnesota Press, 1999).

3. Martin Luther King Jr.'s Theistic Prophecy

1. Raymond Williams, *Marxism and Literature* (New York: Oxford University Press, 1977), 128.

2. Richard Lischer, *The Preacher King: Martin Luther King, Jr. and the Word That Changed America* (New York: Oxford University Press, 1995), 12.

3. David Chappell, *A Stone of Hope: Prophetic Religion and the Death of Jim Crow* (Chapel Hill: University of North Carolina Press, 2004), 87.

4. Ibid., 8. Chappell summarizes the explanatory claim of his book: "The civil rights movement succeeded for many reasons. This book isolates and magnifies one reason that has received insufficient attention: black southern activists got strength from old time religion, and white supremacists failed, at the same moment, to muster the cultural strength that conservatives traditionally get from religion. Who succeeded in the 50's and 60's? Those who could use religion to inspire solidarity and self-sacrificial devotion to their cause" (8).

5. Gunnar Myrdal, *An American Dilemma: The Negro Problem and Modern Democracy* (1944; repr., New York: Harper and Row, 1962).

6. Chappell, *Stone of Hope*, 37.

7. On Myrdal, see Ralph Ellison, "*An American Dilemma:* A Review," in *The Collected Essays of Ralph Ellison*, ed. John F. Callahan, 328–40 (New York: Modern Library, 2003); James Baldwin, "Many Thousands Gone," in *The Price of the Ticket: James Baldwin Collected Non-Fiction, 1948–1965*, 65–79 (New York: St. Martin's Press, 1985); Nikhil Singh, *Black Is a Country: Race and the Unfinished Struggle for Democracy* (Cambridge: Harvard University Press, 2004).

8. Chappell, *Stone of Hope*, on Niebuhr, 26–28, 37–41, 47–54.

9. Martin Luther King Jr., *Testament of Hope* (New York: HarperCollins, 1986), 36, 296; *Autobiography of Martin Luther King, Jr.*, ed. Clayborne Carson (New York: Warner Books, 1998), 25; *The Papers of Martin Luther King, Jr.*, ed. Peter Holloran and Clayborne Carson, 6 vols. (Berkeley and Los Angeles: University of California Press, 1992), 2:166.

10. King, *Testament of Hope*, 40; David L. Chappell, "Religious Revivalism in the Civil Rights Movement," *African American Review* 36, no. 4 (2002): 591; Clay-

borne Carson, "Martin Luther King and the African-American Social Gospel," in *African-American Religion: Interpretive Essays and Culture,* ed. Timothy E. Fulop and Albert J. Raboteau (New York: Routledge, 1997), 358.

11. King, *Testament of Hope,* 88.

12. Sermon quoted in Carson, "Martin Luther King and the African-American Social Gospel," 356.

13. King on Thoreau in *Autobiography,* 14.

14. Reinhold Niebuhr, *Moral Man and Immoral Society* (1937; repr., Louisville, Ky.: Westminster John Knox Press, 2001), 272, 21.

15. Ibid., xxvii, 252, 260, 254.

16. Ibid., 254–55.

17. Lischer, *Preacher King,* 16.

18. Ibid., 141.

19. Ralph Waldo Emerson, "Divinity Address," in *Selected Essays,* ed. Larzer Ziff, 107–29 (New York: Penguin, 1982).

20. Martin Luther King Jr., *Stride toward Freedom* (New York: Harper and Row, 1958), 210. Taylor Branch describes King's encounter with Abraham Heschel, whose great book on Hebrew prophecy had just been translated into English. Prophecy, Heschel said at a conference both attended, "is the voice God has lent to the silent agony." Quoted in Branch, *Pillar of Fire: America in the King Years, 1963–65* (New York: Simon and Schuster, 1998), 30–32.

21. Cornel West, *The Cornel West Reader* (New York: Basic Books, 1999), 101.

22. See especially the essays "Black Strivings in a Twilight Civilization" (87–119) and "Prophetic Christian as Organic Intellectual: Martin Luther King Jr." (425–35), in *Cornel West Reader;* quotation at 427. West finds four major sources of King's thought and politics: "the prophetic black church tradition . . . ; prophetic liberal Christianity; a prophetic Gandhian nonviolent social change; and a prophetic American civil religion" (426).

23. Audre Lorde, "Poetry Is Not a Luxury," in *Sister Outsider,* 36–40 (New York: Crossing Press, 1984); Orlando Patterson, *Slavery as Social Death* (Cambridge: Harvard University Press, 1982); Joanna Brooks, *American Lazarus: Religion and the Rise of African-American and Native American Literatures* (New York: Oxford University Press, 2003); Theosophus Smith, *Conjuring Culture: Biblical Formations of Black America* (New York: Oxford University Press, 1994).

24. King, *Testament of Hope,* 481, 47.

25. Ibid., 10–11.

26. Ibid., 20.

27. Martin Luther, quoted in Lischer, *Preacher King,* 233.

28. King, *Testament of Hope,* 13, 19.

29. Sigmund Freud, *Civilization and Its Discontents* (New York: W. W. Norton, 1961); David Nirenberg, "The Politics of Love and Its Enemies," *Critical Inquiry* 33, no. 3 (Spring 2007): 604–5; Friedrich Nietzsche, "The Anti-Christ," in *The Portable Nietzsche,* 565–657 (New York: Viking, 1968); Hannah Arendt, *On Revolution* (New York: Penguin, 1965).

30. James Lawson, quoted in Chappell, *Stone of Hope,* 69.

31. Arendt on respect, quoted from *The Human Condition* in Richard H. King, "Martin Luther King Jr. and the Meaning of Freedom: A Political Interpretation," in *We Shall Overcome: Martin Luther King Jr. and the Black Freedom Struggle,* ed. Peter J. Albert and Ronald Hoffman (New York: Pantheon, 1990), 151. On impartiality, see Hannah Arendt, *Lectures on Kant's Political Philosophy* (Chicago: University of Chicago Press, 1992).

32. King, *Testament of Hope,* 19.

33. See Charles Johnson, *Dreamer* (New York: Simon and Schuster, 1999) for a truly brilliant novel about King that uses the contrast of Cain and Abel to disclose, and trouble, King's effort to separate love and rivalry.

34. King, *Testament of Hope,* 18.

35. Quote from Michael Eric Dyson, *I May Not Get There with You: The True Martin Luther King, Jr.* (New York: Touchstone, 2000), 188.

36. King, *Testament of Hope,* 87; Richard King, "Martin Luther King and the Meaning of Freedom," 134; "Suffering Servants" quoted in *The Papers of Martin Luther King,* ed. Clayborne Carson (Berkeley and Los Angeles: University of California Press, 2000), 5, 110. Wendy Brown also defends King against Nietzsche; see her "Moralism as Anti-Politics," in *Politics out of History,* 18–45 (Princeton: Princeton University Press, 2001).

37. King story in Richard King, "Martin Luther King and the Meaning of Freedom," 140.

38. King, *Testament of Hope,* 246. On collective self-respect, see Lawrence Goodwyn, *The Populist Moment: A Short History of the Agrarian Revolt in America* (New York: Oxford University Press, 1978), and Charles Payne, *I've Got the Light of Freedom: The Organizing Tradition and the Mississippi Freedom Struggle* (Berkeley and Los Angeles: University of California Press, 1995).

39. Richard King, "Martin Luther King and the Meaning of Freedom," 145.

40. Ibid., 152.

41. For Arendt's illuminating (and self-exposing) exchanges with Ralph Ellison about Little Rock and school integration, see Danielle Allen, *Talking to Strangers: Anxieties of Citizenship since Brown v. Board of Education* (Chicago: University of Chicago Press, 2004), 25–36. Arendt's distinctions between parvenu and pariah and between the social and the political lead her to misrecognize the very politics she values.

42. Sacvan Bercovitch, *The American Jeremiad* (Madison: University of Wisconsin Press, 1978), 177–78, 203.

43. Niebuhr, *Moral Man and Immoral Society,* 240.

44. King, *Testament of Hope,* 301.

45. Ibid., 277.

46. Ibid., 233.

47. Langston Hughes, "Let America Be America Again," quoted in King, *Testament of Hope,* 233–34.

48. Lischer, *Preacher King,* 10, 142, 156–57; Burke quoted on 142.

49. King, *Testament of Hope,* 296, 301.

50. Ibid., 296, 277, 219, 277.

51. Ibid., 296, 277, 219.

52. Ibid., 296.

53. Toni Morrison, "Friday on the Potomac," in *Race-ing Justice, En-gendering Race,* (New York: Pantheon, 1992), xv.

54. From its outset in the late 1940s, the civil rights movement unfolded during a "counter-subversive moment." While struggle against communist influence in the developing world pressured white elites to address the race problem, these elites also authorized a national security state by linking domesticity and consumption to proper femininity, heteronormative sexuality, and suburbanization. Hysteria about communism was tied to (hysteria about) sexual deviance, juvenile delinquency, black culture, and cultural miscegenation through music and drugs. In turn, "racial uplift" took the form of seeking respectability, which meant policing the black community. See Thaddeus Russell, "Queens, Kings, and Citizens: A Queer History of the Civil Rights Movement," unpublished manuscript.

55. Morrison, "Friday on the Potomac," xv.

56. See Malcolm X, *Malcolm X Speaks,* ed. George Breitman (Berkeley, Calif.: Grove Press, 1990); Stokely Carmichael, "What We Want," *New York Review of Books,* September 22, 1966. Also see Huey Newton, "Revolutionary Suicide: The Way of Liberation" and "The Black Panther Party Platform and Program," in *The Sixties Papers,* ed. Judith Clavir Albert and Steward Edward Albert, 167–73, 159–65 (Westport, Conn.: Praeger, 1984).

57. King, *Testament of Hope,* 317.

58. Martin Luther King Jr., *Where Do We Go from Here? Chaos or Community?* (New York: Harper and Row, 1967), 81; King, *Testament of Hope,* 250; Bayard Rustin, "From Protest to Politics," *Commentary,* February 1965, 28.

59. King, *Testament of Hope,* 557–58.

60. Rustin distinguishes between "protest" and "politics" to criticize, not King, but his "black power" critics. For Rustin, the magnitude of the problem of inequality and of black isolation drives them to "frighten white people into doing the right thing." "These spokesmen are often described as the radicals of the movement," but "they are really its moralists" because, despite disclaimers, they seek to change white consciousness. But "hearts are not relevant to the issue; neither racial affinities nor hostilities are rooted there." Rustin, "From Protest to Politics," 25–29.

61. King, *Testament of Hope,* 249.

62. Ibid., 315.

63. Ibid., 234.

64. Ibid., 238.

65. Ibid., 234, 238, 218, 238.

66. Ibid., 240, 640.

67. Ibid., 242–43.

68. Lischer, *Preacher King,* 108, 182; King on Jeremiah 8:18–9:3, quoted in Lischer, *Preacher King,* 182.

69. King, *Testament of Hope,* 275–76.

70. Lischer, *Preacher King,* 189. In his review of Michael Dyson's book, Michael Rogin notes, "the more deeply King saw, the more depressed and directionless

he became, the less faith he had in his original animating vision." Rogin, "The Ugly Revolution," review of *I May Not Get There with You: The True Martin Luther King, Jr.*, by Michael Eric Dyson, *London Review of Books* 23, no. 9 (May 10, 2001).

71. Lischer, *Preacher King*, 193–94.

72. Andrew Sabl, *Ruling Passions: Political Offices and Democratic Ethics* (Princeton: Princeton University Press, 2002).

73. Ibid., 232.

74. Ibid., 233.

75. Lischer, *Preacher King*, 162, 113.

76. Sabl, *Ruling Passions*, 245, 92–93.

77. Ibid., 247.

78. Ibid., 236.

4. James Baldwin and the Racial State of Exception

1. This chapter has benefited from readings by Lawrie Balfour, Mark Reinhardt, and Bonnie Honig. It should be noted at the outset that James Baldwin's work presents great interpretive difficulties. Over forty years he wrote eight major novels, a book of short stories, a play, and a memoir of his years in the civil rights movement, as well as scores of essays published in a wide variety of venues, from the *New Yorker* to *Essence*, from *Partisan Review* to *Harper's Bazaar*. He wrote in different literary genres, through fictional characters, and in his own voice. His work explores every aspect of American life, especially concerning white supremacy, but he also addresses the relationship of race to sexuality and gender, as well as abiding "existential" themes. And though his themes remain constant, he changes his view of American society and politics in important ways, for he witnessed the entire second Reconstruction era, from its early days in Montgomery, Alabama, and Little Rock, Arkansas, to the administration of Ronald Reagan. My sense of the whole is indebted to David Leeming, *James Baldwin: A Biography* (London: Penguin, 1994); my sense of Baldwin's politics is deeply indebted to Lawrie Balfour, *The Evidence of Things Not Said: James Baldwin and the Promise of American Democracy* (Ithaca, N.Y.: Cornell University Press, 2001).

2. James Baldwin, "The American Dream and the American Negro," in *The Price of the Ticket: James Baldwin Collected Non-Fiction, 1948–1965* (New York: St. Martin's Press, 1985), 404. All passages from Baldwin are from this collection unless otherwise noted.

3. "What in the world was I now but an aging, sexually dubious, politically outrageous, unspeakable erratic freak." James Baldwin, *No Name in the Street* (New York: Dial Press, 1972), 18.

4. James Baldwin, *The Fire Next Time*, in *The Price of the Ticket*, 373.

5. James Baldwin, "Fifth Avenue Uptown," 213.

6. Cornel West's *American Evasion of Philosophy* (Madison: University of Wisconsin Press, 1989) remains the best critique of Emerson's racial innocence, and it initiates the wider academic search for a supplement, for some in Du Bois and for others in Baldwin.

7. James Baldwin, "Nothing Personal," 383–84.

8. James Baldwin, "The Creative Process," 317–18.

9. James Baldwin, "Disagreeable Mirror," in "White Man's Guilt," 409. Other passages from Baldwin, *The Fire Next Time*, 370, 375.

10. Baldwin, "Nothing Personal," 388.

11. Baldwin, *The Fire Next Time*, 373–74.

12. Baldwin, "Nothing Personal," 393.

13. James Baldwin, introduction to *Price of the Ticket*, xix.

14. Baldwin, "Nothing Personal," 393.

15. Ibid.

16. Baldwin, *The Fire Next Time*, 379. In Cornel West's formulation, "The most effective and enduring black responses to invisibility and namelessness are those forms of individual and collective black resistance predicated on a deep and abiding *love*. These responses take the shape of prophetic thought and action: bold, fearless, courageous attempts to tell the truth about and bear witness to black suffering, and to keep faith with a vision of black redemption." "Black Strivings in a Twilight Civilization," in *The Cornel West Reader* (New York: Basic Books, 1999), 106.

17. Jonathan Lear is quoted by Eric Santner, *The Psychotherapy of Everyday Life* (Chicago: University of Chicago Press, 2001), 123.

18. There are illuminating analogies between Baldwin's work, therefore, and Judith Butler's recent work, which also addresses a national subject and negotiates the difference between mourning and melancholia. See Judith Butler, *Precarious Life* (London: Verso, 2004).

19. James Baldwin, "Stranger in the Village," 87.

20. Baldwin, *The Fire Next Time*, 373.

21. Ibid., 374.

22. Ibid., 334.

23. Ibid., 335–36.

24. Baldwin, "Stranger in the Village," 89.

25. Ibid., 88.

26. Ibid. Positing black inferiority is *the* way whites ease the contradiction between egalitarian principles and grossly unequal practices. But to sustain this fiction, they must deny the reality they "know," that black women and men are human.

27. James Baldwin, "On Being White and Other Lies," *Essence*, April 1984, 90–92, and "In Search of a Majority," 232, where he explicitly addresses the question of ethnicity. See also Victoria Hattam, *In the Shadow of Race: Jews, Latinos, and Immigrant Politics in the United States* (Chicago: University of Chicago Press, 2007).

28. Baldwin, *The Fire Next Time*, 375.

29. Ibid., 373.

30. James Baldwin, "White Racism or World Community?" 440. In this essay, Baldwin denounces Christianity as an institution, but he equates Stokely Carmichael with the prophets and Jesus, and he suggests that by overcoming the

split between spirit and flesh, it might be possible to "enlarge" and thereby "save" the idea of a god (435).

31. Baldwin, "On Being White and Other Lies."

32. James Baldwin, "Everybody's Protest Novel," 30.

33. Baldwin, "Stranger in the Village," 89.

34. Ibid. References to eyes and blindness resonate with Greek tragedy.

35. See Lawrie Balfour, "'A Most Disagreeable Mirror': Race Consciousness as Double Consciousness," *Political Theory* 26, no. 3 (1998): 346–69, and *Evidence of Things Not Said*.

36. James Baldwin, "Many Thousands Gone," 65.

37. Ibid.

38. Ibid., 66.

39. Ibid.

40. Ibid.

41. Ibid., 68.

42. Baldwin, "White Man's Guilt," 410.

43. Ibid., 410.

44. Friedrich Nietzsche, *Thus Spake Zarathustra*, trans. Walter Kaufman (London: Penguin, 1996), 137–41; James Baldwin, "Color," 319.

45. Baldwin, "In Search of a Majority": The image of "the American boy" suggests "hard work and good clean fun and chastity and piety and success. It leaves out most of the people in the country and most of the facts of life. . . . Beneath this bland conqueror-image a great many unadmitted despairs and confusions and . . . crimes and failures hide" (232).

46. Baldwin, "The American Dream and the American Negro," 403. His speech begins, "I find myself, not for the first time, in the position of a kind of Jeremiah."

47. James Baldwin, "Liberalism and the Negro: A Roundtable Discussion," *Commentary*, March 1964, 31.

48. Baldwin, *The Fire Next Time*, 375.

49. Ibid., 340.

50. Ibid., 373.

51. Baldwin, "Everybody's Protest Novel," 32.

52. Baldwin, "Many Thousands Gone," 72–73.

53. Baldwin, "Everybody's Protest Novel," 33.

54. Ibid., 32.

55. Baldwin, "Many Thousands Gone," 74.

56. Ibid.

57. Ibid., 77. Thus, "the blues are not a racial creation" but "a historical creation produced by the confrontation . . . between the black pagan from Africa and the alabaster cross."

58. Baldwin, *The Fire Next Time*, 376–77.

59. Baldwin, "Many Thousands Gone," 76–77.

60. Baldwin, "Stranger in the Village," 89.

61. Baldwin, "In Search of a Majority," 234.

62. Perry Miller, "The Shaping of the American Character," in *Nature's Na-*

tion, 1–13 (Cambridge: Harvard University Press, 1967). "American studies" and "cultural studies" are founded contemporaneously, each pursuing "culture" as an object, but what is lost and gained by a specifically "American" focus?

63. James Baldwin, "A Question of Identity," 99.

64. Baldwin, "In Search of a Majority," 234. Ellison reads the "joke" of race differently than does Baldwin, in "Change the Joke and Slip the Yoke," in *Collected Essays of Ralph Ellison*, ed. John F. Callahan, 100–112 (New York: Modern Library, 1995).

65. Baldwin, "In Search of a Majority," 234.

66. James Baldwin, "Negroes Are Anti-Semitic Because They Are Anti-White," 428.

67. Baldwin, *The Fire Next Time*, 375–76.

68. James Baldwin, "Faulkner and Desegregation," 147.

69. James Baldwin, preface to *Notes of a Native Son* (Boston: Beacon Press, 1984), xii. For a parallel but more "centering" account of political identification, see John H. Schaar, "The Case for Patriotism," in *Legitimacy in the Modern State*, 15–52 (New Brunswick, N.J.: Transaction, 1981).

70. Baldwin, *The Fire Next Time*, 379.

71. The more famous of Baldwin's critics from a professed "black power" perspective are Eldridge Cleaver, "Notes on a Native Son," in *Soul on Ice*, 97–111 (New York: Dell, 1968); Imiri Baraka, "Brief Reflections on Two Hot Shots," in *Home: Social Essays*, ed. LeRoi Jones, 116–21 (New York: William Morrow, 1966); Calvin C. Hernton, "Blood of the Lamb: The Ordeal of James Baldwin," in *White Papers for White Americans*, 105–47 (Garden City, N.Y.: Doubleday, 1966). For a parallel critique, see Orlando Patterson, "The Essays of James Baldwin," *New Left Review*, no. 26 (Summer 1964): 31–38.

72. Baldwin appeared on the cover of the May 17, 1963, issue of *Time* magazine, not long after *The Fire Next Time* had been published. A banner across the upper left reads, "Birmingham and Beyond: The Negro's Push for Equality." Baldwin's recent biographer, David Leeming, emphasizes that in the article on Baldwin following the lead story, he is cast as a "spokesman and prophet," but William Spurlin sees his sexuality emphasized. "In less-than-subtle contrast to Dr. Martin Luther King Jr., whom the entire article masculinizes as a black leader," Spurlin argues, "*Time* immediately proceeds to claim that Baldwin 'is not, by any stretch of the imagination, a Negro leader. He tries no civil rights cases in the courts, preaches from no pulpit, devises no stratagems for sit-ins, Freedom-Riders or street marchers.'" Spurlin notes that the story goes on to "mark" Baldwin's sexuality, "not only through its comparison of Baldwin to King and Malcolm X, but through its obviously coded description of Baldwin as 'a nervous, slight, almost fragile figure, filled with frets and fears. He is effeminate in manner, drinks considerably, smokes cigarettes in chains, and he often loses his audience with overblown arguments.'" William Spurlin, "Culture, Rhetoric, and Queer Identity: James Baldwin and the Identity Politics of Race and Sexuality," in *James Baldwin Now*, ed. Dwight McBride, 103–21 (New York: New York University Press, 1999). Meanwhile, black critics mark Baldwin's sexuality to discredit him, on the grounds of what he lacks, either middle-class respectability

or revolutionary authenticity. But as Huey Newton, for one, links black struggle to gay liberation, so Marlon Ross notes, "we have to ask why, in current debates about attitudes toward same-sexuality in Black Power discourse, Cleaver is repeatedly quoted as exemplary while Newton's critiques are wholly forgotten." Marlon Ross, "White Fantasies of Desire: Baldwin and the Racial Identities of Sexuality," in McBride, *James Baldwin Now*, 48n16.

73. Howe was reacting to Baldwin's recent publication of *Giovanni's Room* (1956) and *Another Country* (1962); see Irving Howe, "Black Boys and Native Sons," originally published in *Dissent*, Autumn 1963, 353–68, and reprinted in Irving Howe, *A World More Attractive*, 98–122 (New York: Horizon Press, 1963). Says Howe: "Even if all the visible tokens of injustice were erased, the Negroes would retain their hatred and the whites their fear and guilt. Forgiveness cannot be speedily willed, if willed at all, and before it can even be imagined there will have to be a fuller discharge of those violent feelings that have been so long suppressed" (366–67).

74. Norman Mailer, "The White Negro," in *Advertisements for Myself* (1959; repr., Cambridge: Harvard University Press, 1992), 337–58; for Baldwin's critique of Mailer, see "The Black Boy Looks at the White Boy," 289–304.

75. Cleaver, "Notes on a Native Son," 99, 103, 106. In 1964 Calvin Hernton says Baldwin is "loved by white people" because "he does not symbolize the great black phallus that seeks to rape and pillage; rather, he cries for love and forgiveness, and as he soothes white guilt, whites reach out to soothe his wounds, inflicted by racism and the self-hatred it entails." Baldwin "writes about the blood of the lamb, about sin and redemption," not about politics and power. Hernton, *White Papers for White Americans*, 119–22, 124–26.

76. Baldwin, *No Name in the Street*, 63.

77. Lee Edelman, "The Part for the (W)Hole: Baldwin, Homophobia, and the Fantasmatics of 'Race,'" in *Homographesis: Essays in Gay Literary and Cultural Theory*, (New York: Routledge, 1994), 42–59. Also see Anne Norton, "Engendering Another America," in *Rhetorical Republic*, ed. Frederick Dolan and Thomas Dumm, 125–42 (Amherst: University of Massachusetts, 1993).

78. Cleaver thus accuses Baldwin of fraternizing with whites, but he bonds with Mailer in fantasies of phallic power. Still, feminist critics suggest that Baldwin made himself vulnerable to these attacks. For E. Frances White, "It was Baldwin's own narrow vision of masculinity that left him exposed to attacks like Cleaver's." Because he accepted "heterosexuality's investment in rigid and gendered boundaries of desire" and allowed "the terms of masculinity to remain intact and gender to remain fixed, he had no recourse in the face of Cleaver's denigrating insults. As long as gay men could be disparaged as failed men—as essentially women—Baldwin would have no comeback." E. Frances White, "The Evidence of Things Not Seen: The Alchemy of Race and Sexuality," in *Dark Continent of Our Bodies: Black Feminism and the Politics of Respectability* (Philadelphia: Temple University Press, 2001), 176.

79. Kendall Thomas, "Ain't Nothing Like the Real Thing," in *The House That Race Built*, ed. Wahneema Lubiano (New York: Vintage, 1998), 121.

80. Hebrew prophets may initiate the connection between nation building

and sexual policing: They distinguish between chaste wife and whore to police women and to condemn (as promiscuity) the cosmopolitanism that unsettles the stable difference defining peoplehood.

81. Norman Podhoretz, "In Defense of James Baldwin" (1964), repr. in *Five Black Writers*, ed. Donald Gibson (New York: New York University Press, 1970), 145–46.

82. Edelman, "Part for the (W)Hole," 61.

83. See especially Will Walker, "After *The Fire Next Time:* James Baldwin's Post-Consensus Double Bind," in *Is It Nation Time? Contemporary Essays on Black Power and Black Nationalism*, ed. Eddie Glaude, 215–33 (Chicago: University of Chicago Press, 2001).

84. Hilton Als, "The Enemy Within: The Making and Unmaking of James Baldwin," *New Yorker,* February 16, 1998, 72–80; Henry Louis Gates Jr., "The Fire Last Time: What James Baldwin Can and Can't Teach America," *New Republic,* June 1992, 37–43; Julius Lester, "Some Tickets Are Better Than Others: The Mixed Achievement of James Baldwin," *Dissent* 33 (1986): 189–92.

85. Julius Lester laments that Baldwin "abdicated the lonely responsibility of artists and intellectuals to be claimed by nothing but that futile and beautiful quest for Truth." Lester, "Some Tickets Are Better Than Others," 249. In Hilton Als's parallel reading, Baldwin's "voice as a writer" was always compromised by his public role, and by 1968 he "found impersonating a writer to be more seductive than being an artist. . . . In the end, Baldwin could not distinguish between writing sermons and making art. He eventually returned to the pulpit—just where his stepfather always wanted him to be." "Enemy Within," 78, 80.

86. Socrates is "ironic" because he creates a critical distance toward every argument, but he asserts as a matter of faith that a self-examined life is the best life and that it is better to suffer than do injustice. This faith is the axiomatic condition of a life lived by aporetic argument and irony.

87. Jacques Rancière, *Disagreement: Politics and Philosophy*, trans. Julie Rose (Minneapolis: University of Minnesota Press, 1999). By articulating the relation between *parts and wholes,* Rancière avoids both identity politics (which reduces politics to demographic or empirical subject positions) and the reduction of politics to refusal or deferral of identification. Holding in tension the "part that has no part" and a whole constituted by its exclusion, he creates a vision of community never at one with itself, so that the properly political is not exchange within a given field but "dis-agreement" that reconstitutes it.

88. The idea of a space between principle and practice is explored beautifully by Lawrie Balfour's reading of Baldwin in *Evidence of Things Not Said.*

89. Baldwin, "Many Thousands Gone," 78.

90. Baldwin, *Notes of a Native Son,* 145.

91. Baldwin, *The Fire Next Time,* 374.

92. On slavery as social death, see Orlando Patterson, *Freedom in the Making of Western Culture* (New York: Basic Books, 1991), 5–11; West, "Black Strivings in a Twilight Civilization."

93. Baldwin, *No Name in the Street,* 88–89.

94. James Baldwin, "An Open Letter to My Sister, Angela Y. Davis," in *If They*

Came in the Morning: Voices of Resistance, ed. Angela Davis, 19–23 (New York: Signet, 1971).

95. Baldwin, *No Name in the Street,* 64–65.

96. Ibid., 47. In Baldwin's essays written after 1968, comparisons of white Americans to Germans are rife: "We have not absolved the Germans for saying 'I didn't know . . .' But . . . what the Germans did . . . there is no guarantee that we are not doing that right now." "White Racism or World Community?" 441. Correspondingly, he notes that the Warsaw ghetto uprising is not called a riot, while the one in Watts is not called an insurrection. Why is violence heroized in one case and not the other? Partly because "while America loves white heroes armed to the teeth it cannot abide bad niggers," and more deeply because white Americans cannot imagine that "unregenerate horror can happen here. We make our mistakes, we like to think, but we are getting better all the time." Baldwin, "Negroes Are Anti-Semitic Because They Are Anti-White," 428.

97. Baldwin, "An Open Letter," 23.

98. Baldwin, "An Open Letter"; Russel Banks, "John Brown's Body: James Baldwin and Frank Shatz in Conversation," *Transition,* nos. 81–82, 250–62.

99. Baldwin, *No Name in the Street,* 92.

100. Ibid., 139–40.

101. Ibid., 9–10.

102. Ibid., 36.

103. Ibid., 171.

104. Here is evidence of Cora Kaplan's argument that Baldwin distinguishes manly and abject forms of same-sex desire while linking the abject to the feminine. He accepts as fundamental the fact of sexual difference itself, and he represents the failure of that difference as "grotesque." The abject is the phallic mother and lesbian, who are (like) men, or male transvestites, who are (like) women. He demonizes "fags," transvestites, and "dykes" to produce a properly masculine homosexual. See "'A Cavern Opened in My Mind': The Politics of Homosexuality and the Politics of Masculinity in James Baldwin," in *Representing Black Men,* ed. Marcellus Blount and George Cunningham, 27–54 (New York: Routledge, 1996).

105. Baldwin, *No Name in the Street,* 172–73.

106. Ibid., 195.

107. Ibid.

108. Baldwin, *The Fire Next Time,* 379.

5. Toni Morrison and Prophecy

1. Sacvan Bercovitch, *The American Jeremiad* (Madison: University of Wisconsin Press, 1978), 180.

2. Among the critics who do link *Beloved* directly to politics, see Kenneth W. Warren, *So Black and Blue: Ralph Ellison and the Occasion of Criticism* (Chicago: University of Chicago Press, 2003); James Berger, "Ghosts of Liberalism: Morrison's *Beloved* and the Moynihan Report," *PMLA* 111, no. 3 (1996): 408–20; Madhu Dubey, "The Politics of Genre in *Beloved,*" *Novel* 32, no. 2

(1999): 187–206; Cornel West, *Race Matters* (New York: Vintage, 1993); Eddie Glaude, *In a Shade of Blue: Pragmatism and the Politics of Black America* (Chicago: University of Chicago Press, 2006).

3. Toni Morrison, "Unspeakable Things Unspoken: The Afro-American Presence in American Literature," *Michigan Quarterly Review* 28, no. 1 (1989): 12–13. In *Playing in the Dark: Whiteness and the Literary Imagination* (New York: Vintage, 1993), she says, "Romance . . . made possible the sometimes safe and other times risky embrace of . . . understandably human fears," especially "the terror of human freedom—the thing they coveted most of all." Romance also "offered platforms for . . . the imaginative entertainment of violence, sublime incredibility, and terror—and terror's most significant, overweening ingredient: darkness, with all the connotative value it awakened. There is no romance free of what Herman Melville called 'the power of blackness'" (36–37).

4. Morrison, "Unspeakable Things," 16.

5. Ibid., 16–17, quoting chapter 9 in Melville's *Moby-Dick*.

6. Morrison, "Unspeakable Things," 17.

7. Ibid., 18. The scholar whom Morrison praises in her essay, Michael Rogin, separates Melville from Ahab. See Michael Rogin, *Subversive Genealogy: The Politics and Art of Herman Melville* (New York: Alfred A. Knopf, 1983).

8. Toni Morrison, "James Baldwin: His Voice Remembered; Life in His Language," *New York Times,* December 20, 1987.

9. Toni Morrison, *Nobel Lecture in Literature (1993)* (Alfred A. Knopf, 1994).

10. David Walker (1785–1830), born a free black, wrote an abolitionist tract demanding immediate emancipation and defending violent rebellion: *David Walker's Appeal to the Coloured Citizens of the World but in Particular and Very Expressly to Those of the United States of America.*

11. Toni Morrison, *Beloved* (New York: Plume, 1987), 273; further quotations from *Beloved* are cited in the text.

12. Morrison's own success is part of this story: Now honored by an endowed chair at Princeton, she came to national attention when *Song of Solomon* won the National Book Critics Circle Award (1977). *Beloved,* which appeared in 1987, won the Pulitzer Prize. She was awarded the Nobel Prize in 1992.

13. Morrison, *Playing in the Dark,* 63, 65, 90.

14. Toni Morrison, "Friday on the Potomac," introduction to *Race-ing Justice, En-gendering Power,* ed. Toni Morrison (New York: Pantheon, 1992), xiv, xv, x.

15. Morrison, "The Official Story: Dead Man Golfing," introduction to *Birth of a Nation'hood,* ed. Toni Morrison and Claudia Brodsky Lacour (New York: Pantheon, 1997), xxviii.

16. Morrison, *Playing in the Dark,* 47.

17. Paul Gilroy, "Living Memory: A Meeting with Toni Morrison," in *Small Acts: Thoughts on the Politics of Black Cultures* (London: Serpent's Tail, 1994), 179–80. In another interview she says, "I knew I was not in favor of integration. But I couldn't officially say that because I knew the terrors and abuses of segregation. But integration also meant that we would not have a fine black college or fine black education. I didn't know why the assumption was that black children were going to learn better if they were in the company of white children"; cf.

Rosemarie K. Lester, "An Interview with Toni Morrison, Hessian Radio Network, Frankfurt, West Germany," in *Critical Essays on Toni Morrison,* ed. Nellie McKay (Boston: G. K. Hall, 1988), 51.

18. Morrison, "Friday on the Potomac," xxvi–xxix.

19. Thomas LeClair, "The Language Must Not Sweat: A Conversation with Toni Morrison," in *Conversations with Toni Morrison,* ed. Danielle Taylor-Guthrie (Jackson: University Press of Mississippi, 1994), 121.

20. West, *Race Matters,* 23–24. By a jeremiad, West and Morrison reconfigure what Kenneth Warren calls "the damage thesis" and the "culture thesis." Liberals justify state action by arguing that slavery inflicted disastrous damage on blacks. The "culture thesis," used by figures as different as Ralph Ellison and black power advocates, argues that black people created a culture to protect themselves from slavery and racism, that is, from the damage that liberals assert. The damage thesis can pathologize black culture and devalue black agency, while the culture thesis can deny that slavery or racism is damaging, but Morrison and West emphasize trauma while arguing that the cultural forms that *once* protected blacks are failing now. See Warren, *So Black and Blue.*

21. Toni Morrison, "Rootedness: The Ancestor as Foundation of Memory," in *Black Women Writers (1950–1980),* ed. Mari Evans (New York: Anchor Press, 1984), 340.

22. LeClair, "Language Must Not Sweat," 120–21.

23. Morrison, "Unspeakable Things," 3.

24. Ibid., 9; Toni Morrison, "Home," in *The House That Race Built,* ed. Wahneema Lubiano (New York: Vintage, 1998), 5.

25. Morrison, "Unspeakable Things," 11.

26. Morrison in Gilroy, "Living Memory," 181.

27. Ibid.

28. Morrison, "Rootedness," 341.

29. Toni Morrison, "Memory, Creation, and Writing," *Thought* 59, no. 235 (December 1984): 388.

30. Toni Morrison, speaking to Nellie McKay, in "An Interview with Toni Morrison/1983," in *Conversations with Toni Morrison,* ed. Danille Taylor-Guthrie (Jackson: University Press of Mississippi, 1994), 155.

31. Ibid, 155. Morrison's view of a black aesthetic in literature is not only formal. Partly, a defining difference between white and black aesthetics is the absence or presence of "the ancestor." Who is this? "The ancestor is not only wise; he or she values racial connection, racial memory over individual fulfillment." A "black" aesthetic also must "blend the supernatural and profound rootedness in ordinary life." Morrison, "Rootedness," 342.

32. For relating the vernacular to the politics of Morrison's literary form, I am indebted to Dubey, "Politics of Genre." In Dubey's view, black power and cultural nationalist arguments imagined a "black counter-public" characterized by reliance on vernacular culture rather than print literacy and by investment in a politicized notion of racial community. *Beloved* "both resurrects and reluctantly buries" this idea of "a vernacular black art [that] legitimized itself on the claim of its political efficacy for a wider and clearly definable racial community" (203).

33. Wendy Brown, "Wounded Attachments," *Political Theory* 21, no. 2 (1993): 390–410. In his notorious review, Stanley Crouch reads *Beloved* as a "blackface holocaust novel" that trades on victimization in just the way Brown diagnoses. Stanley Crouch, "Aunt Medea," *New Republic*, October 19, 1987, 38–43.

34. The phrase "avows animus but performs ambivalence" is the brilliant suggestion of Bonnie Honig.

35. For the arguments about race that claim "culture" is displacing "politics," see Warren, *So Black and Blue;* Adolph Reed, *Stirrings in the Jug* (Minneapolis: University of Minnesota Press, 1999) and *Class Notes* (New York: New Press, 2001); Walter Benn Michaels, *The Trouble with Diversity* (New York: Henry Holt, 2007) and *The Shape of the Signifier* (Princeton: Princeton University Press, 2006).

36. For the quotation from Douglass, see his "West India Emancipation" speech, New York, August 1857, in *The Life and Writings of Frederick Douglass,* ed. Philip S. Foner (New York: International Publishers, 1950–), 2:426–39. For Morrison's account of the Garner incident, see Gloria Naylor and Toni Morrison, "A Conversation," *Southern Review* 21 (1985): 567–93.

37. Morrison in Gilroy, "Living Memory," 179.

38. Toni Morrison, "Site of Memory," in *Inventing the Truth: The Art and Craft of Memoir,* ed. William Zinsser (Boston: Houghton Mifflin, 1987), 110, 113.

39. Gilroy, "Living Memory," 179.

40. Quoted in William L. Andrews and Nellie Y. McKay, eds., *Toni Morrison's "Beloved": A Casebook* (New York: Oxford University Press, 1999), 3.

41. From an interview quoted in Rafael Perez-Torres, "Between Presence and Absence: *Beloved,* Postmodernism, and Blackness," in Andrews and McKay, *"Beloved": Casebook,* 198n2.

42. Morrison, in Naylor and Morrison, "A Conversation," 585.

43. The founding statement of this vision of American literature is D. H. Lawrence, *Studies in Classic American Literature* (New York: Viking, 1972). For recent versions, see Morrison, *Playing in the Dark,* and Michael Rogin, "Nature as Politics / Nature as Romance," in *Ronald Reagan, the Movie, and Other Episodes in Political Demonology,* 169–89 (Berkeley and Los Angeles: University of California Press, 1987). For haunting as a characteristically modern social phenomenon, see Avery Gordon, *Ghostly Matters: Haunting and the Sociological Imagination* (Minneapolis: University of Minnesota Press, 1996); Jacques Derrida, *Specters of Marx: The State of Debt, the Work of Mourning, and the New International,* trans. Peggy Kamuf (New York: Routledge, 1994.)

44. Carolyn Rody, "Toni Morrison's *Beloved:* History, 'Rememory,' and a 'Clamor for a Kiss,'" *American Literary History* 7, no. 1 (1995): 104.

45. Judith Butler, "After Loss, What Then?" in *Loss: The Politics of Mourning,* ed. David Eng and David Kazanjian, 467–73 (Berkeley and Los Angeles: University of California Press, 2003).

46. Baldwin criticizes Paul for radically splitting spirit and flesh, while Morrison refigures the central related dichotomies in Paul: not only between spirit and flesh, but also between spirit and law, life and death, and particularity and universality. For recent work on Paul and political theory, see Daniel Boyarin, *Radical Jew: Paul and the Politics of Identity* (Berkeley and Los Angeles: University

of California Press, 1994); Jacob Taubes, *The Political Theology of Paul* (Stanford: Stanford University Press, 2004); Allain Baidou, *Saint Paul: The Foundation of Universalism* (Stanford: Stanford University Press, 2003).

47. Orlando Patterson, *Slavery and Social Death: A Comparative Study* (Cambridge: Harvard University Press, 1982) 75, 70. "Slavery, which on the level of secular symbolism was social death, became [spiritual death] on the level of sacred symbolism." The symbolism is congenial to masters because it invokes the actuality of social death only to invest redemption in a spiritual rebirth, but subalterns recurrently give "resurrection" the worldly meaning of overcoming social death. Citing Eugene Genovese, Albert I. Raboteau, and Lawrence W. Levine as corroborating authorities, Patterson quotes theologian Olin P. Moyd: "Redemption is the root and core motif of black theology" (74). For a fabulous account of just this reworking of the symbol of resurrection, see Joanna Brooks, *American Lazarus: Religion and the Rise of African-American and Native American Literatures* (New York: Oxford University Press, 2003).

48. All quotations from Mae G. Henderson are from her "Toni Morrison's *Beloved:* Re-membering the Body as Historical Text," in *Comparative American Identities*, ed. Hortense Spillers, 62–86 (New York: Routledge, 1991), 64.

49. Jennifer Fitzgerald, "Selfhood and Community: Psychoanalysis and Discourse in *Beloved*," *Modern Fiction Studies* 39, nos. 3–4 (1993): 685.

50. Susan Bowers, "Beloved and the New Apocalypse," *Journal of Ethnic Studies* 18, no. 1 (Spring 1990): 72–73. Some critics use "the community of women" to revise Christian ideas of rebirth: "Where redemption has traditionally been understood as a canceling of debt of sin and release from the (deserved) punishment of death, maternal voices speak not of endings and cancellations but of continuity and wholeness. . . . When we listen to a maternal voice speaking of redemption, then, we do not hear that the old is swept away so that all is made new, but that all is finally made *whole*. Rather than an erasure of sin and suffering, redemption exists more as a mosaic that encompasses experience without negating any part of it." Colleen Carpenter Cullinan, "A Maternal Discourse of Redemption: Speech and Suffering in Toni Morrison's *Beloved*," *Religion and Literature* 34, no. 2 (2002): 78.

51. For Linda Krumholz, "Morrison uses ritual as a model for a healing process." Morrison "introduces oral narrative techniques—repetition, blending of voices, shifting narrative voice, an episodic framework—to stimulate the aural, participatory dynamics of ritual within the private, introspective form of the novel." Linda Krumholz, "The Ghosts of Slavery," in Andrews and McKay, *"Beloved": Casebook*, 108–9. For Trudier Harris, "the author-reader interaction for this text . . . is only minimally less powerful than if Morrison were sitting in our living rooms telling us the story." Trudier Harris, *"Beloved:* Woman, Thy Name Is Demon," in Andrews and McKay, *"Beloved": Casebook*, 145. Barbara Christian identifies the novel with a West African "fixing ceremony," whose premise is that, unless the unremembered dead are acknowledged, and "release us from the wrath of the past, the future will be tormented and fractured." Barbara Christian, "Fixing Methodologies: *Beloved*," *Culture Critique* 24 (Spring 1993): 11–14.

52. Doris Somers, *Proceed with Caution* (Cambridge: Harvard University Press

1999), sees Morrison teaching readers to proceed with caution in what they claim to know about a character or event. She pursues a "vitiating strategy" that "gives good plot but takes away the rush of titillating identification" (164). James Phelan, likewise, distinguishes "difficult" and "stubborn" texts: The "difficult is recalcitrance that yields to our explanatory efforts while the stubborn is recalcitrance that will not yield." Phelan, "Towards a Rhetorical Reader-Response Criticism," *Modern Fiction Studies* 39, nos. 3–4 (Fall/Winter 1993): 714. If we say the truth of the text is its stubbornness, we miss the point, for we need to let it be stubborn, to acknowledge rather than know it.

53. Gilroy, "Living Memory," 178.

54. See Anne Goldman, "'I Made the Ink': Literary Production and Reproduction in *Desa Rose* and *Beloved*," *Feminist Studies* 16, no. 2 (1990): 313–30.

55. In "Black Strivings," Cornel West quotes Suggs's speech to exemplify "the love ethic" in African American life. "Every form of individual and collective resistance" to social death is "predicated on a deep and abiding black love." In all its forms love "provides the grounds for the fragile existential weaponry" that "combat black invisibility and namelessness." Cornel West, "Black Strivings in a Twilight Civilization," in *The Cornel West Reader* (New York: Basic Books, 1999), 106–8.

56. Berger, "Ghosts of Liberalism," 179.

57. From one point of view, Sethe enacts a state of exception to moral as well as human law; at the same time, Helene Moglen argues, she "claims the right to *be* the primal mother, giving and taking life without responsibility to a subjectivity other than her own." Moglen, "Redeeming History: Toni Morrison's *Beloved*," *Cultural Critique* 24 (1993): 29.

58. These passages are indebted to Ashraf Rushdy, "Daughters Signifyin(g) History: The Example of Toni Morrison's *Beloved*," *American Literature* 64 (September 1992): 567–97. Morrison shares Beloved's daughterly desire to know her history and maternal origins: Imagining a murdered daughter returning to question her murdering mother, who is herself a daughter full of unanswered questions, Morrison is both a daughter recovering traumatic origins that mix blood and milk and a prophetic old woman nurturing a successor generation by resurrecting ancestors.

59. Naylor and Morrison, "Conversation," 585.

60. Emily Budick, "Absence, Loss, and the Space of History in Toni Morrison's *Beloved*," *Arizona Quarterly* 48, no. 2 (Summer 1992): 135.

61. Dubey, "Politics of Genre," 199.

62. Bodwin is not Schoolteacher or a slave owner but a lifelong abolitionist, though surely also a racist. Still, he provides jobs and housing for the African American community, and Sethe's house is his own childhood home. Morrison points ironically to the moral self-regard and self-satisfaction he gains from black suffering, but she suggests also the value of his support. For a reading of Bodwin as a post-sixties liberal, see Berger, "Ghosts of Liberalism," 190.

63. Some critics therefore make Denver, not Sethe, the key figure of redemption. For Ashraf Rushdy, "Denver not only represents the future, she brings it into being." Her efforts to get help "lead to everyone's salvation: the

reunion of the community" that had been divided. Denver is "the site of hope, the daughter of history." Indeed, Rushdy assures us, Sethe's own "reclamation of herself" will "follow the pattern established by" Denver, whose "personal healing" occurs by learning "her shared history" and making a "successful return to life." Baby Suggs, indeed, comes into Denver's mind and encourages her to leave the house: "But you said there was no defense," Denver responds. "There ain't. Then what do I do? Know it, but go on out the yard. Go on." Rushdy, "Daughters Signifyin(g) History," 244.

64. Berger, "Ghosts of Liberalism," 189.

65. The "Beloved" Morrison invokes at the end of the novel is related to the Silenus invoked by Arendt to end *On Revolution*. For Silenus, who says it is best not to have been born, would use the traumatic violence of slavery to depict the horror of life and senseless death, to ask, What could possibly redeem it?

66. Kathleen Brogan, *Cultural Haunting* (Charlottesville: University Press of Virginia, 1998), 29; Rody, "Toni Morrison's *Beloved*," 102.

67. In David Eng's words, "The militant refusal of the ego . . . to let go . . . is at the heart of melancholia's productive political potentials." David Eng and Shinhee Han, "A Dialogue on Racial Melancholia," in Eng and Kazanjian, *Loss*, 365.

68. Maggie Sale notes, "Despite this plurality, *Beloved*'s method of revisioning the past does not authorize all perspectives equally: Schoolteacher's perspective is articulated but it is not sanctioned," and the positions of the Garners and Bodwin are "deeply problematized." Sale, "Call and Response as Critical Method," *African American Review* 26, no. 1 (1992): 48.

69. Lawrie Balfour helped clarify this argument.

70. Lawrie Balfour clarified this claim as well. For a parallel argument, see Phillip Brian Harper, "Nationalism and Social Division in Black Arts Poetry of the 1960's," in *Is It Nation Time?* ed. Eddie Glaude Jr., 165–88 (Chicago: University of Chicago Press, 2002).

71. For versions of this "new nationalism," see Michael Lind, *The Next American Nation* (New York: Free Press, 1996); Michael Kazin, *The Populist Persuasion* (Ithaca, N.Y.: Cornell University Press, 1995). The mediation of (racial) part and (national) whole and the typical sacrifice of race to advance a "progressive" nationalism were also demonstrated in the contrasting speeches of Al Sharpton and Barack Obama at the 2004 Democratic Party National Convention, and the issue remains crucial in Obama's presidential campaign.

72. The first version of this argument appeared in a paper given at the American Political Science Association Annual Meeting in September 1999. The paper was reprinted as "Narrating Clinton's Impeachment: Race, the Right, and Allegories of the Sixties," in *Theory and Event* (February 2000), along with two responses: Mark Reinhardt's "Constitutional Sentimentality" and Ebony E. A. Chatman's "Clinton's Black 'I'." A revised version appeared in *Public Affairs,* ed. Paul Apostolidis and Juliet A. Williams (Durham, N.C. : Duke University Press, 2004).

73. The Talk of the Town, *New Yorker,* October 5, 1998.

74. My sense of these dimensions is indebted to Stuart Clarke.

75. Lawrie Balfour suggested the way Morrison, uncharacteristically, figures community through victimized men, not the women they victimize.

76. The Talk of the Town, *New Yorker*, October 5, 1998.

77. "To GOP, Christians Urge Punishment and Prayer," *New York Times*, September 19, 1998.

78. The problem with marriage as a trope is that it romanticizes institutions ostensibly based on consent; adultery as a trope, conversely, suggests that our difficulties arise not from the institution of marriage itself or the inevitable ambivalence about it but from willful culpable infidelity. For a brilliant defense of adultery in fact and as a trope, see Laura Kipnis, *Against Love: A Polemic* (New York: Vintage, 2003).

79. On the relation of liberalism, self-control, and "virtue" to white supremacy, see Winthrop Jordan, *White over Black: American Attitudes toward the Negro, 1550–1812* (New York: W. W. Norton, 1977). Morrison reads fascination with Clinton's body racially, but she ignores how his extramarital, nonprocreative, and nongenital sexuality elicits homophobic fascination.

80. Laurie Goldstein, "Christian Coalition Moans Lack of Anger at Clinton," *New York Times*, September 20, 1998.

81. Kevin Sack, "Blacks Stand by a President Who 'Has Been There for Us,'" *New York Times*, September 19, 1998. Clinton repeatedly turned to black churches to show repentance and receive forgiveness; by going to African Americans for love, he of course replays another aspect of the racial imaginary.

82. Kenneth Warren, "'As White as Anybody': Race and the Politics of Counting as Black," *New Literary History* 31, no. 4 (Autumn 2000): 723–24.

83. Cf. Bonnie Honig, "Dead Rights, Live Futures: A Reply to Habermas's 'Constitutional Democracy,'" *Political Theory* 29 (December 2001): 792–805.

84. Philip Roth, *The Human Stain* (New York: Houghton Mifflin, 2000), 2.

Conclusion

1. Alexis de Tocqueville, *Democracy in America*, 2 vols. (New York: Vintage, 1990), 1:331, 2:319.

2. George Shulman, "Race and the Romance of American Nationalism in Martin Luther King, Norman Mailer, and James Baldwin," in *Cultural Studies and Political Theory*, ed. Jodi Dean, 209–27 (Ithaca, N.Y.: Cornell University Press, 2000). I am fudging the difference between Tocqueville's "majority tyranny" (in volume 1) and the forms of "democratic despotism" he links to "public opinion" and an administratively centralized state (in volume 2). But his example of majority tyranny, not coincidentally, is that "free" blacks in the North are not allowed to exercise the political rights they formally possess.

3. Tocqueville, *Democracy in America*, 1:357–59. He goes on: In the North, "the prejudice which repels the Negroes seems to increase in proportion as they are emancipated, and inequality is sanctioned by the manners while it is effaced from the laws of the country" (360). He is certain that slavery is a wrong and predicts that it will be ended by race war. Whereas Garrison argues that such violence can be averted by white repentance and black emancipation, Tocqueville argues

that emancipation will create enmity. For in the South as in the North, "[a] white majority will deprive blacks of almost all their civil rights." Enslaved and formally free blacks will internalize this racism: "Having been told since infancy that his race is naturally inferior to that of the whites, the Negro assents to this proposition and is ashamed of his own nature. . . . he would willingly rid himself of everything that makes him what he is." But seeing that they "cannot become the equals of whites, they will speedily show themselves enemies" (378).

4. He never notes how the "consensus" he depicts as "universal" (among whites) is challenged by insurrection in the South and by abolitionists and feminists who link slavery and patriarchy to confront Northerners about exclusion. Yet reformers join the spirits of liberty and of religion whose generative tension birthed his theory of democracy in America.

5. Tocqueville is typically called "prophetic," but he is anomalous in crucial ways. Partly, he is called "prophetic" because he "predicts" the spread of equality as a "providential fact" that will advance despite what people wish or do. But if French aristocrats "accept" equality as fated, he argues, they could devote energy and action to making it a condition of political freedom. (Still, what prophet depicts a God whose decree so fundamentally threatens human freedom and dignity?) Likewise, he is called prophetic because he "predicts" democratic despotism, but he is warning of it as a *contingent* future that the enfranchised can forestall if they sustain the "art of freedom" bequeathed by their founding. (Still, he sees danger in God's decree of equality, and he seeks not repentance or rebirth but ongoing practices of cultivation to "mitigate" the "natural instincts" fostered by "equality of social condition.") A book could be written, therefore, about the relationship between Tocqueville and Sheldon Wolin, his greatest (re)interpreter, in the substance of their arguments about modernity and democracy, and in their (prophetic?) form and tone. See Sheldon Wolin, *Tocqueville between Two Worlds: The Making of a Political and Theoretical Life* (Princeton: Princeton University Press, 2001).

6. William Connolly, "Pluralism and Evil," in *Pluralism*, 11–37 (Durham, N.C.: Duke University Press, 2005), and "Letter to Augustine," in *Identity\ Difference*, 123–57 (Ithaca, N.Y.: Cornell University Press, 1991).

7. James Baldwin, *The Fire Next Time*, in *The Price of the Ticket: James Baldwin Collected Non-Fiction, 1948–1965* (New York: St. Martin's Press, 1985), 379.

8. Bryan Garsten argues, "In contrast to persuasion, which treats different audiences differently, justification treats different audiences similarly . . . to show why any reasonable person should accept our view, but not necessarily why these particular people listening here and now should do so." The "modern liberal tradition of justification assumes that people can find some shared point of view and asks how they can engage in deliberation within the boundaries" it sets. Garsten, *Saving Persuasion: A Defense of Rhetoric and Judgment* (Cambridge: Harvard University Press, 2006), 5–6. The key presumption is that "private" judgments do *not* harbor partial truths and insights to draw into deliberation but are "too subjective and dogmatic," "analogous to the Puritan claims of conscience that Hobbes thought had turned controversy into intractable conflict." Rawls, according to Garsten, thus treats "major threats to liberal constitutionalism as various forms of religious zealotry." That is why people must alienate private

judgments to public reason. And by attacking conscience and rhetoric, Hobbes initiates this search for "a basis of social cooperation upon which all citizens can unite and that all can potentially endorse as their own even when they do not share more particular private opinions and judgments." Of course, "the decision to alienate one's judgment to such an authoritative perspective is itself a judgment that must be instigated by rhetoric." Garsten, *Saving Persuasion*, 182, 179.

9. William E. Connolly, "Tocqueville, Religiosity, and Pluralization," in *The Ethos of Pluralization*, 163–98 (Minneapolis: University of Minnesota Press, 1995). It is worth noting that Tocqueville sees religion not as merely a form of social control, for in volume 2 he argues that religion can sustain agency and solidarity against the "propensities" toward withdrawal and docility that he attributes to individualism.

10. Michael Sandel, quoted in Garsten, *Saving Persuasion*, 184. Garsten adds, "If we think our primary worry now is at heart similar to the one that Hobbes faced, then perhaps adhering strictly to a narrow language of public reason is the best solution." But "the frustration of being left out of the rewards and discourse of western liberalism," an "alienation" only "intensified by the liberal preference for toleration over engagement, has produced responses to modernity that are as dogmatic and dangerous as the religious fanaticism that liberalism was meant to contain" (17). Indeed, "liberal strategies of political and moral disengagement . . . tend to produce forms of opinion more dogmatic and less prone to deliberative engagement than those they initially sought to displace" (185). In effect, "sentiments of alienation often present themselves as manifestations of religious fervor." If religious zealotry is provoked by the alienation that liberal strategies impose, then democrats need an "alternative strategy" that "engages more directly with religious opinion" (17–18).

11. Michael Sandel, *Democracy's Discontent: America in Search of a Public Philosophy* (Cambridge, Mass.: Belknap Press, 1996); Carl Schmitt, *The Concept of the Political*, trans. George Schwab (Chicago: University of Chicago Press, 1996) and *Political Theology: Four Chapters on the Concept of Sovereignty* (Chicago: University of Chicago Press, 1985).

12. Chantal Mouffe, *The Democratic Paradox* (New York: Verso, 2000); cf. William Connolly's generous critique of Sandel in "Civic Republicanism and Civic Pluralism: The Silent Struggle of Michael Sandel," in *Debating Democracy's Discontent: Essays on American Politics, Law, and Public Philosophy*, ed. Anita L. Allen and Milton C. Regan, 205–11 (New York: Oxford University Press, 1998).

13. William E. Connolly, *Ethos of Pluralization*, introduction and chap. 1, passim; and *Why I Am Not a Secularist* (Minneapolis: University of Minnesota Press, 1999), introduction, chaps. 1 and 6, passim.

14. I mean to say: Race signals that Schmitt is mistaken to absolutely juxtapose liberalism and political theology, and the critique of his view of the friend–enemy distinction also begins with white supremacy under liberalism.

15. On relating Schmitt's friend–enemy distinction to American politics, see Bruce Rosenstock, "Capra contra Schmitt: Two Traditions of Political Romanticism," *Theory and Event* 8, no. 4 (2005), http://muse.jhu.edu/journals/theory_&_event/toc/archive.html#8.4.

16. The alternative to willful innocence is not guilt but acknowledgment;

indeed, if guilt arises because we do not act on what we "know," as Baldwin and Cavell argue, then acknowledging what we know enables action, which ends the disavowal and inaction that generate guilt. The point is not to reiterate innocence and guilt as moral categories, to create a "guilty" subject, but rather to imagine responsibility in political and existential rather than moral terms.

17. Baldwin, *The Fire Next Time*, 334, 379.

18. Ibid., 373, 375.

19. Norman Mailer, *Presidential Papers* (New York: Berkley Medallion, 1970), 25–26.

20. Abraham Heschel, *The Prophets*, vol. 2 (New York: Harper, 1958), 59–62.

21. Stanley Cavell, *The Claim of Reason* (New York: Oxford University Press, 1979), 26–27.

22. Ralph Ellison, *Invisible Man* (New York: Vintage, 1995), 581.

23. Carl Hulse, "The 2006 Election; G.O.P. in House Gears Up for New Leadership," *New York Times*, November 15, 2006.

24. Nietzsche says, "The need for *redemption* is the quintessence of all Christian needs. . . . the Christian wants to be *rid* of himself." Nietzsche, *The Birth of Tragedy and the Case of Wagner* (New York: Vintage, 1967), 191. The Christian seeks redemption from the very history and suffering that constitutes him and from "the fundamental pre-requisites of life." Cf. George Shulman, "Redemption, Secularization, and Politics," in *Powers of the Secular Modern: Talal Asad and His Interlocuters*, ed. David Scott and Charles Hirschkind, 154–79 (Stanford: Stanford University Press, 2006).

25. Talal Asad, *Formations of the Secular: Christianity, Islam, Modernity* (Stanford: Stanford University Press, 2003); also see Patchen Markel and Candace Volger, eds., "Violence and Redemption," special issue, *Critical Inquiry* 15, no. 1 (Winter 2003). The editors' introduction (1–10) and the essay by Michael Warner, "What Like a Bullet Can Undeceive?" (41–54) are especially illuminating.

26. Friedrich Nietzsche, *The Gay Science* (New York: Vintage, 1974), 73; Philip Roth, *The Human Stain* (New York: Houghton Mifflin, 2000), 37.

27. For a wonderful example of a "tragic" approach to politics, besides William Connolly's work, see Peter Euben, *The Tragedy of Political Theory: The Road Not Taken* (Princeton: Princeton University Press, 1990).

28. It is striking to note the parallel ways Thoreau and Arendt link redemption to nature. By a naturally recurring phenomenon, *dawn*, Thoreau depicts beginning or natality not as a miraculous rupture *of* natural processes but as a miracle enabled *by* nature, if we are awake to it. As recurrence of dawn supports faith in our own capacity to begin, so Arendt makes *birth* (into life and kinship) the natural correlate of capacities for rebirth by political action. By a metaphor, she bridges the abyss between nature and politics that characterizes her theory.

29. Bonnie Honig and Peter Euben helped clarify these thoughts.

30. Karl Marx, "Contribution to the Critique of Hegel's *Philosophy of Right:* Introduction," in *The Marx–Engels Reader*, ed. Robert C. Tucker, 2nd ed. (New York: W. W. Norton, 1978), 64.

31. Lauren Berlant, *The Anatomy of National Fantasy: Hawthorne, Utopia, and Everyday Life* (Chicago: University of Chicago Press, 1991), 202–7.

Index

Abelove, Henry, 54, 266n19

abolitionism: Baldwin as abolitionist, 166; defenses of, 266n15; deportation of Burns back to slavery and, 44; initial demonization of Brown's violence, 76–77; Melville's way of voicing Parker's, 179; Thoreau's abolitionist prophecy as politics, 51–55

Abzug, Robert, 264n3

acceptance: as Baldwin's conception of redemption, 92, 93, 133–34, 135, 241; black agency and, 151–54; black criticism of Baldwin's trope of, 160; from disavowal to, 140–41, 150–51

acknowledgment, 30, 92, 235; as alternative to willful innocence, 135, 136, 137, 291n16; confronting refusal of, 19, 180, 241; "facts" used by Thoreau to move people from disavowal to, 45; King on eliciting white, 117; relation to world/others dependent on, 243

action from principle, 48–49, 53, 55, 83, 108, 133; redemption in, 91

adultery as trope, 289n78

Afrocentric identity politics, 191

Agamben, Giorgio, 27, 263n46

agape, 108–14, 117, 127–28, 129; black power critics on, 119; criticisms of, 109–10; as egalitarian political theology, 110; King's practice of, 108–14; meaning of, 108–9

agency: coming to terms with constitutive power of the past as condition of, 234; relationship of origins and, 35–37. *See also* black agency

aggression in prophetic claim making, 244–47

Ahab: Morrison on, 178–79

ahimsa, 108

Allen, Danielle, 129, 274n41

Als, Hilton, 164, 281n84, 281n85

ambivalence: Baldwin's answer to white disavowal with ambivalent engagement, 157–58; generative, toward political identification, 34–35; tension between attachment to community and aspirations to universality, 34

"American" culture: Baldwin's self-identification within, 92, 93; King's self-identification within, 92–93; Thoreau's self-identification within, 92

American Dilemma (Myrdal), 100

American exceptionalism: fraudulent, due to black exclusion, 115; King's reworking of, by jeremiad to whites as national subject, 114–18; liberalism joining faith in rational planning to narrative of, 100; national identity and, 114–18; Obama and redemptive promise of, 226; Tocqueville and, 236

American Jeremiad (Bercovitch), 175–76

American nationhood: accepting centrality of racial domination and initiating nation building, 157; Clinton's victimization by power

GEORGE SHULMAN is associate professor at the Gallatin School of Individualized Study at New York University and the author of *Radicalism and Reverence: The Political Thought of Gerrard Winstanley.*